ARGUMENTS WITH ENGLAND

# Arguments with England

## *A Memoir*

MICHAEL BLAKEMORE

*faber and faber*

First published in 2004
by Faber and Faber Limited
3 Queen Square London WC1N 3AU

Typeset by Country Setting, Kingsdown, Kent CT14 8ES
Printed in England by Mackays of Chatham plc, Chatham, Kent

A CIP record for this book
is available from the British Library

ISBN
0-571-22445-8

2 4 6 8 10 9 7 5 3 1

For Conrad, Beatie and Clemmie

*With this advice, found in a letter
from Anton Chekhov to his actress wife, Olga Knipper:*

You must stop worrying about success or failure,
your business is to work step by step, from day to day,
softly-softly, to be prepared for unavoidable mistakes
and failures, in a word, follow your own line
and leave competition to others.

Translated by Jean Benedetti in his collection
*Dear Writer, Dear Actress:
The Love Letters of Olga Knipper and Anton Chekhov*

# Author's Note

Without the encouragement and occasional finger-wag from Robin Dalton, Claire Tomalin and David Hare I might still be halfway through this book. My thanks to them, to my literary agent Mark Lucas, for his patience and unaccountable optimism, and to my editor Dinah Wood, for another kind of patience. I must also thank Irving Wardle for checking the accuracy of my theatrical history, and Philip Drewe, from whose exemplary *The Masterpiece* I derived my short account of the Sydney Opera House. Finally, I must thank my family for their forbearance when from time to time and over a number of years they have had to put up with living with a writer.

# Contents

# Illustrations

13 Just married. It's nine o'clock in the morning and I'm off to rehearsals.

14 Holofernes in *Love's Labour's Lost* with James Ottaway (Sir Nathaniel).

15 Sir Toby Belch up to no good in the Middle Temple Hall.

16 Badger in *Toad of Toad Hall*. The performance owed much to the prime minister Harold Macmillan (photo: Dilys Minnikin).

17 My father prepares his fishing tackle while I watch.

18 My American grandmother. Her house on Sundays was a refuge from The King's School.

19 In the school uniform with little to smile about.

20 Joe Melia and Zena Walker, incomparable in *A Day in the Death of Joe Egg* (photo: Zoë Dominic).

# ARGUMENTS WITH ENGLAND

# The Beginning and an Ending

In the case of a singular artist, which is the more important encounter – with the man or with his work? I first met Laurence Olivier in person when I played a small part in *Titus Andronicus* in 1957, but we were more crucially acquainted, at least from my point of view, some twelve years before. The first screening in Sydney of Olivier's *Henry V* took place at eleven o'clock one Friday morning at the Embassy in Pitt Street, and I was there. For months I had been charting the film's triumphant progress on its way to Australia in the pages of overseas magazines, and now, like a long-expected meteorological event, Hurricane Harry had arrived.

To be frank, it was Agincourt that I was really looking forward to. How, I wondered, would it compare with the battle on the ice in Eisenstein's *Alexander Nevsky*, which I had seen on the wobbly projector of a film society? I was not to be disappointed. However, returned to the daylight of Pitt Street, something odd began to happen. What lingered in my mind was not the French cavalry accelerating across those green Irish locations, incomparably exciting though that had been, but the rhetoric of the mighty speeches and the outline of the performer who had spoken them. Not for the last time would the tattoo of Olivier's extraordinary delivery go on beating in my head for days after I had heard it. I was sixteen at the time, aspiring to be a film director and rather sceptical about the theatre; but, like the greylag gosling not long from the egg, I was ripe for imprinting. Laurence Olivier now joined Orson Welles and James Cagney as one of the actor-heroes of a rather solitary, skinny boy who in no way resembled any of them.

HMV produced a *Henry V* album of four hefty 78 rpm records, complete with William Walton's rousing music and the sound effect of

the arrows of the English army leaving their longbows. Olivier, somewhat cockily, played all the parts. It was soon alongside my other
albums, the Tchaikovsky symphonies, *The Rite of Spring* and a random
collection of Sidney Bechet records. Played endlessly at disco volume
on the walnut-veneer panatrope it brought transport to me and exasperation to the other tenants of the block of flats in Ocean Street. Soon
I could accompany most of it by heart, and my only difficulty was in
deciding whether to speak the words or hum the score. In the semi-
tropical Australian night outside my window, two versions of Olivier's
refined, explosive diction competed with the crickets. I was hooked.

Show business usually contributes to the heat in the hothouse of
adolescent imagination. With maturity most people leave that flushed,
sticky world behind, and look back at it, if at all, with wry embarrassment. However, disguised among that dreaming population of the
young are dotted a handful of greylag geese who will keep the faith
for the rest of their lives. They have contracted a holy disease, passed
from the afflicted of one generation to the chosen acolytes of the next,
against whose mysterious outbreaks national or class differences are
no quarantine. Some will simply be fans, haunting the lobbies of film
clubs and old theatres, their dreams preserved in an aspic of photographic emulsion. Others of a more challenging disposition, and perhaps
with a dash of talent, will want to have a go themselves. Australia, as
far away from the centres of infection as it was possible to get, was
about to have a minor epidemic, and Laurence Olivier was the carrier.

Every so often the theatre throws up an actor of such accomplishment and charismatic energy that he manages, at least for a while, to
nudge the playwright from his position centre stage. If he is a director
as well and the play familiar, by an author long dead, the illusion that
he has somehow invented the entire evening is all the more persuasive.
It is never true, of course. Only the right words can release the genie
from the bottle.

However, this power that certain very rare actors possess to seem
to take the theatre's creative high ground for themselves can have useful
consequences for the profession at large. When Irving arrived in London
with *The Bells*, an unimportant play raised to a different level by his
hypnotic ability, the whole town wanted to be there to watch him. An
actor of this calibre is like a recruiting sergeant for his profession, not
only pressing the shilling into the willing palms of the stage-struck but
mustering back into their seats that intelligent audience of sceptics

who are always on the point of giving up the theatre for good. Acting seems to become the thing it mostly isn't, a career of originality and immense power, and young people, whom common sense would have kept well clear of the stage door, now follow the stairs to the whore's apartment. Not all become actors – some decline into authorship or direction; but the results of this new and unexpected intake will become apparent ten or fifteen years later. I have met too many of them not to know that the extraordinary vigour of the post-war British theatre owes much to a generation who in the forties were marked by the work of Laurence Olivier.

Now the great seducer was on his way to Australia, and in two disguises. We would be seeing him huge, black-and-white and flat on film as the Prince of Denmark, and small, coloured and three-dimensional on stage with the Old Vic Company. On another Friday morning I was back at my post at the Embassy, waiting for the first showing of *Hamlet*. Olivier had been knighted during the filming and I had seen photographs of him at the Palace in frock coat and with bleached hair. This time I knew the text well and was anticipating more than the clash of steel upon steel.

That afternoon in my room at St Paul's College I began scribbling a review for the university newspaper *Honi Soit*. At once I hit upon the perfect headline – THE FILM'S THE THING! – and with my lead paragraph improved upon perfection, 'A magnificent new film is verifying a current furfy that we have with us now in Sydney the theatre's most brilliant personality.' 'Furfy' was a word I had never used before (nor since for that matter) but at the time was much favoured by Australian journos. When my piece appeared the following week I thought it only fair to share it with the man himself, then appearing at the Tivoli Theatre, so I wrote him a letter with cutting enclosed, explaining that I was a reluctant medical student who preferred to play truant at the movies. I hadn't really expected a reply but back one came, brief, charming and signed magically in blue ink 'L Olivier'. Not since the age of thirteen when The Great Levant, also by chance playing the Tivoli, had answered my letter about my conjuring ambitions, had I received such interesting post.

There had never been a tour of Australia quite like it, and probably there never will be. It was like a present for helping win the war. In Laurence Olivier and Vivien Leigh were combined the theatre's most prestigious couple, Heathcliff and Scarlett O'Hara come down to earth.

*Richard III* was the hot ticket of the three plays on offer, and an all-too-Australian one-liner was in circulation, 'Richard d'Turd or Dick the Shit'. There was no box office as such; you applied for seats like shares in a privatised industry, posting a cheque and keeping your fingers crossed. Not long into the Sydney run Olivier slipped a cartilage in the Battle of Bosworth, but played on gallantly using a crutch. If he hadn't the public would probably have burnt the theatre down.

My first sight of him was the long hobble to the footlights at the beginning of *Richard III*, and after *Hamlet* he seemed a very long way away. We were a restless house and took a while to subdue. But what amazing sounds the actor sometimes made! 'A horse! A horse! My kingdom for a horse!' – the fabric of the theatre seemed to be vibrating with it, one of those pitched sounds that can crack a tray of glass tumblers. By the curtain, like the marvellous George Relph's Duke of Buckingham, we had all sunk to one knee.

However, for sheer pleasure it was the other two shows that opened my eyes. I hadn't read either text, so what would happen next became very important. Olivier not only played in *School for Scandal*, he directed a production of great fluency and invention. The play's most celebrated moment – Lady Teazle discovered behind the screen – was staged with typical Olivier panache. The screen was upstage left and an unknowing Sir Peter had just executed a brisk semicircular walk towards it. As it fell, revealing his wife, the old husband stopped dead in his tracks, his back half towards us, one knee bent, one heel raised. In the auditorium laughter melted away to a complete and prolonged hush as we read his pain from that frozen outline.

For audiences hankering for a glimpse or two of Scarlett O'Hara, *The Skin of Our Teeth* was the perfect third play, American and fast-moving, with Vivien Leigh in black stockings, brandishing a feather duster. Olivier, exploding with zest and mimic resource, played the sort of part you'd expect Walter Huston to do in the movies. On that tour he couldn't have chosen three more extraordinary vehicles. The contrasting body-work was amazing, but what held you captive was the veiled hum of the identical motor within.

After this wondrous theatrical dispensation and the Old Vic Company had sailed on to New Zealand, I wanted even less to be a doctor like my father, even more to be a director, and, a new thought, maybe an actor as well. Whatever I was to become, one thing was clear: somehow or other I had to get to London! Ronald Colman never yearned more passionately for Shangri-La. I didn't know it, of course, but wherever the tour had played in Australasia there were other young people secretly making the same resolve. On winter afternoons in the fifties on the other side of the world I would meet some of them, like me buying a threepenny cup of tea and a swallow of hope in a café not far from a London theatre where they were auditioning actors.

Another great star in procession around the Antipodes was to provide me with my means of escape, and in this case meeting the man was an influence quite as significant as his work. In 1949 Robert Morley enjoyed a rather different reputation from that of the boulevard star of his later career. He had made a name for himself, and sensationally so, in *Oscar Wilde*, the play banned by the Lord Chamberlain but given to great acclaim at a club theatre. He had gone on to perform in Bernard Shaw at the Old Vic and to star in long-running West End hits. In Australia we had seen him stealing the reviews in prestigious films like *Marie Antoinette, Major Barbara* and *The Young Mr Pitt*. A unique performer but also a playwright of distinction, he was now in Sydney starring in his own *Edward, My Son*, in which he had just concluded two immensely successful years on Broadway. What persuaded him to take the long way home to London via Australasia I never knew, unless it was to retrace the steps of another actor-playwright famous in his own day and still at work in the mind of his successor, Dion Boucicault. Morley liked to quote his description of Sydney: 'Manchester with a harbour backdrop'. It was one of a number of remarks that left his listeners unsure whether to be flattered or insulted; a fairly usual predicament, it must be said, in Australian dealings with important English visitors. At any event here he was, with his wife Joan, two young children, Sheridan and Annabel, their nurse and, completing the retinue, a twenty-seven-year-old whiz-kid manager, whom he had brought with him from New York, Morton Gottlieb.

At this time I had just solved the problem of how not to be a doctor by doing no work and failing all my third-year examinations. But this drastic solution had left a nasty aftertaste of diminished self-esteem. I was thoroughly depressed. Even if I had wanted to, there was a six-month wait before I could repeat the year, and in the meantime my father was insisting that I get a job. He made it clear he hoped it would be a sufficiently unpleasant one to bring me to my senses. Somehow or other I had to make something happen which would alter the course of my life. But what? I made some enquiries about working my passage on a ship to England, but had no idea how I would live when I got there.

One evening a friend invited me to a small party he was giving for the dynamic Morty Gottlieb. We were hungry for inside information on the Morley visit, and Morty obliged. The star had declared war on all aspects of Australian sloth. He fought first with the stage staff who had refused to do overtime at the dress rehearsal. They responded by sabotaging the first night; pieces of scenery arrived in place late, and standard lamps went on and off mysteriously in the course of the action. Morley, not in the least perturbed, ad-libbed where appropriate, and on waves of applause the play sailed on to its final ovation. The reviews were excellent, but the business, especially in the light of the standing-room-only conditions he had just left behind him in New York, left much to be desired. For this he blamed an ossified and complacent management. His differences with them had begun in America, where they had asked him to sign their standard contract, of which not the least impertinent clause was one that forbade actors to keep drink in their dressing rooms. He had taken a pen and crossed most of it out. However, his most indignant complaint was about their lack of interest in any form of publicity. Where were the posters and the handbills? Where were the stories in the press?

Even as I listened to Morty I was working on a secret plan. Would Robert Morley, I asked him, be interested in being interviewed by a university newspaper? As roving arts correspondent for *Honi Soit* I might, in my own small way, be able to help in the drive for publicity. Fortunately I was addressing a positive thinker. Morton said he would arrange a meeting in the star's dressing room between the next mid-week matinee and evening performances.

For four feverish days I worked on the details of my plan, one born of desperation and a guardian innocence. Robert Morley wanted publicity for his show. Had I not successfully promoted the St Paul's College Mummers, of which I had been a founder member? Very well then; having gained entry to his dressing room and concluded my interview, I would spring some quite brilliant ideas on him and immediately be offered a job as publicist. This was the strategy, and by far the most extraordinary thing about it was that it worked.

I arrived at the stage door of the Theatre Royal at the appointed hour, carrying in my briefcase a notebook and sketch-pad (being also something of a caricaturist), and Morty led me down a corridor to the star's dressing room. It was like being ushered into what, had it been fifty times larger, might have been a chamber at Versailles. There sat the King as big as a walrus, removing his wig and make-up before rising to pee in the hand-basin and step into trousers held ready by a kneeling dresser. All the time from front-of-house and backstage cheerfully deferential people came and went, while I crouched in the corner with my legs tucked in, asking questions when I could, scribbling and sketching when I couldn't. From time to time he would stare at me with the frank, unruffled gaze of a bird of prey. I was in the presence of the most flamboyantly confident person I had ever met.

He was standing over me, dressed for the street. 'Where do you live?', he did not so much ask as announce.

I told him.

'Good. It's on my way. Let's continue this absorbing conversation in the car. I want to say goodnight to my darling children before tonight's performance.'

Morty, his watchdog, would be coming with us, but it had not escaped me that his would be the first stop. We set off from the stage door with Morley at the wheel of a small hired Austin, me beside him, Morty behind. I calculated that I would have the star to myself for the time it took the car to descend to Rushcutters' Bay and rise up again to Edgecliff, my destination. The picture of Morty is still with me as he leant in the window to say goodbye. The back door slammed, the car started to move, and I remember my dry mouth and terrible resolve as I lurched into speech.

'Mr Morley, I understand you're worried about publicity. I happen to have a few ideas that I think might interest you.' I started to talk and fumbled for some papers in my briefcase, which I couldn't read because of the movement of the car. I went on talking anyway. I talked all the way down the hill and all the way up. Morley stared at the road and never said a word. I suddenly realised the car was at a standstill; it was my turn to get out. Still he did not look at me. If I had been brave before, now I was heroic. 'Mr Morley, I've still got a few more ideas that I'd like to tell you about. Drive on and I'll catch the tram back.'

Without a word he started the car. I talked all the way down to Double Bay and all the way up to Point Piper. Again the car pulled up. By now I, too, was silent, a spent and trembling ruin. Morley gave me a long cool stare. 'So you want a job?' It was another of his announcements.

Ragged with exhaustion I could only mutter, 'It's just these ideas . . . If I could just give them a try . . . I'll work for nothing . . . '

He cut me short, but his reply was mischievous and amused. 'My boy, never do anything for nothing! Ring me in the morning.'

Of all the celebrities who have ever visited Australia I had had the amazing good fortune to accost the one whose whimsical impulses would include finding me work. With the rest I doubt if I would have got past the stage door. However, just as I had conceived a plan listening to Morton, so Robert had been amusing himself with an idea listening to me. That was probably why he had been so silent. If the management was not prepared to publicise the show, then why shouldn't the star hire his own personal press agent to do the job instead? Without knowing it, I was being pitched into the front line of one of his exuberant battles.

By the time I rang the next morning it had all been arranged. I would be paid six pounds a week, would be responsible only to Robert and his co-star, Sophie Stewart, and would work under the supervision of Morty. I was asked to come at once to meet the family, and I remember Joan Morley, already well acquainted with the aberrations of a born gambler, studying me closely lest I be one of the worst. That evening I went down to the theatre and met everyone there. As Robert left the dressing room to begin the play, now complete in costume and make-up, he turned, shook me by the hand and said, as if it was a sly quote from a backstage movie, 'Delighted to have you on board!'

I wish I could say that this scene dissolved at once into a noisy montage of theatrical triumph. Unfortunately, in getting the job I seemed to have exhausted my supply of chutzpah and gall, and I swiftly declined into what I normally was, a rather diffident young man. What saved me was that I was quite good at my job, which was to collect (and sometimes invent) news items that would promote the show. With these neatly typed out I would do the rounds of Sydney's various newspapers, offering exclusives to the gossip columnists, whose paragraphs were then a daily feature of the Australian press. The most welcoming of these veteran journos was mostly drunk and happy to have me write copy for him.

Here's an example: 'Robert Morley's eight-year-old son Sheridan competed in the Cranbrook School Sports last Wednesday. Before he left for the sports ground, Sheridan asked his father what he would give him if he won the gold cup for the best all-round performance.

"My boy," answered Morley, eyeing a figure which strongly supported Mendel's Theory of Genetics, "I shall give you the Harbour Bridge." '

This was printed as I wrote it, except that the reference to the Theory of Genetics was cut, thereby robbing the story of any point it might have had. However, it led to a lively correspondence about insults to the Harbour Bridge, so one way or another we stayed in the news.

At a rival paper there was another columnist, far from friendly, who treated me with impassive disdain, as if he suspected me of being Robert Morley's catamite and had half a mind to pass on this impression to his readers. It was a stressful job, and I sweated profusely as I knocked on important doors, but many of my stories were published. At the least sign of slacking Morty was on my tail, and his expectations of me were very American. Enthusiasm was what I was expected to express; anxiety was what I was expected to feel. Both at all times.

Each evening before the show I had to report the day's events to Robert in his dressing room. 'What's new!?' he would invariably announce, barely looking up from the small magnifying mirror in which he did his make-up, and I would trot out something I'd already prepared and which I hoped might amuse him.

Like all actors at that time he believed in the full slap; sticks of Leichner blended together until the face came up a burnished tangerine, followed by rouge on the cheeks, blue on the eyelids, and the whole lot swamped with powder, which would then be reduced by scrubbing the face with a very soft brush. A cloud of talcum would sink slowly to the floor like stage smoke. The effect was as startling as a totem pole, but highly effective from the front, where you could see those penetrating blue eyes from the back row of the theatre. During these preparations anyone who came into the dressing room, and most could, was expected to be amusing. He had no time for shyness, which he considered a product of laziness and pride. If you didn't put up a fight on behalf of your own personality he tormented you until you did, or, worse, just dropped you to one side like a dull magazine.

The most alarming thing about him was his low boredom threshold, and few things were as discouraging as seeing those eyes glaze over in the middle of your sentence and that lively mind go wandering elsewhere. By the time you reached the point of your story you were speaking in a dead monotone like a gramophone which someone had forgotten to wind. No one got off lightly, not even a weary journalist sent to interview him, inarticulate even by Australian standards and further afflicted by a terrible stammer. I sat mesmerised in my usual seat in the corner while the poor man was taken apart, longing for a referee to stop the fight. But this was only one aspect of an abundant and recklessly generous personality, whom it amused to enlarge the pleasure in life of those who collected around him. He was in his early forties, at the height of his fame as a performer and a playwright, a prodigious earner and blessed in his private life. Resolve and talent accounted for part of this, but, as he often insisted, so did luck. Like a big winner at the race track he wanted to spread some of that good fortune around, and did so by the handful.

Not the least to benefit were the audiences. *Edward, My Son* was a sweeping comedy melodrama about the contradictions of worldly success and love. It followed the rise of a tycoon, Edward Holt, who, discarding friends, mistress and wife, invests his dwindling moral store in an obsessive concern for an only child, Edward, a bad lot who remains throughout offstage. The story is told in flashback with Holt his own advocate and the audience invited to be jury. The play began with Morley, bulky and elegant in astrakhan-collared coat and homburg hat, coming in front of the curtain, centre, to tell his story. At once he set a tone witty and aggressive. 'It doesn't mean you have to like me,' he would announce, his head butting up towards the gallery, followed by a level stare at the stalls – 'Or I you, for that matter.' Within a line or two the house was his. It was an early lesson which I would not forget in the efficacy of direct address. Night after night the audience fell straight into an ambush of laughter. Throughout the tour Morley was an indefatigable performer, and whatever the house or his own frame of mind, I never saw him give a slack or inconsistent showing.

This professionalism was at odds with a provocative flippancy about the theatre in general. In Sydney he changed the afternoon of the midweek matinee so that he could enjoy a day at the races. While approving of comedy because it gave audiences (and himself) a good time, he pretended to baulk at dramatic scenes. 'Couldn't we get Freddie Valk in to do this bit?', he would ask, referring to the distinguished German-born actor who had just had a big success in London as Othello. Yet, in a radio broadcast before an invited audience, I saw him give a simple and intensely felt performance of Crocker Harris in *The Browning Version* which it would be hard to better. Because he was an actor through sheer force of personality, with only one voice and one shape at his disposal, his moments of emotional exposure had a kind of autobiographical authority about them. Areas of pain and longing, left behind somewhere in his youth, were unexpectedly on show, and the effect could be extraordinarily touching.

It hardly needs saying that as actors Laurence Olivier and Robert Morley were some distance apart, but it may be of interest to compare them in an identical role. I was a witness when both accepted an invitation to address the students at Sydney University. The Olivier visit was a very respectful affair. He was attended on the dais by a semicircle of academics, who sat behind him while he stood talking into a microphone. His speech was unexpectedly constrained, flowery at one moment, stilted the next, and disappointing if you came expecting the relish of his stage work. Those personae were completely out of sight. He had one highly effective moment, however. Having just ridiculed the pains taken by scholars to wring some meaning from Hamlet's lines, 'the dram of eale / Doth all the noble substance of a doubt, / To his own scandal,' he suddenly pretended to remember the distinguished gentlemen sitting behind him and swung round, arms extended in humble apology. On stage it would have been even more effective; here it was a shade contrived.

In contrast Robert Morley was spontaneity itself. No professors were in attendance, and the first thing he did was come forward and sit down on the edge of the dais with his feet hanging over like someone gone fishing. He spoke as if he had a million things to say, and no time to say them in. His theme was the liberty of the young and their need to defend it. The students were exhorted to mistrust their elders, heed their own instincts and invent their own lives. It was astonishing, hilarious and passionate enough to grace the platform of a nineteenth-century anarchists' meeting.

Robert was a firm believer in shaking people up. In manner and dress an upper-class Englishman, he was enthusiastically wooed by Sydney society, whose rigidly conservative dinner tables he then reduced to silence by a witty espousal of socialism. In Melbourne a journalist asked him the not-unfamiliar question, 'How d'ya like Australia?', and received a harangue about the loathsomeness of our drinking habits. Next day a headline ran: MORLEY ACCUSES MELBOURNE OF 'HOGARTHIAN SQUALOR', and at the performance that evening there were boos from the gallery and counter-clapping from the stalls. In its high spirits, Edward, My Son was more like a campaign than a tour, and my employment was but one small cause among a number to which he rallied. Also, I think, just as Olivier had discovered Peter Finch in Australia, he felt it appropriate and amusing that he, too, should have a protégé, and I had been the first to apply.

We were coming to the end of the Sydney run and the question arose whether my employment should be extended to cover the Melbourne engagement. This would mean an air fare and an increase in salary since I would no longer be living at home, and Robert appealed to the management for subsidy. When they turned him down he wrote them a letter: '. . . I go to a great deal of trouble to find you a budding publicity genius to mend the damage done by our disastrous opening . . . I have repeatedly asked that the head of your publicity department in Melbourne should contact me personally in order that we might work out the details of a campaign, but he or she has not even bothered to write to me. Why must I always prod you out of this regrettable tendency to let sleeping dogs sleep on? For heaven's sake take my advice about Blakemore, because if you don't Miss Stewart and I will employ him anyway, and shall not feel we are in the least obliged to protect the firm's interest in any publicity releases. Yours ever, Robert.'

So I went to Melbourne, but my usefulness as a publicist would soon be abruptly curtailed. My first responsibility was to go on a couple of days ahead of the main party and approach all the newspapers with the request that they leave the Morleys unmolested on the day of their arrival in Melbourne. This would allow the family to settle into their rented house and the star to rest before the dress rehearsal. The following day there would be a full-scale press conference when Robert would give interviews and photo opportunities to anyone who wanted them. I was an eloquent persuader; no reporters, I begged, at the airport or the house for the sake of the two tiny children. Somewhat grumpily all the editors (I had gone to the top) agreed. And, indeed, there was no press at the airport, nor at the house. The entourage was allowed to unload and unpack without annoyance. I was on hand to help. It was decided to feed the children at a table in the rear garden, where the rest of us could enjoy a drink at sundown. We had barely settled when over the paling fence separating the Morleys' house from their neighbours an unfamiliar figure came climbing. He approached with the backward and forward motion of a dog making friends. It was a reporter from *The Sun*, intent upon scooping his rivals.

Robert, bemused by the man's initiative which had cost him a tear in his trousers, agreed to a chat. Immediately a second figure hoisted himself to the top of the fence and swayed there precariously with an enormous press camera. Robert decided he, too, deserved marks for resourcefulness. The family and Morton arranged themselves for a group shot while I stood to one side, aware that things were not proceeding quite as they should. Noticing my expression the photographer beckoned me into the group.

'Come on, Michael! Come on!' everyone yelled, making room for me at the table. I hesitated, but not for long. I had never had a picture taken alongside my illustrious employer, and surely my scrapbook demanded one. I wish I could say that it was the last time in my life that vanity triumphed over prudence. When the flash went off I was grinning as zealously as a Presidential hopeful. The next day story and picture appeared at the top of page two. Simultaneously the door of every newspaper in town slammed in my face, including, the cruellest injustice, that of *The Sun*.

What then was to be done with me? Robert concocted a few errands that spelt mischief for the management. One night during the performance I had to go behind the set with pencil and pad, and from the back of each tarnished canvas flat take down the names of all the previous shows for which it had been used. The stencils read *The White Horse Inn*, *The Maid of the Mountains*, *The Desert Song*, each flat like a much forwarded envelope that had been circulating in the post for twenty years. Perforce my usefulness decreased with each day, until one evening in the dressing room Robert announced a brand new assignment: the children, aged two and eight, required an education and I was to be their tutor.

Thereafter, each morning at 8.30 I took the half-hour bus ride through the swelling Melbourne heat to the Morley household. Annabel, the youngest, soon made it understood that she was not yet at the age of instruction, but Sheridan and I sat in the garden, surrounded by the racket of Australian insect life, slowly making our way through a history book about Attila the Hun and Alaric the Goth. Inside the house we could just hear Robert, still in pyjamas and dressing gown, tapping away on an idea for a new play. Joan Morley would make us all lunch, and the summer days passed pleasantly.

If Melbourne did little to advance me professionally, it did wonders for me privately. Beyond the borders of New South Wales for the first time in my life and away from the opinions of a peer group I seemed to have had nudging me since kindergarten, I was meeting new experience on my own terms. I had my first full-blown affair, with a policeman's daughter, Etruscan both in her pagan good looks and the generosity with which she bestowed them on me. Technically I had already lost my virginity in one of the scattering of drunken fumbles, mournful and finished in the light of day, that passed for a young man's love life in the Sydney of that period. This was different. Each time I slipped into bed secure beside my Melbourne lover, it was like coming home after an exile that had lasted as long as my twenty-one years.

New Zealand, next stop on the tour, was looming. Morty had done Robert's finances and had discovered serious overspending on items such as the Christmas party for the company. Economies were in order and I had to be one of them. One morning Robert asked, 'Well, my boy, what are you going to do with your life? You want to work in the theatre, but as what? Publicist?'

I murmured that I didn't think publicity had proved to be my métier.

'What then? Actor?'

I said that, yes, I'd thought about acting, but what I really wanted to be was a director.

Robert reflected upon this for a beat. 'You'll have to develop a great deal more personality than you have at the moment if you want to be a director,' he said.

By now I was beginning to take these annihilating observations of Robert's in my stride, but only just. I have never forgotten the exact wording of this one, nor the bland stare that accompanied it.

He carried on blithely: 'Be an actor. There's much more work available. But if you're going to be an actor you'll have to audition, so I think you'd better audition for me. Work something up, and you can give a performance for us all on stage one night after the show.'

This was a challenge which I don't think he expected me to accept. But, beyond fifteen minutes of total humiliation, what had I to lose? Besides, I had a stubborn itch to re-engage his interest, and except for shows of insane courage, I had run out of options. I would do it!

The Australian temperament inclines towards spells of wilful idleness interspersed with periods of frantic entrepreneurial energy. I was now in the grip of the latter as I planned my debut on the stage of the Comedy Theatre. Like so many young and innocuous aspirants to the profession I was drawn to villainous parts, perhaps because I found in their murderous exercise of power something conspicuously absent in my own life. Olivier had just done *Richard III* so I had second thoughts about that, and in retrospect I can only thank God for it. I decided on Edmund in *King Lear*, but needed to find a Gloucester to read the scene with me. I began to make approaches within the company. The elderly actor most suited to the role laughed me out of his dressing room, but Eric Rieman, a gentle Estonian with a marked accent, was too kind to say no. However, he was not such a fool as to agree to rehearse, so he put me in touch with a drama coach of his acquaintance. This lady, dressed like a gypsy palmist and so theatrical in manner I had difficulty holding her eye, did her best with me, but I was unyielding clay, the usual novice compound of awkward embarrassment and innocent conceit. I did better work on my own, declaiming to the four walls of my bedroom the soliloquy which opened the scene. 'Thou, NATURE, art my goddess.' 'Thou, Nature, art my GODDESS.' 'Thou, Nature, art MY goddess.' I ran through the possibilities.

The night of the audition had arrived. In an unoccupied dressing room on the top floor, wearing the better of my two suits, a blue pinstripe double-breasted made to measure by Sydney's only posh English tailor, J. H. Cutler, and now too small for me, I applied the bright orange mask I had so often seen Robert assume downstairs. Like rumour of a public execution, word of my coming ordeal had spread quickly, and as I walked that last mile from the dressing room to the stage, mouthing my words, the air was electric with morbid expectation. I knew my lines by heart but Eric would be reading his. He was waiting for me below, the *Collected Works* clasped in two hands, his expression a grimace of sympathy, exactly like Pat O'Brien as James Cagney goes to the chair. Gathered around Robert in the middle of the stalls were some others in the company, a small body of witnesses. The stage management had provided lights, and there was a brief discussion as to whether we would use the curtain. I thought it might be helpful. Down it came. Eric and I assumed our positions. Up it went again and I was on. 'THOU, NATURE, ART MY GODDESS!!' Not one word throughout the scene went uninflected.

Afterwards Robert took everyone for coffee and sandwiches at a café nearby. I was in such a state of shock I remained completely silent, shivering intermittently like someone overtaken with a sudden attack of malaria. I saw Robert eyeing me with a new curiosity from the other end of the table. 'You did very well, Michael,' he announced.

'Unlike most beginners you made the wise decision to remain stock-still more or less throughout. When in doubt stillness is very useful on stage. I think we should send you to RADA, the Royal Academy of Dramatic Art in London. I'll write a letter to the Principal telling him about you. At the conclusion of the two-year course perhaps you will be able to attempt a movement or two.'

Robert volunteered to write another letter on my behalf, this time to my father. He knew that my decision to go on the stage would be made in the teeth of fierce paternal opposition. This was a time when Robert and Joan Morley took very good care of me. One day, travelling in the car with them to a matinee, Joan said, 'Your real decision is actually which country are you going to live in? If you're serious about the theatre then it probably means going to England and not coming back.' In those days it was probably true.

'But what if I get there and *fail*?' I pleaded.

'Well, of course you might fail!' said Robert. 'Lots of people fail. That doesn't matter. You just do something else.'

'Like *what*?' I said a shade indignantly.

'Anything! Open a corner grocery shop; become a carpenter. There are endless possibilities!'

This was a revelation to me. For so many years I had been drilled in the limited options of Australian respectability – the necessity to succeed, the few things it was permissible to succeed in – that it had never occurred to me that I could be free of all that simply by deciding to be so.

I wish I still had my copy of Robert's letter to my father. It began 'About this son of yours . . . ' and ended, 'When he comes to London I shall, of course, keep an eye on him, possibly a blind one.' It was humorous and very sympathetic, not only to my aspirations but to my father's misgivings. When I left to return to Sydney I took the precious letter with me to post on arrival.

My parents were divorced and the person I had first to tell about my new life was my mother. She was, as mothers will be, mostly concerned with my happiness, and I was clearly a different person from the sullen student of the previous year. 'Robert thinks I should have two years with RADA,' I said.

She looked baffled for a moment then said, 'Of course, dear. But don't you think two years is rather a long time?' The only RADA she knew was Rada Penfold Sherlaw, heiress to the Penfold wines fortune, recently gone to London and notorious in Sydney for a profligate love life. After I explained, she said she'd help with the fees. No mention was made of the fact that her only child would soon be packing up his room and travelling twelve thousand miles to another hemisphere.

Now I posted the letter to my father. I left a full day for safe delivery before going to see him. He was hosing in the garden and seemed in a surprisingly benign mood. He made no mention of the letter. Sybil, his second wife, asked me to stay to dinner, and throughout a cheerful meal it still wasn't referred to. I grew uneasy. Finally, over coffee on the veranda I brought the matter up myself.

I tried the casual approach. 'By the way, what did you think of Robert Morley's letter?'

'What letter?'

'The letter about me going to England . . . and becoming an actor . . .'

There was an awful pause. Sybil intervened. 'Oh dear, I think it must be my fault. There was a letter in the box when I went shopping this morning but it wasn't there when I got back. It's probably those kids next door.'

I'd had an intimation something like this might happen, and in my breast pocket I had a copy. We sat in silence a long time as his eyes travelled along each line and his jaw moved fractionally from side to side. He folded the letter up carefully and returned it to me.

'I don't pretend to know much about the theatre,' he said, 'but I think I can see when someone has what it takes. And you haven't got it.'

But Robert Morley had equipped me in armour. The scepticism that I seemed to have feared all my life glanced to one side.

Likewise when one of my most intelligent friends, studying law with excellent prospects, said to me, 'What do you bet? This time next year you'll be back doing medicine, and grateful for the chance,' I knew it was his own interests he was defending, not mine.

I now resumed the enquiries about working my passage to London that I'd begun six months before. It was difficult to swing, but someone important in one of the shipping lines knew my family. Ironically I was to make the trip in the most uncomfortable way imaginable through the power of my Australian connections, the last time for many years they'd be of much use to me.

I was due to board the RMS *Otranto* no later than ten o'clock one balmy autumn evening. There was just time to drop in on what might be my last Sydney cocktail party. Drinks were being served outside in a lush garden with a smell of cut grass as potent as scent. Below us a mile away the stretching waters of the harbour were corrugated by the nor-easterly breeze which after each warm day blows in from the Pacific to cool and clean that remarkable city. A contemporary of my father's, in real estate, approached.

'Just a word of advice, Mike,' he said. 'This was said to me thirty years ago by old Theo Wilberforce; your mother will know him. I was just starting up and he said "Be patient." That's all. Be patient.'

I was very touched, not so much for the excellent – and prophetic – advice, but because someone who'd known me all my life and who had no interest in the things that interested me, had nevertheless wanted to say that he took me seriously.

Two staunch friends, Joanna Fitzgerald and Andrew Clayton, who if they had their doubts about me kept them to themselves, drove me down to the docks with my two suitcases. I waved into the dark from the top of the rickety gangplank and then vanished through the side of the huge iron ship. I was off.

# TWO

# The Promised Land

Getting to England! There was another reason, apart from my avowed one of pursuing a career in the theatre, why I had to make the journey. My passport was Australian but it described me as a British subject, the dichotomy of colonial life. In the Australia of my growing-up the British influence was as endemic as the eucalyptus was to the bush. Even the railed promenade at Bondi Beach owed something to Blackpool. British animals romped through our children's books, and at the height of summer we opened Christmas presents decorated with emblems of snow and holly. The classroom of my preparatory school was dominated by the lugubrious sepia presence of a stooped King George V in scout uniform. My father's surgery was in a building called the BMA, and when I walked with him through the lobby of the Royal Sydney Golf Club we ran a gauntlet to left and right of signed royal photographs, sleekly mounted behind glass. In our courts judges and barristers wore wigs and looked to the House of Lords for final appeal. All our institutions owed something to a British model, at times for good, at others, as in the case of my education, for something less.

The King's School, at which I boarded from eleven to eighteen, was described by a visiting English observer during my stay there as 'Rugby in 1870'. Dr Arnold himself would not have been displeased with its martinet discipline, its compulsory games and its endless chapel attendances. All that was missing was any passion or feel for education, which hardly mattered since the school's traditional intake was the male offspring of prosperous graziers, for whom the school was a way of filling in time before they turned their hand to the husbanding of their vast acres. What our fathers were buying for us was a brush with the coded world of an exclusive institution, and this was energetically provided. We all wore a bizarre military uniform, on which it was possible as one grew in seniority for small bits and pieces to accumulate, signifying status. We were divided into competitive houses, which took to the rugby field for tribal skirmishes, then united in Zulu wars against other schools. There were incessant roll-calls before prayers and before each dreadful meal. Two school chaplains were on hand to preach sexual abstinence and the dire consequences of solitary indulgence, and in this they were abetted by a history master, self-elected to the task, who smelt of perfumed talc and who had a habit when discussing what he euphemistically called 'this dormitory business' of stroking his face with a plump right hand and letting the tip of his little finger find its way into one or other nostril where it would wriggle in an exploratory fashion. In each dormitory he had an informer stationed, who would report back at the least sign of undue restlessness beneath the bedclothes. Had Kim Philby appointed himself Director General of MI5 it would not have been a more inappropriate delegation of authority.

Every adolescent in the school lived under the threat of madness, blindness and the growth of hair in the palm of the hand, as everyone did what none of us dared admit. Only at a certain time of the year when a huge tree of tropical origin overhanging the approach to the chapel would drop to the ground big sticky pods which smelt unmistakably of semen, would our shared smirking amount to a confession. Gawky boys shuffled about on the gravel drive in their black school boots, grinning slyly at each other, until bugle and drum brought us to attention and we were marched in to worship the King of Kings after whom the school was named.

Lest any of us failed to take this deranged, invented world with due seriousness it was enforced by the genial application of terror. The school was policed not by its largely apathetic staff, but by an elite of senior boys, the monitors, whose authority was absolute. You could be beaten for anything – running on a brick path where you were meant to walk, walking on a grass field where you were meant to run. You could be beaten for infringing rules you never knew existed. Punishment, in fact, preceded crime as if inventing it, and the queue of the guilty waiting to be beaten outside the monitors' study last thing at night was of an always similar length.

The headmaster of the King's School, imported for the job, was Mr Hake, a cultivated Englishman who wanted change but was more or less captive to a heavy brigade of Old Boys who thought the school just about perfect the way it was. It didn't help that he was headmaster during the war years, nor that he was a fervent believer in the idea of the English public school, even as expressed in this quaint Australian mutation. However, I owe a number of things to the intercession of this anxious, displaced figure.

Similarly, the Warden of my University College was a delightful English clergyman, Felix Arnott, who encouraged us to form a drama group, the St Paul's College Mummers, but was hardly a match for the traditionalists. At no time in my life was the word 'tradition' more often invoked than during my Australian education. These traditions were mostly dubious and sometimes disgraceful, as in the ritual torment of freshmen endorsed by the college. Not everyone participated, but those that didn't seemed paralysed by the maudlin justifications of the small core of senior students who did. 'Tradition' was the licence that permitted a handful of usually drunken, vicious young men to haul slightly younger men from their beds at any hour of the night, herd them naked into the quadrangle and then submit them to a variety of ingenious and sometimes painful indignities. The freshers had an 'F' written on their foreheads with silver nitrate, a brand which would remain until new skin had erased the smudgy stain. They were made to eat rotten eggs held fast in a cupboard for six months by some psychotic senior. One year the practice had been to group the freshmen in a rough semicircle so that each held the genitals of whoever stood beside him; the two end men were then connected to the engine of a motorbike which, when kick-started, sent an electric charge pulsing around the loop. It was argued that these and other depravities in some obscure way upheld the British connection. Even our building, a Victorian sandstone homage to Oxbridge, was transformed when the sun was strong into something more Islamic than Gothic. And yet, in a way not intended, these claims to a British tradition may have been the plain truth. There are still vestiges of Australian life which are like an acting-out of some dull memory of the country's first brutal settlement. At King's in the 1830s, so the Latin master once told me, small boys were given leave on Saturdays to see the convicts hanged, a dispensation, no doubt, of the school's odious founder, the Revd Samuel Marsden.

I rebelled against the college as I had against the school, but with the zeal of a reformist, not a revolutionary. There were two reasons for this. The first was self-interest; the system I'd been put through had one useful end product, membership of Australia's rough and ready notion of an upper class, and I was not yet ready to renounce it. The second was more idealistic. Surely it was not the *idea* of such institutions that was at fault; only these Australian parodies of them. I had just been bowled over by *Brideshead Revisited*. Was the book a complete lie? Somewhere the life we aped, the ideal of gentility, was being lived as it was meant to be, and from everything I had read or been told, that place was England.

The education I've described touched on the lives of few Australians, but they tended to be influential ones whose Anglophilia was reflex and unquestioning. The one unpardonable sin in the circles in which my parents moved was to be 'anti-British'. My mother came from a family of sheep-breeders, and, as a girl, had been taken on the Grand Tour of Britain and the Continent. In her accounts of that trip her week in Florence came a poor second to seeing Fred and Adele Astaire live on the London stage. Like similar Australian young ladies abroad, she had had the opportunity of being presented at court, but declined because her knees wobbled when she was nervous. This was a family trait which would reassert itself in the next generation on certain exceptionally tense first nights.

Immediately after their marriage my parents came to London and lived frugally in rooms in Paddington while my father studied for his FRCS. They bought cheap seats for what may have been the first London performance of *Uncle Vanya*, and my father was heavily ironical about a man who could fire at a target six feet away and miss. The play had been given on a very small stage.

Back in Australia they would begin to make long-term plans for another trip. At least once in a decade, more often if you could afford it, you caught the boat to England to brush up on your notion of style, perhaps to acquire the new tortoiseshell frames for my mother's glasses which no one in Australia was yet wearing, or a fresh supply of made-to-measure shirts for my father. Armed with this symbolic attire and a few new ideas they would return to the underside of the world to get on with their lives. These trips fed the myths of my childhood.

Britishness was not imposed upon us; we assumed we needed it. We needed a 'somewhere else' to prop up our frail sense of who we were. Even in as populous a city as Sydney there were days when you looked into the depth of the Australian sky and felt the glare bleaching out all your hard-won scribbles of identity. Until air travel only a brave man could face the yawn of the Australian vastness without a reassuring glance over his shoulder to faraway England.

The RMS *Otranto* was taking me on a voyage of discovery, therefore, not to one country but to two: the Britain I needed to believe in, and the other Britain, the one that actually existed. Pulling these two images into focus was to consume a great deal of my energies over the next five years.

The first Englishman I met on board was consistent with my expectations. I had been instructed to report to the Second Steward, who would inform me of my duties over the next five weeks. He was the typical British NCO figure of which our school Sergeant was but one of many Australian examples, and he told me that I would be waiting on one side of a long table for sixteen, two sittings for each meal. 'And if you don't work I'll have your guts for garters,' he said, with the malign jocularity of men whose uniforms denote the bottommost rungs of the ladder of authority. I then found my way to the cabin which I was to share with seven other stewards, and here I was to meet some Englishmen who did surprise me. It wasn't just that their accents were so heavy I had no idea what they were saying; nothing about them was recognisable. In Australia we knew about the British worker mostly from entertainers with the neutered good nature of George Formby and Gracie Fields. There was nothing neutered about the stewards on the *Otranto*. They were as foreign to me as if I had found myself among Turks.

The *Otranto* would not be your first choice to travel on or serve in – a battered Orient Line vessel which, within a few years would be sent to the scrapyard. She was a one-class passenger ship whose list on this voyage was an unhappy mixture of Australians getting to London on the cheap and disgruntled English immigrants for whom Down-Under had proved the greatest mistake of their lives. The star passengers, if any can be so described, were athletes from the Canadian Empire Games Team on their way home after competing in New Zealand. Some had been assigned to my table. The crew of the *Otranto* derived from the bottom of the seafaring labour market: first-timers, young men avoiding the call-up and others with even more urgent reasons to be out of the country. They were not a conscientious bunch. Those doing the washing-up saved themselves trouble by levering open the

grill across the porthole and simply tossing the dirty dishes overboard. By the end of the voyage crockery was in such short supply
that there were long waits between courses while the few plates that
remained were doused in scummy warm water and recirculated.

The stewards with whom I worked were Liverpool-Irish. This was
the accent which had been so impenetrable to me. No Jean Gabin
or James Cagney had dignified Scousers on film; no books like *The
Grapes of Wrath* or *Christ in Concrete* had examined their lot. They
were, at least to me, un-represented. As the voyage proceeded and
I began to learn more about their lives I realised that, as far as their
own country was concerned, they were also pretty much expendable.

There were two moments of high drama on the voyage, one in the
first week at sea, the other on the very last day. Both were triggered by
drink. We had sailed across the Great Australian Bight to Freemantle,
last port of call before the long haul across the Indian Ocean. I was
one of a skeleton crew kept on board while the rest went ashore on a
morning's leave. By 12.30 only a handful of stewards had returned to
attend to their lunchtime duties, and they proved to be seriously drunk.
Almost the entire ship's company had succumbed to the West Australian beer, much stronger than English bitter and on sale throughout the
day. I found myself having to wait on not eight but sixteen dissatisfied
people. Complaints from the passengers reached a crescendo when the
increasing number of those stewards who had returned stumbled with
laden trays of slopping food and quarrelled noisily amongst themselves. When this aggression turned on the scandalised passengers the
dining room quickly cleared.

Down the far end, a fight with dirty crockery had developed. Plates
flew in one direction across the saloon and smashed cups in another.
I was too busy to give it much attention, until I noticed that one of the
combatants had disengaged himself from the battle and was coming
down the length of the saloon in my direction, holding in his hand
some fragments of broken china. His name was Murphy and during
the week I'd been on board I had seen him watching me with a hostility as disconcerting as it was unexplained.

'Hey, Lofty!' he said, and then came very close to me. 'Take this
fookin' cup to the Captain and tell him you fookin' broke it.'

I was tired and fed up, and told him loudly to bugger off. It was not
a sensible thing to do. In an instant I had become the focus of the
saloon. The battle had stopped, and from all directions Murphy's

companions were approaching with the ominous stateliness that precedes a dog fight. They clustered round, hungry for something to happen. Murphy came even closer and swayed. I looked down at him, at his heavily brilliantined wavy hair and a face all triangles. He lifted a fragment of broken cup and gently scratched my chin with it.

'I could slit your fookin' throat with this,' he said, and added, 'Before we're five days into the Indian Ocean you'll be over the side.'

I was in trouble. Had they all been a shade less drunk I would have been in even worse trouble. As it was, the head waiter bustled in amongst us, broke up the group and, in the few seconds in which they were distracted, spirited me into the galley. I was then pushed into the silver locker and confined there for the two or three hours it took for everyone to sober up. Murphy went ashore again that afternoon, but was later arrested by the police wheeling a stolen motorbike on board, and much to my relief was never seen again.

I had encountered violence before, of course, but being of the institutionalised kind, it had two distinguishing features. The first was that you could see it coming from a long way off (in the case of punishment this was often the intention), and the second was that however unpleasant it turned out to be, there was always a scrupulously observed limit placed upon it. What I had just narrowly escaped was a violence that was spontaneous, random and of unforeseeable dimensions. It was another world.

The other eruption of drama occurred within sight of the Cliffs of Dover. This time it was the passengers who had been celebrating. Particularly drunk were the Canadian athletes, on eight of whom I had been waiting throughout the voyage. Up to now they had been very well behaved, if of voracious appetite, sitting down to each gigantic meal in their neat red blazers. The middleweight wrestling champion, a French-Canadian absolutely cubic in shape, who spoke no English and whose usual job was as a bouncer in a Montreal nightclub, used to take a pencil to his menu and inscribe a number before each course. It was his way of saying he wanted not one but three servings of fish, four plates of steak, four apple crumbles. I was kept busy.

On our last day at sea the team rolled into lunch with much merriment and hungrier than ever. The wrestler smiled foolishly as I put plate after plate in front of him. However, when I returned from the galley with his fifth chop I noticed that his mood had changed. He was arguing violently in French with his neighbour. All around the dining room people began to stare. Wanting to avoid a scandal, a senior member of the team rose from his place further down the table and tried to calm the wrestler by placing a hand on either shoulder. His touch had a contrary effect to the one intended. The wrestler was galvanised. With something between a grunt and a roar he rose up from his seat. The sound was evidently a signal with which his red-blazered companions were only too familiar, because immediately all seven of them swooped to subdue him.

Under constraint the wrestler responded by taking hold of the underside of the long table and attempting to overturn it. Since it was firmly bolted to the deck this was not easy, and for some seconds he was frozen with effort, as neither he nor the table moved and only his colour changed, from pink to red to bruised purple. We all watched disbelieving, like onlookers when Samson heaved between the twin pillars of the temple. There followed a sequence of snapping, rending sounds as iron and wood yielded, and the meals of sixteen people slid away from the horizontal. At the final, splintering crack, as the table and all its loading toppled to one side, the whole dining room rose to its feet and women started screaming.

King Kong was now, as it were, out of his cage, and the enveloping circle of athletes took a cautious step back. Only the flyweight boxer was brave enough to approach in one last effort in conciliation. The wrestler cuffed him to the ground with the offhand brutality of a grisly bear. White with rage, the boxer leapt to his feet and, in the most astonishing blow I will ever see delivered, virtually left the floor, levitated for a moment like a tiny Superman, and knocked the wrestler cold. Quickly the red blazers closed ranks and dragged the unconscious cube from the dining room, in the same way that at the end of a shameful corrida, galloping horses drag the dead bull from sight.

The month that separates these events was one of monotonous and relentless toil. I had never worked like this in my life. The routine was the same every day, seven days a week. Up at six, two sittings for breakfast, two sittings for lunch, then afternoon tea and two sittings for dinner. By the time the second lot of passengers had left the dining room and we had eaten ourselves (often on a scale to match the Canadians), there was perhaps three-quarters of an hour free before the next meal. I would make straight for my bunk and immerse myself in a few more pages of *Point Counterpoint*, the Aldous Huxley novel about depravity in fashionable London. My body may have been confined in one version of England, but for a couple of hours each day I was deep in the world of another.

At night sleep fell upon me with Pentothal swiftness. As the voyage proceeded, and I laboured, ate and slept, I began to feel an unfamiliar sort of physical well-being. Complaint was hardly affordable, nor illness, in this state of animal docility. I saw how a whole lifetime could slide by, just getting through one day, then another, until one day your body let you down and you died.

I made some friends among the crew, and found decency and even talent dispersed in about the same proportions as they would be anywhere. There was a natural comic among the stewards who, throughout the working day, kept up an extraordinary monologue whether people appeared to be listening or not. It seemed to come out of some bottomless well of humorous invention. We liked to queue up behind him in the galley when we were loading up with dishes, just to hear the topic of the moment. Another spirited Scouser told me with touching earnestness of his determination to make his way in the world. He had first tried to box his way out of an impossible life, but after a couple of professional fights was left with nothing but a badly broken nose. Now he had just read his first book, and had decided it might be worth carrying on. He wanted me to make him a reading list.

'What was the book?' I asked.

'*How to Win Friends and Influence People*, by Dale Carnegie,' he told me. 'Do y' know that one at all? It's verra, verra gude.'

I thought of all the books I'd ever read from Beatrix Potter to my current Huxley. Where could I begin? And how could he ever catch up?

I got ashore on two afternoons, the first at Colombo. Before television other parts of the world could amaze you. I had never seen such density of glistening humanity. They seemed to be living lives of an order as strange to me as that of the teeming colonies of soldier crabs I had left behind on the Australian beaches. This shore leave much improved the morale of the crew. They returned to the boat after visiting Port Said talking loudly of wogs, their spirits raised by this reminder that in the pecking order of Empire there were others placed lower than themselves.

The most useful friend I had on the ship, because he commanded a healthy respect from that section who had toyed with the idea of throwing me overboard, was an ex-Royal Marine commando named Fred Malthouse. He was heavy-jawed with a somewhat shuffling walk

as if he'd just got out of bed, and, like me, was odd man out to the
extent that he came not from Liverpool but from Newcastle, the only
Geordie on board. His was the top bunk on the opposite side of the
cabin to me, and I learnt much about his chequered life. He'd just
spent three months in jail for razor-slashing a man in a pub who'd
been pestering him for a drink. The victim's face required twenty-three
stitches, so Fred felt it had almost been worth it. Not long before, his
wife, a seventeen-year-old Italian girl, had died of tuberculosis. The
sicker she got, he told me with a dreadful grin, the more often they
had each other and the better it was. Left with nothing to do, Fred's
thoughts turned at once to sex. In the mornings while the rest of us
were getting dressed, he'd lie naked on his bunk with the nature of his
reveries unambiguously on display. Though preferring women he was
a sexual omnivore and would proposition anything he fancied. He
had, however, one unexpected area of restraint. Stretched out on his
bunk he would never touch, or only for a moment, his engorged member. Instead he would talk to it: 'We're savin' up, aren't we, you 'n' me,
till we get somewhere to put you.' Our History master would have
been proud of him.

In spite of being a creature of appetite, Fred had his moments of
gentleness. A stoic melancholy would come over him when he went
on deck and looked down at the baffling magnificence of the Indian
Ocean with flying fish leaping from the bow wave. In the tropic nights
when the crew drank the warm ale with which we would be issued at
the end of the working day, Fred and I would sit together with our flat
pints looking up at the tropic stars, I, no less than he, silent and diminished beneath those feverish constellations.

I arrived in England in the spring of 1950 with £21 in wages and
£20 in tips. I was also the richer by a pair of socks, purchased in Port
Said, which a woman passenger, undoubtedly a first cousin of Barry
Humphries' Edna Everage, had pressed into my hand as a gratuity for
waiting on her every mouthful over the 12,000 miles of the voyage.
The RADA term began in the autumn, assuming, that is, that I passed
the entrance test. I had a summer to come into my long-awaited inheritance: knowledge of the country Australians incorrectly called 'Home'.

At the top of my list of people to look up was my English godmother, Helen, with whom my parents had gone to tennis parties at
Richmond during the twenties. She and her husband, Guy, were now
dairy farmers in Sussex, where they tended a herd of twelve or so

velvet-nosed pedigree Guernseys. The name of each animal, appropriately cow-like – May-Belle, Daisy and so on – was chalked on a board above its stall. So great was the affection lavished upon them it was more like milking a dozen very large labrador dogs, animal husbandry of a very different order from that on my uncle's property in the Monaro, where nameless sheep shifted in huge, soiled congregations over the dry pasture.

Helen was a small, energetic woman of a cheerfulness that had a hint of reprimand about it, and like many busy people seemed always to be leaning out of the present into the future; as she served up one meal she was already thinking about laying the table for another. Her husband, on the other hand, was a shy Old Etonian who seemed to be leaning in the other direction, backwards and away from whatever was going on. His hesitant, almost asthmatic courtesy concealed considerable rage, and the two often fought – hardly surprising, given the long, inescapable hours they worked, rarely out of each other's company. They had no money to speak of and did everything for themselves, something about which Helen never complained but was not beyond dramatising. It was almost as if the war years had given her an attachment to the stiff medicine of hardship. When she offered me a pair of reeking Wellingtons and suggested a trudge through a small lake of manure to inspect the newborn calves I never felt I rushed to pull them on with quite the enthusiasm she thought fitting.

They lived in an ancient flintstone cottage of great charm and greater discomfort. In the sitting room the veneer on the Queen Anne furniture was buckled and bleached from the combination of sunlight in the summer, when all the doors and windows would be thrown open, and damp in the depths of winter, when with some reluctance they would be shut. The main source of heating in the cottage, constant throughout the four seasons, was the fuel-burning Aga stove in the dining room, and seepage from this source of warmth was meant to make its way down two short steps to the sitting room, glide over the polished brick floor, which four hundred years before had been laid straight on the Sussex earth, take a right turn in the hall, ascend a steep flight of stairs and at last bring comfort to the two upstairs bedrooms.

The one in which I slept was very prettily decorated with wallpaper applied wherever there wasn't a beam, but it was shaped more like a cave than a room. You stooped to enter, then moved cautiously beneath serrated diagonals of wormy black wood. My first winter in England I made the mistake of visiting them and catching influenza. Only when my temperature was about level with the Aga was I put to bed beneath an eiderdown the weight and pliancy of lead sheeting. I looked in the direction of the audible draught and noticed that my bedroom no longer had a door. When I asked Helen about this she explained that it had been needed for the bullpen.

'You're not the only one who thinks he should be cosseted, Mike, dear,' she said, thumping down a tray of bread and lemon jelly.

It must be said that on the sunny spring day on which I first saw the cottage it looked idyllic, and Helen and Guy could not have been more welcoming. I think they were a little surprised to find an aspirant to the stage so rigidly on his best behaviour. They didn't share my father's absolute prejudice against the acting profession; it was a perfectly acceptable career if you were sufficiently affected and brainless to be unsuitable for anything else. Clearly someone as sober as I appeared to be should be thinking along more sensible lines. Helen was to point the way.

We went for walks on the Downs and drank in Sussex pubs, where I sensed but could not decipher nuances of hierarchy in the apparently uniform warmth with which she greeted everyone on both sides of the bar. A neighbour drove us in his sleek Bentley to an agricultural event featuring beribboned cattle. We took sherry in the middle of the day with an elderly baronet who had weekend rights over a National Trust property in the village. We motored to high lookout spots and Guy pointed to the distant features of the beautiful, utterly subdued countryside, a garden three counties wide to which I could respond with nodding admiration but little feeling. Sometimes in the evenings I would be taken to a cocktail party where twenty or so focused, emotionally neutral conversations produced a sound as uniform as that of massed birds. Similar occasions in Australia tended to be loose, rowdy quests for laughter and mockery. I could see the advantages of coherence and social discipline, but I didn't enjoy them.

Back on the train on Sunday night, I reached into my carry-all and took out D. H. Lawrence's *Kangaroo*. In Australia I had read about England; now in England, and for the first time with any passion, I was reading about Australia. No book had ever suggested to me before a clairvoyant aspect to literature. It was uncanny that an Englishman visiting the country for a bare six weeks should be able to get so to the heart of the Australian character, to prophesy its politics and empathise with its landscape. I read with wonder Lawrence's description of the coastal wildness south of Sydney, an area where I had spent many Christmases during my growing-up. As the ordered fields sped past beyond the window this other landscape of limitless ocean and grey bush had never seemed more real to me. The nearer we approached Victoria Station, suburbs giving way to the grimy backs of stunted brick terraces, the more confused my feelings about these weekends in Sussex became. I was being offered something which I knew had value to others but which I didn't really want.

There were other parts of southern England I got to know. Robert Morley, as good as his word, asked me down to Berkshire for Sundays with the family. His particular cottage was more of a house with the right stress on creature comforts. There were always people coming and going or dropping in for tea, most of them conspicuously successful actors and writers. It was a bit like being back in the dressing room once again, waving the flag of your own personality as everyone else waved theirs. Mine was about the size of a small pennant. I was not yet even a drama student, simply waiting to be one, and I felt quite inadequate when confronted with the languid assurance of these fortunate achievers. Robert would shoot me a glance occasionally, sympathetic and perhaps a little impatient, but no one can rescue the young from the pain of their own self-absorption or from the genuine void of the future they must face.

I once wondered aloud to Robert how long it would take to get anywhere. 'For your sake I hope not for at least fifteen years,' he said. 'By that time you may have learnt enough to deal with it.' Fifteen years! That was only six years short of the time I'd been alive.

It didn't help that his friends were always telling me on no account to be an actor. Sewell Stokes, author of Robert's first success, *Oscar Wilde*, spent an entire afternoon tea detailing the awfulness of the life. It wasn't intended as a reflection on my hypothetical talent, but the suspicion remained that I hadn't made the liveliest of impressions. At that time Robert was rehearsing *The Little Hut*, and one Saturday he asked me to join some of the company for lunch at a Charlotte Street restaurant. I found myself sitting next to the play's director, Peter Brook. A man of aggressive curiosity, he soon began winkling out the circumstances in which I'd come to know Robert. I finished my account, quite pleased with myself, and there was a pause.

'Look, I have to advise you,' he intoned gravely. 'Don't be an actor. There are far too many actors already. This would be my advice to anyone.'

I had travelled a very long way to be told yet again I had made a mistake, and I decided to be impertinent. 'Maybe I should be a director then. There aren't too many of them around. Good ones anyway.'

Brook rather liked this show of spirit. 'Well, yes! Why not? By all means! Be a director then.' Whether Robert Morley's prescription for me had been spell or prophecy I have no way of knowing, but it would be exactly fifteen years before I would have an opportunity of acting on Peter Brook's advice.

Like most green young men, I had the firmest sense of myself and the most fun among my own contemporaries, and that summer there were a number of my Australian friends in London. Their intention was not as mine, to stay for ever, but they were engaged in the same romantic exploration of the Mother Country. Foremost of these was Maitland, the friend at whose table I had first met Morton Gottlieb. He had arrived in London some months before me, and with two high-spirited sisters from Sydney had started an accommodation service, called 'Searchers' Agency', which operated from a small office in Shepherds' Market, off Piccadilly. The business depended on an ancient motorbike which Maitland had acquired and on which he would drive all over the more genteel residential areas of London, copying down from the noticeboards in newsagents' windows details of rooms and flats available for letting. The two sisters, Jill and Beth, then put this information on file according to district and price, and satisfied customers paid them the equivalent of a week's rent.

It was therefore to Shepherds' Market that I first made my way when the train from Tilbury Docks deposited me at St Pancras Station. Maitland had a furnished room reserved for me for 35 shillings a week on what would now be described as the borders of Maida Vale. I had barely settled in when I was politely asked to move to more suitable premises. A slightly neurotic cleanliness was one of a number of unwelcomed Australian attitudes I had brought with me to the Britain of ration cards and austerity, and the landlady had discovered I expected a hot bath every morning. Working a twelve-hour day in the salt mines of weekly rep would one day cure me of that. I packed up and moved to the smallest room I have ever attempted to live in, not only six feet square but six feet high, dimensions compensated for to some extent by its magnificent address. For an extra five shillings a week I was living in the heart of Mayfair, directly opposite the rather more spacious accommodation of the Duke of Westminster. Before long I had moved again, to a mews around the corner, Adam's Row, where for the next two years I was to occupy a slightly larger and certainly higher room facing a brick wall above a garage hiring out chauffeur-driven Daimler cars.

By this time I was on the staff of Searchers' Agency. The accommodation side of the business was going well, and now they wanted to expand into other fields; hence my employment. Surely they could do more for their mainly Australian clientele than simply finding them a roof over their heads? Why not introduce them to London's best restaurants, dressmakers, tailors, dry-cleaners and so on? Or, if not the best, then anyone prepared to pay the agency a small commission? My job was to approach various posh Mayfair establishments and entice them into our scheme, in which case I would be paid a commission of the commission they paid the agency. Maitland also had plans to turn the basement immediately below the office into a club where clients, with half an hour to spare in the West End, could browse through Australian magazines over a cup of fresh coffee. First he had to clear this with the landlord, who turned out to be a reserved and watchful redhead, Sandra Masters, somewhat in the mould of the British screen star Greta Gynt, who entertained gentleman callers in the mysterious upper reaches of the building during the afternoons. She was at the upmarket end of her profession, and in the mornings when we arrived for work we would often encounter her in full riding gear returning from a trot in the park. After lunch, expensive cars would draw up at our front door to disgorge little old men, whom we would hear scampering up the flight of stairs beside our office. Half an hour later and with less nimble tread they would descend. Miss Masters agreed to let us have the basement for an additional £2 a week.

It was expensive at the price. Smelling of mould with a distinct component of leaking gas, the room had only one source of natural light: a tiny, recessed window high up at pavement level, through which you could just catch glimpses of the passing ankles of the Market's streetwalkers, and hear the businesslike staccato of their high heels as they hunted back and forth. At the weekend we zealously set to work painting these premises and re-upholstering some second-hand furniture in garishly dyed sacking. We laboured in vain. A few people – mainly friends of our parents wanting to be encouraging – coughed up the entrance fee of thirty shillings, but after five minutes underground they struggled upstairs again, never to return. The truth is a canary would have died down there. One day I noticed a tiny hole in one wall. If you put your eye to it you had a view of the lavatory of the sleazy barber's shop next door. It had been bored as a peephole for the hairdressers in the days when our entire building had been let out to tarts.

Most of the time I was out and about the byways of Mayfair trying to drum up business for the agency. I liked the splendid architecture and the certainty every day of catching sight of a famous face – Sam Goldwyn in Cork Street, Rex Harrison in Piccadilly and a bearded and monocled Gulbenkian boarding a taxi at the entrance to the Ritz. At least I was on the same planet as these people, which you some-times wondered about in Sydney. However, the evidence of my eyes also told me that the West End was a less glamorous place than I wanted to believe. In Berkeley Street a three-piece band of be-medalled amputees, veterans of the First World War, offered a plucky rendition of 'Roll Out the Barrel'. The one with the hat saluted passers-by and called them 'Sir', appealing to that same chauvinism that had cost them their limbs. Occasionally there were quite shocking displays of arrogance as young men, in the upper-class uniform of bowler hat, rolled umbrella, striped shirt and starched white collar, comman-deered taxis that others had hailed, or had loud conversations, one at the top of a tube escalator, the other halfway down, over the heads of twenty or so people they gave the impression of not even seeing. My most vivid recollection is of an elderly man, also dressed to precisely reflect his class in the cloth cap and greasy choker of the thirties and somewhat out of place on the top deck of a Knightsbridge-bound bus. The pores of his skin were impregnated with dust and he was ashen with some kind of pulmonary disease, rotting him from within as a lifetime of labour had rotted him from without. What was so distress-ing was the mute apology with which he crouched in his seat and struggled to contain his wheezing. It wouldn't have surprised me if, without a murmur, he had slumped to one side and died. Such sights, and worse, have returned to the streets of London, but this man's atti-tude of passive, broken dignity is a thing of the past.

My job laid me open to some devastating put-downs. At Anderson and Shepherd, the Savile Row tailors, a smirking salesman showed me to the door with the words, 'We only make for old customers and the sons of old customers,' a tune they have doubtless had to modify since. Snobbery had been alive and well in Australia, but of the artless sort which serves mainly to feed the pretensions of those who entertain it. Here snobbery had teeth, and class was a game in which everyone seemed to be involved whether they wanted to play or not. I had better luck at a shirt-makers off Jermyn Street where I was ushered into the managing director's office by an underling with a sly smile. In no time we had clasped hands on a deal, after which the managing director offered me lunch at the Bath Club. I had three pink gins, met a peer or two and ate gulls' eggs for the first time. Afterwards he took me by taxi on a tour of London, and we circumnavigated a sooty-black St Paul's, standing in majestic isolation among the cleared bomb sites.

The managing director's hospitality didn't end there. I was frequently asked to join him for further pink gins in various parts of Jermyn Street. After the agency had brought him a little business, he invited all four of us to join a party he was taking to the Embassy nightclub. Among his other guests was a dour Englishman, the first I had encountered with whiskers on an otherwise clean-shaven face, growing high up on both cheeks like a pair of auxiliary, inverted eyebrows. 'Funny thing, Orstralia's a place I've never wanted to go,' he told me as if I should be interested. It was a remark that in those days and in various wordings you heard all the time. Coming from the Antipodes, it seemed, was about as interesting as arriving second class on the train from Bradford. You were just another sub-species of Briton, and the pressures to jettison one's first identity and by mimicry become a proper Englishman were considerable.

I knew a number of Australians who tried. Best at it by far were the attractive girls. They lacked the inflexibility and pride of their male compatriots, and accepted the challenge for what it was: passing an entrance test. Also they were better mimics, and within a week so of arrival had learnt a passable Sloane Square patois. They looked on London simply as a larger Sydney, which it wasn't, but the innocence of this conviction was enough to open doors. Hard-headed without being hard, ready laughers, wanting to conform yet capable of blurting out the truth, above all determined to settle for nothing but the best, a few of them cut a swathe through whichever circle they set their sights on – South Kensington respectability, the upper reaches of

Bohemia or, in one case, minor European royalty. Jocelyn Rickards, who arrived the year before I did, gives a good account of such a progress in *The Painted Garden*, in which names are not so much dropped as thrown in handfuls at the ducking reader.

The story of the first few months of my own invasion of England is recorded in two accounts: one a journal I was keeping at the time, and the other a bundle of letters I wrote to my mother, which I discovered tied with string in a bottom drawer after she died. Both, in their different ways, make embarrassing reading, the most interesting thing about them being common to both, some hard facts about food. I dwell on the items to be usefully included in food parcels from home, on the single chop and lone egg my ration book allows me each week, on the fishy taste of the whale steak available at the Italian caff in Shepherds' Market. For the most part the journal is otherwise one long self-remonstrance: how I am too shy one day and too brazen the next, how I am not serious enough and at the same time insufficiently light-hearted, how I must stop being lazy and work, work, work to achieve what I want. What a contrast to the letters! These are a facetious, shallow celebration of the romantic Tory dandy I half-imagined myself to be. Partly this was a matter of cheering up my mother, but I'm afraid I genuinely believed in the importance of the bespoke Savile Row suit on which I had spent £30 of my hard-earned *Otranto* money. I learn from these letters that I could not afford one of the really smart umbrellas from Adeney, Swaine, Briggs in Piccadilly, but that I acquired a passable facsimile for thirty shillings at the Railway Lost Property Office. Nor was there money for a curly-brimmed bowler from Locke's, and in retrospect I can only say, thank God!

On paper it looks as if I wasn't doing too badly. Friends of my godmother's took me to the Fourth of June at Eton, where I spent the day wondering whether I was wearing the right suit (I wasn't). A Melbourne department store heiress was having a grand wedding at St George's in Hanover Square and the Agency was invited. Dressed in Moss Bros gear, and feeling agreeably foolish, Maitland and I escorted the girls from Shepherds' Market to the church and afterwards to the reception at Claridge's, sporting the black silk hats which Maitland had insisted were far smarter than the usual grey jobs. I heard Noël Coward sing his own songs ten feet away at the Café de Paris. I was asked to a ball beneath a painted ceiling at Greenwich, and another at the Savoy Hotel, where young men blew hunting horns and I had my picture snapped for *The Tatler*. This was the life we had read about in novels or heard in descriptions of our parents' trips. It didn't matter that one world war and then another had robbed that life of any innocence it might ever have possessed; nor that it would one day be bought up by American Express Gold Card holders and marketed in in-flight magazines. This was the world we were determined to penetrate, and, if that wasn't possible, then for a few short months invent.

I thought I might be getting somewhere when, in a short story of Evelyn Waugh's about a young man living in Mayfair, I read a description of a room in a mews flat above a hire-car business exactly reflecting my own accommodation. One morning I was astonished to come face to face with the celebrated author in person as he walked towards me down the Burlington Arcade, dressed in checks like a titled farmer in town for the day. I, too, was wearing a carefully considered new suit, and we both swung umbrellas. I can't be sure but I think those blazing button eyes scrutinised me with a certain approval. He was undoubtedly smiling. Perhaps it was just that he had recognised someone other than himself in fancy dress.

These letters to my mother make very curious reading because the word 'gay', in its archaic meaning, recurs like a hiccup in almost every line. 'I had a very gay night,' 'I met a very gay old boy,' and so on. I wrote truer than I knew. One is inclined to forget, now that Sydney is the gay capital of the world, the ferocious taboos that once applied there. Certain gifted people, like the artist, Loudon Sainthill, were allowed out of the closet because no force on earth would have kept them inside, but this liberty was not extended to dentists and architects, for whom the occasional overseas holiday had a particular importance. They came to London the way Englishmen had once sought anonymity on the Continent. That summer London was full of Australians of my parents' generation, and my already busy social life included a number of parties that might just as well have been in Double Bay. Some were snobbishly correct affairs where men and women in brand new clothes struggled to tame their vowel sounds in sub-let Mayfair apartments until one Martini too many got the better of them. Others were rather more unbuttoned.

A hostess who presided over gatherings of the latter sort was that same Rada whom my mother had confused with the drama school. Rich and inordinately generous, she gathered round her a mixed bag of Australian artists, waifs and visitors. Here I was to encounter a surprising side to one or two middle-aged men I had hitherto thought I knew well. It was a bit like being propositioned by an uncle. If I was shocked it was not by their inclination, but by the fact that they no longer regarded me as out of bounds. Did going on the stage make you fair game, even when someone knew your mother?

Other surprises followed. I was told to watch out for the managing director of the Jermyn Street shirt-makers; his patronage of a young man like myself was unlikely to be disinterested, which explained the smile on the face of the sly underling. He had never made a move, but I wondered what loop of film had been running and rerunning in his head over those innumerable pink gins?

By the time Searchers' Agency had foundered – we didn't lose money, we just couldn't make enough – it was hard to avoid the conclusion that the enduring values of Mayfair were Folly, Money and Lust. Perhaps that was what the novels of Waugh and Huxley had been saying all the time. Our High Life adventure died in the summer. Of the many fine doorways we had found standing open upon our arrival in the Old World most had led eventually down well-trodden steps to an airless room where a stooping barber pressed one blinking eye against a peephole. In time Maitland and the two sisters melted back to Australia, and I had to take a temporary job as a shoe salesman in a children's outfitters on Baker Street. In the storeroom when no one was looking I read the Penguin edition of the letters of D. H. Lawrence, and spent my lunch hour looking at pictures round the corner in the Wallace Collection, a very slightly wiser man.

If I've given the impression that my social activities had taken precedence over my theatrical career this was not quite the case. Indeed the most crucial day of that entire summer was the one on which I did my audition for a place at RADA. I was living my life in two sealed compartments, the busy foolishness I've just described and my solitary preparations for the stage. For my entrance test I had to attempt first an allotted speech, some Hotspur from *Henry IV, Part 1*, and then something else of my own choosing. Waiting my turn with a roomful of others I felt nerves that were not just another part of the excitement of putting on plays for fun, but nerves in deadly earnest, upon which one day my self-respect and even my next meal might depend. I looked around at my competitors drawn from various parts of the British Isles, overdosed on adrenalin, stricken, pale and trembling. Each of us had come from a place where a spark of possible talent had made us special to another where that spark was not only commonplace but would perhaps be extinguished. Among these terrified strangers this seemed nothing short of lunacy.

The large room in which we had six minutes to change the outcome of our lives had a line of tables at one end behind which sat what seemed the entire staff of RADA. A couple of flimsy lights on stands, such as you might find in the studio of a seaside photographer, pointed towards the contestants. I began with my Shakespearean speech, an Olivier imitation standard in all respects except that I hadn't remembered his knees wobbling. No one applauded; in fact to the extent that I could see them through the cigarette smoke they looked decidedly unimpressed. The piece of my own choosing was from a play called *The Prodigal*, about a ne'er-do-well son, thought to be dead, who returns unexpectedly to plague his father, a blind industrialist. Three years later in rep, I would be sprinkling my hair with baby powder to play the blind industrialist. Now I was attempting the son.

During this particular speech, he helps himself uninvited to a plate of cold chicken and so speaks throughout with his mouth full. I had thought about bringing along a real chicken leg in my breast pocket, but had decided it would take too long to unwrap. Instead I had an old toothbrush, on which I had carefully rehearsed my eating – large, succulent bites from the bristle end, nibbles at sinewy morsels along the handle. The speech itself was quite funny, when, in my interpretation, swallows, burps and the smacking of lips permitted you to hear it, and after it was over I looked up to find smiles beaming at me beyond the lights. I was in; dental hygiene rather that acting had secured me a place at the Royal Academy of Dramatic Art. These days, with one student accepted for every several hundred who apply, I doubt if it would be enough.

I left the RADA building in a better frame of mind than I had entered it, and on my way out was greeted by the Registrar, Miss Brown, whom I had met at an earlier interview. Miss Brown called you 'dear' but otherwise was quite restrained in manner, unlike her two colleagues, whose florid theatricality not even my gypsy drama teacher in Melbourne could approach. This was something I would have to get used to, but in the meantime I was relieved that they were both at their typewriters.

In due course I was notified that I had been accepted for a place. Between them my parents agreed to share the cost of my fees and

living expenses – fairly sporting on my father's behalf given his prejudice against the whole idea. From the commencement of my studies
I would have £6 a week to live on. Until then I was expected to fend
for myself. The agency had never been able to pay me much, so prior
to the shoe shop I looked for a supplement in freelance journalism and
had a few small successes. The story of my voyage on the *Otranto*
appeared in the *Australian Women's Weekly*, and the *Sydney Morning
Herald* accepted an interview with Peter Finch. They offered big by-
lines but tiny fees, enough to pay for a few theatre seats but not to
make ends meet. I wrote what I thought was another amusing letter to
Laurence Olivier, reminding him of the jokes in my first addressed two
years previously to the Tivoli Theatre, but my request for an interview
was blocked by a chilly reply from a secretary. It was one thing to be
a young Australian hopeful in Australia; quite another in London.
You waited your turn with all the other refugees of Empire. I understood the justice of it. We would begin by taking far more than we
could give from this undemonstrative and rather snappish mother lion,
with, however, milk in her dugs for those who could prove their hunger.

I was beginning to perceive the scale of London. In the theatre alone
there were major stars playing in a dozen theatres. In Sydney we were
lucky if we saw them one at a time. I was accustomed to a single
museum where now in South Kensington the 74 bus drove past a line
of them standing side by side. It was difficult to know where to begin,
and choice almost had the effect of diminishing appetite. I managed
to see dazzling work from Scofield in *Ring Round the Moon* and Rex
Harrison in *The Cocktail Party* but had sharp disappointments as
well. It was surprising, in the face of such abundance, how precise my
likes and dislikes were becoming. This was the era of the star virtuosi,
of whom Edith Evans was perhaps the great exemplar, spellbinders,
whose talent was a mystery of which they themselves were the jealous
guardians. One rung down from these luminaries was a style of well-
spoken, vacant acting in which all three syllables in words like
'Grosvenor' or 'different' would be enunciated very loudly straight out
front. In drawing-room comedy the effect was brazenly snobbish;
in verse drama solemn and high-minded, and I disliked it intensely.
I realised that the thing I had loved so much about Olivier's work in
Sydney was that at some point his performances touched the earth.
He was a bridge between the verbal sophistication of the British theatre
and the skill and raw energy of American film actors. But RADA was

approaching when I would have a chance to test these prejudices against practice.

Not long before the term was due to start two things happened, small and unrelated, which nevertheless gave me a moment's pause about the profession I was on the point of entering. One day I picked up a copy of the weekly entertainment magazine *What's On in London* to find in the theatre section a full-page photograph in a backless evening dress of our erstwhile landlady in Shepherds' Market. Underneath I read, 'Miss Sandra Masters, the actress [*sic*], wants all her friends to know that she will be holidaying in the South of France for the next two weeks.' The second small shock was post I received from the Royal Academy of Dramatic Art. The envelope contained a cyclostyled form, such as you might find on a church noticeboard, informing new students of the things they would need on the first day of term. The list began with a copy of the *Complete Works of Shakespeare*, and went on to include ballet shoes, a leotard and tights. It was the last item on the list that I stared at longest. Was this a usage particular to the theatre, or simply a typing error on the part of one of the lady administrators whose attention had wandered? I had no idea, but I read: 'Men will also require cockstraps.'

# THREE

# Primary School

At the end of the grey autumn day that was the beginning of the RADA term I felt I knew three of my classmates well, and they were all American. One of them I had already encountered a few days before, following instructions, as I was to acquire ballet shoes from Anello and Davide. Since it was clear neither of us were dancers it followed we were probably starting at RADA, and we fell upon each other with relief. Amanda Steele had a long oval face, interesting rather than pretty, and an engaging East Coast manner that suggested private means. The second American I had met within minutes of arriving at the Academy. The new students had been directed to a classroom on the first floor, where we were to wait upon an opening address by Miss Brown. As this group of strangers filed through the door the figure ahead of me turned and, extending his hand with the vigour of a karate chop, announced, 'My name's Theodore J. Flicker!' He was stocky, bespectacled, irresistibly cheerful and gave the impression of being at the centre of things, or at any rate determined to be so.

With the third American it took a little longer to get acquainted. I had first noticed him while we were waiting for Miss Brown to arrive, a gathering as listless and uneasy as newly penned cattle. He was a slight, dark man with a brooding stare, somewhat older than the rest of us, dressed in jeans and an old sheepskin US Army Air Force jacket with a Mickey Mouse insignia on the back – curious attire, it struck me, at least for the first day of term. He chewed gum and blinked very slowly, as if distancing himself from the prevailing nervousness around him. His black hair was oiled and combed back in the pompadour fashion that I had seen on countless American servicemen in Sydney during the war. I wasn't sure that he and I would get on.

I changed my mind about that later in the morning, when I found myself assigned a locker next to his in the changing room where we were told to store our ballet gear. I had hung up my tights and my leotard and was looking for a peg for my jockstrap when I heard him say, 'I see you reached the same compromise I did. On the list we were all sent – that last item was a little difficult to find.' He was one of those people whose smile not only takes you by surprise but is like a window opening on their intelligence. Ted Flicker had overheard us and now joined in. 'I searched every shop in London,' he said, and the three of us were united by the first of what would be many sustaining laughs during our two years at Gower Street. The older man's name was Jack Salamanca, and he was attending RADA on a GI grant, to which his service in the Pacific War entitled him.

My immediate affinity with these three made me realise for the first time since I had arrived in England that, like them, I was in fact, a foreigner. They came from a different USA than the one that exists today. Although the Korean War had started that summer and the Iron Curtain was a term that had now entered the language, the sense of a world rigidly divided into two armed camps, with Senator McCarthy the snarling guard-dog, was yet to come. This was still the abundant America of the Marshall Plan, at least it seemed so on this side of the Atlantic. In a variety of ways my three new friends were to provide me with a Marshall Plan of my own, and as I moved into my first London winter I would need it.

For one thing I was going a funny colour. I realised this not only when I looked in the mirror, but when I found I could spot other Australians in the street simply by their skin tone. Years of over-exposure to a sun of which we were now deprived left us all a kind of jaundiced grey. Our older citizens, men and women alike, proclaimed their nationality by having necks like lizards. I would catch sight of them in Piccadilly, warily on the move, and dressed very correctly in clothes of so little style it was a style in itself. Losing a suntan was like being stripped of a layer of identity.

Other aspects of self-definition were also under threat. By the end of my first term at RADA it was clear that there was a single distinction between one student and another of any importance: talent. Most of us were adequate performers; no more. That was not enough. What counted was ability that was in some way exceptional, and we watched each other jealously for signs of it. Talent was not just a matter of being better than the rest; it was the only thing you could depend on to save you from the pain of being judged ineffective by watching, competitive eyes. Sometimes I lay in the bath in the mornings before setting off to the Academy, the winter mist twisting outside the window, in a state of complete disbelief. What was I doing on this grey side of the world? And what on earth had I got myself into? Once you decided to become an actor it was impossible not to become obssessional, even desperate, about your work; the self-exposure it involved left you no choice.

Actually, that first term I managed to hold my own. Conceit helped. I was twenty-two, whereas most of the British students were still in their late teens, and with the exception of some of the Americans, I was the only one to have worked in the professional theatre and be the friend of a star. I felt I was positively entitled to be as good as anyone else. It was like the start of a horse race, and without much justification, I was confident of my mount. Each term would be a hurdle, re-disposing the field, until some two years hence we passed the finishing post of the Public Show with its Bancroft Gold Medal for the winner. At that time important managers, agents and casting directors would be invited to see us perform one afternoon in a proper West End theatre, and for a lucky few there would be prizes and even contracts.

What made it an easy ride that first term was a number of exceptionally sympathetic teachers. There was Mr Ranelow, a little roly-poly man who might have stepped from a Charles Dickens illustration, and who, in less circular days, had played Macheath in the famous twenties revival of *The Beggar's Opera*. He taught voice. There was Mr Colebourne, who for many years had run his own company with Barry Jones and had given the first performance of Bernard Shaw's *Geneva*. He directed us in *A Midsummer Night's Dream*, and spent the first morning going round the class and chatting with great courtesy and at length to each student, exactly as if we were now members of his company. It was hard not to do your best for such a man.

Amanda gave her Boston Titania to my gum-leaf Oberon, Theodore J. Flicker played Puck like a Hollywood agent, and Jack Salamanca was somehow mislaid in the tiny part of Starveling. Even so he managed to be memorable, and seemed suspiciously content to bide his time. If Jack was the dark horse at this stage, there were two front runners. One was a pretty girl called Eve with a triangular face usually cocked to one side, and strong rather hefty limbs like a print of an eighteenth-century dancer. I had first noticed her, pale with terror, on the day of my audition. She also played Puck in the second of our two performances, and was the only one of us who seemed to light up from inside when she acted. The other was undoubtedly John Glendenning, who spoke in a musical tenor voice, reminiscent of Gielgud's, which everyone at the Academy held up to us as a model. He was accounted the best of the three Robert Brownings in our next production, *The Barretts of Wimpole Street*. I was one of the other two, and suspect now that Paul Hogan would have given a similar performance, if a more amusing one. Again we had an encouraging director, Miss Black, who promised me I had promise.

All these plays were given by daylight in a bare classroom to the rear, where we also did our ballet, fencing and movement. In our second term we would be performing under lights in the tiny theatre located in the basement of the main building, and I looked forward to the help I could expect from costumes and the suggestion of a set. In the event these proved frail props indeed. The play was *She Stoops to Conquer*, and in its director I was about to encounter the first of the three RADA witches who would come close to undoing me. Let us call them Miss Ecks, Miss Wye and Miss Zedd.

There was no malice in Miss Ecks; only irritability operating at the level of bloodlust. I had never seen anyone become quite so deranged with exasperation. She had once been a well-bred young lady who had become an actress in an age when it was difficult for someone of her background to do so, and to add to her difficulties I would guess that at some time or other she had been the victim of a martinet director. She made the common assumption that the pain and humiliation that had been the making of her would also benefit us, and she passed on this legacy with fervour. It was rather as if my godmother, having once on an unlikely impulse gone on the stage, was now seventy, skinny as a tree in winter, and wracked with some involuntary muscular tic which perturbation only made worse.

My first mistake with Miss Ecks was volunteering to be the stage manager. I had assumed this to be a suitable post for a mature student, seasoned in the ways of authority by seven years at the oldest school in Australia. Others, wiser in the ways of the theatre, like Jack, knew that, except for those with a bent for it, stage management was among the most irksome and bruising jobs there were. Blame attached to it almost by definition, since the only time it attracted attention was when something went wrong. In my hands it often did. I was given the job of prompter, following the play on the page, and such was the tediousness of the task and my preoccupation with the problems of my own part, that my mind wandered. In vain actors would look at me for help as I searched frantically up and down the text, trying to recall the last thing said. An awful silence would reign, but never for long. Out of the corner of my eye, as lightning precedes thunder, so I would see the twitching of Miss Ecks' frail shoulders presaging the blast to come. She would then begin screaming at me, and thrashing the floor with her walking stick.

*She Stoops to Conquer* was to be given two performances on successive days, swapping the parts around. In the one I stage-managed I had the small role of Stingo, the innkeeper with whose station the two arrogant young leads confuse Mr Hardcastle, owner of the country house at which they are expected as guests. In the second performance I was down to play Hastings, a part so bland that I felt acutely self-conscious in it. This did nothing to endear me to Miss Ecks. Having rehearsed the play for some weeks in a classroom, one morning we were given our first opportunity to step onto the RADA stage. I was doing my best with an insipid love scene of fine phrases and delicate sentiments, playing opposite another American in our class, Helen Taylor. She was a fair, frail beauty of fiery dedication, and one of the few actors in the school of truly professional standard. It can be quite disconcerting sharing a stage with someone who is as certain about what they are doing as you are unsure. The flashes of intention from Helen's pale blue eyes quite unnerved me.

From the blackness at the back of the auditorium I heard first the squeak of a seat under duress, then Miss Ecks' familiar scream.

'MICHAEL!! You're standing there on *both legs*!!'

Bewildered and speechless I turned and squinted into the dark.

'YOU STUPID BOY!! Go to any West End theatre. Professional actors don't stand on *both* legs! They stand first on *one* leg then on *another*. First their *right*, then their *left*. SURELY YOU SEE THAT!!'

Miss Ecks was in despair, and I was to follow her thence. Where before my Hastings had been merely wooden, now he became fossilised. I saw the terror and pity in Helen's eyes as she realised she would be playing opposite an Easter Island statue.

Jack Salamanca had the part of the put-upon Mr Hardcastle, casting of which I was sceptical. I knew him to be a good actor because I had seen him in a production of *Of Mice And Men* which the American students had put together over the Christmas vacation. However, this was a part as essentially English as our genial voice teacher, Mr Ranelow. How could he be expected to get to the heart of it? Jack had been a professional actor in New York at a time when American theatre had been the most exciting in the world, and I had listened absorbed to his forceful exposition of his theory of acting and to his account of a Broadway season that had seen Lee J. Cobb in *Death of a Salesman* and Marlon Brando in *A Streetcar Named Desire*. He was a believer in the Stanislavsky Method because in those two Kazan productions, he'd experienced a wondrous demonstration of it. There was nothing dogmatic about his likes and dislikes, however, and he gave glowing descriptions of Alec Guinness in *The Cocktail Party* and, indeed, Robert Morley in *Edward, My Son*, both of whom had been in New York that same season. We agreed that much of what we were asked to admire on the London stage was glib and emotionally thin, but I doubted whether 'The Method' had much relevance to a classic comedy almost two hundred years old.

Jack set about the part with quiet stealth. His concentration alone was interesting, and made you want to go on watching. It even had a calming effect on Miss Ecks. He had a good ear, and before long had invented a more than passable English accent for his character. Jack had grown up in rural America, and had a strong feeling for the plain courtesy of country people. This is what he went for. I watched with astonished and rather resentful admiration as his Mr Hardcastle began to emerge. Not only did he manage to absorb himself in what he was doing, so that what he said and what was said to him became an unbroken ribbon of storytelling, he also had the knack of allowing his thoughts to drift laterally, in a sort of free association, so that at the end of a rehearsal his performance would have accrued half a dozen delightful new touches.

There was a moment in the scene with the two young men, when one of them, having been offered a drink, quaffed it down in one gulp and demanded a refill. Jack took the tankard and, incredulous at the rudeness of his two guests, ran a finger absent-mindedly around the inner rim of the vessel, as if unable to believe that what had been full some moments before was now empty. It sounds a small thing written down, but in the context of that particular rehearsal it was funny, moving and above all, true. Reluctantly I had to concede that a gifted and intelligent twentieth-century American of Spanish descent could make as good a guess at the behaviour of an eighteenth-century English country gentleman as anyone in the building.

But how did he *do* it, I wanted to know. For one thing how did he keep his *mind* under control? One cross word from Miss Ecks and mine was sparking and fusing like defective electrical equipment. Instead of Jack's steady, inviolable hum, my concentration would break down and go dead, and the more Miss Ecks cursed the machine the less hope there was of it starting again. Running from the room in tears was not an option open to me, but it was frequently what I felt like doing.

There was one thing, however, at which I shone. My skills as a schoolboy caricaturist stood me in good stead when it came to make-up, in the art of which Jack was fortunately rotten. For my smaller role as the innkeeper I had planned something really spectacular, and on the morning of the performance arrived with the cleaners to begin my preparations. After an hour or two I was padded to thrice my size, and further disguised by false nose, false eyebrows, blacked-out teeth and a generous overlay of raspberry-coloured greasepaint.

It was at these final performances that our work came to judgement before the Principal, Sir Kenneth Barnes. He sat in his own box at the back of the auditorium, always in the company of his elderly spaniel, Marsha. At my entrance as Stingo the dog raised its head from Sir Kenneth's feet, elevated itself on its hind legs, took one look and barked – something of a compliment given the number of performances Marsha had attended unmoved.

Sir Kenneth had been appointed Principal of the Royal Academy of Dramatic Art at its foundation early in the century and was now in his seventies. He came from a family with two distinguished branches, one ecclesiastical, the other theatrical, and indeed would have looked splendid in a bishop's gaiters had not theatre won the day. His sister had been the Edwardian star Dame Irene Vanbrugh, whose daughter, herself a successful actress and something of a beauty, had married in Australia while on tour there. I'm not sure that this latter connection didn't incline him to a curiosity about me and a tolerance toward my shortcomings. Like the great actor-managers of his younger days his passion was to make the theatre as respectable as the other professions, and he saw his task at the Academy as forging the largely suburban student intake into performers at ease in the stage drawing rooms of

Oscar Wilde and Sir Arthur Wing Pinero. In old age his snobbery was unabashed, and the constitution of the student body reflected this. Thus the niece of the Duke of Devonshire, Philippa Hunloke, a sweet and able girl with a sleepy manner, found little difficulty in getting a place, though no one, including Philippa, had a burning faith in her abilities as an actress. Such well-bred souls, however, were a leavening to the surrounding ambition and neurosis, and Philippa, with her intense interest in the social life of the Academy, has to this day served our class well as oral historian.

In spite of his inclination to maintain the tone of the place, Sir Kenneth was enough of a pragmatist to realise that talent comes in all shapes and sizes, and as students we sensed that at the end of the day we would probably get justice from him. He was the Court of Appeal from the sharp opinions and occasionally the malice of the middle-aged women who dominated his staff, and he projected good sense quite uncompromised by the tiresome ups and downs of talent. His manner towards us was one of gruff, frequently exasperated benevolence as he launched into some critical observation of the work of one of us with the words, 'Now look here . . .'

The class always had a meeting with the Principal after he and Marsha had attended one of our performances. We would gather in the dark corridor outside his office until the precise time of our appointment, when, after some nudging and jostling, one of us would essay a knock. We would then respectfully tiptoe into the small room, the first through the door getting the two chairs, the bulk of us joining a yawning, stretching and rather smelly Marsha on the carpet. Sir Kenneth would then consult his notes before proceeding to give each of us in alphabetical order his observations on our work. After *She Stoops to Conquer* he waxed eloquent about Jack's Mr Hardcastle, but about my Hastings said not a word. Stingo fared a little better. 'Good make-up,' Sir Kenneth remarked before moving on to the next student. For the remainder of 1951 it was practically the only thing I would hear from him.

Compensations were at hand in my social life, thanks largely to the Americans, who were the only people in our class who could afford to live in flats rather than rooms. Ted was nicely installed in St John's Wood, Mandy in Ebury Street, and both encouraged visitors. Television was in its infancy and no one had a set; powerful hi-fi equipment was yet to come. We reached out for each other's company, and whatever we did was, perforce, an event – going to the movies, sitting long hours in cafés over a cup of threepenny coffee, attending one of Ted's memorable bottle parties at which I arrived with my rolled umbrella and some Spanish red at 3s 9d a bottle.

Jack, who was married and whose wife, Mimi, worked at the US Embassy in days when to demonstrate outside it would have been as unthinkable as an angry crowd in front of St Paul's, had a flat in West Cromwell Road, the door of which was permanently ajar. I look back now almost with shame at the limitless hospitality with which the Salamancas sustained me during my years at RADA. Like many skinny young men I was a prodigious eater, and Mimi would return each night laden with forbidden delicacies from the Embassy commissary on the off-chance that Jack would have returned home yet again with the hungry Australian or some other undernourished British student. Jack and Mimi were both from the South, and it was my first experience of that sense of community that was once so much a part of American life away from the big cities. RADA was now their community, and we were all to be included in the events and rituals of the American year, Thanksgiving and Fourth of July parties, lavish Christmases and New Year's Eves.

I was learning many things about Jack, and all of them were interesting. He was exceptionally well read, particularly in verse, and had the gift of being able to memorise, sometimes at a single reading, any poem he'd taken a liking to; after a couple of drinks Browning, Keats, most of Housman, all the American poets would come tumbling out of him, spoken in the incantatory fashion poets use when reading their own work, but improved by an actor's sense of presentation. I got the impression he could go on like this for hours. When he spoke about the war or the humiliations of being an actor in New York his mood turned black and angry, but at other times he reflected the quiet virtues of a scholar. I admired the orderly way he would follow through on a subject that had come to interest him, whether it was the anthropology of Malinowski or Sir James Jeans writing about the planets. The information would be patiently absorbed, then make a lucid and enthralling reappearance in conversation. He was the first person I'd met whose talk seemed to have the precision and the shape of the written word. Eventually I learnt he was at work on a long novel based on his own growing-up in West Virginia, which he said it would take some years to complete. I was never in any doubt that one day it would be finished. I realised I had the luck to have as a friend a truly gifted man.

What Jack thought of me is another matter. I was younger, of course, and far more impressionable, so I was getting rather more than I could give. I think he was initially suspicious of my patrician Australian ways, and found inexplicable and rather ludicrous my attachment to symbolic possessions like my rolled umbrella and my bespoke suit. What we shared was a cast of mind in which much of Jack's brooding indignation found a release in my lighter qualities of mockery and ironic defence. We both agreed that the world was a pretty awful place. He reminded me that it could also be mysteriously beautiful, and I reminded him, perhaps, that from time to time it could be very funny. When he described his passionate attachment to the southern landscapes of his youth, it began to dawn on me that being Australian had less to do with the hybrid society that had been spread as thin as butter over that vast continent, than with the childhood experience of the place itself: its colours, smells and remorseless light. Even in the cities this presence made its way into the bones of all Australians and was our true, perhaps our only, claim to uniqueness. Had the melancholy of the New World, which all my life I had felt hanging there in the Australian sky, something to do with this severance between a private, incommunicable sense of landscape and a human society that had not evolved within it but had been cobbled together out of borrowed attitudes and errant memories of elsewhere? Was this the source of our contradictions and insecurities, and was this why mercantile ugliness met so little resistance as it ate its way through our country? And finally, was this why in cold, uncomfortable England, about which Jack and I constantly complained and laughed, we both were beginning to feel so oddly at home.

None of these reflections had much application to the art of acting, which was still causing me some bother. I was navigating a second lake of fire, and her name was Miss Wye. I can remember nothing about the play we did under her guidance except the aptness of its title: *Dance with No Music*. Miss Wye provided no woodwinds, brass or soothing strings to ease us through our rehearsal period; her only instruments were condescension and scorn. She was a handsome woman with a sweep of greying hair gathered at the back, and unlike Miss Ecks, she was a cool, even amused tormentor who addressed all her students as 'ducky'. I bear you no more ill-will, she seemed to imply, than a gardener does his weeds. Her aunt had been the famous actress Dame Madge Kendall, and at some point or other this information in various roundabout contexts was conveyed to every class she taught. In the corridors students made jokes about it, but surreptitiously, nervously, never to her face. Miss Wye was as serious about blood-letting as someone engaged on a cull of baby seals.

I knew at once she had me in her sights. The self-consciousness that had now become my affliction made me the perfect slow-moving target. However, since she never raised her exquisitely modulated voice, I maintained enough presence of mind to protect myself with drollery.

'Ducky, in all my professional experience I've never seen any actor so *hopelessly* stiff and lifeless.'

'I know, Miss Wye, I know. I couldn't agree more. Hopeless. But it's the time of day.'

'The time of *day*, ducky!?'

'It's ten-thirty in the morning. And look, it's raining outside. Could I have another shot at five past eleven? I may have un-stiffed a bit by then.'

This did not particularly amuse Miss Wye but the class laughed, a political reality she had to take into her calculations. She grew wary of me.

Others were not so fortunate. The sweet-faced Eve, who had been an outstanding Puck for Mr Colebourne, was so terrified that when addressed she could hardly follow what was being said to her.

'Pardon, Miss Wye?' she murmured one day.

'*Pardon*? Did I hear you say "*Pardon*"? It's frightfully common to say "Pardon". Didn't you know that, ducky? How *common* it is to say "Pardon"?'

On the attack Miss Wye had a way of looking around the class with a despairing smile, as if the rest of us were endorsing her every word. Eve's blush seemed to go on for an age, achieving ever more humiliating depths of colour. We watched, helpless, as over the next few weeks all the life went out of her. Miss Wye gave her no mercy. She became truly lifeless. The following term she had gone.

At last *Dance with No Music* had its heavy-footed performance. There followed Sir Kenneth's notes, after which we would normally have seen the last of Miss Wye. However, we had barely filed out of the Principal's office before she began shepherding us, somewhat surreptitiously, into an unoccupied classroom. She told us she had something important to say to us, and began by disagreeing with most of Sir Kenneth's assessments, which in her view had been far too kind. She then announced that she would like to read us something. I peered at the spine of her much-handled volume, but could not make out the name of the author except that it began with an 'N'. The passage she was now mellifluously delivering concerned the long arduous quest for a true leader. When at last that leader had been found (and his disciples would know him at once) it became their holy duty to submit their wills utterly to his and to act without question upon his every commandment. I listened incredulous. There was little doubt who the leader was that Miss Wye had in mind, even if a question mark still hung over the worthiness of some of us to be disciples. She closed the book.

'Those are the words of Nietzsche,' she said, 'And I hope none of you will ever forget them.'

In the King's School chapel, when I had been likewise seized by an agony of giggles I had managed to disguise my irreverence by slipping into an attitude of silent prayer. This wasn't altogether appropriate, so instead I crossed one leg and tried Rodin's 'Thinker'. Alas, I had already caught Amanda's eye, and I became a sculpture rendered not in marble but shuddering jelly.

Our tuition did not consist entirely of rehearsing plays. We were for ever going up the RADA stairs and down again, from one room to another, against the current of other classes also on the move about which we as yet knew little. We searched their faces for signs of a new Garrick or Bernhardt, hoping for and threatened by authentic mystery in some pretty girl the back of whose neck we had once studied in the canteen queue. Most of our classes were with teachers who taught a particular skill, and without exception I recall these specialists with affection and in some cases gratitude. Pert Miss Scott taught the technical aspects of voice, and she set about our defective consonants and wayward vowel sounds with the unshakable optimism and encouragement more often extended by saintly teachers to the handicapped. Her catchphrase, 'Lips, teeth, tip of the tongue!', was delivered with such wholesome force that we all desisted from the obvious lewd jokes. Mr Froeshlen taught fencing; he was a man so mild and permanently amused, one wondered how he got involved in anything which even hinted at bloodshed. Head and shoulders taller than his colleagues was the inestimable Clifford Turner, whose book *Voice and Speech in the Theatre* was the standard work. Allowing for the fashion of the day, he had a magnificent instrument himself, resonant, mellow and with just a hint of the pulpit. One afternoon in the Forbes Robertson room he intoned Shelley to us, whilst outside the bolted windows a yellow fog, one of London's vanishing pea-soupers, gathered force. That night the buses would creep through the city at the pace of a man walking, and old people would cough and die, but our lungs were strong and we found it exciting to leave the building and confront a transformed street where the world ended at half a dozen yards.

Mr Turner's head was an oral library of Shakespeare and the poets, and he often gave highly regarded readings in public, something that set him apart from most of the staff. He dressed conventionally but with a certain flamboyance, like a maverick bank manager, and the nicest and, in some ways, the most touching thing about him was that he could never quite take himself seriously. When he least expected it his gravity would be rent apart by his own foghorn laughter. Some years after my time at the Academy, and when his own children had grown up, I heard that he'd left home and in a furnished room in Bloomsbury was living the life for which, even in the days when we had known him, he had evidently been pining. Young men came and went. Not long after, and without warning, he died.

A handful of us, as an optional extra, were studying for the London University Diploma. This was an academic course on theatre-related subjects, and was supposed to be useful if any of us fell upon teaching. Its greatest benefit, however, was to bring us into contact with a remarkable scholar, Muriel St Clair Byrne, who taught the history of costume. She came to class invariably dressed in a severely tailored jacket and skirt in men's suiting, worn with a blouse and a necktie, and the effect completed by pince-nez and a broad-brimmed felt hat of vaguely Andalusian provenance. Miss Byrne had for many years been an intimate of Dorothy L. Sayers, and sometimes on winter evenings the two gifted ladies would leave the Academy together, attired in identical fur coats, made from some robust little animal, possibly a raccoon, and reaching all the way to their ankles. With their flat-brimmed hats they looked like a couple of hidalgos, adventuring into the coldest reaches of the Andes. As a kind of advance guard for Women's Liberation they were probably well advised to wrap up.

Miss Byrne spoke carefully in a low voice which can only be described as creaking, possibly because where another would take an inflection up she invariably went down. But her manner was always gentle, even on occasion demure. During the magic lantern shows which accompanied her lectures on costume, she would pass over with haste any period in which fashion briefly allowed some mild indecency. Unaccustomed to topless bathing or even *Playboy* magazine, the class would sit bolt upright as a series of slides came and went in split seconds like the windows of a passing train.

She took us on some memorable outings; to see the Hilliard miniatures in the Victoria and Albert Museum or the Tudor Room at the National Portrait Gallery, where by some osmosis of her reserved but fierce enthusiasm a little of her immense learning passed through the membrane of our resistant ignorance. Twenty-five years later, when I served on the RADA Council, one of my fellow councillors was Miss Byrne, frailer obviously but remarkably unchanged, and a few years after that in her eighties her major work on the Tudor correspondence of the Lisle family was published to acclaim.

It was summer again, the end of my first year at RADA, and notwithstanding Jack's mockery I was having another Savile Row suit made. How I could afford this I can't quite explain, except to observe that irrational craving usually wins in any contest with prudence. In my need to resemble what I had absolutely no wish to be – a stylish stockbroker, perhaps, or a young wine merchant – it seems I was prepared to put up with almost anything. I had certainly lived a frugal year. My mother, anxious about standards, may have put a little towards the cost. The Salamancas, with their lavish subsidy of free food, can also be regarded as contributors. At any rate such a suit carried a purchase tax of £12, which, on an Australian passport, I could legitimately evade by exporting the suit to the Continent and wearing it back on the returning boat. I calculated that on the amount thus saved I needn't come back but could stay on in France for about ten days, if I avoided hotels and stuck to youth hostels. Someone had told me that at Biarritz on the Bay of Biscay there was a surf rolling that was recognisably Australian. I just about had the resources to hitch-hike there and back.

Leaving my suit, embalmed within its box in fleecy tissue paper and still unworn, with American Express in Paris, I caught the Metro to the Porte d'Orléans and stood by the side of a road, smelly with dilapidated traffic, my thumb in the air. I had with me a sleeping bag and a tin billy, both attached to a rucksack on the back of which I had sewn a small Australian flag. Hitch-hikers were comparatively few in 1951 and were benevolently regarded. Soon I was creeping down the map of France, rarely on the direct route, but on a course determined by the destination of whoever picked me up. The most memorable of my lifts was with a man in a broken-down Renault, one side of whose face was swollen with an abscessed tooth. He wore a beret and a little moustache and, as a third permanent fixture, a cigarette screwed into the corner of his mouth; he might have stepped out of a grainy, pre-war French film. Looking for a conversationalist to take his mind off his pain, he had had the misfortune to choose me, and for mile after mile we had an exchange of single words, which I had first to find in my pocket dictionary before either comprehending or replying. It was agony for me, but worse for him. I marvelled at his stoicism.

Sometimes I slept under a roof; once in a vineyard where I woke wet with dew. In the evenings I allowed myself a meal in a modest restaurant, and noticed that however humble the surroundings there was wine on the table and the food was delicious. I had a sharp sense with these Frenchmen that in the small but dependable compensations of their lives there was an unbroken thread going back into a past that stretched as far as you cared to trace it. In London, notwithstanding the architecture and the museums, the thread frayed and snapped somewhere in the nineteenth century. For Miss Byrne and other educated people the Tudors still lived, but did they in any real sense for the likes of my sick workman on the Knightsbridge-bound bus or Fred Malthouse aboard the *Otranto*? Not in anything they ate.

I arrived at the coast by night, and settled into the Biarritz youth hostel where the Pyrenean flea existed in plague proportions. I had been warned of this, and now dusted the sleeping bag and myself so copiously in DDT powder that in poisoning the flea I probably did lasting harm to myself. Every time I rolled over I gave off a cloud of white dust through which tiny black skydivers could be seen plunging towards the floor.

I awoke to a diamond-sharp September morning. The hostel was on the cliffs, high above the beach, so I set off down a dirt road with my tin billy serving as a kind of lunch basket, stopping off at various small shops along the way to select my picnic. A Dutch hitch-hiker had told me he had lived for eight weeks on nothing but raisins, so I bought some of these, but also some peaches and one huge tomato cleft all over like a cluster of tiny sunburnt buttocks. This was produce of a succulence I could hardly believe. At the bottom of the hill I turned a corner and there, blocking out my view of the sea and standing in the middle of the beach like a pink wedding cake the size of a cathedral, was the Hôtel du Palais. I walked beyond its enormous wrought-iron gates down to the ocean.

The scoop of the bay terminating in two rocky headlands reminded me of Bondi, but there were, to say the least, differences. One was the possession of the amazing grand hotel. Another, as I was to learn over the next few days, was that every cliff-face, every promontory and inlet, was adorned with mile after mile of gardens and promenades, built in the last century for the public to enjoy and presumably at the public expense. In comparison poor old Bondi was dressed in rags. I walked by myself along the edge of the turbulent water as I had times without number along beaches on the other side of the world, attracting a few curious stares, and staring myself at women of an almost forbidding sexiness and chic. Even their suntans looked as artful as if they had been applied by powder puff. There was an orderliness about this beach life – one of ball games, expensive canvas gear and elaborate lunch baskets – that was very un-Australian. But all this was to my left. To my right was the ocean, and with this at least I felt completely at ease. Waves came out of the horizon, and moved towards the shore in majestic lines, authentic messages from home. This was a place to which I hoped to return.

At the start of the autumn term there was a lovely newcomer in our midst, and everyone was talking about her. Rosemary Harris, already an accomplished rep actress of two or three seasons' experience, had seen in RADA the possibility of a London shop window. Likewise, RADA has seen in her the possibility of a star graduate. She had so little to learn that Sir Kenneth allowed her to skip the first year altogether, and join a class that was preparing for the Public Show the following term, to which she could make a mutually advantageous contribution. Just the way Rosemary dressed told us she was a pro, never extravagantly but always with a certain flair, as if every day was an audition.

One of the curiosities of my time at RADA was that the students who were to achieve immediate success were all women. A few years later when Albert Finney, Peter O'Toole and Tom Courtenay were part of the same intake, they would all be men. We had Zena Walker, who would soon be playing Juliet at Stratford, Margaret Tyzack, Sheila

Hancock and any number of Rank starlets who were signing contracts even before they left. However, the three most spectacular beauties, at least as far as I was concerned, were Rosemary, Diane Cilento and a teenager called Joan Collins. At one time or another I was in love (though by no means successful) with all three.

A mere glance was all that it took with Joan. There may have been fairer girls at RADA; none so awesomely desirable. In her presence my hormones went on red alert and I lost the power of speech. Attractiveness on this scale has its penalties for a young girl as well as its advantages, not least the rigid enmity of the staff, and Joan occasionally gave the impression of being baffled by her own packaging. One problem was that, like the rest of us, she, too, was falling in love with Joan Collins, at least the bits that moved into her line of sight. Her eyes would glaze over as she looked down at an exquisitely turned calf and ankle or the swell of a breast. After school the students drank coffee at nearby Olivetti's, the walls of which were lined with mirrors. Here three or four Joan Collins held court, all of them looking slyly sideways at each other, like figures in a Balinese painting.

One lunchtime I was sitting in the canteen with Ted Flicker when Joan came in dressed in jeans and a top not much bigger than a pocket handkerchief. Ted was cooler under fire than I was, and Joan liked him for this. She stood beside our table and supported herself on one superb arm, which she and I then regarded with slack-jawed wonder. Her bosom was level with Ted's nose. 'Stop staring at me,' he said in a passable Groucho imitation, and departed bent at the waist and smoking his fountain pen. I was alone with Joan and knew it was a challenge I had somehow to meet. Bearing in mind Miss Scott's advice, 'Lips, teeth, tip of the tongue,' I tried to remember how words were formed: 'Dinner . . . with me . . . to have . . . would you like?' Joan shrugged and said all right.

I had a dish for just such an occasion, a pasta covered in a sauce made with ingredients from one of my Sydney food parcels. I called it 'Spaghetti Dinkum', which most people found amusing, though not particularly Joan when I told her what I had in mind for us – a quiet evening at home. My room in Adam's Row was on the second floor, the kitchen on the first, and I thought it best to spare Joan contact with the other tenants, who would also be cooking their evening meals at the same time. I doubted, for instance, whether she would take to Mr Henney, a once dynamic businessman in his sixties, who had fallen on bad times, and who, since the bathroom was upstairs, after dinner scrubbed his false teeth in the kitchen sink. He and I did not get on. He flew into unexplained rages if he ever caught me sitting still reading a book. Or there was Miss Barke, a saleslady in a Knightsbridge hat shop, who had had a private telephone installed in her room. Whenever she wanted to use the lavatory she would ring us in the kitchen a wall away and ask us to clear the corridor. We were a very mixed assortment of tenants with only one thing in common: the delusion that it was better to live in discomfort in Mayfair than at ease at a lesser postal address.

I whisked Joan upstairs and installed her in my room, explaining that I would have to dart down to the kitchen from time to time to ensure that my sauce wasn't turning to charcoal at the bottom of the pan or that Mr Henney hadn't commandeered my gas ring. I had uncorked a bottle of Spanish red, but the neck was trembling so much when I poured that it arrived in the glass effervescent. Conversation became rather disjointed because of the number of trips I had to make downstairs. When I at last appeared puffing from below with two generous platefuls of Spaghetti Dinkum Joan was beginning to look at me with the detached concern a nurse extends to a sinking patient. The concern I liked; the detachment I knew was ominous. She took no more than a few sips of her aerated red, then put the glass well to one side. Sluggish bubbles circled at the brim. Most of her spaghetti remained untouched. Talk grew spasmodic. She allowed me one chaste kiss then asked me to escort her to the nearest Underground.

The story does not conclude until twenty-five years later. I was at a cocktail party with Joan just before her return to the States and megacelebrity on television. I greeted her with the special enthusiasm you show to a friend indelibly featured in the memories of your youth. She looked friendly but quite blank. 'RADA!' I said, thinking she must be joking. She still looked blank. 'Ted Flicker! Jack Salamanca?' These names elicited a response, and with further prodding I got her to agree that we had certainly been at drama school at the same time. However, as to our evening together, or even who I was, she hadn't the least recall.

Rosemary Harris is a better story. We remain firm friends, and thirty years after RADA had a rich collaboration in the Wyndham's Theatre revival of *All My Sons*. Amanda had invited her to share the Ebury Street flat, and I spent many evenings with the two of them and whoever else had turned up among Rosemary's numerous suitors. I think Rosemary liked me, but she was a grown-up young woman who had complex expectations of any man who hoped to be welcomed into her life, and she watched me closely for signs of the one thing I didn't have, maturity. There were others in attendance who did: a delightful solicitor with whom I discussed American literature and a journalist who had just become editor of *The Spectator*. In a way I felt less grown-up, less certain of what I was, than I had been in Australia. In the process of re-inventing myself, I had the vulnerability of a creature between skins.

My feelings towards Rosemary veered from the intensely romantic to a fearful confusion about commitment. I was tormented by sex, but unwilling to accept that the solution to this lay in accepting a degree of responsibility for what I desperately wanted. This probably went for most of my fellow students. RADA was no more or less sexually permissive than any other educational establishment catering to a similar age group. Whatever the strengths of the impulses drawing the young into each other's beds there are powerful contrary forces keeping them apart: a sudden fastidiousness, a priggish insistence on the ideal, a failure of nerve. It was this last that undid me with Rosemary. We almost made a couple, but never quite; something that has given an interesting charge to the friendship that followed.

Diane Cilento was remarkable in all sorts of ways. She was sharply intelligent and endowed with a swing of long, blonde hair, and the big green eyes of a cat. She was also another of the Academy's Australians. In summer she walked through the streets of London in torn clothes as if barefoot on a Queensland beach – a trailer of the coming sixties. We had an immediate, wry understanding of each other, in which perhaps there was a hint of competition. Every story she had about shark attacks near Surfers' Paradise I could match with one about giant stingrays at Bawley Point. This complicity of experience brought us together, even as it sharpened our scepticism one to another. Diane was strikingly beautiful, but had either of us come all this way to encounter what we had left behind? We had many things going for us but not mystery, something which Diane possessed in spades among the English. In spite of this, almost against our wills, we kept drifting back into each other's company, hungry for a familiarity we resisted and yet were grateful for. We were as honest with each other as siblings, and became each other's reserve player. These days our meetings are years apart, but it only takes an instant to pick up on a lasting rapport. And on something else, too, very Australian: mockery at odds with a secret hunger for belief.

Of these three singular girls Rosemary was the only one to have the respect of the staff. Joan and Diane were treated almost with contempt, as if their somewhat bolder good looks could not possibly co-exist with talent. This was preposterous. Joan could do then what she later was to do in films and on television – all she needed to be a star. This became apparent when she left RADA, and at once picked up a Hollywood contract. Similarly, in no time Diane was in the West End, then on Broadway, playing Helen of Troy in Giraudoux's *Tiger at the Gates*. Both were victimised by a small clique among the staff who seemed positively affronted by the attributes of youth, and their voices were powerful. 'Look,' they seemed to say, 'we who are so much more worthwhile than you have been denied the rewards which are about to fall into your undeserving laps. Let us do our best to amend this injustice in advance.' Enter, on cue, and upstage centre, the third and last of the weird women, Miss Zedd.

I intend to be hard on Miss Zedd, because of the three she was the one with talent, which is to say an instinctive understanding of how it should be done. There was much she could have told us, but she preferred to keep it to herself. This was her revenge, and it was also her power. She took a rehearsal the way I remembered the Professor of Anatomy at Sydney University conducting an oral examination, turning the skull over in his dry fingers to point to some bony excrescence or minute canal. He, who knew everything, remained silent. You, who (in my case) knew nothing, were expected to talk. The Professor of course was obliged to hold his tongue. Miss Zedd was not. She would sit watching rehearsals with her shrewd, pale-blue eyes, exasperation slowly building within her. Usually this could be diffused with sarcasm, but occasionally, overwhelmed by our incompetence, she would leap to her feet and execute a few angry, grotesque pirouettes of acting. The intention was to show you what *should* be done, but never *how*. She was a judge, not a teacher, and each student was issued with more than enough rope to hang himself. Once you were dangling, Miss Zedd made it her business to ensure, within the inner councils of RADA, that burial followed. Only Sir Kenneth could dig you up again, and indeed it was to be his spade that came to my rescue.

Miss Zedd had had an interesting professional career, the high point of which had been to play male leads at the Old Vic during the First World War when more exact casting was serving at the front. Her most important roles were Henry V and Richard III, and vestiges of these two successes still clung to her, the one in her Agincourt haircut characterised by a severe grey fringe extending all the way round her head, and the other in the beginnings of a hump which the passing years were adding to her upper back. She was a good actress, still got work occasionally, and had just been seen perfectly cast as the prime suspect in one of Agatha Christie's genteel murder mysteries.

I had already done one production with Miss Zedd, *The Merchant of Venice*, in which Jack's Shylock had sent a tremor of excitement throughout the building. People from other classes slipped into the theatre between lessons to catch a moment of it. I played a rather rigid Antonio. Now under her direction we were to do *Hamlet* with Jack as the Prince. Miss Zedd's pleasure in merciless assessment was well exercised at the beginning of the rehearsal period with two or three days of casting, and at the end with her interminable costume parades, which in feeling were more like a police line-up.

As had Miss Ecks, I knew Miss Zedd had me pigeonholed for somewhat stolid second leads, the category in which since *She Stoops to Conquer* I felt most acutely self-conscious, and as we read the play back and forth, auditioning for various parts, I sensed that I was being mustered towards the one role in which I was totally miscast – Claudius. I had only the vaguest idea of my proper range, but suspected that it might be in the area of character comedy. When, somewhat diffidently, I suggested myself for Polonius, Miss Zedd snorted with laughter and declined to let me read.

We rehearsed in a room at the front of the building, which in the afternoon caught the full force of summer. Trying to act in great squares of sunshine was difficult enough without the alarming interventions of Miss Zedd, who would leap from the shadows with a cry of scorn to display a courtly bow or a moment of swordplay. It was like trying to rehearse with no clothes on. Clothes, however, were not much help when it came to the dress parade.

The RADA wardrobe consisted mainly of soiled donations from professional companies, the bulk of which derived from Sir Herbert Beerbohm Tree's tenure of His Majesty's Theatre at the turn of the century. Made of the heavy furnishing fabrics of the day, maroon brocades and velvets in khaki and blue, they had begun their lives before dry cleaning, and in the armpits the sweat of old stagers commingled with that of generations of terrified students. You only had to wear one for five minutes to have fifty years of theatrical history unfold in a pageant of odours. Miss Zedd decided that my legs were too skinny for Claudius and insisted that I pad. This meant climbing into a pair of stained and ragged long-johns of quilted cotton half an inch thick, such as an elderly prospector in the Yukon might have welcomed to see him through a particularly bad winter. This, however, was summer. I then donned a costume that seemed to have been made from old tasselled cushion covers, antimacassar and swags of rotting plush. In a junk shop someone would have sat on me to test the springs.

After being kitted out in the wardrobe the students returned to the rehearsal room and stood in line awaiting one of Miss Zedd's meticulous and sarcastic inspections. She moved slowly from one to another, spending most time over the costumes of the prettier girls, her long, freckled hands moving slowly forward like fish to glide over the fit of a waist or the cut of a bodice. These days such attention would risk the description of sexual harassment in the workplace, but in 1951 it went as unremarked as cockstraps, at least among the more respectful English students.

If I have dwelt at some length on the shortcomings of Miss Zedd and those of her predecessors, Miss Ecks and Miss Wye, it is partly because I've recalled them through the eyes of intolerant yet vulnerable youth, but also because these three women came to typify the sort of directors that later on as an actor I would most resent: the martinet, the guru and the politician. All directors occasionally have these roles thrust upon them, but in the professional theatre our behaviour is moderated by the fact that rehearsals are moving towards the imponderable of a public judgement which will have a bearing not only on our self-esteem but on our livelihoods. In these RADA productions our directors were also our audience and our critics, and their derision was unlike anything I was to experience later. This is not to deny them their share of human virtues outside the rehearsal room. I once met Miss Ecks in the street not long after *She Stoops to Conquer* and was quite taken aback by her civility and charm.

The performance of *Hamlet* was a sticky affair. Polonius, making final adjustments to his huge Santa Claus beard and snowy wig, missed his cue, and so failed to interrupt the kiss which Miss Zedd had instructed me to bestow on Gertrude. The kiss went on and on as, with our eyes tightly shut, we heard the urgent hissings of crisis in the wings. Wondering what had gone wrong but still kissing, we decided independently to pop open our eyes at the same moment, and the effect was so startling that my Gertrude began blowing bubbles down my throat. It was the laughter of panic. At last Polonius was pushed on, dressed in black and looking like a horsehair armchair with a sleeping white cat on top. We went on to play the scene as best we could, arranged in a paralysed triangle like a three-piece suite.

If I was dejected after the performance Jack was even more so. Hamlet was a part he knew he understood, and playing it had become a crucial personal test. That afternoon was the first time I had ever seen him nervous, or have to struggle like the rest of us for presence of mind under the lights. His reading was intelligent and deeply felt, and yet in terms of that all-important magnetic field which comes into play whenever an audience gathers to see a performance, and which partly consists of assumptions that may be no more than passing fashion, his performance did not work; no more than that of Alec Guinness that same year, who was roundly chastised by the critics for wearing a beard and being too short. Hamlet, it seemed, in clear defiance of the text, should be clean-shaven, blond and willowy. The truth of the matter was that in the most banal understanding of the term, both actors were miscast, at least for 1951. Jack was dismayed by the fickleness of it. So began his withdrawal from the theatre.

At least he had established his talent in other roles. I was on less firm ground. Nothing I had yet done had made anyone actually sit up, always excepting Marsha. Certain things gave me hope. In *Mourning Becomes Electra* I played Ezra Mannon's death scene with a relish on which even Sir Kenneth remarked. O'Neill's melodrama, redeemed by his granite sincerity, was material in which I felt at home. It helped that I had a full beard and a New England accent to hide behind. Also that my rival in the part, who would be playing it at its second performance, was a seven-foot Persian student with a very uncertain grasp of spoken English. He had the most spectacular good looks I had ever seen, like a warrior from a frieze in the British Museum, but because of his great height the effect was odd, like a handsome man seen in a funfair mirror. My performance could not help being the better of the two, and Sir Kenneth conceded this briefly after first complimenting me on my make-up.

I could sometimes be surprising, too, in the improvisational classes. Once, when we were asked to invent a story about a bell, a bird in a cage and a little girl, Ted Flicker and I proposed a scenario in which a poppet rings a stranger's front door and is promptly fed to a giant vulture behind bars in the front parlour. I played the verminous bird and did so with abandon. But then with improvisation you were writing your own material even as you acted it, and the mind was fully engaged. Playing a part like Hastings I learnt the words then turned to wood. Now, to add to my worries, I was certain I could hear Miss Zedd sharpening her axe in the teachers' common room. I had failed at medicine; it was insupportable to think I might also fail at this. Desperate measures were required.

Jack was a Stanislavsky actor, an approach not favoured at RADA. If it worked for him, why not for me? I had read *An Actor Prepares* in Sydney, and its propositions then seemed so simple as to be self-evident. Now with winter approaching I began to study it seriously, like a technical manual, making notes chapter by chapter. In the light of my ineptitude it became a revelation. In particular I fell upon the exercises to help concentration: how one could make use of all those arbitrary scraps of reality that were under one's nose in the rehearsal room: the chair that wobbled, the dust accumulating on the tabletop which, brushed away, becomes included in the fiction of the scene; how listening is just as important as speaking because it furnishes the impulse for the next thing you say. I learnt that all parts begin with yourself, to which is then appended a whole list of suppositions or 'ifs'. *If* I was forty not twenty, *if* I was a king not a student, *if* I lived two hundred years ago, not today, then what would I be like?

I was groping my way slowly towards the most important thing the student actor can learn: what it actually feels like, the sensation of rehearsing properly. This state of mind – receptive, open to possibility – once discovered becomes the blank sheet of paper on which the actor is now at liberty to inscribe his part, and as I was to learn the feeling was very akin to the pleasure I took in improvisation. Good actors take this state of mind so for granted that they would never think to remark on it, and 'The Method', even in America, has long been discredited for its self-indulgence and cavalier attitude towards text. Nevertheless I can think of no better way for the student actor to approach his craft than through Stanislavsky's fervent simplicities, in which there is no place for pride or affectation or even embarrassment. At any rate the Russian patriarch rescued me.

It was Christmas by the time I had finished my extracurricular studies, and once again in the vacation the American students would be preparing a production of their own, this time *Night Must Fall*, in which Jack had the lead. I was asked to join them and play Hubert, the stiff and correct Englishman who is suitor to the young woman in the play, an invitation which I accepted with a certain wryness since Hubert was characterised as having the same awkwardness that I mostly displayed when I acted. In the light of what I had just learnt perhaps something could be made of this. The director was an amible American student called Charles with a voice like Orson Welles and a harmless conceit about his ability to wear period clothes. I once found him in the wardrobe stroking the mottled velvet of his Tudor cloak and crooning to a circle of admirers, 'I love the texture of things.'

On the morning of the first rehearsal he clapped his hands together and announced, 'OK, people, let's use the stage!' For two days we hurried left to the French windows, right to the fireplace, executed circles round the sofa or paced up and down stage like something desperate behind bars. We soon had no idea what the play was about, and the rehearsal room became a place of gloom and exhaustion. Even Charles began to wonder what to do next. Very gently, and careful to preserve Charles' already tattered dignity, Jack began to intervene in the process. He suggested we all sit down and simply read the scene a couple of times. The things he then said about it were so pertinent and helpful that immediately our spirits recovered. Soon these discoveries suggested moves and we were on our feet. No one took a vote on it – we didn't need to – but over the next few days Jack became our director.

I was seeing the natural evolution of that particular role: how any group of actors, if inadequately led, will seek out the person in their midst who holds the most lucid view of the play. If that person can also demonstrate disinterest in his judgements and real pleasure in seeing his ideas extended by the talents of others, then you have a director. Historically this figure has sometimes been an actor, sometimes a writer, sometimes a designer or a stage manager. But I believe he has always been there, even if unacknowledged and unnamed, sitting out front and supplying an objective opinion that others come to trust: a kind of yeast that can immensely speed up the process of fermentation.

Jack was precisely such a figure, concerned less with generalities than with concrete details. He had an infallible nose for the false or unfulfilled moment, and would build a scene by supporting it from beneath with an infrastructure of things to think and do. These derived not from previous theatrical practice but from the life all around us. At the same time he didn't neglect the inherent pacing of the dialogue, or the fact that we were doing one sort of play rather than another, a form with its own strengths and limitations. Rehearsals became immensely exhilarating, particularly for me; I had a director who understood and sympathised with my own private quest.

One morning I arrived at rehearsal in a state of utter dismay. I had received a letter from RADA informing me that I was to be kept down for a term. This did not affect my chance of eventually gaining my diploma, but it did mean I would be excluded from the Public Show and thus the chance of competing for prizes and professional offers. Others in my class were in the same position, including Gertrude in *Hamlet*, a very pretty girl and more than competent actress who apparently I had taken down with me as we clung together in that protracted kiss. Miss Zedd's axe had fallen. There was little sense or justice in the names that had been picked, and I knew it was simply a way of thinning the ranks of those who expected parts in the Public Show, but it was devastating to find oneself amongst them.

Jack was sympathetic but rather formally so. He seemed more concerned with making a start on the morning's work. I wanted everything to stop, all day if necessary, so that we could fully explore my iniquitous treatment. Alas, others didn't seem all that interested. The scene we were to rehearse had Hubert, the repressed suitor, proposing and being gently turned down. I had never felt less like acting. However, use everything, Stanislavsky had advised, including presumably the mood you bring to the rehearsal room; including even the fact that acting was the last thing on earth you wanted to do. Pride came to my rescue. I hid my feelings and we started to work.

I had already found a way of turning my own stiffness into an attribute of the character I was playing, and, in inverted commas as it were, no longer my own but Hubert's, that stiffness had made people laugh. Now, to my astonishment, as I concealed Hubert's longing and disappointment beneath the understated English banalities of the text, I found I was making people cry, or at least touching them. Helen Taylor, who was playing the old lady in the wheelchair, and who during *She*

*Stoops to Conquer* had never hesitated to express an opinion about my inadequacy, was giving little squeals of delight as she sat watching the scene from the side of the room. I felt a rush of pleasure as I realised I had my small audience in thrall. Up till now I had relied as an actor on my small store of sophistication and assurance, and had got nowhere. Only now when I was making use of the most vulnerable and naked aspects of myself had I come up with something of real interest. I began to see that notwithstanding its occasional triumphs, its conspicuously public success, there was at the heart of an actor's life an aspect of public confession, something perplexed and even grieving.

For the moment all I felt was astonishment that the door had opened for me. 'Genius!' hyperbolised Helen Taylor as we finished the scene, and Jack conceded me the grin of the satisfied trainer. I had learnt how to do it! And immediately, since success has a monotony which struggle doesn't, the story becomes less interesting. Sir Kenneth attended the performance of *Night Must Fall*, and at his notes afterwards I found myself being studied for the first time with real curiosity. 'You have a distinct bent for comedy,' he told me almost with irritation, directed, however, not at me but at those who had persuaded him otherwise. Thereafter he was to become a staunch defender of my interests.

In my last two terms at RADA I had a succession of plum parts and the guidance of some exceptional teachers. Now that I had a sense of what I could do the right parts seemed to be effortlessly coming my way. Tattle in Congreve's *Love for Love* was wonderful casting for me and I rehearsed it with a new single-mindedness and confidence. When I met weeping girls on the stairs, desperate because they felt poorly represented in the Public Show, or upstairs in the canteen overheard obsessive conversations about the agents and casting directors who would be there on the big day, I felt almost relieved to be out of it. Whilst others fretted about their careers, I was getting on with my work.

In any case, the Public Show was proving to be a shamelessly rigged affair. It was billed as an open competition, but like so many other aspects of British life, the winners were decided in advance. So indignant were the American students to discover this that they petitioned the Registrar, but Miss Brown was as lofty and unyielding as a Cabinet Secretary. Jack expressed his disapproval by refusing to participate. We all knew who would win the Gold Medal – Rosemary Harris, whose long scene in *The Heiress* was the centrepiece of this all-important afternoon at the Wyndham's Theatre. However, in her case British hypocrisy had a point, since she clearly deserved to win. I watched the event with Jack from a box at upper circle level, and it had its moment of bitter hilarity. My candlelit death scene in *Mourning Becomes Electra* fell to the seven-foot Persian actor, but as he was buried beneath a full black beard on a stage so underlit as to be almost pitch-dark, his amazing good looks counted for little. Nor could you understand a word he said, a dilemma compounded by the girl who was murdering him, an uninhibited Czech student also encumbered with a heavy accent. Sitting there in the dark it was a bit like tuning in by accident to a radio broadcast from the Middle East, in which listeners were exhorted to some sort of indecipherable bloodshed.

The Public Show came and went; my parts got better and better. The last thing I did on the RADA stage was the lead in an interesting play of thirties despair, *Musical Chairs*, and in the audience was one of those important agents whose names had been whispered in connection with the Public Show, Ronnie Waters of Al Parker Ltd. He liked my performance enough to recommend me as a novice actor to the Theatre Royal, Huddersfield. So in the end it turned out that I was among the lucky ones who could leave drama school with a job to go to.

This turn in my fortunes after *Night Must Fall* coincided with the arrival in London of my mother, the first of a number of trips she would make from Australia throughout the fifties to visit me. Since her divorce she had worked in the dress business, an interest in wearing clothes being the only enthusiasm with which her correct but erratic education had furnished her. These visits were carefully budgeted affairs, this one partially financed by a temporary job in the fashion department of Fortnum and Masons, and they became important to both of us. We enjoyed, a shade self-consciously, one of those crisp, companionable relationships between mother and son you find idealised in plays and novels between the wars. This belied the origins of a bond forged twelve years before in a period of great distress for both of us, that of her divorce. In lieu of alimony my father had offered her a trip to England, and at the age of nine I was deposited in the left luggage of a boarding school to await her return. Weeping inconsolably, I had waved a sheet from the veranda of the old Government House building which had become Cranbrook School, myself at one corner, the school matron at another, hoping to send a signal to the departing liner on the harbour below, a slow, slow arrow aimed at that tiny red target at the top of the map. My grief was, of course, identical to that of thousands of English children whose parents had sailed away in the opposite direction to administer larger areas of red. It was another of the mimicked agonies of a colonial growing-up. The nine months of her absence was an occasion of misery for me, and, I suspect, lasting guilt for her, and it was to draw us particularly close when she returned.

My mother moved easily into the circle of my new friends, pleasantly surprised that none of them turned out to be the theatrical grotesques she had half-expected, and they in turn responded to the well-groomed reserve and the open-mindedness that was part of her code. I was two people during the months of her stay: one weekend visiting my godmother in Sussex, I would be the old version of myself, and the next, with the Salamancas, I would try out the new. She gave me back the comfort of my old identity when I needed some respite from change, and in return I could now offer her the particular gift that a grown child can extend to a parent: some participation in what will happen next. She still had the curiosity and the vigour to make the most of it.

She came to RADA to see me act in a Granville Barker translation of a Spanish play, *The Romantic Young Lady*, in which I had an excellent light-comedy part. Afterwards I introduced her to the director, Nell Carter, a sweet-natured actress who had been an ingénue in Beerbohm Tree's company, and who, in her sixties, was still a woman of porcelain prettiness with a fringe of little grey curls and a lively dress sense. Miss Carter sang my praises, and the two women chatted about my prospects as they eyed each other approvingly on the RADA stairs. Towards the end of her visit she arranged an appointment with Sir Kenneth, who repeated his revised opinion on my abilities, then roguishly turned the conversation to my mother.

'But look here, you haven't the least trace of an Orstralian accent!' he exclaimed, beaming. She was of a generation to take this as the highest compliment. But even in 1952 younger Australians weren't so sure. When Sir Kenneth counselled me to get rid of my accent offstage as well as on, I said nothing but inwardly fumed. This was advice never offered to Americans; why to me? I wasn't proud of being Australian, but I'd learnt enough about England certainly not to be ashamed of it.

As our last summer as students approached so did the London University Diploma exams. We had lecturers other than Miss Byrne who taught, for example, the history of stage architecture. The teacher with whom we studied dramatic literature told us not to overlook the minor Jacobean playwrights, particularly John Webster, on whom she thought there might be a question. She warned us, however, that Webster would be tedious to read, burdened with archaic language and built around plots which, when not incomprehensible, were distastefully melodramatic. I'd found much to argue with in her previous opinions and deduced she was likely to be astray in this case, too, so I hurried home to read *The White Devil* for myself. Out of such perverse impulses do we learn.

*The White Devil* astonished me more than any play I'd ever read. Far from being obscure the writing sometimes had an almost confessional force, and, notwithstanding the verse and the play's exotic locale, many of its images had the immediacy of daily experience. Here was just the cast of mind I felt I had been waiting for, a perception of the darkness of the world sufficiently like that of my own beleaguered youth that I might have been reading it with the ink barely dry. As for the melodrama, I found it wonderful – pessimism exalted by poetry and evil redeemed by passionate regret. In a state of great excitement I ran downstairs to the kitchen to telephone Jack.

Unknown to me he, too, had had doubts about the judgement of the teacher, and my call interrupted him a few pages from the end of the play. Our reactions to it, even to certain lines and moments, were a match. It was extraordinarily exhilarating to claim these responses as one's own, but then with literature, as with most things, the vanity of personal discovery can help mightily in authenticating what you feel. We poured scorn upon our poor teacher, but we were actually in her debt. Who else had set us on the path? Perhaps it's time to include Miss Ecks, Miss Wye and Miss Zedd in this mellower judgement. Before the end of the week Jack and I had both read *The Duchess of Malfi*. Like *The Godfather, Part II* it was the same but even better. In our private cosmology, Webster became our dramatist just as Housman was our poet, spokesmen for a sweeping pessimism that was sustaining rather than defeatist, because we believed it described the world as it was, not as it emerged from the pages of newspapers or the mouths of our elders and betters.

That time of my life is now some fifty years away, and I'm relieved that our assessments then were, if not wrong, certainly incomplete. Being alive has proved a good deal more various and surprising than simply an experience of the world's oppression and the perception of one's own physical decay and approaching death; at any rate for those who reach the plateau of a fortunate middle age. Nevertheless, for a young man with his eyes open, still tender-hearted and with as yet no hold on the world, it wasn't a bad way of steeling oneself for the hypothetical onslaughts to come. 'The thoughts of others / Were light and fleeting, / Of lovers' meeting, / Of luck or fame. / Mine were of trouble, / And mine were steady, / So I was ready / When trouble came,' Jack would intone as he reached for the Bourbon purchased from the Embassy, and my skin would prickle.

In truth, of course, luck, fame and lovers' meeting occupied a great deal of my thoughts, and would continue to do so until I had had fair-sized helpings of all three. That I also thought on better things was largely due to Jack's encouragement. His influence on me was not entirely to do with his formidable intelligence. Like many American artists who grew up during the Depression there was an ethical concern at the heart of his thinking which carried over into his everyday conduct. The Salamancas always seemed to have the time and patience for anyone who turned up on their doorstep, and many did. I, on the other hand, had little tolerance for people I didn't especially like, and would wriggle out of any responsibility to catch, say, a screening I had been looking forward to at the National Film Theatre. Jack's moral authority, in small as well as in more transcendent matters, gave his opinions a forcefulness that was not without its dangers, since among his many interesting ideas there were inevitably one or two duds, and one tended to swallow these as enthusiastically as the rest. For instance, it would be some years before I fully grasped that moral imagination was not, alas, invariably an attribute of talent.

Increasingly his energies were turning away from the theatre and towards literature, and he urged me along the same path, but I knew I lacked his subterranean confidence. Besides, I was now making some headway with acting. 'Mimicry!' he scoffed.

So concluded my two years at RADA. In a sense it was the beginning of my true education. Armed with not one but two diplomas, the beginnings of a craft and a half-baked philosophy, I turned my face away from London and peered to the North.

# FOUR

# North and South

A few years ago, travelling from Sydney to London, my plane was queuing to take off from Bombay Airport. On a patch of land slap up against the runway, the long grass of which was tossed and flattened all day long by the blast of jet engines, people were trying to live. You could see them moving slowly from one flapping shanty to another, heads lowered against the roar and stench of the huge wings which passed them by. There were children's heads visible and signs of cooking. One could not begin to imagine what such a life would be like. In 1952, on the last lap of my journey from London to Huddersfield, aboard that nineteenth-century equivalent of the jumbo jet, the steam locomotive, I had had a glimpse of another Bombay closer to home.

I had made the mistake of travelling on a Sunday, changing from one sluggish train to another as we meandered first up the length of Britain, then sideways through the Pennines. Most of the journey had been grim, rattling through the bleak, monochromatic Midlands, or sitting stranded in a railway intersection so huge it was like a harbour clogged with a seaweed of dirty steel tracks. This last section, however, was spectacular in its awfulness. As the train wound through the devastated beauty of the hills, each valley was revealed as a sink of smoke from which, like neglected washing-up, bits of township projected – a chimney stack, a church spire, the long spines of terraced housing sloping upwards. A Sabbath deadness hung over each community (that stale haze was the residue of the previous working week) and only a few people walked the streets.

Sydney had had its share of poverty and squalor, but at least a uniformly disposed sunshine bleached the laundry in the most cramped back yard, and anyone could escape for an hour or two to the harbour or the coast. But down there entire lifetimes were ticking away as remorselessly as a chronic cough. I was appalled. Why had nobody spoken to me of this – not my godmother living in the orderly pastures of Sussex, not my teachers at RADA nor my fellow students? It was if a bomb had fallen on half of this small island, and for a century or more the other half had simply pretended it hadn't happened. I'd been in Britain two years and thought I was part of it, but all I possessed was a sketchy understanding of a couple of patches of southern England and a dozen London bus routes. I experienced the indignation and shock of a grown child who learns something disgraceful about a parent.

What had the North of England signified for me in Australia? At the age of six it had been Stanley Holloway intoning 'Sam, pick oop thy mooskit' on a scratchy portable gramophone. I was meant to find it funny, but secretly I thought it dull and, in some obscure way, *tame*. Later, at the pictures, the North was Gracie Fields trilling at the head of a column of workers on the march, or George Formby smiling with oriental vacancy through one of his ukulele ditties. Like so much popular British entertainment these films were a jolly enough way to spend an hour and a half, but they were shot through with a social acquiescence I could not have begun to define but which I instantly sensed and disliked. It was the same with the English comic cuts, *Film Fun* and *Radio Fun*, so bland and formulistic when compared to the American strips competing for our pocket money. *Dick Tracy, Flash Gordon* and *Tarzan* had a sweep, a vividness and, even to a boy of ten, a blazing sexiness which left their British competitors limp and unread on the newsstands. Anything could happen in the American comics, a trip to Mars or a wrestle with a lion. The English ones went round in cramped, uneventful circles.

If the industrial wasteland I was passing through on my way to Huddersfield spoke of the selective blindness of those fortunate enough to live elsewhere, it also said something about the perverse social obedience of the thousands dumped in the middle of it. Similarly the fondness for secrecy among those who governed, of which I had had a slight experience at RADA and would have more in theatres all over the country, could only be indulged by a constituency happy not to know. I could see that the class system, the acceptance of which was so incomprehensible to an outsider, was shored up most crucially by its victims, a population obsessed with deference. These were the obvious things about Great Britain which I imagined I was discovering. However, generalisations, even correct ones, could not begin to describe the complexity of Britain in the way that generalisations were frequently apt for a country as recent and as homogeneous as Australia. Exceptions were everywhere and, for someone intent upon it, this multitude of exceptions could provide a very real personal liberty. By the mid-sixties England would be a country in which I felt lucky to have found refuge. By the mid-eighties, as the old heartlessness found new ways to assert itself, I would be less sure.

I haven't much affection for my time in weekly rep. It was a harsh, frequently stultifying way of acquiring a craft. The plays were mostly dreadful and the working conditions on a level with those aboard the RMS *Otranto*. You were the working class of the theatrical profession, and as such you were expected to climb a ladder with no rungs. Mostly it was a twelve-hour day. On Monday you dress-rehearsed in the afternoon and opened that night. The next morning, beginning at ten, you walked through all the moves of the play which would be presented the following Monday. We followed exactly what the original London cast had done, transcribed faithfully into the pages of a French's Acting Edition. After the second performance of the current show that night, you returned to your digs and learnt an entire first act for rehearsal the following morning. The next night, between the hours of eleven and God knows when in the morning, you learnt Act Two; the night after, Act Three. On Saturday morning you put the whole thing together, then, after lunch, went on to do two shows. On Sunday you rested and revised your lines for Monday, when the treadmill began its next cycle.

There was actually something called twice-weekly rep – a new play every three days, but this was an abomination I managed to avoid. Only the very gifted could benefit from this punitive employment. Sir Henry Irving was one, whose beginnings in the provincial stock companies of his day show hundreds of parts played within a single year; but then he had a photographic memory and the double incentive of poverty and genius. For most of the thousands of actors processed through the wringer of weekly rep a century on, it was no more than a job until a better came along, if indeed it ever did. Weekly rep was not kind to talent.

The leading man at the Huddersfield Theatre Royal was Maurice Durant. He had begun in rep before the war, then, like so many of his generation, had had a huge bite taken out of his career by his army service. Now a man in his early forties, he had come back to where he started. He had the slightly battered good looks of a Trevor Howard or a David Farrar, and with better luck might have done well in films playing taciturn pipe-smokers of quiet charm. In those days each rep had its designated leading man, as well as its leading lady, character man, juvenile lead, etc. Maurice had a sharp sense of his territory and of the prestige and few extra pounds that went with it. He had also become expert at making the most of the life, and lived not in digs but in a large, airy flat, a bus ride from the theatre, atop the green hills overlooking the nearby town of Halifax. This he shared with his leading lady, with whom he was having a turbulent affair, and to help with the rent had invited me and one of the stage managers to occupy the other two bedrooms.

Maurice insisted on a certain formality in the way we lived. Arriving home from the theatre after the show, we always sat down to a proper meal, which it would have been the turn of one of us to shop for at the open-air market next to the theatre. Rationing was still on, and I was used to one egg, four ounces of butter and one lamb chop a week. In Huddersfield produce slid straight from the surrounding farms into the butcher's stall with no questions asked, and a cheerful girl with spots behind the counter, a supporter of the theatre, made sure that every night we fed on huge slabs of animal protein.

Precisely three-quarters of an hour was allowed for supper, after which Maurice would ready himself for the work ahead. First he would make a half-gallon of tea in one of those huge metal pots you once saw in transport cafés. With this gargantuan brew and a pouch of pipe tobacco he would then retire to his bedroom to do battle with next week's script. It was a matter of professional pride with him never to go to bed until he'd learnt every last line of the act, by which time, since he only played leading parts, it was often dawn and the pot would contain nothing but cold leaves. After a couple of hours sleep he'd arrive at rehearsal almost cross-eyed with study but somehow in command. It was an almost perverse display of character, more suited perhaps to his war years than to his career as an actor.

By Monday he'd have his performance ready, and it was frequently a good one. There was only one problem and it applied to everything he did. Though he always knew his lines there was never time for them to become comfortably absorbed in the muscular memory of lips, tongue and thorax. Consequently, he'd acquired the habit when speaking of both rocking slightly from the waist and just perceptibly twisting his head, the sort of small struggling motions people make when dreaming. Presumably it helped in pumping out those hundreds of new sentences each week, but it also marked him ineradicably as a rep actor. In the next few years I would encounter other veterans with different wounds: a character man who, making the most of a bass voice, applied an identical inflection to everything he said; a leading lady who never met your eyes but stared fixedly at a point in the middle of your forehead as she launched into her next speech. The only direction you ever had was 'Pace! Pace! Pick up your cues!' and there was something desperately trancelike about some of the performances, particularly on a Monday night.

It has to be said that as weekly reps went, Huddersfield was one of the best. It operated on the visiting star system, which meant that most of our productions featured a celebrity who would join us briefly before taking the same performance on to another company. These visitors fell roughly into two categories: pretty Rank film starlets trying to get some theatre experience (and badly in need of it), and old stage stars keeping busy at the end of their careers by trotting past successes around the provinces. This combination of innocence and experience in our top billing led to a variable standard. Among the starlets that season was the yet to be celebrated Kay Kendall, who a few weeks before I arrived had come up to play Sadie Thompson in *Rain*. By Thursday it was clear she would never be able to learn her lines. In desperate straits, the management decided to change the play to *Pygmalion*, in which she had starred a few weeks previously in Bradford. Maurice Durant forgot about the two acts of *Rain* he already had under his belt, and set about learning Professor Higgins in what was left of the week. Likewise the designer was obliged to build Covent Garden in a day. Somehow or other they had a fully mounted show by the Monday.

These pretty young women often felt as displaced and lost in Huddersfield as I did, and I would sit with them in the star dressing room, each trying to cheer up the other. A fortnight was more than enough to become mournfully infatuated, but I was too junior a member of the company ever to act upon my longing. One of these beauties, Jean Lodge, was also an excellent actress, and I doted on her. She joined us to do *The Barretts of Wimpole Street*, in which I made my professional debut as the elderly physician who prescribes a daily glass of porter to his lovely patient. Jean was nice about my make-up (false nose and bushy white eyebrows) but I could tell it was not sexually enhancing.

Our artistic director was also called Maurice, the only thing he and the leading man had in common. They were barely on speaking terms. Since a working rapprochement with the actors was the least of a rep director's responsibilities, this did not affect the quality of the shows. What was of more consequence was his impulse to cast himself, often in grossly inappropriate parts. You felt he almost longed for someone in the company to fall sick so that he could step in and take his place. When this happened, there was Maurice, seated at the vacated place in front of the dressing-room mirror, making up with one hand and turning the pages of the script with the other in a curious state of shivering terror and self-importance. In another it might have seemed courageous; in Maurice it turned the business of acting into a matter of unseemly compulsion, like the imperatives of a drag queen. What made this exhibitionism doubly uncomfortable, and beyond the realm of comment, was that as a child he had been badly crippled by polio, a disability that was only magnified on stage.

Maurice's direction consisted of sucking up to the visiting stars and bullying junior members of the company like myself. However, I preferred his spite to his friendliness. In the pub after the show I dreaded being beckoned into his circle, where I would have to endure a string of servile theatrical anecdotes about our betters, the rich and famous of the West End theatre. He referred to them, like royalty, by their first names, and gave adoring impressions in his ripest theatrical tones. 'A HAAAND BAAAG!' he would shriek, as Edith Evans, in Lady Bracknell drag, made a spectral appearance in our group. Others in the pub would look in our direction, then glance away quickly, as if they had spotted something disabled about the lot of us. I would clutch my glass of soapy bitter and wonder, if this was the life of an actor, what on earth was I doing living it?

But in one important respect – my encounters with some great, if fading performers – Huddersfield could not have been a more instructive and sober introduction to the professional theatre. Tod Slaughter, the melodrama king now in his seventies, came up to give us his most celebrated performance, in *Sweeney Todd, the Demon Barber of Fleet Street*. A big man, who rehearsed in a worn homburg hat and wrapped up in a vast entrepreneurial overcoat, he had the preoccupied manner of the

actor-manager who has spent a life juggling the concerns of performing with those of the nightly take. He had sent on ahead a description
of how the lethal barber's chair should work, and the stage carpenter
had sawn out a trapdoor stage centre. It was a big show, with period
costumes and many changes of scene, and the dress rehearsal seemed
fraught with danger, as miscued scenery flew in from above and the
trapdoor opened from below. These Monday afternoons loom large
in my memories of Huddersfield – hanging on to our lines by our
fingernails, those nervous waits we could not afford when something
technical went wrong, the onset of that cold lethargy at the prospect
that one's tawdriness would soon be on public display.

On this occasion I shall not forget the desperation and nervousness
of our star, stoically endured, as he readied himself for a part he had
already played perhaps a thousand times. As it would twenty-five
years later, when I caught sight of Ralph Richardson's shaken face
after a first preview of *John Gabriel Borkman* at the National, it
seemed somehow awful that an old actor with so much behind him
should still have to be frightened.

That night I felt very differently about Tod Slaughter, and indeed
about the theatre, as I watched him, head lifted to catch the full force
of a green spot, knees bent like Irving in *The Bells*, deliver his soliloquy on guilt and retribution. It was tosh, of course, but done with
blazing panache. I felt I was gazing on not one, but a whole line of
actors, stretching back and back through a succession of childhoods
thunderstruck by a visit to the theatre.

Sir Henry Irving was still a presence in the building. Billy, the oldest
stagehand, a little bent Yorkshire elf who had started work at the
Theatre Royal as a boy, remembered seeing him on his last tour. So
had Fred, the nightwatchman, who lived beneath the theatre in one of
the underground, windowless dressing rooms. He slept all day, then,
just before the show, donned his heavy black boots and fireman's uniform, and roamed the theatre till dawn. On one occasion, unbeknownst
to Fred, the designer was working late on the paint frame to the rear
of the stage. From a distance she heard Fred's inimitable approach,
heavy measured footfalls sounding from beneath. She followed their
progress along the dressing-room corridor, up the circular metal staircase, then across the stage itself, where they came to a halt by the
footlights. The designer peered from behind the stacked canvas flats.
Fred stood with his back to her, stage centre, arms raised towards the

yawning auditorium. 'The bells!' he cried. 'THE BELLS!' then turned, left the stage and resumed his lonesome patrol.

The theatre, which had a beautiful Victorian interior even if its dressing rooms left something to be desired, was demolished in the sixties in favour of a car park, so neither Sir Henry's agonised cries, nor Fred's for that matter, have anywhere now to echo.

Another of our visitors was Claude Hulbert, lesser brother of Jack, a comedian with a line in lovable upper-class twits. His trade, and the respectable background he'd deserted to pursue it, left him the victim of constant anxiety. That week of rehearsals was one of deep gloom, and of ominous warnings to myself. In welcome contrast was another comedian, Lupino Lane, the Cheekie Chappie whom I remembered from *Film Fun*, and whose acrobatics had made him a fortune in the original thirties production of *Me and My Girl*. He arrived with his ex-chorus-girl wife, who towered over him by a good six inches, and both were as cheerful as old troupers in a backstage movie. You would never have known that the last years of his career had ushered in a string of catastrophes. A mistimed pratfall that toppled him into the orchestra pit had left him with injuries that now obliged him to walk with a stick, and he'd lost all his money when, after the war, he invested it in a West End theatre, only to find that it had been so badly shaken by the bombing that it had to remain closed. He remained slyly irrepressible, on stage and off. While we waited in the wings to go on, he showed me how to roll a bowler hat down my arm. I responded by showing him a conjuring trick with a half-crown piece. At the end of the week he gave me a signed copy of his book *How To Be a Comedian*, in which were described bits of physical business, some of it going back probably to the *commedia dell'arte*. I kept it for years, then my seven-year-old son spotted the title, borrowed it and, alas, I never saw it again.

However, the star who turned out to have the most influence on me was the one from whom I expected least, Henry Kendall. There was a photograph of him on the board front of house announcing forthcoming attractions. It showed a plumpish man in evening dress, with the flared nostrils of Somerset Maugham and the same look of amused disdain, probably a still from one of the London revues in which he'd had his greatest successes. Maurice, our director, took delight in alarming me with his description of this mercilessly camp West End sophisticate who would soon be in our midst. It was an accurate enough account, but far from complete. What he neglected to mention was Henry Kendall's dazzling and generous professionalism.

The play was his London hit *On Monday Next*, which made fun of just the kind of rep company he had come to visit. He was to play the Artistic Director. He took one look at our own and decided to handle the production himself. Almost his second decision was to demote me from soppy juvenile to the lesser role of Ambulance Man, something he did with such directness and obvious lack of malice, that, like a clever dentist removing a tooth, I barely felt a thing. Within a day or two the theatre was buzzing. Rather than him coming to Huddersfield, it was more as if he'd picked up the entire company by the scruff of the neck and dropped us into the middle of Shaftesbury Avenue. His dress rehearsal, unlike the gloom of most Monday afternoons, was a marvel of lightning authority and optimism as he fired off succinct notes in all directions to actors, stage management and crew, each appended by a first name. I would not see such a concise and productive use of available time until I worked for Tyrone Guthrie seven years later.

*On Monday Next* was undoubtedly the most achieved show of the season. That night, playing to the usual cut-price Monday house, I heard laughter such as I had never heard before, at least on the receiving end. It was almost as if Henry Kendall was conducting it. Then a very strange thing happened. On Tuesday night the theatre was almost empty; similarly on Wednesday and Thursday. We were all bewildered, until, by way of the friendly girl at the butcher's stall in the market, an explanation got back to us. Our audience, upon whose loyalty we depended to get through our most moribund productions, didn't care to see their theatre mocked.

One could hardly blame them. A night out in these industrial towns was a choice between the pubs, the movies and, occasionally, a rep theatre. We were supported through desperation. Even a city like Sheffield closed down completely after eight o'clock at night. There wasn't a restaurant or even a corner shop open to differentiate those grey streets. In Huddersfield on Sunday the sun need hardly have bothered to rise. The centre of the town was as dead as Angor Wat. With nothing better to do I would walk the streets past locked buildings which spoke of nothing but another Monday of work and money. It wasn't a town; it was a utility. Only on Friday nights, payday, when in communities all over the North the workforce enjoyed a few hours of anaesthetic drunkenness, did the streets come truly to life. The hordes discharged into the drizzly night at closing time rarely gave trouble. Their aggression had been poured back down their own throats. After the theatre we waited at the terminal among the legless but orderly crowd queuing for a last bus home. With a full load aboard, the vehicles would set off quite recklessly, like the helicopters that evacuated Saigon, with passengers spilling off the back or being dragged along the street as they clung doggedly to a handrail.

Was this where I was to spend my life, stepping over vomit at some shivering bus stop or enduring Maurice's shrieking triviality down at what he liked to call 'The Fun Factory'? For some it was already too late. The company's juvenile lead, who gravely smoked a pipe, was trapped in one room with a wife and baby twins. After the show one Saturday night, I found him applying Max Factor pancake to the circles under his eyes before setting out to some local dance in search of girls. Every aspect of his life seemed compromised and he had barely begun.

There was one escape available to me, as there had been aboard the *Otranto* – books; and the reading I did during my years in rep became a matter of passionate self-definition. At RADA Jack had recommended Scott Fitzgerald and particularly *Tender is the Night*, assuming correctly that the story of Americans drifting back to re-engage Europe would have something to say to an Australian on the same quest. *The Great Gatsby* was available in Penguin, but the other novels were out of print and unknown to me. Jack got me copies from the States, and I gobbled them up one after another in a state of rapt identification. Would that closing sentence about Dick Diver's bruised retreat to America, 'In any case he is almost certainly in that section of the country, in one town or another,' one day signify my own return to Australia? Running out of novels, I turned to Fitzgerald's biography, and after a long afternoon's read I would reluctantly put it aside and set off to the theatre through the autumn evening with doomed Zelda and poor, broken Scott throbbing in my mind. Below me, in the misty valley, the dim lights of Halifax beckoned as mournfully as those over Long Island Sound.

Being smitten by a writer makes you want to write, and my grandfather's typewriter was still part of my luggage. However, my confidence did not yet extend beyond letters, which I dispatched all over the place – to family, to friends in London and Sydney. Those to my mother had become a habitual discipline, and reading them now I'm surprised by their ebullience, given what I remember about my general mood. One describes an improvement in my fortunes at the theatre: 'Astounding change of attitude towards Huddersfield. Last Saturday night I had to take over a large part from another actor with only one rehearsal, and managed it to the *satisfaction of all*. The reason is that next week the local amateurs are taking over the theatre (a mammoth musical production of *The Dancing Years*) and our resident company are being sent out on tour with last week's play. This is *Harvey*, and Leslie Henson is the star.' The actor I was replacing was the juvenile with the pipe and the pancake, who had been given a week off to do a broadcast. I'd had ten days to learn the part but only a few hours rehearsal, so my competence that Saturday morning surprised even Maurice. On the strength of this display I was to be asked back in the New Year.

Leslie Henson was the biggest star of that season, and because he stayed with us an extra week, the one we got to know best. Our leading man asked him to have lunch with us at the flat one weekend. The years of his greatest success had been the twenties and thirties, when he had been the leading comic in a number of famous musicals. He'd made pots of money, and at one time had maintained a yacht in the South of France. One gathered most of it was now spent. Over the meal he regaled us with anecdotes about the legendary figures he'd worked with, and we were willing listeners, all actors being part fans. However, as story followed story, I noticed that however light-heartedly they began, during the telling they drifted into an area of veiled grievance. One tale concerned the great Fred Astaire coming into his dressing room during the show, ostensibly on a social visit but actually to give him a note. He described how Fred moved uneasily about the dressing room, executing a few dance steps, clearing his throat or tapping the mantelpiece with his fingers, before coming out with it: would Leslie mind *not* lighting that cigarette just before Fred went into his second dance? Lost in the story, the old comedian raised his head to look at us, and said, as if the incident had happened just the night before, 'Would you *believe* it!' It was my first experience of something I would find quite incomprehensible until I had tasted it myself: the slightly crazy, bitter edge to success.

Just before Christmas, an outside pantomime took over the theatre, and the company was dispersed until such of us as had been asked back could reassemble in February. I fled to London and to my room at Adam's Row which, miraculously, had just become vacant; to the Salamancas and their hospitality, lavish over Christmas, and to conversation which could include such topics as whether God existed (or, more to the point, whether he didn't). How wonderful it was to be back among the foreigners, with whom one could swap impressions or let one's mockery rip without fear of misunderstanding; to be found funny again and sometimes, even intelligent. My personality, like a passport, had been briefly returned to me. I was free to stroll across the river to the new National Film Theatre or along Jermyn Street, window-shopping at the displays of shirts and handmade shoes.

London, I insisted in my letters, was where I was comfortable. I had yet to accept that discomfort is the more effective teacher, and at least one of the things I had to learn was a more comprehensive understanding of my adopted country. Throughout the fifties I would be forced to abandon the capital to go criss-crossing the railway map of Britain – to Sheffield, Chesterfield, Weston-super-Mare, to Glasgow, Birmingham and Derby, on and on, like a path through some maze, at the far end of which I would emerge, if not English, then English enough to have something to say about it. This was to be the gift of my days in the provinces. Like a long, irksome part, which can't be played until it is studied, I had to learn the country, and it was to take rather longer than the usual week.

In January, although I had work to return to, I decided to do the rounds of the agents in the fanciful hope that some wonderful job would detain me in London. There were certain agents, like Vincent Shaw, who had the reputation of being sympathetic to beginners, and these were the ones on whose doors I knocked. Denton and Warner were two ageing ladies who had an office up three flights of stairs at Cambridge Circus. They would sit you down and stare at you with the benign intensity of psychics, waiting upon some intimation that the young hopeful opposite them indeed belonged to the select few whose future was inscribed with fame and riches. After a séance of about ten minutes they took a sufficient shine to me to suggest a meeting with the husband-and-wife team who ran the Devonshire Park Theatre in Eastbourne. Later in the week that encounter, too, went well, and I was asked to come back after lunch with an audition piece prepared.

That evening I made two triumphant telephone calls, the first to my godmother in Sussex to tell her I had been offered a string of leading parts, beginning with the Leslie Howard role in *Berkeley Square*, at a lovely theatre not ten miles from her farm, and the second to Huddersfield to let Maurice know I would not be coming back. I did not disguise my self-satisfaction to either party. Ten days later, when I turned up at Eastbourne to rehearse, I couldn't understand why I had trouble catching the eye of either of the artistic directorate; not until a good-looking actor, five or six years my senior, with that same sense of territory I remembered in Maurice Durant, strolled on stage to join the new company. The husband now took me aside. It seemed that, after engaging me, they had found an actor they preferred and had offered him the parts promised to me. There was nothing to discuss since my contract specified 'play as cast'. They had a bit part in the first production if I was interested, two weeks' work. I had to accept because I needed the money. Back in London I climbed the stairs to Denton and Warner for justice, but I was giving off a different aura now, and the two ladies shuffled and murmured me out of the door. There were plenty more clients where I'd come from, but the list of employers was finite and no agent could afford upsetting one.

When I told Jack of this betrayal he gave a grunt of bleak laughter. It accorded only too accurately with his experience as a New York actor, and was further evidence condemning a fickle profession. I was all the more touched, then, by his invitation to stay with them until such a time as another job came along. The Salamancas had just returned from a trip home to the States, and they brought back disquieting stories. Over one of Mimi's southern dinners I heard the name 'McCarthy' for the first time, and was introduced to one of the themes of the fifties, the bigotry and obfuscation attendant on the acquisition of a nuclear arsenal. The climate of the necessary lie, not least in Britain, would be with us for the next thirty-odd years.

How long could I expect the Salamancas to put up with me? I had heard of actors being out of work for six months or longer. However, rescue for both of us arrived sooner than expected. I had been staying with them for perhaps a week, and having a much better time than my penniless status would suggest, when one Monday morning, as I sat sipping American coffee with a chapter of Jack's novel-in-progress on my lap, the telephone rang. It was Vincent Shaw, one of the agents I had visited over Christmas. If I could be on a train in two hours there was a job waiting for me in a weekly rep up North, in Bridlington, leading man at a salary of £9 a week. This was a marked improvement on my Huddersfield earnings, and part of me, at least, was elated, but it was also a bit like a call-up in wartime. With a little vacuum of dread in the pit of my stomach I scrambled to pack.

It was dark by the time I arrived in Bridlington, a town about which I knew absolutely nothing. I had been instructed to make my own way from the station to the theatre, where the Artistic Director would be waiting to greet me. The Grand Pavilion was a big thirties pile, more like a cinema than a theatre, and it took me some time to locate the stage door. As I turned the corner at the rear of the building I ran into something which restored my spirits in a rush; I couldn't see the sea but the smell of it was slapping me in the face. In the weak light above the stage door I could just perceive at the bottom of a flight of steps a beach stretching away into the darkness, and beyond that, like a promise of liberty, lay what had to be the North Sea.

Inside the building it was apparent that a performance was in progress, this week's first night. Someone led me through a door and onto the dark perimeter of the stage. On the other side of canvas flats, caged in light, actors barked and shouted dialogue at each other like panicky instructions to stay calm and avert catastrophe. Acting, as it always does when perceived from the wings, seemed about the most unnatural thing in the world. A cheerful face swam out of the darkness. This belonged to my new Artistic Director. What was most immediately striking about him was a trim head of bright yellow hair, about which the black chest-hairs, seen through the V of his open-necked shirt, at once raised questions. However, there was nothing effeminate about Roger. His build and demeanour were those of a plucky lightweight boxer, and he had a slightly off-centre nose to match. Affability itself, he led me back to the corridor, where we could drop the whispering and he could brief me on what lay ahead. I would be playing the lead, he told me, in the next four productions, after which I would be given a play out. 'A play out' meant a fortnight in which I would play the first week, rehearse the second, but not both at once, and was considered a rest.

Roger then suggested that we remove ourselves to the rear of the auditorium where we could watch a little of the current first night. The play was *The Glass Menagerie*, an encouraging choice, I thought, for a seaside rep. The acting was uneven, but given my own premature elevation to leading man, this was no surprise. A girl in her early twenties, with lines drawn all over her face like an Indian on the warpath, was playing the mother, and giving a forceful drama-school performance in a part it would have been better to wait twenty years before attempting. One actor was outstanding. He played the narrator, and his grasp of the American idiom, the ease and conviction with which he took the stage, made it look as if he'd walked in from another, much superior production. I leant across and whispered as much to Roger. His expression went into neutral, then he made a guarded reply. 'Oh yes, Reg. He's the actor you're replacing.'

After the show I met my predecessor briefly at the stage door, going down the line as I was going up. 'Good luck', he said with almost offensive irony. Later that evening I was to learn why. Digs had been arranged for me in the same house as the girl who had had a courageous shot at the mother, Shirley Bush. A late supper had been laid out for us, spam sandwiches and a large pot of iodine-flavoured tea, maturing under a cosy. Having survived a first night, Shirley expressed herself with the frenetic relief of someone who has stepped unhurt from a car smash. Her hair was still damp from the ordeal, and traces of stage make-up showed in her hairline like minor abrasions.

'Isn't he dreadful! Don't you think he's *dreadful?*' she appealed, sucking on a cigarette as if it contained oxygen.

'Who?' I enquired.

'Roger, of course! That's why Reg is leaving! He just can't put up with him any longer.'

It seemed that Roger had engaged Reg on the understanding that they would run the company together. Arguments about the programme of plays, and, I daresay, some professional jealousy had led to a spectacular falling out, which had even made its way into the local paper. Its drama critic championed Reg, a poor look-out for me. I tried to find a silver lining. 'Well, at least Roger occasionally does a decent play.'

Shirley roared with laughter. 'You must be joking! *The Glass Menagerie* was Reg's idea. Roger only agreed because it's cheap – one set and four actors.'

I awoke to a day of brilliant winter sunshine. The digs were in a fussy Edwardian terrace that gave the impression of being compressed from each end of the block, but the windows looked onto an airy street that hinted at the sea around the corner. I set off to the theatre with Shirley, who was now scrubbed and rested, and I was aware for the first time of her striking looks – a classic profile and amazingly clear green eyes that gazed on the sunny day with artless contentment.

The play we were to rehearse was *To Dorothy a Son*, an even cheaper proposition than *The Glass Menagerie*, having one set and only three actors, or rather two and a voice offstage. In the first act a father-to-be is alone on stage talking through an open door to his pregnant wife, a character who never appears. In the second act an American girl arrives and there are complications. In the third act these are resolved and the unseen wife gives birth to an unseen baby. It was a better than average West End comedy, and had been chosen by Reg with himself in mind.

The girl playing the pregnant wife was one of those not uncommon rep performers who had concluded that the road to survival lay in approaching every role with an absolute minimum of effort. She told me she would be reading her entire part from an armchair in the wings. This was Tuesday. By Wednesday lunchtime my failure in *To Dorothy a Son* was a foregone conclusion. I could more or less remember the lines, but, being entirely dependent for cues on a disembodied voice chanting the text as monotonously as plainsong, it was impossible to remember which line followed what. At the end of the morning I was in a state of complete disorientation, with a third of the act unrehearsed.

'Never mind,' said Roger brightly. 'We'll catch up.'

We never did. The run-through on the Saturday morning was a catastrophe, and the dress rehearsal the following Monday afternoon hardly less so. As I waited alone on stage ten minutes before curtain-up, as disbelieving as a man about to be taken outside and shot, suddenly a cinema organ, the existence of which was a surprise to me, exploded into melody. Popular favourites thundered around the auditorium, reaching a climax with an ear-splitting rendition of *There'll Always Be an England*.

'Follow that!' the unseen organist seemed to be saying, and I had the absurd idea it might be Reg out there, turning on his bench to acknowledge his applause, as the lights dimmed and the huge keyboard started to descend.

Nervousness, like pain, has a certain optimal level, and, later in my career, acting on live television before an audience of millions, I would never feel more stricken than I did that night in Bridlington. In a properly rehearsed show nerves are an expression of the superstitious dread that, in spite of all one's precautions, awful things can still happen. Nervousness on this occasion was based on an entirely realistic assessment of what lay ahead. During Act One I lost my way more times than I can remember. My off-stage wife was to receive rather more visits than the playwright intended, as I fled dumb into the wings to be rescued by an uplifted script and a finger jabbing at the forgotten passage. I forgave her everything. The dissatisfaction of the audience, a block-booking by Reg's fan club, was now expressing itself as an indignant murmur such as you might hear from investors milling around a defaulting bank. At the top of the second act Shirley burst through the door with staring eyes and forehead beaded with sweat, her entire part stretching ahead of her like a swaying bridge. Terror was now shared, mine somewhat abated by exhaustion, hers at its peak. Fortunately she was firm on her lines, and somehow, an hour and a half later, the curtain came down, then went up again to a trickle of applause as we willed our exhausted faces into some sort of smile.

I had just learnt the one great lesson of weekly rep; indeed, of the theatre. No matter what you had to go through in the way of fear and sickening humiliation, the experience did not actually kill you. You lived to fight another day. So it was that the next morning at ten o'clock I turned up to rehearse Maxim de Winter in *Rebecca*. Oddly enough, I approached the role with confidence. For one thing I had the right clothes. All rep contracts specified that the actor had to supply from his own wardrobe one lounge suit and a dinner jacket, and mine were superior. Also I had seen Laurence Olivier in the film a couple of times, and felt that with the same moustache and his example I might just get away with it. The text had a certain melodramatic vigour, which meant that it would be easier to learn than *To Dorothy a Son*, and in any case was distributed among many more characters.

One of the members of the company that I was meeting for the first time that morning was the character man, Arthur Reece. He was playing the cad (George Sanders in the film), and even as we shuffled around the stage with our heads in our scripts, sorting out the moves, he was able to project a silhouette of the part. He had come to rehearse with an idea about it, particular, his own. It was startling to be confronted by talent, as self-evident as the plumage of a bird, in the context of this decidedly rum seaside rep. A man in his sixties, Arthur had an air about him, a courtesy, that suggested better days. In the coffee break he approached Shirley and me and said that he was looking forward to seeing the current show, 'But a little later in the week when you two young people have had a chance to settle down.'

The surprising thing is that not only did we settle down, we improved. When Arthur visited us on Thursday night the laughs were clean and plentiful; just as well since the day before the local paper, in what should have been a review but was more an elegy to the departed Reg, murdered me. I pinned my hopes for improving my relations with the press on *Rebecca*. At the dress rehearsal Arthur came on stage perfectly attired for his part. Again he'd been thinking about it, and from somewhere in his wardrobe had found the silk scarf, the blazer and the pressed white flannels that neatly expressed the character. Looking at him I became less depressed about the set, which consisted of last week's canvas flats rearranged around a French window. The great staircase at Manderley was rendered by three treads which vanished behind a wafer-thin cream flat. Some horse brasses on one wall, borrowed from the local pub, were a concession to the feeling of a great country house.

At the first performance that night, and throughout the week, when Arthur wasn't on, he sat in the wings attending to the show. As I grew more confident in my part I would come offstage after Maxim's big scene to be greeted on the Tuesday by a friendly nod, on the Thursday by a complicit grin and on the Saturday night by two thumbs up. Throughout the week he had sat there, under some compulsion never to stop working, precisely calibrating my improvement.

On our day off Arthur invited Shirley and me to a light supper at his digs. He had two rooms, a bedroom and a tiny sitting room, partially furnished with his own things. It was comparative luxury for a life in rep, but one couldn't help feeling the old actor deserved something better. The landlady had prepared spam sandwiches and a jug of Camp Coffee, a concentrate that came out of a bottle like treacly soy sauce, to which you added hot water. Arthur told us his good news. The nearby York Theatre, a well-regarded rep which rehearsed each play an unimaginable two weeks, had offered him a job, and he had given his notice to Roger. We were delighted for him but sorry for ourselves, as we saw more of the talent and all of the experience of our company trickling away. After supper, Arthur produced a huge scrapbook from the bottom drawer of his little antique desk. In the thirties he and his wife had run a successful theatre on the outskirts of London, at Richmond, and there were big, glossy photographs of them in a well-mounted production of *The School for Scandal*, the smiling actor-manager with his pretty leading lady surrounded by their company. It was some kind of high point. He told us that his wife had died suddenly, then he grew reticent and returned the book to its drawer as if he now regretted having ever opened it.

Arthur's farewell performance was to be in another three-hander, *Murder without Crime*, playing an effete villain who wears green suede shoes. A hint of the 'sin that dare not speak its name' was shamelessly used to liven up the sinister goings-on, which involved Shirley dead and stuffed into an ottoman, and myself as a very unpleasant young man, undone by his own cleverness, who brings the curtain down on a rising crescendo of ironic laughter. All the roles were what is usually described as juicy, particularly Arthur's, and doing well in it, as he said goodbye to Bridlington, became important to him.

A letter home describes the first night: 'The dress rehearsal was gloomy and chaotic, and by the performance we were all pretty much exhausted, especially poor old Arthur, who in the course of the play has to crawl all around the stage in the throws of fatal poisoning. The curtain went up and we got through the first scene all right, but in the middle of scene two he dried up horribly, and, getting no help from the prompt corner, lurched into a scene from another act. With lots of all too obvious ad-libbing we scraped out of it somehow, but from Arthur's point of view the evening was in ruins. In the interval he raged and shouted at this new girl on the book, and so tired himself that from then on he forgot practically every other line. How we got by I don't know. The audience, our usual old-age pensioners, started laughing in all the wrong places. After a while it became almost interesting to see just how far things could go wrong without having to bring down the curtain. My chores included breakdowns with either wild sobbing or hysterical laughter. I was amazed I didn't feel sillier.' Whatever the evening may have done to Arthur, who went to York and died there a year later, it's clear that I had become a more resilient performer than the one who had arrived in Bridlington the previous month.

In the weeks that followed other actors took fright, and soon Roger reigned over a company of only four professionals, all under twenty-five. When additional performers were required the backstage staff were pressed into service, and the roles once allotted to Arthur Reece were now played by the stage carpenter, Eric Grono, who rendered West End sophisticates, rear admirals and country squires alike in the broadest Yorkshire. When Roger and his wife made their occasional star appearances they shone like diamonds in mud. Roger's sway extended to the choice of plays and these were becoming odder and odder, comedies about young toffs dredged up from the twenties, with names like *He Walked in Her Sleep* and *Almost a Honeymoon*. In these I invariably had the lead, as I would later in other reps. It was not merely a matter of finding myself trapped by my own tailoring, an irony worthy of *Murder without Crime*; I was actually rather accomplished in them. These creaking vehicles were repositories for all the received ideas about England it had never occurred to me to question during my Australian childhood. Now, with doubt raging, I had sharp insights into the mechanisms of the faith. No one could touch me when it came to swinging a rolled umbrella or wearing a bowler hat. No one could better rattle out the inane, almost surrealistic dialogue so that at some level, well below the intellect, it provoked laughter.

This was the theatre I was doomed to be good at. The theatre I believed in was three thousand miles away where Elia Kazan and Marlon Brando had worked their miracles, and I wondered if I was alone in all England in aspiring to it. I was not to know that in provincial theatres elsewhere there were other young men, often at odds with their colleagues, whose artistic lives were nourished less by the play they performed at seven-thirty than by the screening of *On the Waterfront* that they'd sneaked in to see that afternoon. It was only when, a few years later, I went to see those lucky ones, Michael Bryant in *Five Finger Exercise* or Alan Bates in *Look Back in Anger*, that I realised I had always been part of a generation intent on change.

In what garbage can Roger found some of the plays we did I will never know. Scripts would be distributed on Tuesday mornings, sometimes no more than a soiled and crudely bound collection of blue carbon copies. You would receive, not the play, but the lines of your part. The connective tissue of the things other characters said would be indicated by a series of dots followed by the last three or four words of your cue. There was no choice but to learn the role entirely by rote, rather like one huge senseless speech, and hope that at rehearsals the following morning, when other members of the company arrived with their pieces of the jigsaw, the play would begin to make sense. It was excruciating work, and sometimes late at night with half an act still to go, I would be seized with the hopeless rage of a prisoner set to work breaking stones.

Over the Easter holidays we touched rock bottom with a North Country farce, the name of which I've successfully repressed. It was a shameless steal of stock situations from a hundred similar and marginally better plays: two characters sit at a table with a bottle of whisky between them and take fifteen minutes to get drunk (growing hilarity in our audience); then they stand up and their trousers fall down (absolute pandemonium). The author's name, as printed on the programme, I've likewise forgotten, but not his identity; it was Roger, writing under a nom de plume. He couldn't resist letting the company in on his secret, but remained vague about the necessity for it. We all knew. Easter was the one week in the year of guaranteed box office. As manager and author, Roger would clean up on two fronts, something he preferred to keep from his sponsors, the Bridlington Council.

Despite his gall, it was impossible entirely to resist Roger. Artistic directors, in whatever context, need to be made of cork. He had gone into the theatre at fifteen and battled his way to his present autonomy as actor-manager, and he intended to enjoy it while he could. What he particularly relished was exercising authority over his ragtag company, and he would seize on a minor misdemeanour of one of his actors, such as being a minute or two late for rehearsal, as an opportunity to give a forty-minute lecture to the rest of us on the great traditions of the theatre and the need for discipline. Given that he was unpunctual himself, and most of the time bone lazy, it was as comical a performance and as syntactically bizarre as the constable, Dogberry, addressing the members of his watch in *Much Ado About Nothing*. Yet he was no bully, and had a cheerful shrewdness that was not exclusively at the service of his own survival. If only for his cheek, he deserved his hour in the Bridlington sun.

If Roger sometimes exasperated me, he enraged Shirley. She had been trained at the Old Vic School, where high seriousness had been the rule, and she approached even the most hopeless part with extraordinary willingness. I felt admonished by the lack of resentment with which she set about learning her lines in the evenings. She seemed happy to be working in a theatre, any theatre, and made no demands beyond expecting a similar dedication from those around her. It was sweet to see, but left her vulnerable in the jaded environment of most weekly reps. After one rehearsal, at which Roger had wasted an entire morning by not knowing his lines, she returned to the digs so angry that she put her fist through a pane in the front-parlour bay window. It was one of those displays of counterproductive violence of which only essentially gentle people are capable, and achieved very little beyond setting her back 17s 6d for new glazing.

We were always in each other's company now, at the theatre mornings and evenings, at the movies in the afternoons, or, if the day was sunny, exploring the town together. Both of us were readers, and on wet days we would take our books to some café and, over a 1s 3d pot of tea, sit there for a couple of hours. I was gravitating to those mighty achievers of the early years of the century, Joyce, Mann and, later on, Proust, who posited art as a kind of secular religion, and for whom being an artist entailed the renunciation of the world of their upbringing. Unconsciously, I suppose, I was looking for something to sustain me in my exile from Australia, and for a lofty artistic credo to which to cling through the rough seas of my apprenticeship. I was desperate to prove myself, and desperate, too, with the debit side of ambition – foreboding about whether I was actually talented. It was hard to see the value of what I was doing, and I discussed with Shirley what Jack had suggested: that I abandon the theatre and have a shot at writing.

By now, as has ever been the case with actors who find themselves stranded together in a strange town with a nightly call to their courage, we were slipping into each other's beds. In this blur of sharp need and comradeship, with its tacit understanding that there would be no subsequent demands, we gave little thought to consequences. However, consequences were built into the simple fact that we were spending so much time happily together. I was twenty-four and she was twenty-one, and we were having a love affair as real and easy as buttering toast together each morning before setting out to work. In 1953 this was something young people were expected to wait for.

We were always hungry. After the show at night, to supplement the rudimentary supper waiting for us at the digs, we would call in at a fish-and-chip shop where the catch was of an almost feathery freshness, and feed off great slabs of flaking, white cod. We had discovered an amazing truth: appetite exists to be satisfied. And we made love at any hour of the day and at any location that it pleased us to. We were not without 1950s guilt, of course (nor 1950s terror of pregnancy), but we managed to transmute it into a kind of good-natured defiance, much helped by the fact that theatre people, because of the curious hours they work, exist sealed off from the pressures of the communities in which they find themselves.

After lunch on the day of the Queen's Coronation, with the rain pelting down outside, we went up to Shirley's bedroom and listened to the ceremony on the wireless. A letter home gives this selective account of history in the making: 'The bad weather came to a climax last week with the Coronation. Radios and television sets were going all day, and in the streets Bridlington had risen to the occasion with hundreds of Union Jacks, yards of bunting and other decorations, all sopping wet. Each house has its own patriotic display, and pictures of the Queen are in all the parlour windows. By accident the other day I opened a book and found these lines by Yeats: "A king is but a foolish labourer / Who wastes his blood to be another's dream." '

It didn't seem to have occurred to me that Yeats' lines applied with equal force to the acting profession, though maybe not to its representatives labouring in Bridlington.

By now it was early summer, and the sea was just about warm enough for swimming, but this only made me restless for a bluer, rolling ocean. I knew that over the border from Biarritz there were some Spanish beaches where the waves were good and the living cheap. Shirley and I had both been able to save about two pounds a week, and we decided that when the season finished in July we would take ourselves to the Atlantic coast of Spain and stay there until the money ran out. Meanwhile, on our Sundays off, with the sun shining, Bridlington had its charms. There were picnics to take along the grassy cliffs, and paths to follow through the copses and fields that bordered the coast.

I had never really taken in before the intensity of an English summer, that avalanche of leaves which suddenly engulfs the grey lacework of winter branches. Shirley, who had spent a childhood in the Yorkshire Dales, pointed out trees and wild flowers that were as familiar to her as gum trees and wattle were to me. She was passionate about her landscape, and made a collection of odd things that I would have passed by as worthless: a ringed stone that the sea had polished, a bit of bark with strange colours in it or a curiously branching twig. These walks had a way of clarifying her personality, as she left behind at the theatre the occasionally strident young actress who put her fist through window panes. Like the wildlife that by chance we sometimes spotted, I found myself watching her as one watches a creature too absorbed in the rapture of its own life to know you're there. I began to understand what it must mean to have had an English childhood. The destiny I had always imagined for myself involved one of the worldly, determined beauties I had known in Sydney or at RADA. Now I was almost alarmed to see a future unravelling in quite another direction. I knew there were other young women in the world as good-looking and as lively company; what I found myself defenceless against was the tenderness, the unqualified directness of her gaze as she turned in our walks to share some small thing that had delighted her.

We travelled to the Spanish border as cheaply as we could, sitting up all night in the company of a large French family who had been wise enough to bring along their own provisions. We watched hungrily as bread, sausage and wine passed between them. In Spain we'd been warned always to travel first class unless we liked standing in the company of chickens and goats; in any case, first was as cheap as third in other countries. On the platform at San Sebastian we met a young Spaniard, Raphael, also travelling to our destination, Santander, who had been studying in London and who spoke a lively, comical English. That attribute of youth, the ability to conjure authentic friendship out of nowhere, would be working for us all that holiday. At Bilbao, the Spanish equivalent of those English cities I was getting to know that gave the impression of being at the fag-end of some nineteenth-century mercantile process, we had to cross the dusty, unpainted town centre to make our next connection, and on the last lap of our journey travelled by time-warp.

The rolling stock must have gone back fifty years, and our compartment had the musty, overstuffed luxury of a hansom cab. We were drawn by a miniature engine which wheezed its way up and around the coastal mountains, occasionally affording thrilling views of the moving ocean below. Two or three times the train came to a complete halt, whereupon the passengers, familiar with these interruptions, disembarked and wandered down the grassy slope, picking wild flowers and chatting incessantly in their rapid percussive language. A hoot from the engine-driver recalled them to their seats for the resumption of the journey. It took eleven hours to cover a distance of perhaps one hundred and fifty miles.

We arrived at our destination late at night. An incredibly battered taxi stood outside the station and we handed the driver a piece of paper on which was written the address of our pension. He scowled, shook his head, then drove for twenty minutes all over town on an ostensible quest for our lodgings. We stopped outside numerous bars for him to make enquiries. At one he parked on an incline so precipitous that the vehicle began shuddering downhill in little hiccoughs of movement. Alone in the back seat we stared, unbelieving, down a ski-jump of tarmac to a busy intersection. We'd already picked up speed by the time the driver strolled back across the road, and, wiping his mouth with the back of his hand, jumped into the moving car as laconically as a cowboy mounting a horse. Eventually we drew up at the right address and handed over a ransom of pesetas. Next morning when we drew the curtains there was the railway station just fifty yards beyond the window.

This was a prototypically bad beginning to a memorable holiday. Santander was a large port on an estuary, and the smoke of trade dozed in the sunshine over the wide water and the docks. Many of its old buildings had been destroyed in a devastating fire in 1941, and the architecture that had replaced them was rudimentary, but the town still had its beauties if you cared to look for them. There were a few tourists in the streets, mainly young people like ourselves, but no tourism; this had yet to be invented. Thus a prime reason for travelling to foreign parts – that you should be as different and interesting to the people you are among as they are to you – was still firmly in place. Another new friend, a French student, Alain, winkled us out of our pension and installed us with his Spanish family, who each year filled their apartment with a crowd of young people to supplement the husband's earnings as a civil servant. For the equivalent of £3 10s a week they provided bed and full board. I wondered aloud to Alain whether in a Catholic country our unmarried status might give offence, but he scoffed at such Anglo-Saxon anxieties, and we were duly shown into a room with a view over a monastery garden, a double bed and above it a huge crucifix.

We had come to Santander for the beaches, and these were many and various. The most popular, the Sardinero, was a trolley-bus ride from town, following the estuary to the point where the coast turned to face the open sea. Here were my Australian waves, or very good imitations, and, since no one knew how to body-surf, the holiday afforded me some delicious moments of showing-off. Had I brought my old surfboard with me, as Peter Viertel, the Californian writer, demonstrated a few years later at Biarritz, I would undoubtedly have drawn the town. The young Spanish bourgeoisie with whom we shared the sand, though no surfers, were constantly on the go in other ways. The beach was a battleground of ball games, which the pretty young women would never play without first donning a short towelling robe to prevent too generous a display of their charms. Two-piece bathing suits were forbidden, and if Shirley dropped so much as one of her shoulder-straps to ensure an even tan, a policeman would be standing over her within minutes pointing with his stick. Jaunty Spanish pop songs were broadcast over the beach from speakers on the changing pavilion, and the *Potatas Frittas* man, dressed like a shabby legionnaire, trudged back and forth across the sand for custom, his call rising like a flamenco lament above the Spanish chatter and the breaking waves. It was, literally, bliss.

At noon, like daylight Cinderellas, we had no choice but to climb back into the trolleybus. Lunch was waiting for us back with the family, and our holiday was so tightly budgeted that we couldn't even consider the alternative of a bag of those homemade, olive-oily potato crisps. On Thursdays, when the Señora prepared a stew the principal ingredients of which were large, pale beans, we faced a terrible dilemma. Though delicious, a few hours later, it gave both of us violent diarrhoea, invariably inconvenient given the state of Spanish public lavatories, but we were far too hungry to deprive ourselves of a meal. Dinner at night was an abundant ceremony, presided over by the cheerful Pepe, while his pale, no less good-natured wife went quietly about the business of keeping her huge household of multi-tongued young supplied with food and clean linen. They were a couple of quite remarkable sweetness and dignity.

A less benevolent presence was the sullen old man who was always there whenever you entered or left the apartment building. Though he was dressed in civilian clothes, we were told that he worked for the police, and his job was to report on all the comings and goings in our street. Others were similarly employed throughout Spain. Mostly one was unaware of living in a dictatorship, so it was salutary to be brought up short by something official and vindictive in a doorway. Franco was not popular in the North of Spain, and when you mentioned his name Pepe gave a snort of contempt.

By now we had looked up our friend from the train journey, Raphael, and were mixing in his circle, young men on holiday from the sort of professional studies I had abandoned in Australia. They introduced us to the secrets of the town, out-of-the-way bodegas where, for the equivalent of a few shillings, you could pass an entire evening drinking red wine and feasting off fresh, grilled sardines. Jose, a sleepy, good-looking law student, accompanied the others on his guitar as they sang traditional songs of their province. At one bar, a cellar dominated by huge casks of sherry, we sat a table away from three farmers down from the mountains to sell their produce. A choral competition began between our two groups. The farmers would sing one of their songs, complete with accomplished harmonies, and Raphael's friends would counter with one of their own. The music went back and forth, full-throated and almost barbaric in its precision and absence of urban sentiment. Later in the evening, after the farmers had left, Raphael asked me for a song, but all I could think of was a few bars of a mournful Gershwin standard. Despite, or perhaps because of, their polite, baffled attention, I stopped halfway through. How tawdry and rootless it sounded. It was impossible not to envy them, these young Spaniards whose sense of themselves was so secure, so self-evident, that probably none of them had ever posed the question 'What, exactly, am I?' A need for such clarifications had brought me halfway round the world, and would keep me on the move for the rest of my life.

In the early fifties, with Hemingway alive and revered, it was impossible to think of a trip to Spain without a visit to the bullfight. On three successive Sundays Shirley and I joined the stream of people strolling along the main boulevard towards the bullring on the edge of town. We sat in cheap seats facing the late-afternoon sun and directly above the pen from which the bulls, one after another, would be released into the arena like huge black cannonballs, only to be dragged away some twenty minutes later, inert and loose in death, by a couple of wretched, bony horses. What we saw was, by turns, thrilling and awful. A young South American matador with a reputation to make fought with such courage and fervour that it brought us all to our feet. The famous Ordonez, on the other hand, unwilling to take risks at an unimportant provincial booking, displayed such offhand cowardice that the booing crowd hurled their cushions into the ring.

I was never completely won over by this ritual of inevitable death, but its power as theatre was undeniable. It was theatre, moreover, in which the dead Richard III (and on occasions even his nemesis, the Duke of Richmond) were no longer available to take a bow. You approached the bullring in the dying heat of the day knowing that something was about to happen, wretched or exalting, perhaps both, but in either case indubitably real. I never felt this expectation with more certainty than I did at our first bullfight when suddenly, from a high gallery overlooking the amphitheatre, a tinpot brass band struck up a *paso doble* so familiar it encapsulated every cliché about the corrida from *Carmen* to *Blood and Sand*. To this music the toreadors made their entrance, a parade both slovenly and stately. There were more partici-pants than I expected. Leading were the three matadors, but behind them came a host of old hands, there to be of service to the stars. The tinselled costumes of these veterans had the tight, soiled look I remem-bered from the RADA wardrobe, and they wore them with the same indifference you see in stagehands who are asked to dress up for cos-tume plays when the scene changes are in view. A few of them were still smoking. None of this was of consequence. If anything it heightened one's realisation that something awesome was about to take place.

The memory of Bridlington was a sour joke on a seaside postcard. I decided when I got back to London I would forget acting and try to write.

# FIVE

# Stopping and Starting

Returning to London, we were beset by unexpected woes – a taxi strike in Paris where we had to change stations coinciding with an attack of diarrhoea. We were also completely out of money. An Indian student, with whom we had been discussing our predicament during the wait for a train, produced a ten-shilling note from his pocket. 'Go on, take it. You can pay me back by post,' he said, sitting beside his luggage, arm extended. Even allowing for the solidarity of youth it was an extraordinary display of trust and good nature, and I was careful to take his name and address.

However, worse than these practicalities were the unspoken anxieties that occupied us both throughout the journey. Shirley and I had been together for six months, sealed off from the rest of our lives, first in the confines of a theatre company, then on a holiday abroad. Now we were returning to a London winter, to friends who were more mine than hers and to work which, if we were lucky enough to find it, would separate us. Guiltily I half-welcomed the prospect. We had got beyond the point where one or other of us could carelessly end it; nor did I really want to. At the same time I was terrified of where it might lead – to pregnancy, marriage and a weight of responsibility which I felt would mean the death of all my ambitions. I had so much riding on achieving a degree of success in the arts, with the need to prove that I'd been right to defy my father and leave Australia, that all through my twenties I would live under the threat of a disappointment so wretched I doubted whether I would be able to survive it. To this extent I was wildly, neurotically ambitious. We no longer accept Cyril Connolly's proposition that a pram in the hall is the death of the artist, but at the time, with little money and less luck, I believed it with all my heart. Shirley, seeing life in simpler and better terms, couldn't help but read this on my face. Nor could she conceal this recognition on her own. As the train approached London she leant her head against the back of the seat, eyes closed, her face a mask of reproach and pain. For a moment, I hated her.

Jack and Mimi Salamanca, who now lived in a capacious maisonette off Kensington Church Street and whose generosity seemed without limit, offered to put us up until we had each found somewhere to live. Shirley was bewildered by the special language that had evolved between Jack and me over the three years we'd known each other, and interpreted his teasing as condescension. Matters came to a head at a party the Salamancas gave to which a number of our RADA contemporaries had been invited. I longed to immerse myself in past intimacies, and resented being watched by someone outside them. Recklessly I drank too much and steeled myself to be hurtful. Coming down the stairs from the bathroom as I went up, I met Joan Collins and made a clumsy pass at her. Vastly unimpressed, she continued to the sitting room and told everyone. Later that night I was in a bedroom trying to undress Diane Cilento when Shirley burst into the room, horribly upset. The awfulness of my behaviour now caught up with me, and I moaned and sobbed as Diane, eyes popping, tiptoed discreetly from the room.

It was time to stop abusing the Salamancas' hospitality, and in the morning, sober with emotional exhaustion but wryly together again, Shirley and I set out to find accommodation. Round the corner in Hornton Street there was a big building with an untidy arrangement of about a dozen bell-presses beside the front door: bedsitter land. In those days young people were not supposed to live together unwedded, whatever else they might have been doing, so we were looking for two rooms in the same building. However, the landlord, an elderly American called Mr Rapport, had only one room free, a big attic up four flights of stairs. With much raffish smiling he hesitated over the impropriety of such a let. We hesitated too, though for different reasons. But the room was too special to forego. Perched as high as an eagle's eyrie with a bohemian view over the roofs of London it would be a perfect place to begin my novel. With our few possessions – mainly clothes, my typewriter, Shirley's portable wireless – we nested in secret.

The Salamancas knew where we were, and so did an Australian friend, Peter Heath, who had just arrived in England and who had hunted me down. We cooked a dinner for him on the single ring which branched off our gas fire, and he told us how he'd abandoned Australia to embark on a quest which may have been based on my own. At school I'd known him mainly as an exceptional athlete, and his discontents came as a surprise. So did my new and uneasy role as exemplar.

Shirley was soon off on tour in a play called *Uncertain Joy*, a title drawn from a Scandinavian saying, 'Children are certain sorrow, uncertain joy,' a sentiment with which I was sure her family in York would concur had they known our circumstances. During the next eighteen months she was to have far less trouble finding work than I was, and when unemployed breezed into part-time jobs with little or no anguish – as a dentist's assistant, as a barmaid, as a door-to-door saleswoman. Her good looks helped, but so did the fact that she was without the frail self-importance of the young male, reeling from rebuff to rebuff.

But for the time being, at least, I was a writer. With careful budgeting I thought I could just about hang on until Christmas, when I'd be far enough advanced to judge whether it was worth continuing. I don't remember much about my novel except that it was heavily under the influence of Scott Fitzgerald with Sydney's Palm Beach standing in for Cap d'Antibes. I was embarrassed that it was so derivative, but didn't know how else to proceed. When I sat in front of the typewriter wondering quite what to say next, I would stare down at the city below me and try to find ways of describing it: the distant red buses 'like corpuscles moving through the grey veins of London'. Such observations I would transcribe into a small notebook, struggling to do the first and hardest thing an artist must attempt, confidently to *name* himself. I could more or less call myself an actor and believe it, but as a writer I felt weighted down with imposture. In the middle of a paragraph I would run to the bookshelf and open a novel randomly if only to see how a real author did it.

My letters to my mother are hardly models of self-confidence: 'Some days it doesn't seem too bad, but other days it seems so awful I feel sickened . . . Writing is an irksome business with endless opportunities for self-reproach, deflated vanity, weariness and guilt. This rather takes the fun out of it.' In that same letter I confess that I'm running out of money and doubt whether I can get by till Christmas. As she was to do all through the fifties, my mother came to my aid with a small sum, a bank draft for perhaps £20 or £25, just enough when combined with the couple of notes I was collecting from the Labour Exchange to provide me with the £6 a week I needed to live.

As October turned into November I stared at the grey sky over London, which each morning seemed to draw ever lower and closer, and struggled to move my characters through a remembered Australian summer. By the end of the month, I had fifty pages written, and was desperate for encouragement; or perhaps discouragement. The former I could always get from Jack, but instead I sought out an Australian journalist I'd known in Sydney. The things he said were unanswerable. In the entire country only twenty people made a living writing novels. There was money in playwriting, but that required experience which I was at present foregoing. He advised me to return to what I had first set out to do and continue with my acting career. As for my few pages, they were competent, nothing more. He pointed out a few banalities of expression, and I felt suicidal with shame. But I knew he was right. I did not yet have anything fresh to say, and maybe never would. His assessment was just, but even as I crumbled under it, I thought I caught a glimpse of his satisfaction at thus dispatching my hopes. There was something unpleasantly deft about it, like wringing a chicken's neck, and what little spirit I had left rose against it. He could condemn the work if he liked, but not the impulse to do it. This tiny rebellion saved me. My pilot light, though flickering precariously, was still on, and may-be one day there would be fuel for a book. In the meantime, however, I was as depressed as I would ever be. I returned to the garret through winter drizzle and tore up my pages one by one, like Constantin in *The Seagull*.

My days were now filled with the abject routines of an actor look-ing for work: writing letters which largely went unanswered, doing the rounds of the agents, and the small-time casting directors, shiver-ing by the coin box two floors down with a list of calls and a pocket full of coppers. I quickly became prey to a string of minor illnesses, sinus trouble, a kidney infection, a speck of grit in my eye which I had to go to the hospital to have removed by a kindly doctor, who turned out to be Jill Bennett's father and was therefore sympathetic to the folly of an actor's life. On a visit to my godmother in Sussex, I went down with a high fever and lay in bed, captive to her cheerful accounts of hardship on the farm. Since she'd paid for my rail fare it was difficult to interpret as other than a reprimand her declaration that 'Guy has had to give up hair oil because of the expense.' She had crisp opinions about other things that should be given up, notably my idle and un-successful career as an actor.

Christmas was coming and Shirley was off to York to spend it with her family. Peter Heath and I had an offer from a good friend over from Australia, Rozalind Doyle, whose mother had remarried an Englishman and now lived in some splendour in Hampshire. As if fulfilling the contract for an engagement in weekly rep, I packed my dinner jacket and one lounge suit and set off. The contrast between living in sin in a garret and life in the huge red-brick country house, a subdued exercise in thirties Tudor, could not have been more marked. At the front door a genial North Country butler, with none of the hauteur you expect from the movies, shook me firmly by the hand. Any intimidation I might have felt was dispelled by my hostess, intent on protecting her Australian young. Her husband, like Guy in Sussex another of those Old Etonian elders who loomed over the intermittent episodes of respectability in my life at this time, ushered us into an interior where the sense of discreet moneyed welcome was as all-enveloping and as much of a novelty as the central heating.

The weekend was to be a round of convivial if rather stuffy rituals. The first night there was a Christmas party for the staff, of which there was a roomful, servants, gardeners and so forth, where I learnt later I was awarded points for having real conversations. As is any guest, I knew I was under observation, and was alert to pointers as to the behaviour expected of me. On Christmas Day we went to church, where a red-faced Lord Montagu, recently involved in a homosexual scandal, took his place at the front of the congregation, and we discreetly tilted our heads to left and right for a better look. That night there was a dinner party for about twenty, where, I remembered, you were meant to converse first to one side then to the other, but not across the table, and where, after dinner, the women retired and the men settled to their port, cigars and the somewhat deliberate use of coarse language. 'He's an absolute *shit*,' said my host of some Labour politician in a drawl so effete it was as surprising as finding the expletive embroidered on a cushion. There were long walks in the afternoon past dripping fences, beyond which stationary cows, their muzzles plumed in mist, returned our stares. There were afternoon teas from laden trolleys, consumed in the unstable depths of vast sofas. At a noon cocktail party an elderly man of immense distinction took me for a brisk walk to the end of the garden and back, and asked me good-humoured but pointed questions about what I wanted to do with my life. It was a little as if I was being prepared for some unspecified examination which, if I so wished, it was hinted I could pass. I felt almost neutered by the consideration being extended to me on every side, because it was not feigned but sincere. They were interested in this young man from the colonies who showed promise in a role which with practice he could master. Something surely could be found for me, in the City perhaps or in business. I knew I was an impostor, but at which address, the garret or this house in the country? The answer came one afternoon in a discussion with my host. His money came from that nineteenth-century mix of inherited land, newly augmented by the wealth of industry, and his family had owned coal mines. These had now been nationalised.

'What was the point?' he asked gently. 'We knew how to look after our own people.' However, I'd been there, or near enough, and I knew this wasn't the case. Even as I nodded, my mind softly clicked shut against him.

With the New Year my career prospects suddenly improved. For a start, my writing turned out to be not altogether wasted. The memory of the beach that had been with me at the typewriter I turned into a radio talk about the Australian surf. Our landlord put me in touch with his nephew at the BBC, and the talk went out one morning at nine o'clock and was subsequently published in *The Listener*. Thirty years later I would return to this material in a film, *A Personal History of the Australian Surf*. On the acting front I had been interviewed by the Artistic Director of the Sheffield Playhouse, in London to cast for the forthcoming season, and he thought there might be something for me. What most excited me, however, was an invitation, out of the blue, to spend the weekend with a suave middle-aged couple with high-powered theatrical connections who were neighbours of Helen's in Sussex. He, predictably, was an Old Etonian businessman, but she had once been a successful West End actress and they were intimates of the Oliviers. What else could this be but an offer of a leg-up?

Their weekend farm represented privileged English life at its most beguiling. You entered an old, two-storey stone house to confront an interior of ravishing *things*, old and new artfully commingled. Modern art, masses of it, adorned the walls. I noticed at once one of Bacon's Screaming Popes resonating in a side room. The most seductive part of the house, however, was a big barn, extended to adjoin the main building and converted into an informal kitchen/living area. Country furniture in elm and oak glowed here and there. Its spaciousness anticipated the open-plan living that in the years ahead would become the ideal for anyone with some money to spend as servants melted away. On a big triangle of wall space below the exposed roof timbers the wife had copied to scale a Picasso mural, gigantic and linear, like a crayon drawing, and entitled *Joie de Vivre*. The original was in the South of France, but I recognised it at once because in Sydney I'd seen it reproduced in *Vogue* magazine.

My hostess seemed to be good at everything. She dressed and cooked as exquisitely as she organised her house, and seemed a model of intelligent self-possession. In addition, she had a beautiful daughter, pale and silent, on her way to becoming a much-photographed fashion icon with whom I took walks through the watery winter garden when the perfection of indoors became a shade too oppressive for both of us. In the sixties this rather shy girl would revenge herself on good taste by marrying a working-class pop star. The weekend passed slowly from one Elizabeth David meal to another as I waited for the subject of my career to be broached.

At last, on the Sunday night, as we consumed what my hostess described as a 'scratch meal', something which seemed to me just short of a banquet, she asked me to tell her about my life in the theatre. She listened with sharp but impassive attention as I filled her in with my history so far, my disappointments and my hopes. Eventually I ran out of things to say. There was a beat. With a studied casualness she asked 'Have you ever thought of giving it up?' And, immediately on cue, her husband chimed in, 'I could always give you a job if you wanted one.' His highly successful business was in motor cars, specifically used ones. He was offering me work as a secondhand-car salesman.

I didn't, couldn't reply. The eyes of the family began to reflect my distress. I knew I had changed colour, but whether to red or to a stricken pallor I had no way of knowing. In the silence the penny dropped. I had been set up! This weekend was the contrivance of my godmother. It had the busy fingerprints of her benevolent interference all over it. For the rest of the meal I was so numb with misery it became impossible to speak. At one stage I even wondered if I might cry. In panic, I stared hard at the huge Picasso mural, grinning and gambolling over the Aga cooker.

In bed with the lights out, another kind of awfulness awaited me. The central heating was like a fire under the floorboards, and I thrashed about all night, reviewing and re-reviewing my plight. I knew why I was so reluctant to release my grip on my small stake in upper-middle-class England. I had been taught in Australia that it was my just inheritance and, adrift and broke in what was essentially a foreign country, was it any wonder that I wanted to hold on to it? To anyone from outside coming to England in the fifties, it was hardly possible not to be in thrall to the Posh, so ubiquitous was its value system, so impoverished other social alternatives. Even the Socialists were led by a gang of public schoolboys. In this strange land my only points of definition were my work and my connections. Yet the bitter truth was that the two were incompatible. Just as I had left Australia, I had to let this go too. These well-meaning people, in whose house I lay, were not my tribe, because collecting art was not the same thing as struggling to make it.

In the morning, as cattle lowed in the yard below my tiny seventeenth-century windows with floral curtains as skimpy as knickers, I heard the voice of my host giving rather cold orders to the farmhands who would be tending his property while he did a week's business in London. I could only feel anger with myself that I'd ever imagined that any of this concerned me.

This was a turning point in my life, though not such a clear-cut one as it may seem on the page. The years ahead were not without their odd weekends in the country when the chance came up. And when visiting Australian friends took me to dinner at a club in St James's, with which their Sydney club had a reciprocal arrangement, I listened almost with nostalgia to their sentimental avowals of a Britishness that I knew didn't exist in the way they described, and perhaps never had. Such elegant fictions, though they dressed up real power, were no longer of much use to me, because a life in the arts allowed for luck but not for short cuts obtained through influence.

Let us fast-forward through further experiences of an actual Britain. The Sheffield Playhouse was a fortnightly rep with an incredible two weeks to rehearse and two weeks to play, and was therefore a big step up from the grind of weekly, although I had been offered only the opening production. It was a large-cast historical play called *The Young Elizabeth*, and I would have to make my mark in a small and unpromising part in order to stay on. The Artistic Director, Geoffrey Ost, was a decent, cautious man with a moustache and a pipe, who came to work neatly dressed in a tweed jacket and tie like a bank manager at the weekend, and I soon realised I had as little chance of impressing him with my miserable role as asking for an unsecured loan. I searched in vain through the company for a kindred spirit, but they were a likewise staid lot, lost in the pages of their *Daily Mail* or bent over *The Times* crossword, and stirred to feeling only by prospects of advancement in the company. The first week I had a persistent spot on my nose, and felt like a new boy at an uncongenial school.

However, when the theatre disappointed me, I now knew where to go: inside the covers of a book. I had long devoured the literary columns of the posh Sunday newspapers, Cyril Connolly in the *Sunday Times* and Philip Toynbee in *The Observer*, and had noticed that one name came up week after week – Marcel Proust. From the public library in Kensington High Street I had brought with me the first volume of *Remembrance of Things Past*, and like a channel swimmer was now poised to dive into that ocean of words. The Public Library, the Health Service, the Labour Exchange, these were the things that sustained me during the fifties, but not so vitally as the idea to which they contributed: that your worth was not necessarily related to your bank balance. Being broke in England at that time was uncomfortable, time-consuming and involved queuing, but it wasn't the humiliation it would become some thirty years later. If you could maintain a belief in yourself there were values other than money to keep you afloat. This was perhaps the crucial difference between the country I was living in and the one I had left, and I was just beginning to realise it made up for a great deal.

Even so, in my letters home I am not charitable to Sheffield, which I describe as 'abysmal and horrible', though I provide a lively picture of life in theatrical digs. 'My landlady is a big-bosomed number called Mrs Rhodes. She's very cheery, and has little piggy, roguish eyes. I've given her some tinned meat from a food parcel and she has me neatly categorised as "a nice young gentlemen". Like all landladies, she insists on fifteen minutes a day of one-way conversation, but since she tells her stories so well, I don't mind in the least listening to them.' Among her other boarders was 'a man and wife team of adagio dancers. She's not so bad, a tiny, little blond thing with an urchin face and big, sad, blue eyes, but her lord and master is beyond words, forty-five-ish, small and sallow, with a thick mat of wiry black hair. He struts and sniffs, and has the worst kind of performer's vanity, so transparent you feel almost sorry for him. Yesterday afternoon the three of us found ourselves together in the sitting room. I was trying to read. He launched into a loud conversation with his wife about his plans to improve the act. She tried to shut him up with a few lugubrious remarks, but on and on he went about the laugh lines in the second spot, and should he wear his comic trousers, and had she pressed the jacket of his evening clothes? It was all a performance for my benefit. Eventually he couldn't resist speaking to me directly. They do a turn called "Beauty and the Beast". He's dressed up in a monkey outfit, she in a bikini, and he throws her about. He showed me a tattered snap of them in action.'

In my next letter the tale of the adagio dancers continues: 'Last Saturday after breakfast they sneaked out without paying the landlady. The Beast had the nerve to implicate two of us in the crime. Another actor staying here has a car, and he was asked if he would mind taking their bags to the station. I helped by lugging these two heavy, dirty suitcases through the rain to the car. With their luggage out of the house it was an easy matter to slip away when Mrs Rhodes was in the kitchen. It would take pages to tell you what a weasel the adagio man was. In the middle of the week he insisted that we go up to their bedroom, so that we could watch them rehearse their act in the space between the double bed and the wardrobe. It was not only crude but embarrassingly inept. Of course they made no money in Sheffield. They'd had a booking but after the first performance the club that employed them refused to pay up, presumably because they were so dreadful. After they'd gone, Mrs Rhodes found a crumpled letter in the wastepaper basket addressed to Harry from Mollie; she must have been his real wife. Mrs Rhodes brought it downstairs and we all read it. It said that the kids still had plenty to eat, but could he forward the rent sometime. Mrs Rhodes is a kind soul, and because of the letter probably won't report Harry to the police. But it has cost her six guineas.'

In the same letter I record more scandal at the digs – the tale of Mad Tom. 'He appeared on Mrs Rhodes' doorstep a few weeks ago with a dreadful story about an unfaithful wife, malicious parents and attempted suicide. He had scars on his wrists to prove it. Mrs Rhodes felt sorry for him, and gave him a single room at the top of the house, only to find she had a lunatic on her hands. Tom has a ferocious persecution complex, and he is convinced that everyone calls him "a yellow-livered coward" behind his back. He's about twenty-two with sunken cheeks in a gaunt long face. A few days ago he went into Mrs

Rhodes' kitchen and said, "You know that skinny tall fella, I'll fight him any time!" (He meant me.) Mrs Rhodes asked for an explanation and he said, "I heard him last night before he went to bed calling me a yellow-livered coward." As it happens I'd gone to bed early and was sound asleep at the time of the alleged insult. Mrs Rhodes was scandalised and asked Tom to leave. He disappeared the next day, and the next we heard of him was a headline in the newspaper that said he had been charged with attempted murder. Apparently he'd gone back to his wife, found her in bed with someone else and then gone berserk. At the moment he's being observed in a clinic.'

The digs had one extraordinary amenity: a large, brand new television set. It sat on its own spindly legs in a commanding position in the living room. On my way to work in the morning I glanced through the open door at its blank screen, a milky eye on the point of hypnotising the nation. One night on the evening news we sat watching Armageddon in black and white: a bubble the size of a mountain pulsing through cloud cover, then writhing smoke obliterating miles of sky. This was a test of a hydrogen bomb in the Pacific, and I seem to remember it as the first British test, but it may have been American. It doesn't matter. All distinctions melted away in the face of those images.

Nor was there much to be encouraged about at the Playhouse. All Geoffrey Ost could offer me was the small part of the French valet in *Nightmare Abbey* later in the season. This meant a few weeks waiting around unpaid. However, I decided to make the best of my time by paying visits to the artistic directors of a number of other northern reps – Chesterfield, Derby, Manchester and Liverpool. Robert Morley had advised me, 'Don't write letters asking for work. Write to say you're coming to see them, turn up on their doorstep and pester them until they do.' This strategy would later lead to two jobs. Meanwhile there was *Nightmare Abbey*. Mrs Rhodes was fully booked when I started rehearsals, but I found new digs across the valley.

The front parlour of this latest accommodation had an imposing view over the smoke of the factories to the city centre rising up on the hill beyond, but since no one ever inhabited this room it went unnoticed. The upright piano, the three-piece suite in uncut moquette, the gleaming sideboard were kept in immaculate condition but never used. A waxy, sealed-up smell hung in the air. The family spent all their time in poky rooms at the back of the house. My new landlady had none of Mrs Rhodes' curiosity or determination to be involved in life. Her lined face was a stoic mask of endurance that reminded me of old photographs of Red Indians. She served up abominable meals in silence. I was not reassured by a sign on a shop further up the road which read 'Horsemeat. Fit for human consumption.' Often when she left the room I would grab a sheet of newspaper, wrap up her dark cuts and dispose of them in the fire. Pale, gelatinous gravy hissed and spluttered among the burning coals, but anything was better than incurring her unspoken rebuke.

Her husband sat all day in the corner of their tiny back parlour, smoking his pipe and doing nothing much beyond attending to the ticking away of his old age. If I tried to read in his company he became affronted, and would maintain a stream of stubborn interruptions until I capitulated and put the book to one side. I learnt that he'd started on the railways at the age of twelve, working from six in the morning until six at night, and stayed down there at the station for half a century. Repeating the facts of his life to whatever stranger was staying in the house was presumably his way of trying to make sense of it, and his one release from the depression of retirement. The narrowness of the life that had been imposed on him might have touched me more had it not been for the loyalty he seemed to have for it. Too often life in these northern towns was something I recoiled from, as if it might reach out and take me down with it.

With the summer, my visits to other provincial theatres began to pay off. I was invited by Derby Playhouse for a 'special week' to play the best part, that of an alcoholic American film star, in an otherwise deeply reactionary country-house comedy by Noël Coward, *Relative Values*. It was something I knew I could do well, and set about it with zest. The Artistic Director was a sweet-natured individual with the demeanour of a cheerful clergyman, whose name, Leslie Twelvetrees, precisely conjures up the man. He presided over a talented and restless company who made unmerciful fun of him when he was out of earshot. I found myself sharing a dressing room with another young actor who had struggled, if with rather more determination, to do some writing. We got on at once and he brought in his most recent and as yet unperformed play for me to read. It was extraordinarily ambitious, written in verse and set in the future, as if Christopher Fry and George Orwell had worked in unlikely collaboration. I was struck by the care with which it had been typed, with bold use made of the red as well as the black ribbon. Having the luck to meet a contemporary like this, who seemed of the same mind and who had the same aspirations, could transform one's time in a rep company. To begin with, it meant laughter in the dressing room and in the wings, the distinguishing factor between a harmonious company and a miserable one. The theatre became a place where you were happy to spend twelve hours a day.

The actor with whom I had felt an immediate affinity was John Osborne, whose wife, Pamela Lane, was also a member of the company, as were a Welsh actor, John Reese, and a pretty young woman I'd been at RADA with, Yvonne Savage. The raw experience that would go into the making of *Look Back in Anger* was being played out that summer in Derby, though in ways which differ somewhat from the play. At the Royal Court Jimmy Porter and Alison lived in an attic with a water tank in the middle of the room. The Osbornes, however, put their two salaries to resourceful use and lived with a certain dash in a couple of elegant rooms in a Georgian terrace. Before I left Derby John gave me the telephone number of his London base, a houseboat on the Thames, but for whatever reason, carelessness or the social promiscuity that was the inevitable consequence of shifting about the country from one company to another, I never got in touch.

A few years later I was on my way through Sloane Square to see the hottest new play in London when I noticed ahead of me a young actor whose name I couldn't remember. We greeted each other warmly. 'You coming to see the play?' I asked him, and received the cryptic reply 'I might stand at the back for a bit.' It was only when I sat down and looked at the programme that I realised I had just been speaking to the author.

Today *Look Back in Anger* reads as many another play in the cumbersome three-act convention. Then it had the penetrative force of a shell exploding against the façade of British life, and, rather like the bomb sites still in evidence around London, it allowed you almost improper glimpses of things once hidden – a naked light bulb hanging in a ruined kitchen, fading wallpaper suspended over a void, and fragments of a staircase leading nowhere. 'Get rid of this rubbish and make a fresh start' was the message we took from it, and if you were young and hungry it was a wildly exciting one. The change it advocated was never really political, though often assumed to be by the play's detractors. What it demanded was no less than a change of the English heart. After the show I met John and conveyed my great excitement to him. We arranged to meet a few days later for a drink at the pub adjoining the theatre.

I duly turned up, and had waited twenty-five minutes past the time of our appointment before John rushed in full of apologies. *The Observer* had been interviewing him for a profile next door, and had demanded extra time for a photograph. He decently made light of the exhilaration he must have been feeling, and we managed a conversation not too dissimilar to the ones we'd had in the Derby dressing room. We were both living in the King's Road area and in the next couple of months often ran into each other in the street. I noticed a subtle change in his physical appearance. His complexion had begun to reflect his success, pink and rather glossy. We arranged to meet once more, at the newly opened Kenya Coffee House on the King's Road. John now smoked slim cigars, and sat in profile to me talking languidly of the people he was meeting as an equal, the writers and actors that had only been names to us at Derby and still were to me. I struggled to interest him and became uninteresting in the process. If he was changing, a fatal self-consciousness now changed me more. I hadn't taken the trouble to keep in touch with him before he'd been discovered. Why was I making the effort now? And why should he respond? Our friendship was too compromised to pursue without demeaning myself and perhaps inviting his condescension.

In the next few years I would have to be content with reading about him in the papers – his huge successes, his marriages and affairs, his predilection for champagne first thing in the morning. Later on I would be reading other things, of his feuds, his professional isolation, the onset of illness and eventually of his death. In one's twenties it is difficult to grasp the pointlessness of envy. Eventually, when my own luck turned, John and I started to nod to each other again, and his friendship was always on offer. He wrote me a lovely letter when my novel *Next Season* was published, and turned up regularly at my productions. In the eighties when he and his wife, Helen, sent out jokey invitations to their regular Christmas and summer parties, I was usually a recipient, but for a variety of reasons was never able to attend. There was nothing intentional about this, though I'm not sure it was entirely fortuitous. Perhaps I was protecting the memory of one of those youthful encounters, however brief, made before success had validated either party, and contrasted to which the social life of middle-aged English

celebrities, with their readily expressed exchanges of flattery and camou-
flaged resentments, their anxiety that the people amongst whom they
find themselves may actually be, in Antonia Pinter's phrase 'the second
eleven', has a decidedly oxidised taste.

A resourceful contemporary of mine, Oscar Quitak, slight, clear-
thinking and with the friendliness of a puppy, had helped found the
Buckstone Club with basement premises well situated opposite the
stage door of the Haymarket Theatre. This was becoming the meeting
place of savvy young theatre people, and I had coughed up a subscrip-
tion. Oscar was also behind a theatre company, which, with a cavalier
disregard for the second half of his life, he had called 'The Under
Thirties'. We would all grow old, true, but not within the foreseeable
future. He offered me a summer season by the sea at Hythe in Kent.
This proved to be my pleasantest engagement to date, no less hard-
working than previous jobs but much ameliorated by pretty surroundings, sunshine, and some good plays to perform in the company
of spirited colleagues.

The work had the goodwill and effervescence of undergraduate
theatre. The director, Tony Knowles, our own age and one of us,
worked as hard as his actors, and gave up his Sunday to help demolish
one set and build another. The workload on all of us, though un-
resented, was huge, and towards the end of the season fatigue began
to express itself on stage in hysterical lapses of professionalism. It was
particularly unfortunate that our final play was also our silliest,
because the least mistake during a performance, a verbal slip perhaps,
or a fumble with a prop, would bring on a fit of giggling enough to
stop the show in its tracks. We would stand staring at each other, our
upper torsos shuddering like a rally of veteran cars waiting upon the
starter's pistol, quite unable to speak or move. The play required a set
with a bay window which could be curtained off from the audience.
On one occasion my giggling became so uncontrollable and painful
that I fled into this recess and drew the curtain on myself until I had
mustered sufficient self-possession to reappear and resume speaking.
At the interval we would go down to our dressing rooms genuinely
ashamed, and sometimes with the insides of our mouths bleeding
from the bites we had given ourselves to re-establish a degree of self-
control. From the audience's point of view giggling on stage can never
be defended, but during my rep days the combination of youth, bad
plays and exhaustion could sometimes leave me helpless against it,

particularly if I found myself on stage with someone whose eyes betrayed that same vertigo.

Shirley was on tour in an army farce, *Reluctant Heroes*, earning better money and enjoying more spare time than I was. She caught trains across England to visit me at weekends, and we found a small hotel along the coast at Sandgate where we could spend the odd precious Sunday night. We had known each other eighteen months, were both contentedly in work and summer was at its height. It was a kind of high point for us, and, though I was shaken, I was not really surprised when she told me she had become pregnant: 1950s precautions, a foaming tablet called Gynomin, had been outwitted. Certainly I loved her, but didn't quite know what the word 'love' was meant to describe. Was it the image of crass perfection projected by the popular culture of the time? Was it invalidated by contradictions? We discussed what we should do, but I knew my own mind was made up. How could I 'settle down' when I had built my life around the priority of an as yet unrealised career? I felt I lacked any paternal instinct, not knowing that the presence of a child will soon create one. I still saw the pram in the hall as the enemy of the artist, not accepting that this was merely an idea I had picked up from a book, which could as easily be overturned by another and perhaps better idea. Shirley yielded to my callow inflexibility. And given our situation and financial prospects it may well have been the right decision. However, abortion, regardless of whether in principle it is right or wrong, must always be a step hedged about with doubt. You are making a decision without sufficient information; the essential data lie hidden in the future.

My Australian heiress friend, Rada, had once given me a name for such a contingency: Dr Rosenfeld. In a shadowy and illegal world he was expensive but reliable. Shirley and I visited him at an office in Park Lane. He was a small, well-tailored man with a mournful face, who spoke in a strange, heavily accented wail. 'Do you really want to have this done?' he asked, with what seemed genuine reluctance, looking from one of us to the other. I wondered if we looked like the brother and sister we had sometimes been mistaken for. Eventually it was arranged. The cost would be £60, seven weeks' salary at the Chesterfield Civic Theatre, my next job. Shirley would still be on tour and would have to come down to London for the day. She had explained her plight to a sympathetic company manager, who had her understudy standing by. There were no such things at Chesterfield, so

I would be stuck there, rehearsing by day and playing by night. But first, there was the problem of the money.

I could think of only one person to turn to: Robert Morley. I visited him backstage one evening before the performance of his current West End success. I had barely begun to explain when I saw him reaching for his cheque book. 'How much?' he asked. There was not a moment of hesitation. I murmured that I'd do my best to pay him back. 'Whenever,' he said. It was a most stylish act of generosity, particularly since it ran counter to his own robust belief in marriage and children. However, I appeared to need help, and he offered it on my terms, not his. I visited him again about six months later, when I had scraped together £15, a first repayment on the debt. Robert seemed so astonished and amused to see even a small part of his money again that I'm ashamed to say I let subsequent instalments lapse.

The abilities of the Artistic Director of the Civic Theatre were political not artistic, so it follows that he was constantly engaged in convincing anyone he met of the opposite. He had already persuaded the Board and a surprising number of the company of his creative stature, and the atmosphere at the theatre was once again like school, being expected to subscribe to cant and being penalised if you didn't. He was also bone lazy, and had engaged an assistant director to whom he palmed off the productions of the farces and light comedies on which the theatre depended for income, leaving to him the prestige plays and the annual Shakespeare. He had no talent and was shameless about stealing from other people. At rehearsals I became used to offering up an acting idea, only to have it suggested to me a minute later as an inspiration of his own. He also knew the value of information and played games within the company, dangling good parts in front of us before whisking them away and bestowing them on favourites. He was not, however, a bully, but rather had a canine hunger for approval, and eventually found a convivial niche as a producer at the BBC.

I was now almost through Proust, and whenever possible slipped next door to the reading room of the public library where I could read the final volume undisturbed. The novel astonished me, and had from the first page. First of all there was the tone of voice. I'd been expecting something lofty and mandarin, which would leave me feeling vaguely excluded. Instead I found myself being addressed as if by a newly acquired friend, met by chance on a train journey, or, like John

Osborne, turning up in a theatre dressing room. It was true that this new friend spoke in sentences half a page long, and occasionally laboured a point, but such was his passion to communicate, and to do so with precision and candour, that the prolixity was an aspect of something you couldn't help but revere: the struggle to be truthful.

And how thrilling the writing could sometimes be, unexpectedly concise and to the point as an entire volume seemed to come into focus on a single page. The scope of the work was so huge that a character would disappear from the narrative only to emerge volumes later, like a forgotten acquaintance re-entering your life. Similarly the spine of an idea arching suddenly out of the prose would dive out of sight, then, hundreds of pages later, break the surface again with a splash. In one volume I would read: 'The heart changes and this is our worse misfortune'; weeks later in another: 'It is always thus, impelled by a state of mind that is not destined to last, that we make our irrevocable decisions.'

*This is my experience*, the friend seemed to say. *Use it to help understand your own.* Time and again I would find myself lifting my head from the page as some moment in my own life, previously of little consequence, was recalled for me, now imbued with value. Far from intimidating me with a description of a world I was outside, the book gave me back the simplest and most vivid moments of my own life. Out of such simple building blocks I saw art being made, which, in turn, helped me sort out my own experience. I was having explained to me what I had always sensed but never defined: why being moved by a book or a piece of music was so important to me. It was the mapping of an interior terrain that might otherwise remain unknown. As for the world of fashionable Paris, so lovingly and comprehensively evoked in order the better to be dispatched, it may seem hilarious to compare the Faubourg St Germain with social life in Sydney's eastern suburbs, but all elites have something in common, and Proust's long struggle to detach himself from his own world of seductive appearances helped me, at just the moment that I needed help, to let go of my past. The reality of possessions and connections, regarded with such complacency by those absorbed in them, was ultimately dependent on a greater reality, the comprehending mind. And its priorities were those curious, unwilled moments of heightened perception, triggered often by something modest and unpredictable – a sound, a scent or, in Proust's case, the taste of a humble cake. When that response echoes back through memory to strike a chord in our past we are provided, as in navigation, with the two readings that will begin to tell us who we really are.

Whether, re-reading Proust today, I would respond to the sublime scheme that I then thought I had unearthed, I don't know. The idea of literature as an aspect of faith has been under assault in the intervening years, and in any case grows harder to accept as you become familiar with the endless varieties of error contained within the covers of books. But one thing I'm in no doubt about: the luck of discovering Proust at this particular time in my life. I had found my way to it, over what seemed an immense distance, driven, as in one of the book's mysterious sexual couplings, by particular need. The experience was to make me forever wary of critical orthodoxy, of such things as categories, lists and 'great traditions'. The critic, like the marriage broker, can certainly get you together with a range of suitable matches, but the one thing that matters, a passionate response, is not within his gift. I had read the book, of course, in translation, having abandoned French at the King's School, where it had been taught as not much more than an exercise in enduring tedium. Proustians may be amused to know that in the six months I took to read it, I pronounced in my head the illustrious name of the Guermantes family with three syllables as if it was a word in Spanish.

Shirley's tour was coming to an end. On her weekend visits to Chesterfield she had become acquainted with the company, and to our surprise the Artistic Director now offered her a place in the company, playing Desdemona in the annual Shakespeare and Beatrice in an excellent North Country drama, *Hindle Wakes*, with other parts to follow. We found a couple of rooms in a big, splendid, run-down house on the edge of town, run by a friendly woman who spent all her time tending the garden and let the house look after itself. On half-landings and up unexpected flights of stairs there were rooms with other tenants, but you rarely caught sight of them. Our bedroom and sitting room, with electric cooker on the landing, were tucked away high up in a tower.

I had made no particular friends in the company, but had established good working relations in the three or four months I'd been there. Shirley had yet to learn this common language, and was too intent on doing justice to her roles to see the need to do so. It didn't occur to her that the company might be less than happy about two plum parts going to a newcomer, or that her fervour at rehearsals might be resented by actors who, week after week, had been slogging through farces and pot-boilers. Most dangerous of all, she was too artless to conceal what she quickly perceived, that her director had nothing whatever to offer. Since he'd given her the job in the first place I felt that a little dissimulation was in order, and found myself becoming increasingly upset by her upsets. As a couple, I could feel us being isolated from the rest of the company.

However, notices in the local press for her Desdemona were splendid, and she'd found an ally in the company, Mona Bruce, an excellent Emilia, who'd agreed to private rehearsals of their big scene together. I thought we might be over the worst, particularly as her part in the next play, *Hindle Wakes*, was the perfect vehicle for her qualities of directness and uncompromised feeling. As occasionally happened in rep, when actor and role were perfectly matched, it was as good a performance as you could hope to see, and put to shame the work of the rest of us. It was therefore shocking when the cast list for the next production went up on the noticeboard, and Shirley learnt she had been dropped from the company. The play was a drawing-room comedy, *Birthday Honours*, and a West End smoothie, Hugh Latimer, had been specially engaged to reprise his starring role. Playing opposite him a young actress had been recruited with appropriate South Kensington credentials. It was bitterly unfair, but the play was so snobbish and empty it depended on assured type-casting, and our director was not one to make difficulties for himself.

I hoped Shirley would draw some comfort from the context in which she had lost her job, but she was inconsolable. I couldn't believe it was possible to shed so many tears. For three days she stayed in the tower and wept. Over and over again I told her the play was worthless, the part unsuitable, the Artistic Director's judgement of no account, but nothing I could say was of any comfort. I argued, however, from a very narrow base, and perhaps dared not acknowledge that her grief reflected other losses. For one thing this experience put paid to the idea that it would be easy for us to find work side by side in a congenial company. On the third day the agony of sympathy I felt for her began to cloud over with exasperation. Such rejection was part of an actor's life, I told her. You simply had to put it behind you and go on to the next thing. If you couldn't do this – it was all too easy to move the argument forward – perhaps you shouldn't be an actor.

Wanting the best for her, but wanting also to be disencumbered from a weight of feeling with which I was impatient, I found myself offering her the sort of realistic advice that I refused to apply to myself and which I resisted fiercely when proffered by others. She, however, listened. We both knew that in some ways she was the better actor. What she lacked was my lacerated resolve. Perhaps she felt the raft we were on could carry the weight of only one load of ambition without breaking up. For the second time in a year she was to give up something, and I was to be left wondering about the ambivalence of my influence over someone who looked to me for love.

Shirley went back to her family in York to think about what she would do next, and I struggled on at Chesterfield till the end of the season. Morale at the theatre was low. The box office had dropped alarmingly, and the Artistic Director started a whispering campaign blaming his assistant. This was a disgraceful charge, since the farces and comedies which had been the assistant's responsibility accounted for most of our revenue. However, he prevailed with the Board, and the bewildered man was sacked. In my last week with the company I came out in a scaly rash, and took myself off to the doctor. It was a crisp, sunny, March morning, and I squinted like a creature that had been underground all winter. He shone a light into my eyes and told me I had the theatrical equivalent of shellshock, and needed a rest. This suited me. I'd had about as much of weekly rep as I could take. I determined that when I went back to London I would hang on until a decent company, one with at least two weeks to rehearse, offered me work.

My mother was coming over on one of her trips from Australia, and she suggested a week together in Rome. It was enough to be there for a day to have Chesterfield bleached from my mind. I hadn't expected Ancient Rome to be a presence almost as palpable as the Victorian era was to London. You didn't have to go looking for the architectural marvels of the city; take a walk in any direction and they found you, rearing up as you turned a corner or waiting for you in blinding sunlight at the end of a dark street. One day, without knowing what it was, I stumbled into the Pantheon, and stood amazed. I was in a huge, ancient building that was more than just a row of scarred pillars against an open sky; the place was completely intact. What was so strange was to stand beneath the immense dome of a European temple built without reference to Christianity. On the walls anguished tokens of the building's subsequent conversion diminished to nothing in the face of its brute splendour. It spoke of power, material existence, the world as it is, and I found it exhilarating to be freed for a moment from the ubiquitous iconography of Christian mortification.

My mother had a friend who had married a Roman physician, and the family took us to an open-air restaurant one balmy night, where at least the pleasures of food still seemed to be founded in the pagan past. This, I thought, is how Australians should eat, and of course they now do. The doctor had two beautiful daughters, and later that week they were to show me the Coliseum by moonlight. Having lived with it all their lives the well-brought-up young women gave the ruin hardly a look, and seemed much more interested in widening their vocabulary of obscene English words. They pestered me with such determination that eventually I gave them a short list. This new knowledge delighted them, and they shouted obscenities into the velvety night with that curious Italian dying fall that sounds like a good-natured complaint. 'Fucka!' wailed one of the sisters at the ancient walls, hoping for an echo, but the monstrous wheel of pockmarked stone had heard worse, and wasn't answering. 'Cunta!' yelled her sister. 'Cocka! Cocka!' they persisted in unison. I tried to distract them by asking for the same words in Italian, but the sisters immediately covered their faces with their hands and giggled in hopeless confusion. The more I pressed them the more stricken with shy laughter they became, until eventually, and with the greatest reluctance, one of them conceded me a single word: the Italian for 'bottom'. I could not have had a better illustration of the way we imbue our own language with magical properties.

Back in London I established a base for myself, a tiny room up three flights of stairs in Shepherd's Bush, which, because I had spent a little money decorating, the landlord agreed to let me have at a reduced rent when work took me out of town. This was to happen sooner than I expected. Ronald Russell and Peggy Ann Wood, a husband-and-wife team of actor-managers, ran the Little Theatre in Bristol, a fortnightly rep with a fair reputation. They made me an offer, but with a catch. First, I would have to do a summer season of weekly rep at their other theatre at Weston-super-Mare. This was an eleven-week slog, but it would be by the sea, and a couple of the parts they offered me I had already played at Chesterfield. Shirley, who had joined me in London to do a steno-typing course – learning to do shorthand on a machine as a step towards interesting work – would take over the room in my absence. A natural student, she applied herself to this with the same lack of resentment with which she had once learnt the lines of bad plays, and quickly became the most accomplished in her class.

A friend of ours, who had a car, suggested the three of us make an outing of my journey to Weston, so we packed his Morris with a picnic basket, some bottles of wine and my luggage and set off. His was a qualified kindness, however, since he wanted to get his hands on Shirley, and managed to do so on the return journey. We were still a couple, but the understanding between us had inevitably been shifted by events. My work was going to mean absences of six months or more, meeting, when we could afford the fares, only at weekends. She knew me too well for me to conceal my sexual restlessness, and she took her cue from that. We both had lives to lead. Over the next few years a pattern emerged in this cycle of reunion and departure. As the moment of separation drew closer Shirley would become increasingly miserable, whilst I would take covert sniffs of my approaching liberty. The moment we were apart, I adrift in some ugly town with digs to find, she left behind to continue her London life, the tables would be turned. I became the one to feel friendless and wretched without her; she would only have to turn a corner to see that the world had other things to offer than the attentions of a feckless lover.

Weston-super-Mare depressed all hell out of me. The Bristol Channel was no Bondi Beach. Here's how I describe the seaside resort in a letter home. 'Crowds and crowds of holidaymakers shamble aimlessly through the town. Their favourite pastime appears to be a morning wandering through Woolworth's with grubby children in tow, not buying anything, just looking. Even on a sunny day the store gets more attention than the sea-front. The beach, which is a mixture of mud and sand, favouring mud, lengthens by a mile when the tide goes out, leaving the Grand Pier high and dry and hideous on its barnacled under structure.' On the weekend before Ruth Ellis was hanged, I walked along the front aware that there wasn't a person in that crowd, perhaps in the whole country, who did not have her approaching death ticking away inside their head. The 'rope' was the most ghastly of the many rituals of authority and deference that described the English way of life. This idea of a holiday was another. So was the fare we were offering the holidaymakers at our theatre, plays set in drawing rooms with actors aping the manners of their betters. One of our attractions was the same *Birthday Honours* that had been Shirley's downfall, and which, as a consequence of its West End success, was breaking out in reps up and down the country that year like an epidemic of social grovelling. However, at the very least I was practising my craft. I shared a dressing room with Peter Jeffrey, and our laughter did something to make the work endurable. I learnt my lines late at night in a perpetual state of anger, I fought as usual with the director, and a pretty, plump ASM, who wore a dog collar, I inveigled into my bed. The eleven weeks passed, and suddenly I had arrived in Bristol.

I took to it at once. Perhaps because it was an echo of home, I loved the presence of water in the centre of town and the steep hills rising up from it. I loved the Georgian terraces perched on the heights of Clifton, which surveyed the estuary and the city below with the hauteur of patrons in a circle of private boxes at the Opera. The knowledge that these elegant buildings owed their existence to the slave trade gave them the corrupt sheen of those looming Pasadena mansions in the novels of Raymond Chandler. Most of all I loved my new working conditions: an unbelievable two weeks to rehearse meant the chance to attempt a little more than simply learning your lines. And when the management gave you a play out, there was an entire month when, for the first fortnight, you were free all day, for the second, every evening. It was actually possible to have a life. With this luxury of spare time I began to write again, recasting the material in my abandoned novel as a stage play. This time I would finish it.

Because of the presence of a university, the town was full of young people, and, with autumn deepening, I found my way down steep, watery streets to their coffee bars and meeting places. Sitting amongst them with my cappuccino – strikingly pretty young women, who in London would already have been claimed by someone with a sports car, and sparky, restless young men relentlessly dreaming of elsewhere – I was again to be reminded of Sydney. Provincial life, as lived in a city like Bristol, which in many ways offered more than yearned-for London, was something I understood, and it stirred me.

I first found accommodation above a restaurant in Clifton called 'The Four Seasons', but was thrown out by the proprietor's wife after Shirley had spent a weekend in my room. My neighbour along the corridor, a retired naval commander with a kind of stainless-steel calliper where once there'd been a hand, had evidently complained, and I was ostentatiously drummed out of the building. This was a bit rich since another guest, and the landlady's favourite, a homosexual colleague at the theatre, had had a boyfriend to stay that same weekend. One of the curiosities of the time was that a young bachelor, notwithstanding the law of the land and provided he was discreet, could lead a homosexual life with rather less hassle than a heterosexual one. However, all turned out for the best when, just around the corner, I found an attic flat in a sandstone terrace for just 35s a week.

Only one thing was to sour my stay in Bristol: though the Little Theatre was a step up from my other engagements, elsewhere in the city there was a far better theatre, the Bristol Old Vic, which boasted an eighteenth-century auditorium, the most beautiful in England, and which had not two, but three whole weeks in which to rehearse. Their programme for the season included *King Lear, Uncle Vanya* and *Volpone.* The leading actor was a twenty-eight-year-old Eric Porter, and he played quite wonderfully the name parts in all these plays. After our curtain had come down I would tear across town to catch perhaps the last twenty minutes of these productions, tormenting myself with the fact that there were actors in the company no better than I, who had this particular job whilst I didn't. One of these competitors, however, was clearly a personality to reckon with. I met him one lunchtime in a tiny tea-room next door to the Vic, where he held court with the same sort of expansiveness as a star regular at the Ivy. In his presence you felt positively sucked up by his curiosity about you and his passion for the theatre. He'd only just left RADA, and was playing walk-on parts, though this would soon change. The following season Peter O'Toole would be leading the company. We soon discovered we were both huge fans of Olivier, whose film of *Richard III* had just opened at the Leicester Square Cinema. I'd made a trip to London one weekend to see it. Peter made several. 'I just can't keep away from the damn thing,' he announced. He would burst into a room like a student in *La Bohème*, projecting a slightly ludicrous (but, one felt, probably justified) sense of destiny.

On one of our matinee days he crossed town to see me perform. The part wasn't bad but I knew we were offering tame fare. The Little Theatre was the entertainment side of the business, but, alas, entertainment about thirty years behind the times. In a letter I record the visit to Bristol of the American pop star, Johnnie Ray, who performed in the concert hall that was also housed in the same vast, nineteenth-century civic space as our own auditorium. 'When I came in for the evening performance the road outside was swarming with young people, and there was a sense of real anticipation in the air. I couldn't help comparing this excited horde to our audience of benign grey heads. It was our first night and we found ourselves playing against the distant roar of hundreds of voices in the street below chanting "WE WANT JOHNNIE". Our supporters tried to reassure us by audibly tut-tutting, and they gave us a heartier clap than usual at the curtain. But I'm afraid my sympathies were with the people outside. They really wanted Johnnie Ray, whereas most of our lot would have been quite as happy at a whist drive.'

One thing our theatre couldn't be accused of was pretentiousness, and occasionally we did a play, which, though commercial, demonstrated real skill and talent. Such a one was *Meet a Body*, a comedy thriller by the film writers Launder and Gilliat, and I was excited to be given the lead in what I believed could be a very funny play. At rehearsals I became quite passionate about getting it right – the pace, the timing, the precision that comedy requires – and I sensed my fellow actors deferring to an instinct that they were learning they could trust. It was therefore very gratifying when all three local papers went out of their way to endorse the show. The most severe of our critics was Peter Rodford of the *Western Daily Press*, and here he was writing about us at length and in the tones that he usually reserved for the Vic. My performance he discussed not in a sentence but over a number of paragraphs. I remember exactly where I was sitting and the time of day when Peter Jeffrey handed me the newspaper folded open at the magic page. 'Have you seen this?' he asked. I hadn't, but I already knew the gist of it from something I could discern beneath his smile, that discomforting mixture of goodwill and deprivation with which we respond to the good fortune of a friend. Now it was my turn to hide something, my first authentic taste of professional success; that is to say the exaltation of having one's powers willingly acknowledged by others. Suddenly, and rather unexpectedly, one was through the sound barrier of their indifference.

No one who could help my career saw the performance, nor did it lead to better work. And Peter Jeffrey made his mark in the theatre long before I did. But this production taught me what I needed to know: that here was something I was a little bit more than good at. My time at Bristol was coming to an end. I'd saved some money, and so had Shirley from her new skill as palantypist, and we went off to see some more of Europe, this time Austria.

# SIX

# A Door Opens

In Australia I had skied in the university vacations, wearing a pair of modified army boots mounted on skis passed on by a relative who had acquired them in the twenties. The New South Wales snow country could boast only two hotels, twelve miles apart, and one primitive lift that dragged you perhaps two hundred yards up a modest hill. With a few friends one mainly shuffled along valleys or herring-boned laboriously through the snowbound gums, as isolated as a party of explorers. Now, in Austria, you could take a chair-lift that left you dangling high above the crisscrossed slopes and made going up almost as exciting as coming down. Once on top you faced a precipitous descent measured not in minutes but in miles. And yet I didn't enjoy it as much as I'd hoped. To begin with, all the other skiers were so much better, even the disabled war veterans skiing on one leg or with no arms, even the group of blind skiers I watched traversing the slope with hesitant competence. Nor did I like the sense of being a mere unit in a commercial enterprise that processed thousands through an Alpine holiday. At home as I pushed through the snow I had sung songs to myself, or just stopped and raised my head to take in the white, rolling solitude. At Obergurgle with an instructor breathing down your neck or half a dozen skiers homing in on you like torpedoes, you were as likely to be contemplative as you would be in the middle of Oxford Street. The Alps themselves were an awesome, constant presence, but you saw them only in such snatches as the serious business of skiing allowed. After ten days the snow started melting and big, brown patches began to appear here and there, as if the mountain was soiling itself in disgust at its infestation by humanity. We decided to spend the rest of our holiday in Vienna.

This, too, was not what I expected. The old city clustered around the cathedral was quaint and lovely, but there wasn't much of it. Surrounding and swamping it was architectural propaganda extolling the Austro-Hungarian Empire. Even if history had not subverted its message, this nineteenth-century exercise in self-important town planning would have been very hard to like: circular avenues twice as wide as they needed to be, an open space as bleak as a parade ground to set off some bronze hero astride a bronze horse the size of an elephant. In contrast the imperial buildings in London were almost domestic. However, there was plenty to see, and one morning Shirley and I visited the great flagship of the German-speaking stage, the Burgtheater. On impulse we presented ourselves at the stage door as a couple of young British actors with a keen interest in European theatre. No less than the Intendant himself received us, and I got the impression that he was vastly amused at our cheek, but we were shown around the building and given tickets for one of the plays in the repertoire. No theatre in England could begin to match this one in subsidy, and we were suitably humbled by its working conditions and the scale of its operations.

The performance the following night was the first I had seen in a foreign language. It was a new play, but set in the early nineteenth century so presumably spoken in the German equivalent of Standard English. It was splendidly acted, but it wasn't long before I became aware of two things: firstly, that without knowing the language most of the play was lost to me; and secondly, that the sounds the actors made, though doubtless eloquent to a German ear, had for me as I craned forward to understand more the desperation of someone shaking at a padlocked door. I was reminded of D. H. Lawrence's poem about the gasp a tortoise makes during mating, its only sound in an otherwise mute existence. Sex, concludes the poem, is 'the cross on which our silence first was broken'. Language had come into being not because it was beautiful but because it was *necessary*. In the English classical theatre at that time the spoken word aspired to the golden and the mellifluous. I was now perceiving our effort to communicate with one another as something rather more urgent and surreptitious than an orderly procession of mellow vowels and perfect consonants. I had recently read a book by an academic, John Press, in which he challenged the idea of the music of language and insisted instead on the centrality of sense. He took the famous lines, 'In Xanadu did Kubla Khan/A stately pleasure-dome decree,' and using a sequence of similar sounds in the identical metre composed a line of comic nonsense. Any aural power it possessed dissolved in the absurdity of its sense.

The fifties boasted a generation of British actors of quite remarkable vocal technique. There is no one on stage today who can elicit the pulse of iambic pentameter to such thrilling effect as Olivier, or phrase a passage of verse with the effortless grace of Gielgud. However, the tremolo frequently adopted by performers in Shakespeare impressed me as being a very generalised device to suggest feeling. With the beautifully spoken star there was also some confusion between poetic sensibility and deference to upper-class diction. All these actors had prodigious voice projections and when, for instance, Olivier turned up the volume he could make the fabric of the theatre hum like a tuning-fork. Lesser actors simply made a lot of noise, and a Shakespearean production would typically begin with a young actor covered in make-up bounding on stage like a squash player and belting the opening line of the play as hard as he could against the back wall of the auditorium. This was meant to attest to the vigour of what lay ahead, and I often wondered if I was the only one to find it faintly embarrassing. What a relief and a revelation it was a few years later when a young Franco Zeffirelli staged *Romeo and Juliet* at the Old Vic and had Derek Smith as the Chorus walk on stage and in the most normal tones simply explain to us, 'In fair Verona where we set our scene . . .' Unencumbered by British notions of verse-speaking, Zeffirelli encouraged his young cast to think about what they were saying and forget how it sounded. 'Parting is such *sweet* sorrow,' said Judi Dench to her Romeo, John Stride, and the wearisome familiarity of the line fell away. She was telling you three things about herself at once – her discovery of feeling, the paradox of such emotion and her new delight at being able to play games with words. This landmark production also directed your attention to aspects of the play itself so self-evident they had usually been overlooked: that it was specifically about adolescents, young males with too much testosterone hanging out in a dusty Italian square, closeted girls shyly yielding to sexual curiosity and to passion. It was a Shakespearean production rooted in recognisable life, taking place in an actual Italy at an actual time.

Back in London my first problem was accommodation. The landlord of the room I had sublet to Shirley had suddenly turned nasty and was insisting that I owed him an extra month's rent, which I didn't. Since I'd decorated the place at my own expense, he assumed he had me over a barrel. When I protested, he flew into an astonishing rage, screamed obscenities at Shirley and made a move towards her as if to throw her down the stairs. There were specks of white spit at the corners of his mouth. We stood transfixed at the vision of seedy, rooming-house London revealed to us – poisonous, long-smothered resentments, and worse, body parts buried under floorboards. It was time to go, and as quickly as possible. The following day, when the landlord was out, my Australian friend, Peter Heath, drove us back to the house. We loaded up his car with various belongings including my new curtains and a roll of bright yellow Heal's linoleum which I'd put down in an unsuccessful attempt to give an impression of sunshine. In dismantling a lamp we managed to fuse all the lights in the house, and, for luck, I threw the contents of a bottle of ink all over my splendid wallpaper, also from Heal's. Then we tiptoed down the stairs and drove away laughing like maniacs. An ex-girlfriend from Sydney, who had married a well-off Old Etonian (for her and a number of socially ambitious Australians I knew this latter qualification was rather like a designer label), with whom she now lived in a big house in Chelsea to the considerable unhappiness of both, offered to put me up for a week or two. They didn't much like each other, but in their different ways I liked both of them, and they were to prove staunch friends.

Shirley was already installed in a room around the corner in Oakley Street. We had both found shelter, but now with the money running out fast we needed work. She found a curious secretarial job with an elderly anthropologist in Dorset, who during the thirties had been one of a number of well-born fascist sympathisers and gave the impression he still was. In her job application she had included a snapshot I had taken on our Alpine holiday of her being nuzzled by an Austrian cow, which quite by accident had the appropriate Aryan connotations. The job was hers. I was to find work the day I was down to my last pound, like Bridlington, another of those crisis engagements which involved boarding a train at a few hours' notice. Lesley Storm had written a play called *The Long Echo* based on the Burgess and Maclean affair. It was presently touring prior to a London run at the St James's Theatre. The management was Laurence Olivier Productions, no less, and the prestigious cast included Denholm Elliott and Joyce Redman. I was being asked at extremely short notice to cover the two male leads. There were only two things wrong with the job: firstly, the play was quite hopeless, and had the author's earlier *Black Chiffon* not been a huge success, it would never have got on; and secondly, I knew under-studying to be a mostly no-win situation. Even if you were suited to the part there was rarely enough rehearsal time to make it your own, nor were you expected to; what was required was a carbon copy, inevitably a smudged one, of the principal's performance. However, I boarded the train to Liverpool with luggage and typewriter, glad of the work. *Gum Beach*, the play I had begun writing in Bristol, was almost finished, and the tour would give me the time and solitude I required.

First there were the lines, a great many of them, to be learnt and to be learnt quickly. The director (in those days called the producer) would be coming up at the end of the week especially to rehearse me. As a general rule the worse the play the harder it is to memorise, and I was up until three and four in the morning trying to hammer the two parts into my head, a task which even weekly rep had never deman-ded. At 10 a.m. I reported to the theatre and under the gloomy work-light went through the moves with the other understudies. When not required on stage I stretched out on the floor in the wings and tried to snatch some sleep. This caused such consternation in one of my fellow understudies, a bossy woman who considered it unprofessional, that she reported me to the company manager. When something is wrong in a theatre they quickly become like schools, and matron and prefect figures emerge out of nowhere. By Friday I more or less knew my words, and felt prepared for a visit from the Headmaster. In London, when he'd offered me the job, he'd been as friendly as a pussycat so I was expecting at the very least to be commended for learning the lines. Instead I was in for the worst afternoon of my professional life.

On practically every line I was stopped, then when I became so confused that I started to forget the words, I was attacked for not knowing them. 'No! No! No! No! That's not the line Lesley wrote. And you're not doing it like Denholm! Watch the performance at night! Learn from Denholm!' The young Denholm Elliott, who in the years to come would emerge as an actor of eccentric brilliance, was, in my opinion, giving a mannered and empty performance, and I had no wish to learn from him. In any case, he'd had four weeks to rehearse; I'd had four days. So that all could hear, the Headmaster delivered his waspish disdain from the back of the house, and the element of sadism in it was so undisguised that anger saved me from any depression I might have felt had his remarks been more reasonably expressed. For a director to treat an actor this way is not only out-rageous, it is counter-productive. There are bad actors but very few lazy ones. The prospect of exposure and possible humiliation on a pub-lic stage ensures that actors *try*. They have little choice but to do their best, and, particularly at the early stages of rehearsal, are as vulner-able as chicks pecking out of their shells. There have been a number of famous directors who bullied, but it is never forgivable. Basil Dean, who had a big reputation between the wars, is reputed to have driven one actress to suicide. The rehearsal at last drew to an end. As I left the stage after Six of the Best, Matron was waiting for me in the wings. Her immensely satisfied smirk was perhaps the most unpleasant thing to be endured on that grim afternoon.

Fortunately I had developed some of the scar tissue that all actors need, and I followed my own agenda, which was first to become secure in the parts I was understudying, then to concentrate on my play. My typewriter was installed on the table in my dressing room, and I worked there in the mornings when the theatre was empty and during the performance at night. Occasionally Matron intruded without knocking and ticked me off for not going out front and 'learning from Denholm', but notwithstanding these interruptions *Gum Beach* was completed. It was the first time I had written 'Final Curtain' and I could hardly believe it. Now I was free to watch the performance, and there were two actors from whom I certainly had something to learn. One was Joyce Redman, who gave a very un-English performance, overflowing with feeling. The other was Marjorie Fielding, who had things to teach that transcended theatre. A dignified and accomplished actress in her sixties, she rendered to perfection the ideal of upper-class understatement that was the currency of so many plays of the time. And, more than that, lived it. She had stomach cancer, from which she was said to be dying, yet she never missed a performance or failed to give a good one. The stage management put a chair for her convenient to the set, and I would see her leave the stage and sink into it, her face assuming the horribly private and suspended expression of someone dealing with pain. I have known two actors of my own generation, Colin Blakely and Paul Eddington, who have gone on working at this most exposed of employments aware that their deaths were almost upon them. Long purged of any vanity or self-importance, they went on acting because it was what their lives had always been about, mem-bers of a profession journalists now choose to call 'luvvies'.

After Liverpool our next stop was Edinburgh, my second important encounter with Scotland. The first had been in the pages of a book. In 1950, Boswell's *London Journal*, only recently discovered, had been published to much excitement. Newly arrived in England, I identified at once with this young Scotsman coming down from the North determined to make his way in the Big Smoke. Boswell had a rather more various sex life than I did at the time and much more social energy, but his ups and downs, small triumphs and humiliations seemed a mirror to my own. I decided that a Scotsman was to eighteenth-century England what an Australian was in the twentieth. Now I had arrived in the land of Boswell's birth, and nowhere in the British Isles had I ever felt so at home. The landscape of bare hills as seen through the train window as we travelled on to Glasgow reminded me of the Monaro in New South Wales where I'd spent much of my childhood, and I loved the accent which to a lesser or greater degree, as in Australia, appeared to be ubiquitous. The Scots displayed a courtesy to one another, a kind of informal formality, which spoke of a more briskly democratic ethos than I had ever encountered in England. I had not expected it to be so completely a country with its own character, and one day I would spend three of the most crucial and rewarding years of my career amongst this very particular people.

We opened in London to a poor press and were told we would be coming off after a month. In some ways this was a relief. In the meantime I was grateful for the four weeks' salary and began to enjoy my first West End employment. The St James's was a lovely Georgian theatre (which would be replaced by an office block before the end of the decade), the Headmaster was nowhere to be seen, and, in addition, I had landed a wonderful daytime job playing a lead in the *Sir Lancelot* TV series. Each episode was filmed over the course of a week, and my role was that of Sir Cedric, a foolish knight. I was to receive the princely sum of £75, three times more than I had ever earned for a week's work. Even Matron seemed impressed. So was Robert Morley, who arranged an introduction to his high-powered agents, MCA. After *The Long Echo* my next engagement was a special week at the Croydon Grand, earning only £12 a week, but which I had accepted because I thought it would be an opportunity for MCA to see me in action. In a letter home I describe one of the pitfalls of an actor's life: 'The play was *The Philadelphia Story* and the part a very good one (Cary Grant in the film). The opening on the Monday night went extremely well, and a couple of less important agents were there to see it. But the most important people of all, MCA, came to the fated Wednesday performance when everything went wrong. Props were missing and the sound cues from the panatrope were either late or simply not there. I got stupidly nervous, and had one of those awful nights when one simply loses the knack. I must have been trying too hard or something. The next evening, Thursday, thoroughly disgusted with myself, I went on and gave a splendid performance, but, of course, no one was there.'

Though Shirley and I were seeing each other almost every day, we'd decided not to cohabit. She had her room in Oakley Street, and I was renting a basement studio for a month from a Greek friend who lived a walk away in Tedworth Square. I was looking for somewhere more permanent. It fell into my lap unexpectedly when Peter Heath stumbled upon a two-bedroomed flat in Carlyle Square which he suggested we share. It was 'furnished' only to the extent that it met that legal qualification; a couple of sagging beds and a few broken chairs were enough to protect a landlord against security of tenure should his tenants prove unsatisfactory. The flat was extremely dirty, and the first night I spent there I discovered that the mouldy green carpet in my room was infested with cat fleas. As you walked about in underpants they smelt blood and leapt across your path like grasshoppers. It was soon out in the street, and I got to work with a paintbrush to make the room presentable, three walls grey and the fourth terracotta, though this last proved a mistake and had to be painted over. I still had my Heal's curtains and I bought an elegant Victorian armchair for £4 10s at the Portobello Market, reupholstering it myself in red corduroy. Heat was provided by two gas fires, one in each bedroom, which in winter consumed silver coins like some insatiable animal insisting on food. We suspected the landlord had rigged the mechanism. There was a tiny kitchen, now enlivened by my yellow linoleum, and on the landing a payphone with extensions into the various rooms for incoming calls only.

The building itself was an attractive match to others in the square, but once inside was essentially a rooming house. It was not unusual then in a desirable area to find an odd congruence of neighbours. Adjacent to us in the grandest house in Carlyle Square lived Sir Osbert Sitwell, and we would catch sight of him, stricken with Parkinson's, shuffling slowly from a chauffeured car to his front door. He had a cleaning lady, of a sort you used to see in films played by actresses like

Kathleen Harrison, and we managed to inveigle her away from the manicured interiors next door for half a day a week. She imposed a little order on our squalor with scandalised cheeriness. Class loomed large in British life, but in contradictory ways, because it did not invariably relate to money. Everyone used public transport, which was clean and efficient and it was not unusual to see a Sloane Street matron aboard a 22 bus with her parcels from Harrods, or a stock-broker in a bowler hat bound for the City on a tube. In my first decade in London I don't remember one escalator out of service or one train delayed. In some unfathomable way, which we took for granted, the country *worked*, both on a practical and on a social level, and although intellectually I railed against Britain's complacent assumptions of its own importance, I still assumed that London was somehow the centre of the world. Through force of habit, perhaps, it was granted imperial status by Londoners and visitors alike, and I was proud and excited to be making a life there. What added to the excitement was that change was in the air.

Without particularly meaning to, I had included in my reading many of the books which would set the agenda for the sixties. At drama school I'd read *Coming of Age in Samoa* and *Lady Chatterley's Lover*, the one a now questionable work of anthropology, the other D. H. Lawrence's worst novel, but both of them, for all their shortcomings, espousing a more generous attitude to sex than the one bequeathed to us by the nineteenth century. As a student I'd also read a remarkable memoir by a manic-depressive, *Wisdom, Madness and Folly*, which anticipated the ideas of R. D. Laing by a decade. In the garret I had gobbled up *The Doors of Perception*, Aldous Huxley's herald to the drug culture. In Bristol I read *The Catcher in the Rye* and *Lucky Jim*, and in Carlyle Square *The Second Sex*, then later *The Golden Notebook*. The pendulum would inevitably swing too far with the ideas and attitudes found in these books, and they would soon become compromised by sixties hedonism, but this is not to say that the status quo they challenged was not due for profound change. We were just a decade away from the second of the two most ghastly wars in history. It was customary to blame the Germans, but was not the culture to which we all belonged culpable to some degree? Was Germany the only country in which Jews had been hated or eugenics preached?

One evening Shirley and I went to the new National Film Theatre, now re-sited under Waterloo Bridge, to see Alain Resnais's film *Night and Fog*, which had been made to celebrate the tenth anniversary of the liberation of the concentration camps. Its cool, almost clinical tone was in marked contrast to the newsreels from which we had originally learnt of this absolute of Nazi brutality. At the end of the war the subject had received enormous publicity, the ultimate vindication of the Allied cause, and then, almost as if its implications were as yet impossible to digest, it had gone underground for a decade. Similarly, after the First World War it had taken the same ten years for the full reality of the trenches to make its way into print with books like *All Quiet on the Western Front* and *Goodbye to All That*.

The form of the film was a return journey to the camps as they looked then, in 1956. The memorialising of these places was yet to come, and the weathered concrete and brick, standing among weeds, looked as ordinary and morally neutral as a derelict factory or an abandoned building site. The camerawork was in matter-of-fact colour, and interspersed with this contemporary material was black-and-white footage from the war, very little of which we had previously seen. Familiar with the horrors, we had not taken into account the organisational tedium attendant on an operation as vast as the Final Solution. This was not the work solely of jackbooted sadists but of perfectly ordinary men and women doing what they were told – bureaucrats making lists, clerks bent over railway timetables, construction workers meeting deadlines, industrialists supplying product and people in factories producing it. That smell of uneasy boredom, which so often seems to foreshadow shameful events, permeated the footage. The most affecting moments were often the most ordinary – an apathetic soldier walks beside a stationary train closing the sliding doors of the cattle-trucks; inside one of them an old man stretches out an arm to help. The film concluded with images long familiar, the piles of skeletal corpses, the mass burials by bulldozer, but we were now seeing them in a very different light. It was as if the very qualities on which the West prided itself and which it considered distinguished it from lesser societies – its organisational skills, its mechanical ingenuity, its social co-operation, its science, even its art – had been turned upside down in this mindless celebration of death.

When the lights came up the response of the audience was like nothing I've experienced before or since. We sat there in silence, ashamed. Then the full house rose to its feet and filed out of the cinema without one word being spoken. There was nothing to say. We had been told something about ourselves that it was almost indecent to know. The Holocaust has gone on to become a commonplace of history, the subject of books, factual and fictional, TV series, films and acres of journalism, its meaning more often out of focus than in. For me *Night and Fog* got it indelibly right, and the later much longer *Shoah* was a film of similar power. Primo Levi wrote a sublime account of his experience as a deportee and an inmate, and Peter Weiss's play *The Investigation* wisely abjures drama and simply catalogues the appalling evidence. Lesser treatments have made me very uneasy. The subject is one to be fully comprehended once, and then left alone. The ordinary human qualities that allowed it to happen – indifference to others, the sense of deliverance elicited by another's misfortune, morbid curiosity, to name the least pathological – are always waiting in the shadows to feast at second hand.

And now, in 1956, we were busy preparing for a Third World War, one of even greater, and perhaps final, horror. I could understand the theory behind 'mutual deterrence', but I was not convinced by it. In the long term, 'better dead than red' was a nonsensical proposition, since, if 'red', there was always the possibility, however long it took, of change or insurrection, but, if 'dead', the story was over. For ever. I was also unconvinced by the assertion that nuclear weapons had kept the peace for ten, twenty, thirty or however many years. Even if the bomb kept the peace for ten thousand years before it was used, it would still have proved the supreme miscalculation. Indeed this proof may be waiting for us.

What those of us who hoped to live out the remaining two-thirds of our lives most resented was the shallowness of the public debate about this, the most metaphysical, apocalyptic and plain evil of all man's inventions. Britain, as even Nye Bevan was soon to say, could not 'go naked into the conference chambers of the world'. He might just as well have been talking about a Savile Row suit – the nuclear weapon as fashion accessory. This posturing on the world stage by successive prime ministers would go on for the rest of the century, to the irritation of the rest of the globe but the apparent approval of the British electorate. And this is what most amazed me: people from all points on the political spectrum were united in wanting their bomb, and no party could get elected without supporting it. By 1958 a window card at any post office showed you how the National Cake was divided; one huge slice of 28 per cent went on Defence, a sliver on

Education and for the Arts one-tenth of one per cent in crumbs. An already impoverished nation might just as well have taken its banknotes out into a field and made a bonfire of them.

It was Suez at the end of 1956 that dramatically exposed to the country the way it was governed, and surprisingly few seemed to mind. Perhaps the event meant so much to me because I possessed a little inside knowledge. Peter Heath had a job with a charter airline which did business with the government. In the weeks leading up to the military operation he'd been in and out of Whitehall running errands for his company. In the evening he'd return with stories of government and military officials buzzing like self-important hornets as they made clandestine preparations to go to war. The headlines later were all too predictable. Whereas this sorry story of arrogance and mendacity would have united another country in protest, here it divided it. Alone among newspapers, *The Observer* and *The Guardian* told the truth about the collusion between the invading powers, and were castigated for treason. The circulation of both papers fell away, in the case of *The Observer* leaving it disadvantaged for many years to come. It was as if the readers of the *Washington Post* had penalised it for covering Watergate. For me its scrupulous and courageous stand was a rallying cry, and I was exhilarated to find myself part of a swell of passionate opinion which had been waiting for something like Suez to provide a focus. In discovering exactly where I stood over this issue, I had found a way to be at ease in my adopted country.

A new kind of Englishman: that's what *Look Back in Anger* earlier in the year had suggested. Or perhaps it was the re-emergence of a much older type of Englishman, one who predated those nineteenth-century institutions which had once propped up an empire but now suffocated British life to no purpose. The public schools, the hierarchic rituals of power and governance were for the most part as recent and about as authentic as those Victorian churches in the Gothic manner that were falling into neglect all over the country. A few people in England lived extremely well; others, like myself, were lucky in the work we were allowed to do. But, apparently, I was not alone in thinking that too many British subjects were fobbed off with something instead of a life – a daily dose of self-esteem accruing to a people that had once had an empire and been on the winning side in two world wars. Even if their own lives were cramped and diminished they were British, and that meant better than anyone else. And who needed culture, when you were allowed to stand outside in the rain and watch the Royal Family going about their solemn and sumptuously lit fancy-dress party?

It was surely time for change. The journalist Henry Fairlie had already identified what he described as the Establishment, that unofficial network of top people whose influence was felt in every aspect of the national life. Now they had been rumbled, and were given notice that they could no longer take deference for granted. In *The Spectator* Bernard Levin in his 'Taper' column described the Prime Minister at the time of Suez, Anthony Eden, as 'this weak, vain man' – language of unprecedented bluntness from a political commentator, and in the same journal he wrote an article announcing the arrival of the new British radical, who would be distinguished less by his political affiliations than by an unintimidated intelligence prepared to question anything. The battle lines were drawn, and there was a contingent on my side standing right at the front, the British theatre. Of course, we misidentified the enemy, or anyway chose a secondary one. Our target was the upper-middle-class Establishment, retired military men writing indignantly to the *Telegraph*, or Palace officials complacently censoring our plays. What we failed to take into account was that the censor believed as strongly as we did in the importance of what we were doing; otherwise he wouldn't have tried to suppress it. Even the retired colonel was a supporter of the theatre, provided it went no further than Noël Coward. Our real enemy, Margaret Thatcher's constituent, was biding his time in the suburbs, sponging down his car on a Sunday morning after a week in the city, and looking suspiciously over the hedge at his neighbour's plans for an extension. He couldn't care less about censorship, because he didn't give a toss about art, and against this absence of belief there would be no defence. In the meantime, the Royal Court, Joan Littlewood's Theatre Royal, later the RSC and the new National would, in the next twenty years, take the theatre to the heart of the national debate. The stage was suddenly important and seriously fashionable; it was a wonderful time to be part of it.

In Charing Cross Road I ran into John Osborne, and he told me he had just finished a new play. 'This one's really going to shake them up,' he said. Like him, spurred on by Suez, I, too, had started on another play. It was to be a protest about how nostalgia for the war seemed to have the British psyche in a headlock. Week after week the Sunday newspapers provided space for the memoirs of generals like Montgomery, who re-fought tidier versions of their battles, or officers who had escaped from POW camps or hurled themselves from planes in airborne landings. These accounts were strong on heroism and resolve, weak on confusion and horror. In the cinema Kenneth More clambered legless into his spitfire with a plucky grin, and Richard Todd bombed a dam and lived to light his pipe. My play covered the same ground (if to rather less effect) as *Catch-22*, in that it proposed there were two enemies: the official one, and the one standing right behind you pushing you into battle. Since the play also contained a great deal of Osborne-type rhetoric I was at first shy about mentioning it, but eventually I did so. 'It's definitely not for the Noël Coward audience,' I said. And he replied, 'But those aren't the sort of people we're trying to reach.' A new sort of Englishman: at that time it almost seemed possible. I'm not sure that the best of the sixties didn't really take place in the second half of the fifties. The ferment then had a moral seriousness far removed from the self-gratification that was to come with the acceptance of an altered social order. Protest and change were not yet generating big money, nor did anyone expect them to.

When, a few months later, Laurence Olivier went to work at the Royal Court for £60 a week playing Archie Rice in *The Entertainer*, it was as if an important politician, perhaps even the Prime Minister, had crossed the floor of the house to vote with the opposition. You could almost hear the 'Ah' of astonishment. Henry V was forsaking the royal purple and donning the bow tie of a seedy, lower-middle-class comedian – and, more, actually identifying with him. His first entrance, coming on fast from stage left in a showbiz shamble, which I can only describe as energetically clapped-out, was something that I have only to think about to see. This wasn't Olivier 'characterising', the way a posh actor of the day occasionally went slumming to show us his skill with an accent or a strut. It was a performer owning up to things about himself we'd never guessed at – his vulgarity, his cynicism, his weary vulnerability – and what made it joyous was that, above all, he was celebrating his own artistic renewal. *The Entertainer* was one of those rare congruencies of a national mood, a particular event (in this case Suez and its aftermath) and wondrous talent, resulting in an evening of quite exceptional intensity. Sometimes such an occasion has led to a riot, like the famous O'Casey first night in Dublin in the thirties; sometimes to an overflowing of public emotion, like the Moscow Art's first great success with *The Seagull*. What they all attest to is that, on however small a scale, theatre can matter, and this was something on which a number of us were betting our futures.

On another level, of course, my life was no different and just as absurd as it had always been. I was still getting excited about the possibility of a new suit, that is to say dressing myself in the uniform of the enemy, and had gone so far as to save up and have some shoes made to measure in St James's. I was still thinking too much about sex, getting luckier at it and occasionally managing a promiscuous afternoon tryst. I was still finding reasons not to work on my play, or, having started, finding reasons to stop. I was still reading magazines when I should have been reading books. On a bad morning I was still getting up at eleven, and eating so much at lunchtime I needed a nap afterwards; still sitting idly in my room doing nothing much beyond picking my nose or letting my thoughts drift. Yet somehow better things got done. I'd sent my only other copy of *Gum Beach*, the carbon (how that brings back the period) to the producer, Hugh Hunt, who was running the Elizabethan Theatre Trust in Australia, and he'd written back showing some interest. I was halfway through my new play. And I'd written dozens of letters pursuing work, one of which had paid off spectacularly.

Douglas Seale was Artistic Director of the Birmingham Repertory Theatre, the most esteemed provincial company in the land. He had built a reputation on his brilliant productions of the Shakespeare histories, notably the cycle of the three parts of *Henry VI* and *Richard III*, which in the sixties would appear in a new staging at Stratford under the general title *The Wars of the Roses*. He had also had a great success with the two parts of *Henry IV* and now intended to round this off with a new production of *Henry V*, in which he had cast a young actor straight from drama school, Albert Finney. I'd written to Dougie and he'd replied almost at once suggesting we meet. Talented people are often the most approachable, and one afternoon towards the end of the year we shared a pot of tea in that same Kenya Coffee House in the King's Road where I'd sat with John Osborne watching him smoke his cigar. I was delighted and rather astonished to find myself in easy conversation with this highly regarded director, and an hour went swiftly by. Before we parted he said, yes, he could probably find something for me in the production.

I thought I would be ideal for the French court, playing the Dauphin perhaps, or the Constable, but instead I got Exeter, the King's uncle, a part more suited to a heavyweight character actor in his fifties, not a skinny young man of twenty-eight with an aptitude for comedy. However, I had a strong voice and a well-stocked make-up box, so I hoped I would get by. My first shock was Birmingham in the middle of January, which in a letter I describe in a now familiar whinge as 'about the most unpleasant city in England'. I found digs of a most peculiar sort in the house of a very old and frail maiden lady, Miss Bagnol, whose life revolved around the Catholic Church. 'There are little shrines and holy pictures everywhere, in the hall, up the stairs and in all the bedrooms. Against one wall in the dining room there is a great stack of holy pictures with frames damaged or glass smashed, which have either blown down in the night or been set upon by atheist lodgers. There is also a cat, and an ancient Victorian water-closet with an intricate motif of flowers and herbs decorating the enamel bowl.' It was the first time I had ever slept on, or more accurately in, a feather mattress, and once I'd got used to the idea that it must have been at least fifty years old and that I was lying where generations had lain before me, it had a weird cosiness.

At the theatre I had few complaints. In the same letter I wrote: 'This is the first time I have seen a play really produced. The director knows his script inside out, as well as having a thorough knowledge of the actual history which he uses to amplify what's in the play. He is also a performer, and a very inventive one, and I get the feeling that there's probably not a part that he couldn't have a pretty good shot at. This is sometimes a little daunting.' Douglas Seale was a small, graceful man with a charm that on first encounter you might describe as elfin. On closer acquaintance, as you watched him prance through rehearsals with a driven, nervy energy, the image of the elf occasionally made room for the satyr. There was something a little dangerous about him that all of us in the company were careful to respect. He was to be the first of a number of gifted directors for whom I would work in the next few years, something which, when I became a director myself, was to make me thankful for my time as a performer. Actors are in a position to observe and assess a variety of directors at work. A director, however, is familiar with the process in only one rehearsal room – his own. Some years later Douglas Seale moved to North America where he continued directing but also resumed his career as a performer. When, in 1983, I was casting Noises Off for its New York production, Dougie came in to the office to read for the part of the elderly

burglar. He had changed very little: the same smile of misleading blandness, the same brown eyes as alert and nervy as a squirrel's. I was
delighted to see him again, though it seemed almost improper that I
should be the one now doing the interviewing. Fortunately, he read so
well I was able to offer him the part on the spot, and he went on to
perform it brilliantly for over a year.

If at the start of one's career the theatre seems a vast and impenetrable kingdom, such is the rate of attrition that it soon shrinks to a
small, accessible one, and the survivors cross and re-cross each others'
paths throughout their lives. *Henry V* was to be my first encounter
with Albert Finney, but by no means the last. We were all curious
about this nineteen-year-old who was getting such an extraordinary
break at the very start of his career – curious and perhaps a little
resentful. He, in turn, appeared to be on his guard, thrown into the
midst of this company of largely middle-class pros, and he wore his
North Country background like armour. I wanted to like him and be
liked in turn, but I was too proud to defer to him as I might to a leading man my own age or older. Like many very young and very talented
people he was a disconcerting mixture of vulnerability and arrogance.
One evening we found ourselves sharing a table in the restaurant on
Platform 4 of New Street Station. This served generous portions of
things like fried plaice and gammon steaks, both with a mountain of
chips, and being next door to the theatre was popular with actors who
wanted to eat before the show. Albert wore a sweater and I daresay
I was in one of my effete, hand-stitched tweed jackets. Hoping this
might be a chance to get to know each other better, I started asking
him about himself – were there other actors in the family? What did
his father do? The answers shot back – 'No!' and 'Plumber!' – as if
putting a full stop to this line of conversation. As I was later to learn,
his father wasn't a plumber but a bookmaker, quite a successful one,
an occupation Shirley's father had adopted rather late in life after a
series of false starts. We might have gone on to have a conversation
about it, but such intimacy would have to wait.

Throughout what must have been a testing rehearsal period for him
Albert showed remarkable nerve. At the dress rehearsal we learnt that
he had decided to go on without make-up, something unheard of,
particularly in Shakespeare. The accepted wisdom (quite untrue) was
that without a layer of greasepaint and all sorts of subtle lines and
shadows an actor wouldn't light properly. Dispensing with make-up

was almost tantamount to going on stage naked. Besides, it meant abandoning a ritual that many actors believed calmed nerves before a performance and raised self-esteem. It didn't bother Albert that his face had a few teenage spots and a winter pallor which first night nerves would do nothing to diminish. Henry V himself probably looked much the same just before Agincourt. He had a triumph in the part, as good a performance as any in his career. There was an underlying anger, a sense of scores to be settled, which made this and much of his early work so arresting. The text was spoken plainly and in his own way, without so much as a nod to any of the leading actors of the day. Dougie had staged the scene before the walls of Harfleur with Henry's exhausted troops huddled at the very front of the auditorium where the orchestra pit normally would be, as if they had retreated to the security of a trench. He had Albert crouch on the lip of the stage immediately above them and give the speech, 'Once more into the breach, dear friends, once more / Or close the wall up with our English dead,' in a desperate whisper, restlessly moving back and forth along the line. This was clearly the turning point of a military operation that could go either way. It was an audacious break with the rhetorical tradition, in which the outcome of the battle always seems a foregone conclusion.

The founder of the Birmingham Rep was Sir Barry Jackson, still at seventy-seven the presiding figure at the theatre. Without him and one or two other private individuals – Miss Horniman at Manchester, Lilian Baylis at the Old Vic, Granville Barker at the Royal Court – there would have been precious little serious theatre in the first half of the twentieth century. I describe him in a letter: 'Sir Barry Jackson himself came to see rehearsals yesterday, still sprightly and dapper. He is reputed to have supported the British theatre over the years to the tune of a million pounds from his own fortune, acting as a private patron the way the state does on the Continent. His definition of a successful theatre is not one which necessarily makes money but one which plays to packed houses.' Sir Barry's family had made their pile in industry; for most of his life he'd been giving it back. He always presented a respectable appearance, very upright in a dark, three-piece suit with fob watch. His expression was as habitual – an intent look of expectation, as if he was certain that something interesting was just about to happen. It was exactly the look of the dedicated theatregoer, already in his seat, just at the moment that the curtain rises.

In the most discreet way possible, Sir Barry was gay, and he had a private secretary, not, I think a partner, who, unlike his employer, did not attempt to curtail a certain extravagance of manner. I often used to run into him at lunchtime at the railway restaurant and we would eat together. Tom was always in and about the theatre and was often to be found watching the show from the wings. One *Henry V* matinee I caught his eye just as I was about to make an entrance as Exeter and throw the gauntlet down to the King of France. It was my most diffi-cult scene, particularly as the director had insisted that it be played very aggressively and at shrieking volume. I kept on thinking how much better C. Aubrey Smith, the Hollywood actor famous for his British colonels, would have been in the part. I was dressed in full chain mail (actually coarse string netting painted silver), consisting of a jersey with hood above and, below, what was effectively chain-mail panty-hose. Just as I was psyching myself up for a bellicose entrance, Tom shot me a twinkling aside. 'You and your Dorothy Ward legs!' he whispered, comparing me to the famous pantomime principal boy. That afternoon the scene lacked a certain gravitas. Shirley came up the following weekend to see the show, and said afterwards about Albert, 'He's a real star, isn't he?' That I could more or less take, but her next remark was offensive not only to me but to the memory of Dorothy Ward, 'And he has the best legs in the company!'

One lunchtime, coming down the steps to the railway restaurant, I found a mass of strange people strung out along the platform. Some were sitting on their luggage, silent and apathetic, others talking in worried little groups. You could tell from the small differences in the cut of their clothes and from the cast of their features that they weren't English. In the restaurant I was told that they were Hungarian refugees who had managed to get out after the Russian invasion, now on their way to be resettled in various parts of Britain. It was a grim winter day, and the view of Birmingham along the diminishing railway tracks can't have been encouraging. I had just finished *Darkness at Noon*, Koestler's devastating indictment of Russian communism, and this sea of anxious faces endorsed his every word. The tanks had rolled into Budapest just five days after the vainglorious Suez gamble, yet no British paper, not even, I think *The Observer*, had dared to suggest a connec-tion between the two interventions. It would have been too shaming. My belief was that had not the West squandered its moral capital at Suez, the Russians would have thought long and hard before invading Hungary.

In the theatre one piece of luck tends to engender another, and for the first time in my career I found myself on something of a roll. Because of its young star *Henry V* had attracted national attention, and one of our visitors had been the hugely prestigious Shakespeare Memorial Theatre. As a result I was now contemplating the most exciting offer of my career: the European tour of Peter Brook's production of *Titus Andronicus*, starring Laurence Olivier and Vivien Leigh. This had been the hit of the previous season at Stratford-upon-Avon, and the only actor, apart from spear carriers, not available from the original company was James Grout. It was his part, the Roman Captain, that I was being offered, not a large role but one with a good speech that paved the way for Titus' first entrance and a clear line through the production. I would be named in the programme and no doubling required.

I kept a journal during the rehearsals which records a typically neurotic start to the engagement. On the first morning I was so preoccupied by what would be appropriate attire that I left the flat later than I intended and, seeing not a bus in sight, panicked and caught a taxi. I asked the driver to let me out at Cambridge Circus, thinking perhaps that it would be less ostentatious if I walked to the Scala Theatre rather than be seen arriving at the stage door by cab. Once there, I realised I'd made an awful mistake, and that rehearsals were being held not at the Scala but at the Stoll. With only five minutes to spare I ran back along Tottenham Court Road looking for yet another taxi, and managed to hail one exactly where the previous cab had let me out. I reached the Stoll with a minute to spare, sweat running down inside the legs of my trousers and seven shillings out of pocket.

On stage, among the gathered company, there was time to get my breath. A few yards away were the great stars, Laurence Olivier and Vivien Leigh. I watched them reuniting with the other principals, like important arrivals on a railway platform who exchange kisses and hugs among the porters and the passers-by. They didn't yet know me, but I knew them, their faces, their voices, the way they moved almost as well as my own family. On screens all over Sydney I'd seen their eyes, as big as headlamps, mist with feeling; I'd seen them laugh, kiss and lament in monochrome and colour. And here they were, a few yards away, tinted miniatures of their other selves, stars whose two-dimensional image had been among the first to spread across the world like a new virus. In that brief period of 'the talkies', before the theatre had lost its prestige with the general public, before television had made screened entertainment commonplace, this acting elite held sway in both mediums, playing to audiences whom a surfeit of drama had yet to break down into that more sluggish and sceptical component, the viewer. They were famous, rich, lacquered in glamour and magically skilled. And unique among this unique generation was Laurence Olivier, who had somehow juggled huge celebrity with artistic achievements of the highest order. Was it any wonder that I found this day significant, a completion to a journey of twelve thousand miles and seven years? Here I was, on 22 April 1957, sharing the stage with the greatest actor of his generation.

Such intimations of destiny are important to young actors, whose lives are mainly contingent, depending on chance and the whims of other people. But as we started on the day's work reality was quick to intrude, and the subterranean struggle between generations to begin. Here is my first day's comment: 'Seeing Sir Laurence across the stage from me with his script in his hand and his glasses perched on the end of his nose was to realise that he was just another actor like me, a man who had to shave in the morning and probably feels sleepy after lunch. I look at him now like a puzzle to be solved, a nut to be cracked, and watching him just today, moving about the stage with his relaxed comedian's rhythm, I think I'm already getting at his secret.' Most of the newcomers to the cast were young males in the lower half of the company, and, as the week progressed and our excitement at landing the job diminished, rehearsals became an agony of watching and hoping to be watched. I studied these contemporaries as they assumed expressions or struck attitudes which would testify to their untapped abundance of talent and keenness, saw the foolishness of it, but at the same time couldn't help doing the same thing myself. I watched Olivier constantly, while appearing not to do so, and one of the things I noticed was that he was often watching us. His eyes kept swinging over the newcomers, assessing us perhaps or just practising which name went with which face. I also noticed that Olivier smoked Olivier cigarettes, a brand, like others named after famous performers, Du Maurier and De Reske, no longer on the market; that in the first week he never wore the same outfit twice, and that he and Vivien Leigh frequently gave rather rehearsed displays of affection, as if the rest of the company, like a theatre audience, weren't really there. Apart from the brittle artificiality of these moments he seemed in exceptionally down-to-earth good spirits, and no wonder. He had just finished the run of *The Entertainer* at the Royal Court and was now embarking on a revival of his most striking success in a classical role since the days of *Richard III* and *Oedipus Rex*.

It was, however, Peter Brook who most dominated my first week. *Titus Andronicus* was quite as much his triumph as Olivier's. He had not only directed it, but composed the music and overseen the ground-breaking design, an austere, monochrome conjuror's box which would unexpectedly open up to reveal a splash of luminous colour. It did not reject conventional theatricality with quite the flourish of his later *Midsummer Night's Dream*, but was already pointing in that direction. It was like nothing we had seen before. Since I was the only newcomer with lines and with an important speech that came early in the play, I was quickly thrown into the thick of rehearsals, but Brook responded to my situation with tact and quickly earned my trust. He had that concentration, in which empathy and detachment are somehow combined, that I was beginning to recognise as the mark of a good director. It was a pleasure to watch him as he watched us, his small, bright eyes flicking here and there, taking everything in, his expression one of involved amusement – a signal to all of us that though we were working we were also at play. He could sometimes be sharply impatient, and I record one such occasion. 'At this afternoon's rehearsal Peter Brook really put his actors through the mill. Not me, fortunately, though I felt strongly for those concerned. It reinforced my conviction that it helps if a director has some experience of acting. All of Brook's points were perceptive, but the remedies were needlessly painful. He hammered away at the externals – inflections and movements – until the poor actors were quite undermined and confused. Just a word or two at a slightly deeper level would probably have done the trick in half the time. If an actor has the right concept of a scene then the rest follows. If he has the wrong one, then no amount of detailed direction can help him.' This, of course, is the actor speaking. As a director I wish things were as simple. Occasionally Peter had a go at me, but I never found it upsetting, because it always seemed to be about the work upon which we were both engaged, not about me personally. 'Peter Brook,' I wrote, 'has the knack of treating everyone exactly the same from the stars down. Yesterday he buzzed about the auditorium, stinging indiscriminately.'

By and large, however, I was having the time of my professional life. One day's entry begins: 'I am beginning to mistrust myself; I am too happy in this job. I keep thinking that the next day's rehearsal will bring me down to earth again.' This never happened. Just being on stage with Olivier and hearing him pitch that extraordinary voice to the back of the auditorium with the precision of an arrow was excitement enough. He was forty-nine, at the zenith of his powers and luxuriating in the relaxed ride occasionally afforded by the theatre when a great success is given a second lease of life. Every young actor in the company knew his opening speech by heart, and impressions of his unique delivery resonated along corridors and in dressing rooms. On came the war-weary old soldier to a solemn march, accompanied by the coffins of his sons killed in battle, and raised one hand in a Roman salute.

> Hail, Rome, victorious in thy mourning weeds!
> Lo, as the barque that hath discharged her fraught
> Returns with precious lading to the bay
> From which at first she weighed her anchorage,
> Cometh Andronicus, bound with laurel boughs,
> To re-salute his country with his tears,
> Tears of true joy for his return to Rome.

Most of this he spoke in one sustained breath, making a sound as assured in its reserves of power as a plane as it starts to move down the runway. And if ever a performance took wing it was his Titus. The Street Scene about a third into the play remains the most extraordinary fifteen minutes I have ever experienced in the theatre. I watched from the side of the stage every time it was rehearsed, at every performance on tour and in London, and never ceased to be amazed by it. In a way it was the justification for doing the play in the first place, and nothing that followed, either in the writing or the acting, could match it. Olivier cobbled the rest of his part together with a series of vocal and physical surprises that owed as much to theatrical guile and experience as they did to imagination. The Street Scene was on another plane.

On the page it is an improbable string of horrors redeemed to some extent by language. It begins with Titus pleading for the lives of two of his sons as their judges escort them offstage to arbitrary execution. A third and only remaining son tries to forestall the sentence, only to suffer banishment. Next Titus' brother, Marcus, leads on his daughter, Lavinia, who has first been raped, then had her tongue cut out and her hands lopped off to prevent her putting a name to her assailants. Titus' misfortunes are not over. Aaron, the Moor, appears and offers him a grim bargain; if he will allow his own hand to be cut off it will be accepted in exchange for the lives of his condemned sons. Titus agrees and his betrayal becomes absolute. A Messenger enters returning his hand to him together with the severed heads of his two sons. It is now given to his brother to lament. Titus says nothing.

> MARCUS  Why art thou still?
> TITUS  Ha, ha, ha!
> MARCUS  Why dost thou laugh? It fits not with this hour.
> TITUS  Why, I have not another tear to shed.

The production handled the physical horrors with a discretion that by distancing them purged them of melodrama and gave them an ominous credibility. Lavinia's mutilations were suggested not by stage blood but by red ribbons spilling from her wrists and mouth. When Titus lost his hand to Aaron it was with his back to the audience, conveyed by a spasm of the shoulders and the horrific sound of the chop, and the two heads and the severed hand were returned to him in wicker cages, so that Titus at first could only guess at the contents within. In England the production had been praised as a brilliant interpretation of a ghoulish and unlikely play, but when we performed it in Poland and Yugoslavia, countries in which the memory of the Nazi Occupation were very much alive, its horrors were accepted as the literal truth. Recently I read of an incident in South Africa in which some youths occupied a house randomly chosen in a prosperous white suburb and held the wife captive. As each of her three children returned from school they hanged them one by one in front of her. When the husband returned from work he, too, was hanged. Only then did they kill the woman. It was Olivier's comprehension, tapping into some recess of melancholic dread inside himself, of what it must be like to experience the very worst that life has to offer, that gave the scene its mesmeric power; that and the paradoxical actor's relish of knowing that he was on to something that could freeze an audience in its seats.

He charted Titus' agony stage by stage. With his beloved daughter he was like an animal in a trap that in its misery turns on itself.

> What fool hath added water to the sea,
> Or brought a faggot to bright-burning Troy?
> My grief was at the height before thou cam'st,
> And now like Nilus it disdaineth bounds.
> Give me my sword, I'll chop off my hands too.

The text is shot through with imagery of the sea.

> For now I stand as one upon a rock
> Environed with a wilderness of sea,
> Who marks the waxing tide grow wave by wave,
> Expecting ever when some envious surge
> Will in his brinish bowels swallow him.

The metaphor reaches its height when, having sacrificed his own hand, he likens his daughter to the raining sky, himself to the ocean. His brother, Marcus, has counselled him: 'But yet let reason govern thy lament,' and Titus replies:

> If there were reason for these miseries,
> Then into limits could I bind my woes.
> When heaven doth weep, doth not the earth o'erflow?
> If the winds rage, doth not the sea wax mad,
> Threat'ning the welkin with his big-swoll'n face?
> And wilt thou have a reason for this coil?
> I am the sea.

And here Olivier took a huge, strangled breath, a guttural intake which suddenly exploded on the next sentence.

> Hark how her sighs do blow.
> She is the weeping welkin, I the earth.
> Then must my sea be moved with her sighs,
> Then must my earth with her continual tears
> Become a deluge overflow'd and drown'd.

The text tumbling out of him like lava from a volcano, he suddenly rose and propelled himself to one side of the stage as if his pain was something physical from which he had to shake himself free. The speech over, he stood quite still, the only sound his exhausted breathing, the only movement on stage the rise and fall of his chest. Into this stillness came the Messenger with the heads of his two sons. It was then that Marcus asks his question, 'Why dost thou laugh?' And Titus replies, 'Why, I have not another tear to shed.'

The French star Pierre Fresnay once described an actor as 'a sculptor in snow', and Olivier was fond of quoting him. Titus was above all a shaped performance. In the Street Scene he left outlines of himself trailing in one's mind as graphic as an illustration by William Blake, and he organised the verse into great blocks and ascending steps of language, welded together by the remorseless pulse of the iambic pentameter. It was acting as soaring as architecture, the way the structure in one of Brahms' great orchestral finales can sometimes seem almost palpable. What rescued it from contrivance were those moments of behavioural truth, insights into Titus' plight, that were not only psychological but physiological. At one performance I was amazed when, at the end of the speech I've described, his breath came in stops and starts, with moments in between in which he seemed to have stopped breathing altogether. Doctors are taught this is symptomatic of major shock. He had intuited it, perhaps hardly aware of what he was doing or how powerful it made the moment, because it was the only time it happened.

Yet there was a catch. Titus, like all of Olivier's stage work, was such a constructed thing, beginning with how the man looked (another of his brilliant make-ups), how he sounded and moved, combined with the inventiveness and flair for the theatrical moment that were his hallmark, that if you saw him on one of those odd nights when, as it were, the Force wasn't with him, his performance could fall away into its component parts. Contrivance was all his detractors could ever see. The actor with whom I was assigned a hotel room on the tour was one of them; he compared him detrimentally to the great pre-war actors of the continental theatre, none of whom, incidentally, he had ever seen. The miracle that I thought I was witnessing each night passed over his head.

Few of Olivier's great stage moments survive translation to the screen. On film he tries to repeat by an effort of will that which, in the theatre, the presence of a willing audience elicited from him. He could smell their attention, their stillness and eventually their submission, and he stalked them like prey. 'Got 'em!' he is said to have whispered to his fellow actors on the first night of *Oedipus Rex*, as he turned away after his famous and protracted howl of recognition and despair. At the height of one of these great moments – the audience riveted, the auditorium ringing with his voice – there was something in the performance almost akin to relaxation, as if what we were seeing was only a part of the power available to him. On film you sense exertion, and the results to those who loved his work on stage are often unsettling because what you see is the very opposite of what you experienced in the theatre – the limitations of this sort of acting. There is one precious strip of film, taken during a live charity performance of *The Entertainer*, that captures the great performer as he was at his best. Like Fred Astaire dancing he might just as well be airborne. Later in life he insisted he no longer enjoyed acting, but I don't think this was quite true. When the juices were flowing he probably enjoyed it too much. But increasingly a triumphant night left him with misgivings about being able to repeat it, and when this was compounded with fear about remembering his lines his pleasure in acting was all but eroded, at least until he was actually on stage. Besides, his performances were so audacious, characterised by moments in which there was always the possibility of humiliating misjudgements or even physical danger, that, like many great artists, he became intimidated by the very standards he himself had set. He was an actor of the greatest courage, the more so because he had the intelligence to know exactly the risks he was running. This could leave him moody and beleaguered when preparing a new part, but on *Titus* we saw none of this until the dress rehearsal in Paris.

What distinguished both our star and our director was their curiosity. Nothing that went on at rehearsals, on stage or off, failed to engage them. One morning I had rehearsed my brief speech, and in spite of some tactful direction from Brook, couldn't get it right. That afternoon, feeling quite depressed, 'I was standing at the side waiting to make an entrance when Sir Laurence suddenly turned to me and said, "You've got a very good voice, a fine voice, but if I might just suggest, try pitching it further forward. Up here." (He tapped his frontal sinuses) "Just for a day or two to see how it goes." More than this excellent advice what bucked me up was the fact that I had been noticed and, however briefly, thought about. Those few considered words warmed my entire afternoon.' On another occasion when we had our first run-through in costume I was just about to go on and make my speech when the stage management thrust on me a huge military standard, twelve feet of metal piping crowned with a top-heavy emblem of skull and horns. This was a complete surprise to me. I struggled on stage with it, hopelessly out of step with the music, and tried to say my lines with the standard swaying about in front of me like a tree in a high wind. I may have had a banner but my part vanished through the cracks in the stage floor.

During a break between scenes when the company had gone back to their dressing rooms, I returned to the empty stage and tried to work out how to handle this huge prop. Olivier had spotted me from the back of the auditorium and was now on stage. 'Look,' he said, 'If you hold the thing here, you can get a purchase with your other hand here, then when you have to speak, you can put it down and swing it clear of your body – like this.' For some reason his use of the word 'purchase', seemed very characteristic and apt. In my journal I conclude: 'In the way he put it down and turned to the auditorium with a slight heave of the chest and a lift of the jaw, he gave me a clue to the playing of the scene that could never properly be explained to me in words.'

That afternoon I felt bold enough 'to mention how much I'd liked *The Entertainer*, and he chatted with me most unaffectedly for ten minutes or so, making sly fun of the producer, Tony Richardson, who apparently had tried to bring the Stanislavsky Method into the rehearsal room. "I didn't tell him that *An Actor Prepares* had been passed around the dressing rooms when I was at the Birmingham Rep," he said. "We all read it thirty years ago." I felt ridiculously flattered to be granted this conversation, as it were actor to actor, although why one should be surprised by civility in a powerful and successful man I don't really know. I suppose you're always so conscious of how easily they could harm you that you're overcome with gratitude when they don't.' This last observation clearly indicates that I am trying to keep my head, but, like most of the company, I was by now thoroughly seduced. Doubtless this had also been part of his intention.

If these anecdotes are a shade reminiscent of old Red fables about how Uncle Joe Stalin, walking in the country, comes across a comrade struggling to change the tyre of his tractor, and, unrecognised, rolls up his sleeves and does the job for him, it's because even this tarnished and preposterous propaganda, once so widely believed, says something relevant to the gift of leadership. As I would later learn, Olivier was no better and no worse than the next man (or more accurately he was a lot better and a lot worse), but he was also one of those uncommon individuals who see in the authority that comes their way the opportunity, even the obligation, to exercise their better qualities. As an actor-manager he led from the front, taking more risks than his subordinates, assuming a heavier workload and great responsibilities. These are Roman virtues, and his assumption of them added to his credibility when he played a general like Titus, or a warrior like Coriolanus.

His concern for young actors at the beginning of their careers was genuine. In the acting profession he believed in the importance of succession, the torch being passed from Garrick to Kean to Macready to Irving and now to him. Fifteen years later, when I worked for him at the National Theatre as an Associate Director and we held general auditions, I often saw him brighten the day of some beginner just as he had once brightened mine. Whatever the age or inexperience of the terrified actor who came into his presence he always dignified them with the appellation 'Mister' or 'Miss' so-and-so, and occasionally had them stay a while so that he could pass on some vocal technique or trick of relaxation that he thought might help. Once an actor had established himself, of course, it was a different matter. Now he had a competitor, and he assessed them according to their weaknesses, not their strengths, and often with a marked lack of generosity. After he left the National and his health had gone, he once told me that one of his big regrets was that he had never held any master classes in which he could have passed on to the young the things he'd learnt about playing big houses, techniques that allow one's physical and vocal presence to register in the last row of the uppermost balcony. These are dying skills, and perhaps redundant ones now that sound ampli-fication and lighting can do so much for the performer. During the dress rehearsal of the first musical I directed on Broadway, *City of Angels*, I would see our talented but inexperienced ingénue acquire, in the time it took her to get miked-up, a stage presence which in the fifties would have taken ten years' work. Even so, to stand in the very back of a theatre watching a performance by someone like Maggie Smith, confident that there will not be a word, a look or even a thought from which one will be excluded, is to realise that something is being lost.

'This is the last week of rehearsal,' begins my entry for 8th May. 'And on Monday we at last got around a piano to bash out a standard version of the funeral chant we all have to hum in the first scene. While we gathered at the footlights Peter Brook went into the orches-tra pit and picked out the tune with an index finger. Seeing him there standing before the piano, very short and upright and nodding his head fiercely to each note, I had a picture of him as he must be when he works on a production at home – the door closed, the text open and ideas coming fast and furious. I imagine a good deal of striding about, of humming and scribbling, all the more intense for being private. At rehearsals he is a pleasing man to watch at work. When things go well he stands wrapped up in his raglan overcoat looking rather like a scientist surveying with amused satisfaction the installation of some huge piece of sophisticated equipment. When things go wrong he is transformed into a precocious schoolboy, furious because some stupid adult has been fiddling with his chemistry set.'

The following week we were in Paris. Here's how I describe events leading up to our first night at the Théâtre Sarah Bernhardt. 'The day after we arrived we had a stopping dress rehearsal, which went on from about three in the afternoon till twelve at night. Our minds were still on the Channel crossing and finding suitable accommodation, and the rehearsal was a dead labour. The afternoon light of Paris seeped into the theatre from the flies to ridicule our efforts, and the French stagehands seemed positively obstructive as they muttered and argued with each other over the public address system. In the auditorium there was a dense pack of journalists and photographers on the hunt, and all afternoon the cameras were clicking and snapping like some ominous massing of insects. When the stars made their entrances the noise became positively orgasmic. This dress rehearsal was an agony for Olivier. He covered the distance as if it were a desert, plodding on through endless hold-ups and delays with only the presumption of disaster ahead. Between scenes he would slump onto a step with what seemed complete exhaustion, generally to the accompaniment of a muttered oath. I was seeing the other side of the talent penny, and I couldn't help remembering all those doom-laden dress rehearsals in rep. We made four false starts on the Street Scene, and each time he returned to his mark and sank down on the steps with, first, an "Oh God," then an "Oh Christ," then an "Oh Jesus," and, finally an "Oh fuck." At one point I heard him say "They're going to laugh us off the fucking stage." I felt for him, but I was also curiously elated to find that this, the most renowned of actors, could be deserted by his muse at a dress rehearsal. Besides, I was certain in my own mind that the show, and particularly its star, were going to enjoy a huge success. Is this depression on the way to a first night an unconscious way of reserving vitality? It follows the bigger the actor, the greater the gloom.

'The performance the following night suggested this was certainly the case with Sir Laurence. Towering is the only word for his perform-ance. The evening was successful beyond all our expectations. To ensure the smooth running of the show the cast had been asked to vacate the wings when they were off between scenes, and I realised that for the first time I wouldn't be able to watch the Street Scene. As the others went back up the iron steps that led from the stage to the dressing rooms, I dawdled behind and waited unobserved on the bottom step. I argued to myself that technically I wasn't *in* the wings; I was elevated nine inches above them. Even in the dark, seeing nothing but a spill of light, it was as thrilling an experience as I've had in the theatre. I couldn't believe the sounds coming from the stage. It was as if the building itself, never mind the people in it, was holding its breath in awe. The entire cast were surpassing themselves, particularly Anthony Quayle as Aaron the Moor, and the last act was played by an assured company, who knew with certainty what to expect at the curtain. Or rather thought they did. The reception was, literally, fantastic, and could have gone on till dawn. Clapping, stamping, cheering with the entire house on its feet. Eventually Peter Brook took a curtain, and the uproar started all over again. Finally there was nothing for us all to do but just stand there, grinning like children, allowing that ocean of enthusiasm to splash over us like warm, noisy surf.'

On the following Thursday, at a special matinee we gave for the French acting profession, many of whom were working themselves in the evening, Olivier was to top even his first night. There was no longer a prohibition about being in the wings, so I was able to watch. At the end of his 'I am the sea' speech there was an explosion of applause and some of the audience rose to their feet, the first and only time I have ever known this happen in the middle of a scene. Those few weeks in Paris represented the life of an actor at its most intoxicating. We had captured the city, and every night hordes of the celebrated and famous came to see the show. Afterwards there was usually a social event of matching glamour, one night a candlelit reception in a refurbished Renaissance palace at which, among the guests, a young and exquisite Elizabeth Taylor drew the eye like a tiny pearl in this opalescent shell of a building; another a party on a boat on the Seine which the novelist Irwin Shaw threw for the entire company. We were invited to a reception at the British Embassy, and to a matinee of *Cat on a Hot Tin Roof* where we were entertained afterwards by its star, another ravishing young woman, Jeanne Moreau. On 22nd May Laurence Olivier had his fiftieth birthday, and a group of us, on our way back up the iron staircase after the performance, were waylaid to have a drink with him in his dressing room. He poured us champagne with a hairy arm, dressed in the old-fashioned woollen vest he wore under his Titus costume, and gave a performance to suit this attire, that of a weathered old pro enjoying a drink with his fellow actors. During the day, and sometimes drunkenly late at night, the company separated and simply wandered the streets of Paris, only to re-encounter each other around every corner until finally it became a kind of joke.

All this was fun and exactly what I had hoped for from this most enviable of jobs, which would soon be taking me on to Venice. But, in truth, nothing that was to follow could match the excitement, or the privilege, of the weeks of rehearsal leading to those first few performances, and before we left Paris my journal, which I had intended to maintain throughout the tour, peters out in an uncompleted sentence.

# SEVEN

# And Another Closes

The Fenice in Venice was the most beautiful theatre I had ever seen, and in it we gave the worst performance of the tour. On opening night the boxes were filled with Venetian nobility, who were occupying their usual seats for no better reason than that it was customary. All we received from the packed house by way of response was a mild curiosity. One wondered if this was the sort of house people like Mozart had had to play to. You could feel their apathy from the moment the curtain rose, and, after Paris, the cast's surprise and discouragement. Sensing disaster, I went on and did my speech with all guns blazing, but they weren't impressed; neither with me nor with Laurence Olivier, who was on next. Before the Street Scene I saw him go to the prop table, tilt his head back, and with an eye-dropper run two streams of glycerine tears down his cheeks, the only time he ever stooped to this desperate measure. There was one ray of sunshine. At the post-mortem afterwards Peter Brook upbraided the company for not fighting back, but singled me out as the exception, and later that week in the local paper my performance in the part of 'Un Capitano Romano' actually got a mention. I still have the cutting, now as beige and dry as a pressed leaf and in a language I don't understand, somewhere at the bottom of a battered suitcase at another address.

Now the tour was under way a certain worldliness was beginning to nibble at the supremacy of the evening performance. Our days were becoming as important as our nights. There was so much to see, not to mention our eventful social life in the tireless charge of Vivien Leigh. If I haven't had much to say about our other great star up till now it's because her part in *Titus* was a small and not particularly suitable one. The brilliance of her work in films, and in particular her enduring

Scarlett, needs no endorsement from me. However, she was at least ten years too old for Lavinia, and although she still looked breathtaking on stage, once she had lost her tongue, her hands and her virginity, there was little for her to do but stand around as an emblem of suffering. And Vivien was not a person to stand around. If she couldn't be at the centre of the play, she was determined to be at the centre of the company's offstage life. Unrecognised by most of us, she was at the beginning of an upswing in one of her periodic bouts of manic depression. All we were aware of at first was that this famous, pretty woman, her face alight with delicate energy, was standing up for our interests. She never accepted an invitation unless it included the entire company, and by the time we had arrived in Warsaw she was organising social occasions of her own for us. One morning we were shepherded to the airport for a day trip to the ancient town of Cracow. On boarding the plane we discovered that we were one passenger too many, and since I had an eye infection and was feeling off-colour, I volunteered to drop out. Displeasure registered on Vivien's face like a light going out. She herself was indifferent to ailments, and besides, she had been looking forward to a stand-up fight with our Polish supervisor. Earlier in the week she had packed the company into two buses and we were driven far into the flat Polish countryside for a picnic by an ominous-looking lake. We had been told to bring our swimming costumes so a dip was obligatory. It was here my eye became infected, and here, too, that Vivien, splashing about in the brackish water, trod on a broken bottle and gashed her foot. We helped her to the shore, and someone remembered that I had once been a medical student, neglecting to observe that I was also a failed one. I examined the nasty cut and knew enough to advise an anti-tetanus shot as soon as we returned to town. In the meantime I poured vodka into the open wound and bound it up as best I could with a clean handkerchief.

The sensible course would have been to cut short the picnic and go back to Warsaw, but Vivien wouldn't hear of it. She hobbled about gamely for the rest of the afternoon without a word of complaint, and at the end of the day joined in the singing aboard the bus as we made our way homeward. It was impossible not to admire her pluck, though by this time we had grasped that it had an edge of craziness. She reminded me a little of some *principetta*, absolute in her whims, reigning over a small state in Renaissance Italy. The company was her principality, and she could be as charming or as deadly as the mood took her. By turns I was in her good books and her bad, and both experiences were alarming. At a reception at the British Embassy in Belgrade I found myself, drink in hand, unexpectedly standing beside her. She looked up at me with devastating sweetness and said, 'I hear you're Australian. I love Australians!' Her long affair with Peter Finch was common knowledge, so this was not a little provocative. She had barely finished the sentence when, from across the room, Olivier came swooping down upon us, and with a steely smile of unambiguous warning, directed first at her then as an afterthought at me, took her by the elbow and swept her out of sight. I was to taste her displeasure much later when we were playing in London at the Stoll Theatre. We had run into each other ascending the stairs to our dressing rooms, hers on the first floor, mine at the top of the building, and for want of something better to say I remarked on a cartoon that had appeared that week in the *Daily Express*. It showed Vivien protesting about the demolition of the St James's Theatre, where for some years Olivier had been actor-manager. At once I was made aware that I had said the wrong thing, but exactly why I had no idea. For some weeks thereafter, as far as Vivien was concerned, I might just as well have been in Siberia.

The complexity of touring a huge company to five countries in almost as many weeks was an invitation to human fallibility, and we had soon catalogued any number of narrow escapes as actors almost missed trains, almost got lost in strange cities or almost failed to appear for the evening performance. One afternoon in Venice I went searching for the Rialto with another member of the company, drawn ever deeper into the enthralling maze of streets. Over a dozen bridges, through as many squares, we turned and twisted for an hour and a half. Only when we stumbled on the famous bridge did we think of looking at our watches. In panic we saw that we had ten minutes before we were due back in our dressing rooms for that night's performance. A motor launch stood by in the Grand Canal. We each handed over what amounted to half a week's pay, went speeding down that wide, majestic loop of water and arrived at the stage door breathless. Later, when we consulted a map we saw that on our expedition we had progressed through a huge, irregular circle, and that the Teatro La Fenice and the Rialto were a few minutes' walk apart.

Our next stop was Belgrade, a long overnight journey that took us off the map of the familiar Europe. No English-speaking company had ever penetrated inside the Iron Curtain, and we had little idea what to expect. The first surprise when we woke in the morning was the beauty of the Yugoslavian landscape, sliding past us in a series of sudden valleys and rearing wooded hills, which some thirty years later I would see again in television news reports as a background to horrible events. The propaganda of the Cold War almost led one to believe that Technicolor would give way to black and white as you crossed the border, but my first impression of Belgrade was of the sameness of life wherever it is lived. Ticket collectors, garbage men or the man in some sort of peasant costume and a huge Serbian moustache whom I saw digging up the street – no political system could do much about the way most people were obliged to earn a living. There were many striking differences of details – the man with the moustache was one – and there was clearly less prosperity than in the West, but an exotically pretty woman was no less sexually assured as she walked along the pavement for having run up her dress herself from some remnant of material. Indeed, after Paris and Venice it was interesting to see people enjoying their lives in bars, restaurants and modest night spots despite having their acquisitive instincts tempered. Whatever was wrong with it, Tito's Yugoslavia was not Communist Russia.

Belgrade itself was not much of a city, having been bombed and vandalised by the Germans, and it was hardly improved by the muggy June heat. Its new buildings were ugly and utilitarian, and the Ottoman past was like a dusty residue in the streets. The wide Danube, not blue but khaki, passed by the city, and one day we watched a dead horse gliding downstream on the buoy of its own bloated belly. At the theatre, however, we were completely at home. As much as any embassy it was part of that sovereign territory to which theatres all over the world belong. The day we arrived a ballet was in rehearsal backstage, and along the corridors you could hear the stop and start of a piano and the distant thump of dancing. I opened a wrong door by mistake and came upon a girl so beautiful I felt my jaw go slack. I had caught her just as she was about to change out of her rehearsal gear. She recognised me as one of the British visitors and answered my grimaces of apology with a shake of the head and a devastating smile. Then silence. The lack of a common language left us either side of a sheet of glass. I had to turn away and shut the door on what at that moment had become the love of my life. Later, queuing up for a glass of lemon tea in the theatre canteen, I caught another glimpse of her, but she'd melted through the door with a second smile just as I was being served. I hung around the stage door for half an hour, hoping for quite what I wasn't sure, but didn't see her then or on any of the days that followed. Others were succumbing to the yearning induced by foreign travel, and every time the train pulled away to some new destination there would be a member of the company who, on the basis of a shared cup of coffee or just a look, would feel himself severed from the promise of bliss. Like an army on the move, the young men were permanently and mournfully on the lookout. We were never anywhere for more than a week, and only the gays, who went around in a surreptitious, light-hearted pack, seemed to have any idea about how to get what they wanted.

The opening night in Belgrade more than made up for the tepid reception in Venice. Between his scenes Olivier walked up and down in the wings trying to memorise a sentence in Serbian, which he'd asked someone to write out phonetically on a scrap of paper. When he spoke these few words at the curtain call it was as if the entire audience were stretching out their hands to him. So many flowers rained down on the stage floor that, like a snowfall, they obliterated it. It was a reception to match Paris, but with a difference. Here the intensity of goodwill was a coded but unmistakable message: we are your friends, and only the politicians and the military shake their fists at one another. Afterwards at the stage door the entire audience seemed to have reassembled. When the Oliviers appeared there was renewed applause, and again flowers, hundreds and hundreds of individual blooms, which, as the crowd parted to allow them passage to their waiting car, were thrown in their path like a carpet unrolling. It was very moving, one of those occasions when what people are permitted to express is fed and intensified by what they are not. You felt that this event would resonate far beyond the walls of the theatre.

In Zagreb we were back in a more familiar Europe. Its Austro-Hungarian past was visible everywhere you looked, in the pretty buildings and parks, the neglected but still functioning cathedral, and in the enormous turn-of-the-century hotel in which we were billeted. This last was now run with exceptional inefficiency by the State, but it was still luxurious, with spacious bedrooms, and in the adjoining bathrooms gigantic porcelain tubs fitted with polished taps as sturdy as brass bells. In the circular dining room you waited an eternity for breakfast whilst a dozen waiters stood against the wall shifting from foot to foot. On our last night in Zagreb there was no performance and instead the company was entertained at a big gathering in the hotel. I met a young, dark girl with a simplicity of manner and a beauty so natural that immediately I was in love again. I reached for her hand beneath the table and found it to be trembling. Later, on a park bench under some trees we spent the rest of the night clinging to each other, our faces as close and framed as the reflections in two hand mirrors. We taught each other single words in our two languages with rapt playfulness. It was unconsummated perfection – less a contradiction in terms than it first appears – and boarding the train next morning was like going into exile. Her name was Karolina Bevc, and I wrote to her from our next stop, Vienna, but the censor, the postman or her own prudence got in the way and I never had a reply. Much later, when war divided the country, I wondered what had happened to her, this person whom I knew for only five or six hours of my life and with whom I had had an experience perhaps commonplace but which I can recall almost minute by minute.

Away from the theatre we were seeing less and less of Olivier and more and more of Vivien Leigh. She was at the height of her manic phase and needed no more than an hour or two's rest a night. Her husband, exhausted not only by her demands but by those of his part, was using the daylight hours to catch up on his sleep. Zagreb boasted one state-run nightspot, the Ritz Bar, where after the show you could dance or just sit in a banquette with a drink. It attracted actors from the company and, every night, Vivien, who had her regular table. She was attended by a Yugoslavian official assigned to watch over her, whom we all supposed to be a secret policeman. Interpreting his constant presence as a challenge, she determined to wear him down, and one night he sank drunk and unconscious underneath the table. The following day, we had a special noon matinee for schoolchildren. I arrived at the half-hour to find panic backstage. Vivien had disappeared. Having succeeded in giving the slip to her minder, she'd stayed out all night. In the auditorium you could already hear the expectant children gathering. They were chirruping in their hundreds, like birds massing for some migratory flight. It seemed appalling to deny them their Scarlett O'Hara.

With only ten minutes before the curtain was due to rise Vivien appeared at the stage door. She was somnambulistically drunk, not in the least unruly but quite stunned by sleeplessness and alcohol. She was spirited away to her dressing room like someone being rushed to Intensive Care. The waiting understudy was stripped of her costume, and Vivien, as passive as an articulated doll, was dressed and made up. The company watched her come down from her dressing room and onto the stage, the delicate drapes of her costume billowing behind her as if she was walking under water. She was in another element.

The performance began, and we all watched holding our breaths. She never forgot her lines, but there was always a dislocating pause before each speech like one of those international calls when the satellite is playing up. Nor did she forget her moves, though she took an age to get from one position to another and always arrived late. Olivier, ever conscious of his responsibilities, was pulling out all the stops, but his efforts to compensate only accentuated Vivien's strangeness. Basil Hoskins and I, waiting in the wings, found it such an agony to watch we turned away. 'I AM THE SEA!!' declaimed Olivier. Then we heard him step up the volume with each succeeding line until at last he was still and silent on the other side of the stage. This was the moment that in Paris had brought the French profession to their feet, but in place of their applause Vivien had decided to make an observation of her own. Her words were not angry or loud – the tone was almost affectionate – but they had the piercing clarity of a child's voice and penetrated every corner of the theatre. Basil and I stared at each other, hardly believing what we'd heard. We darted back to have a look. There stood Larry, leaning against the set and staring into space like a body strung out on barbed wire. A few feet away was Vivien, swaying gently back and forth like seaweed, and regarding him with the detachment of some delicate, sniffing animal. About this great moment of theatre she had given her verdict. To him, to the entire cast and to a thousand Croatian children. 'Silly cunt,' she had said. It was hideously, mortifyingly funny, and in the wings on the opposite side of the stage I could see other incredulous members of the company bent double as they tried to smother their laughter.

It was also extremely sad, but for the moment none of us could see that. Art had slipped on a banana skin, and Olivier, invincible in Paris, had become ridiculous in Zagreb. He would never forgive her, though as a couple they had probably long been doomed. And what an easy thing it was to puncture the presumption of an artist – to slash a picture, burn a book or humiliate a performer. No wonder the question people in the theatre are always asking each other is, 'What are you doing next?' There is not much safety in the present, none in the past, but in the future it can at least be imagined.

There was trouble of a different sort in Vienna. We were to play at that same Burgtheater that I had visited with Shirley at the end of our skiing holiday. The building had been damaged in the war, and in the restoration afterwards great care had been taken to give the auditorium a perfect acoustic. This, however, was the acoustic of engineers, not actors, who failed to understand that reverberation and a touch of echo can be very helpful to the spoken word. The old theatres in which we had been playing were typically structures of wood and plaster, and they resonated with the human voice. On the stage of the Burgtheater, soft and loud were barely distinguishable and even the applause seemed muted. Our perception of the opening night was that it had been lifeless. Later in the week Olivier had a mike installed at the front of the stage with speakers turned not in the direction of the audience but back towards him. Their function was not to increase audibility but to give back to the actor what had been taken from him, a sense of his own voice.

The first performance was further diminished by the magnificence of the reception laid on for us afterwards. The Burgtheater is monumentally round and at an upper level there is a gallery which encircles the building. Guests approached this gallery up a grandiose staircase where, drawn by the sound of a distant chamber orchestra playing Mozart, they proceeded in a huge curve towards the source of the music. A trail of candlelight led the way. Eventually, on the opposite side of the building, one came upon the musicians and the rustle of the gathering party. It was brilliantly organised, in flawless taste and extremely theatrical. In Britain there was no theatre as secure in its civic importance or as generously endowed as this. It was what we didn't have, a proper National Theatre. I wondered if our host, the Intendant, would remember the young actor who had previously gate-crashed his stage door, but he recognised me at once and greeted me with a courtesy even more amused and ironic than the year before. I also met some of the actors that I'd seen perform on that earlier visit. They, too, were friendly, but it was hard to gauge their response to the performance. Later that week they invited a few of us to see the sights of Vienna. We were standing on a hill overlooking the city when, rather guardedly, they began discussing the show.

'We don't do that anymore,' one of them said with a faint smile.

'What?' I asked.

'Roll our R's,' he replied.

It was true. Olivier's first words were 'Hail, Rome', and because he said 'Rrrome', so with my opening speech, 'Rrromans, make way,' did I.

'You still do that in England? We stopped doing that in the twenties.'

I felt myself blush. I was suddenly seeing our work from another's perspective, and it was as if someone had pointed out a gross imperfection in a loved one, which up till then I had either overlooked or been content to live with. No longer. I had seen the work of these actors and their judgement was not something I could easily dismiss; after all, they belonged to what was at that time the most sophisticated theatrical culture in Europe. In seconds my mind had riffled through the production looking for other vulnerable areas. For a start there was the performance of my compatriot, Frank Thring, who played Saturninus with the villainous grimacing of a silent-movie actor. What must they have made of him? In as little time as it takes for the sun to go behind a cloud, my faith in the production had been shaken, and this betrayal had come as much from within as without. In my subsequent career there would be many other occasions when some small thing – a single bad notice among a number of good ones, the murmured dissent of a friend – would be enough to topple the edifice of artistic belief. Yet somehow one must learn to buttress and protect it, because, finally, it is the only thing one has.

Fortunately, belief in the show came back with a rush at our next and last date of the tour, Warsaw, where audiences responded to it with the same heartfelt enthusiasm we'd experienced in Yugoslavia. Olivier was back on form, and even if he did roll his R's he was magnificent. I would continue to roll mine in an act of solidarity. Nowhere did the grim events of the play seem more plausible than they did in Poland. Every person one met had some extraordinary and horrific tale to tell about the German Occupation. Our interpreter, a pleasant plump girl in her late twenties, had worked for two years as a slave labourer in a factory, sleeping by her machine. Someone else had almost killed himself leaping from the end of a moving train as the Gestapo, on a hunt, came closer carriage by carriage. These were commonplace experiences. In a tentative, almost apologetic way our Polish hosts wanted us to know a little of what they had been through during the war, and one morning we were invited to a film show. We were told that, with defeat approaching, Hitler had decreed that the Poles, being a Slav people, were not entitled to a capital city, and teams of soldiers with dynamite and flame-throwers were dispatched throughout Warsaw. First each and every building was crudely numbered with white paint, then as systematically destroyed street by street. As always cameramen were on hand to record the achievement, and it was their footage that we were shown. I was embarrassed because so few of us had turned up.

Later that same day we were taken to the Old City, and I asked why the Germans had left this particular part of Warsaw intact – these ancient streets and lovely baroque churches. 'But this is all new,' I was told. I could hardly believe it. There seemed nothing approximate or 'neo' about these buildings. Down to the smallest carving on a stone lintel they had a look of complete authenticity. Somehow this country, though impoverished by war, had mustered the will and the resources to resurrect at least a part of their beloved city and the past that it embodied. I was told that it was really Canaletto who had rebuilt Warsaw. On his visits in the eighteenth century, the artist had made an immensely detailed record of its streets and buildings. It was his work, preserved in Venice, that enabled the Poles to rebuild the Old City with such passionate fidelity. This reconstruction, a testament to belief, was not the city's only architectural wonder. The other was the hideous Palace of Culture, Stalin's gift, and the only tall building in Warsaw, a testament to cynicism. It loomed over the city about as invitingly as the watchtower of a prison camp.

The Iron Curtain tour of *Titus Andronicus* was coming to an end. The company boarded a plane chartered from British European Airways, and we took off for London. A weary Sir Laurence spoke to us over the public address system quoting *Henry V*, 'Where ne'er from France returned more happier men.' Ahead of us was a ten-week season in London, booked into a huge barn of a theatre in Kingsway, the Stoll. We were the last show to play there before it was demolished. *Titus* had been my first long engagement, and I was experiencing, as I would later with my own productions, the curious sense of a show's life. First a production is born, in an atmosphere of excitement, risk and often pain. If the birth is successful there follows a splendid youth, when every performance is special and the public comes pressing in to greet the new arrival. Then comes a consolidating maturity, sometimes a matter of months, in some cases years, when the production settles down to become one participant among many in the cultural life of the town. Quite suddenly, the way a cat grows old, there is a sense of the end, quickly followed by a death, and the show is history. You pass the theatre where it played, and almost wonder if it ever happened. A new growth of photographs and hyperbolic press quotes has sprouted across the front of the building. Most of the time you're happy to see a production go, but not invariably. For instance, I can't pass the Virginia Theatre in New York where *City of Angels* played for two years without a flicker of that indignation felt by someone who comes home to find squatters in residence. I had invested so much belief and invention in the show that it was awful to see it killed off.

Even though *Titus* was to play twice as long in London as it had on the tour, I had the feeling that we were on our last lap. For one thing, Olivier was running out of steam. It was not only fatigue; he seemed to have gone with the part as far as he could go, and I suspected he had now grown weary of it. On the first night at the Stoll he made a weird curtain speech of flowery phrases and uncomfortable jokes, in which he almost gave the impression he was apologising for the evening. I stood by my watch at the Street Scene every night, and though his performance never altered in detail nor diminished in professionalism, that spell which had once been the rule became the exception. Sometimes when an old friend like John Mills was in front something would happen and he would amaze me all over again, but the sheer size of the theatre, over two thousand seats, and his own exhaustion made such occasions less frequent. On these special nights I longed to smuggle a tape-recorder backstage and preserve at least the sound of him in that one scene. I made enquiries with the company manager but was told that anything of the sort would be strictly forbidden. So the run came to an end, Laurence Olivier's performance died in the air, the theatre he had played in was cleared away as rubble, and I went on to my next job.

The new director of the Birmingham Rep, Bernard Hepton, had invited me back, this time for an entire season. It was just the sort of job I had been hoping for, and I would have been over the moon had it taken me to somewhere like Bristol. But Birmingham! And for six months! However, there was no question of turning it down. It was August and I had a spare fortnight before the first day's rehearsal, so I decided on a trip to Bude in Cornwall, where my father told me he had once caught some waves. This had been in the twenties, when he was studying for a postgraduate degree in London, and, so unfamiliar were the Cornish locals with the sport of body-surfing, that they sent a boat out to rescue him. I, too, found my waves, and thereafter for the next ten years if I found I had some spare time between jobs in the summer, I would take myself off to the West Country for a week by the ocean, and acquire a little of the scrubbed fitness I remembered from Australia.

Shirley, who had landed a promising new job working for a Rank executive at Pinewood Film Studios, joined me for the weekend. We faced another of our long separations, and had decided after many rueful conversations, to give it a certain formal standing. This time we would be officially apart, not necessarily for ever, but for as long as the job lasted. Couples were just beginning to use the term 'trial separation'. Circumstances and, on my part at least, inclination meant that infidelity was being built into the relationship. There was no one in my life of more importance, and I doubted if there ever would be in quite the same way, but the fact remained that something in me was still on the hunt. Perhaps it always would be. One of the principal reasons young men leave home for the big city, W. H. Auden said somewhere, is to find lots and lots of sex, and the sexual revolution, even if articulated in the language of Bloomsbury, was well under way in the fifties. Like all movements in which the line between principled argument and personal gratification is blurred (market forces would be another) there was a price to pay. In the meantime I was off to Birmingham and wondering whom I would meet.

Other surprises were waiting for me in this Midland city. To begin with the sun was shining, something that had never happened during *Henry V*, and I became aware of the sooty grandeur of the nineteenth-century architecture surrounding me – the vast railway stations and colonnaded civic and commercial buildings alive with pigeons, which had so adopted the protective colour of their habitat that sometimes it looked as if the Corinthian pediments were shifting and sprouting the odd wing. Like a flow of lava, this ponderous Victorian city had swept over a forgotten and more elegant Georgian one, just as in the sixties the Birmingham I was getting to know would again be obliterated under a second and much uglier flow of concrete.

I had arrived in autumn, a season which in England I dreaded because it meant the end of summer and the imminence of winter gloom, only to be taken aback year after year by its filtered beauty. Soon great flocks of migrating birds were swinging back and forth above the charcoal buildings like some giant Venetian blind opening and closing against the sky. At night, mist settled along streets steeped in the smell of the steam trains that cut through the city on tracks as wide and black as rivers. The place began to have the smudged romance of an old etching, the sort of thing you might have found covered in dust in that line of second-hand bookshops, stacked one beside another along the Edgbaston Road.

The Birmingham Rep occupied a narrow Art Nouveau theatre opposite the railway station that I considered the best space I had ever played, a perfect balance of intimacy and scale. Most of the audience were seated on a single steep rake rising away from the stage. A performer looked out not to a distant exit light or the blank front of a circle, but to a close bank of attentive people. As any visitor to the bullfight knows there is something about looking down at the action that generates feelings both of danger and of safety from it. It was from trees and high places that people once avoided predators or waited to ambush enemies, and this is perhaps why the galleries of Victorian theatres, in spite of their discomfort and distance from the stage, once encouraged a more excited response than that experienced in less vertiginous parts of the house. The pleasure of theatregoing has its precursors in much primitive behaviour. When, from an upstairs room, we watch unseen an incident in the street, we are doing precisely what we do when we go to the theatre – trying to extract a narrative from words and body language apprehended at a distance. The stadium from which we look down at the struggle of a sports event, the cathedral which takes the eye upwards to other possibilities, the empty building behind a wall at which we peer on tiptoes and which invites us to explore it – all can contribute to the excitement of a theatre space. And the reason so many modern theatres are dull is that they hardly acknowledge such things. They appear to know so little about us.

The first play of the season was Peter Ustinov's *Romanoff and Juliet*, one of his Iron Curtain comedies that capitalised on differences in national character. It was far too good-natured to say much about the murderous realities of the Cold War, but it was written with a flawless ear and was a delight to play, particularly as I had a part for which I was well suited, that of an innocent young American. With almost a month to rehearse it was a pleasure to go to work. Birmingham had two excellent critics, Rosemary Anne Sisson, who was also a playwright, and J. C. Trewin, whose paper, the *Birmingham Post*, had a similar prestige to the *Manchester Guardian* and was distributed nationally.

I kicked off the season with splendid notices from both. Albert Finney had returned to the company to play leads in the first three productions, so our audiences often contained high-powered visitors from London. Our fourth show was a musical, *School*, which was still uncast and about which there was much interest and speculation. It was based on Tom Robertson's Victorian comedy about a girls' school and the beaux the young ladies attract. Douglas Seale would be returning to direct. There were no trained singers in the company, so three of the leads had to be cast from outside. There was, however, a fourth lead, the more comic of the two young men who form attachments with the schoolgirls. (Thinking about the play again after so many years I'm suddenly aware how very curious the material was. At the time nothing could have seemed more wholesome.) This role also required some singing, but of the Rex Harrison rather than the Nelson Eddy variety, and it was a part I knew I could do well. The composer and lyricist, Christopher Whelan and Redmond Philips, visited Birmingham to ascertain the company's musical potential, and I gave a wobbly rendition of 'You're getting to be a habit with me', which I'd recently heard at the National Film Theatre in *Forty-Second Street*. Christopher took me through some scales, and a few days later I was told the part was mine.

Not unnaturally, I was extremely apprehensive on the first day's rehearsal. There was already talk of a West End transfer, so success in the part was not just important; it could change my career. I noticed that Dougie Seale seemed far more edgy than he'd been in *Henry V*. I was also aware that my part, this Victorian swell, Jack Poyntz, was one he could easily have played himself as a young man, and I thought I detected a certain scepticism in the way he was eyeing me. To be an actor is to make a brother of paranoia. Dougie's career had recently blossomed and he'd made the common mistake of accepting all the work which was now coming his way. He was running around the country from one production to another. As I would later learn, the first few days of a rehearsal period are the most demanding for a director. It's his responsibility to overcome the natural inertia that applies to any group at the start of a common endeavour. People look to him for ideas and answers when, like everyone else present, he may still be making up his mind about the best way to go. It needs preparation and thought beforehand to get through the first week comfortably; otherwise you're dependent on energy, bluff and someone else to blame.

On the third morning we were rehearsing a scene that involved the entire company. Dougie, like a barking terrier, was trying to marshal it into shape. Until I'd learnt a part and knew what I was doing with it I tended to stare into my script and mumble my lines. The terrier leapt at me and bit. 'More energy! More energy!!' he shouted.

I tried to excuse myself. 'It's just that I'm trying to get the character's thoughts sorted out,' I murmured.

Dougie turned red. 'THOUGHTS!' he exploded, 'CHARACTER? *What* thoughts?! *What* character?! This isn't your bloody Method rubbish! This is a musical comedy, boy! Eyes and Teeth! *EYES AND TEETH!*'

He was so angry that I had a detailed view of his own eyes and teeth only inches from my face. He had succeeded not only in shocking me but shocking himself, and abruptly he went as quiet as everyone else on stage. We pretended to continue with rehearsals, but under the watching eyes of the company I felt myself beginning to pulse with misery. I could cope with bullying, but not such sincere, inexplicable rage from someone I admired. At lunchtime, Kenneth Mackintosh, one of the more senior actors in the company and as an ex-POW doubtless familiar with worse humiliations, took me to the pub to cheer me up, but in all kindness there is an element of voyeurism and my involuntary signals of distress were too shaming for me to stay long in his company. Alone, I wondered if I would lose the part. Or become so self-conscious I would be incapable of playing it. I was convinced I knew exactly how the role should be approached. From old Punch cartoons of Victorian toffs I had Jack Poyntz's silhouette clearly in my mind – how he should stand, wear his clothes, comport himself – and I wanted him to affect the fashionable weak R of the period. Far from rolling them, Jack wouldn't bother with his R's at all. What was I to do? There was only one course open to me: to go home, learn and rehearse the entire part and return to the theatre as fully prepared as I possibly could be. When a few days later the director suggested we run my first scene I was certainly nervous, but I had something up my sleeve. We made a start and I felt a surge of confidence. Then from the darkness of the auditorium I heard a solitary chuckle. As suddenly as I had gone into the woods I was out of them. I had just received the highest commendation any actor can hope for from a director, more sincere than words. In this particular case it was also possibly a kind of apology. From then on we were to work wonderfully together.

*School* was a sell-out success for the Birmingham Rep and a personal one for me. The press was ecstatic and, in that eighteenth-century phrase, we drew the town. It was my first experience of a musical and of the high spirits that take possession backstage as the overture comes over the tannoy and one by one the numbers resonate up the stairs and along the corridors. This excitement is a little too adrenalin-driven to be described as happiness, but when a show is a success it is the next best thing. *School* was wonderful for the company, as actors revealed aspects of their talent that took their colleagues by surprise. Albert was cast as an extra and had nothing to do except stand around in the crowd, but contributed by doing so with generosity and goodwill. Ken Mackintosh played a desiccated old fop in a red wig, and Arthur Pentelow a jovial, singing Headmaster. The most arresting performance, however, was that of Geoffrey Taylor, an actor whose work up till then I'd tended to dismiss. Older than most of us, he'd been at the Rep for some time, and was inclined to treat young newcomers to the company like myself to an initial period of disdain. Once you'd won his trust, though, he revealed a sweet nature. The war had taken a bite out of his career, but it had been for him what was called 'a good war', leading to a commission and the surprise for someone of his background of finding himself accepted as an equal by his fellow officers. This widening of horizons, which a number of soldiers experienced, and which would never have been possible in peacetime Britain, was one of the more positive things contributing to the post-war climate.

Geoffrey had recently married the Wardrobe Mistress of the theatre, Rosa, a Jewish-Australian lady of tiny stature but outspoken opinions. They were devoted to each other and one would often spot them walking to and from the theatre, hand in hand. You felt two rather odd but particular people had had the good luck to find each other. He usually played, with rather too much enunciation, well-spoken parts in the classics. In *School* he played the villain, a nasty schoolmaster who prowled the premises grinding his teeth and bending a cane between two clenched fists. It was a funny, weird performance which drew on Dickens and possibly elements from his own childhood. In the close confines of a permanent theatre company actors become acutely aware of the limitations of those they have to work with and grow accordingly impatient, but they can be remarkably generous when one of their number comes up with a performance of freshness and originality. For all of them it breaks the circle of predictability, and helps justify the artistic aspirations of the profession by bringing to the light of day something which would never have existed had not the actor made that special effort. Even in the modest context of our musical, Geoffrey and I had been lucky enough to land parts which encouraged that effort, and it led to a certain fellow-feeling between us.

Newcomers to the company, engaged for just this production, included a packed dressing room of pretty young women to play the singing schoolgirls, James Maxwell to play the romantic lead, and our one star, Eleanor Drew, who had made her name in London in Julian Slade's *Salad Days*. If less whimsical, *School* was rather the same sort of show, as eager to be liked as a puppy, though its blandness was not apparent to us in Birmingham due to Dougie's vigorous staging and the huge welcome we were given by our audiences. Eleanor and I played opposite each other and we had a number of funny, well-written scenes, in the last of which I had to woo her in the full-dress uniform of a Guards officer, my head half-buried beneath a bearskin. This headdress was to have an agenda of its own. Eleanor had a lovely, insinuating singing voice but she was also an expert comedienne, and we were able to trigger huge, clean laughs as precise as gunfire. The pleasures of stage acting, particularly comedy, are largely to do with this delicious sense of control, usually described as timing. You touch a button and the house explodes. Unfortunately in the contest between you and the audience control can never be taken for granted; hence the inescapability of nerves.

The West End was now showing considerable interest in a transfer, the front runner being the Jack Hilton management, and they had made a number of visits to assess our chances. For some weeks we were on tenterhooks as a transfer seemed to be first on, then off, then on again. Just before the New Year it was confirmed: *School* would open in London in March. This was the news we had all been waiting for, but it did involve a gamble. Actors who went with the show would leave gaps in the permanent company which new recruits would have to fill. There would be no coming back. Arthur Pentelow, who had settled down with his family to a life in the Midlands, took the safer course and elected to stay put. He was to remain contentedly with the Rep for many years. All the other principals decided to take their chance in the metropolis.

We were obliged to start rehearsals with the part of the Headmaster uncast, so auditions were held in the lunch breaks. Far and away the best candidate was a big, bluff actor called Wensley Pithey, but Dougie rejected him in favour of an elderly comic whose best recommendation for the role was that he slightly resembled his predecessor, Arthur. My misgivings increased when it became apparent after a week's rehearsal that the replacement was having great difficulty learning his lines. I guessed this was a long-standing problem, because he had developed sly techniques to help him scrape through. At our first preview he had scraps of text written on his handkerchief, on his two white cuffs, on the inside of his mortar board and on bits of paper on his desk. He was not the only old actor I would encounter in my career who chose the possibility of humiliation over the loneliness of sitting unwanted in a furnished room. So deft had he become at hiding his liability that I'm not sure audiences knew it for what it was, but they would certainly recognise a performance devoid of all drive and purpose.

There were other worries. The sets followed the Victorian convention of a series of painted cloths which in the intimacy of the Rep had seemed appropriate, even charming. Re-situated to the vastness of the Prince's Theatre, they had a decidedly skimpy look, especially in the light of the competition just about to open down the road at Drury Lane – *My Fair Lady*. Another worry was that one of our more important schoolgirls had lost all her zest and was looking drained and preoccupied. It emerged she'd got pregnant during the Birmingham run, and had gone into rehearsals not knowing what to do about it. There were a few pluses. We now had a proper band, and it was exciting to hear the familiar score beefed up with witty orchestrations. When our first preview went far better than expected, hope returned, and I began to feel we had a real chance. On the day of our first night I was practically numb with nerves, and went to the theatre in the early afternoon because I couldn't bear staying at home. There I met James Maxwell, and the two of us went wandering around the West End with the incredulity of comrades about to be shot. We would catch sight of each other sighing and yawning, and do our best to find it funny. An hour before the curtain the company met in the auditorium for a final word from the director. After the last 'Good luck' when we were about to make our way back to our dressing rooms, Dougie called me aside. 'You've got that wonderful entrance with the bearskin,' he said. 'But before you begin the scene with Eleanor, why don't you take it off? We need to see more of your face.' This seemed like a good idea.

I settled in front of my dressing-room mirror for the ritual of making up. Laid out in front of me were the sticks of Leichner greasepaint, the lake-liner, the eyebrow pencils, the spirit gum and the small pieces of gauze sewn with hair which would become the moustache and sideburns of a Victorian dandy. The wig-maker usually delivered a full moustache in one piece, but I'd learnt the trick of cutting it into two to give the face mobility and minimise the risk of one side of the moustache pulling free. I set about my face-painting and my gluing with the care of someone making a model aeroplane, and at last Jack Poyntz was looking back at me from the other side of the mirror. Fifteen minutes later when I spoke my first line, my voice seemed to have gone up an octave, and my left knee, the bent one, was trembling in exactly the way my mother had told me that hers had trembled on certain critical occasions. I wondered if the audience could see my trousers flapping from the impact. Soon my first number was bearing down upon me, and I counted the bars leading to my musical entry as if my life depended on it. With that first song behind me I knew I was over the worst, and by the time we had reached my big Act One scene with Eleanor I was actually enjoying myself. When the interval came I returned to my dressing room by a route that took me under the stage and I distinctly remember thinking, almost complacently: so this is what a West End success feels like. This premature congratulation was a mistake I would never make again.

For some reason the second half was a little down on the first. What had they been saying to each other in the interval? But I still had my final scene with Eleanor and felt confident about it. I made my entrance wearing my bearskin, and there was a strong laugh and some applause. Now was the moment to take it off. As I lifted the sleeping black animal off my head it awoke to malevolent life. The chinstrap swiped at my top lip and took the upstage half my moustache with it, and in a state of appalled disbelief I watched it flutter to the floor. The scene, of course, had to continue. My motor memory dealt with that, whilst the rest of my mind, now ice-cold, computed the possibilities open to me. Since the audience could see only one side of my face they would assume I was wearing a full moustache. But three or four speeches ahead I had to move to the rear of the bench on which Eleanor sat and face out front. There was only one option; as I circled the bench I would nonchalantly stroke my top lip, removing the other half of my moustache. I finished the scene clean-shaven, but some fifteen hundred people were aware that things were not quite what they should be. Their attentiveness had given way to speculation, and those beautiful clean laughs had become tentative and ragged.

It was only when I left the stage that I lost my nerve, and began running in all directions. I had one more scene to play and I rushed into my dressing room, grabbed an eyebrow pencil and inscribed something on my sweating top lip. As a moustache it was about as convincing as Groucho's. Afterwards a member of the audience said to me 'I assumed it was deliberate – shaving off your moustache when you joined the army. It was only when you painted it back that I realised what had happened.' Actors always forget that audiences will usually give them the benefit of the doubt. At the curtain call I clutched Eleanor's hand and bowed as bravely as I could. There was reasonable applause. Then suddenly from high, high up there came another sound, riding over the clapping like the arrival of something unpleasant from another planet. The Gallery First Nighters were booing us. This group of regulars, who each paid a few shillings to sit in the gallery at every London opening, had recently hit on a strategy to make their opinion count. There would be a conference at the interval, then an exchange of nods at the curtain, and the theatre would be filled with the sound of loud and concerted booing. The first time this happened it was headlined in every newspaper the following morning, and the power, for people who had never had any, went to their heads. Managements had to endure having their entire investment jeopardised by a small group of people whose combined ticket sales were hardly sufficient to carry the cost of a single costume. Later in the year the theatres would put a stop to it. In the meantime the gallery was booing us with self-righteous malice, the sound of which was like nothing I had ever heard before. Now that the game was up, I listened to it almost with detachment.

*School* ran for a fortnight. The notices were not so much bad as tepid, but we knew we were doomed, and dragging oneself to the theatre for the second night's performance, exhausted by adrenalin depletion and with nothing to look forward to, was agony. However, after a few days our spirits revived somewhat, the show recovered its old verve, and we began to play to small bands of enthusiastic believers. For two weeks I occupied a star dressing room and received a West End salary. Then the final performance came and went and I packed my make-up back into its biscuit tin, left the stage door, and slid down the snakes and ladders of a theatrical career to the bottom of the board.

However, there had been a few gains, the most important of which was the least visible, experience. I'd been taken on by a reputable agent, Fraser and Dunlop, and had been seen in the part by a number of casting people who as a matter of routine covered all the London shows. Like one of the horses at the start of a race I was recognised, if not as a favourite, at least as a contender among the push of young actors in London, who had reached the point where they now had an agent to pester and a few contacts to give them hope. An actor's life is always lived under the shadow of rejection, and the failure of *School* was particularly hard on the older members of the company whose years at the Birmingham Rep had protected them from London and left them untutored in its harsh ways. Ten or more years older than I was, Geoffrey Taylor was now having to do the things that, hopefully, I'd put behind me – writing letters which would go unanswered, supplicating for an agent, sitting for hours on a draughty bench outside an office in the hope of half a day's work on an advertising film. He and Rosa had found accommodation, somewhere less pleasant and more expensive than their flat in Birmingham, and were barely getting by. One afternoon, having spent the day trudging from one disappointment to another, Geoffrey came home to find Rosa out and the flat empty. Unwanted as an actor and adrift from the life that the war had seemed to promise him, he must have decided he'd had enough. When Rosa came in later the whole flat smelt of gas. She ran into the kitchen to find her husband dead beside the stove. Good friends took her to stay with them, and eventually, with their support, she seemed to be coming to accept what was beyond acceptance. Left on her own one day she went into the bathroom and slit her wrists. I can think of no starker instance to demonstrate how cruel a life in the theatre can sometimes be. It taught me never to take my own good fortune for granted, because to make the best of one's opportunities is something owed not just to oneself but to those many others who, like Geoffrey, may have some talent but much less luck.

For people my age, the second half of the fifties was the time when the theatrical tide, having turned, was coming in in full flood and lifting us all up with it. The visit of three foreign companies contributed to this sense of things waiting to be achieved. One was the Moscow Art Theatre, which came to Sadler's Wells with three Chekhov plays. This institution was one of the few in the Soviet Union which Stalin had left unmolested, and the company had an unbroken tradition going back to its beginnings in pre-revolutionary Russia. Indeed, the productions we were about to see were virtually the same as the ones that Stanislavsky had unveiled around the turn of the century, and frequently looked it. The sets, for all their wall-to-wall realism, had the flat look of production photographs fifty years old. Even the acting, about which we'd all read and heard so much, was hardly uniform in its excellence. The most famous company in the world had yet to find a way of compensating for differences in talent. However, when these actors were good they were sublimely so, whether in an ensemble moment such as the end of the first scene of *The Three Sisters*, when one of the young men starts a top spinning during the party and the whole room becomes hushed by the spell of its hum, or in the work of a great individual performer such as Gribov, who in the same production played the demoralised doctor. In the last act he sat motionless in a chair on the porch of the house, his unread newspapers on his lap, doing nothing and everything, after he brings the news that the Baron has been killed in the duel.

These moments had nothing to do with the assertive dazzle you could expect, indeed demand, from one of the great performers in the West, an Olivier or an Orson Welles. They came out of months and months of rehearsal, not to mention years of playing, acting that became a distillation of the essence of the play. Curiously, what was to leave the most lasting impression on me during that season was not a performance but some noises off. The Moscow Art eschewed recordings and amplification for its sound effects and insisted on a natural acoustic, which was recreated in the wings at every performance using a variety of props and gadgets. Only the actors were considered to have the sensitivity and timing to do justice to this element of the production, and it was they who produced and orchestrated these offstage sounds. Their storm in *Uncle Vanya* was so lifelike, so reinforced with unexpected details, that you could have sworn the air was heavy with moisture and that water was cascading down the gutters outside the theatre. It began with very distant thunder which came closer until it was overhead. Then you heard the first heavy drops of rain, hitting the dry earth one by one. When the downfall came the timbre of the rainfall altered as the ground became increasingly sodden. Finally the rain lessened bit by bit and the storm passed, leaving behind a vacant silence interrupted by the plop of drips landing in puddles beneath the eaves of the house.

One marvelled that someone had gone in search of a real storm, had carefully annotated it and then by trial, error and sheer ingenuity had found a way to give it a second life, out of sight in a dusty corner of a stage. We know that Chekhov expressed some impatience with Stanislavsky's obsession with sound effects, especially when distant frogs and corncrakes interrupted a scene which would have played perfectly well without them. However, the storm in *Vanya*, like the effect at the end of their third production – that shocking report of axes notching the trunks of the cherry trees – were sounds central to the action, and their fidelity filled the stage with life. It was naturalism executed with such attention to truth that it was almost poetry.

Concurrent with the Sadler's Wells season, the National Film Theatre was showing some archival material of the Moscow Art Theatre shot in the thirties. There on the screen was the same production of *The Three Sisters* with some of the same cast, but in parts more suited to their younger selves. Thus the actor I had seen as the Schoolmaster was here playing Tussenbach. It was a little claustrophobic, but such continuity of work was amazing to us. At their curtain call, the demeanour of these Russians, like that of the actors in Vienna, their modesty and lack of show-business bluff, suggested a professional life that we in England could only dream about.

For directors and designers, however, it was the visit of Brecht's Berliner Ensemble in 1956 that had been the eye-opener. Overnight the painted canvas flats and rather fusty humanism of the Moscow Art and its American offshoot, the Actors' Studio, were consigned to the past. Here was a way of telling stories on stage which could come to grips with the tumultuous events of the twentieth century, a new kind of theatre in which individual destiny, until then the staple of drama, took second place to an understanding of the historical forces which are always shaping it. Whether you consider Bertolt Brecht a great playwright depends, as it does with a Catholic writer, on whether you agree with the doctrine his work espouses. In his play about the emergence of Hitler, *The Resistible Rise of Arturo Ui*, Marxist theory accords more or less with historical fact and it can be marvellous theatre, even if its power owes as much to its author's more ordinary fascination with American gangster movies. But when, as in *Mann ist Mann*, he writes to affirm the proposition that human nature is exclusively a matter of social conditioning, scepticism intervenes. As a man of the theatre, however, with a new idea of what theatre could be,

Brecht was undoubtedly the most influential figure since the war. It was as if he had replaced an old, elaborately carved cuckoo clock with one of those immaculate timepieces below a dome of transparent glass, in which all the polished moving parts are on show. Such a clock not only told the time accurately; you could see *how*. It was grown-up theatre. You were asked to watch the performance with your judgement awake. Nor were you offered magic and illusion. Everything on stage would be what it seemed – wood would be wood, metal metal. Only such elements of reality as were needed to tell the story would be carefully selected and placed for your inspection – the porch of a house, an old motor car or Mother Courage's wooden cart rattling with her wares. You wouldn't be seduced by empathetic emotion, at least not deliberately. The glue that held the evening together would be sheer aesthetic exhilaration, arrived at after months of preparation, with inventive staging that deployed a superb ensemble of actors and sets as spare and considered as sculpture. The productions would be as carefully practised as a high-wire act at the circus, and as thrillingly exposed. The Berliner Ensemble was that paradox, a political theatre which believed in art for art's sake. It offered a scene change so fluent and ingenious that it was as spellbinding as anything else in the evening.

Some years later, when I was at the Glasgow Citizens' Theatre and planning my own production of *Arturo Ui*, I persuaded the Board to allow me a trip to East Germany so that I could see for myself the famous original production which I had missed when it visited London. British directors spoke of it in awe, and I needed to know what I was up against. I flew into East Berlin to be met by an earnest young woman who was to be my guide and minder during the visit. That night I saw not *Arturo Ui* but *Mann ist Mann*. I was most impressed by the production, but this didn't prevent me from having reservations about the play. It was curious experiencing this didactic evening in the confines of a beautiful and exquisitely well-maintained baroque interior. But then ambiguity seemed to be built into Brecht's theatre, though no one spoke of it. The great man was not long dead, and the atmosphere of political correctness surrounding him and his works was palpable.

I had the good sense to keep my mouth shut the following day when I was taken on a tour of the institution. In the evening I at last caught up with *Arturo Ui*. The production was again remarkable, though not as intimidating as its reputation. I suppose that's what I'd hoped to discover. Before I caught the plane back to Scotland I was granted an interview with Brecht's widow and keeper of the flame, Helene Weigel, who was now running the theatre. She received me like a preoccupied head of state, and was almost impossible to impress. I had with me some production photographs of another Brecht play I'd staged at the Citizens' the previous season, *The Visions of Simone Machard*. This concerned a young French girl during the German occupation, who sees herself as a Joan of Arc figure and becomes a focus for the Resistance. It was far from Brecht's best play, but he was very fashionable at the time so getting the rights for the first professional production in Great Britain was something of a coup. Weigel, her face a mask of severity, shuffled through the photographs as if she was examining X-rays. Then she gave her judgement. 'Brecht said Simone Machard must be played by a child. You have cast an adolescent!' I murmured that the sixteen-year-old actress, who looked about thirteen, was by far the best we could find for the part. 'Brecht insisted that she be played by a child!' she said, turning the volume up. 'Had I known about this I would have forbidden the production.' I was beginning to get irritated. In my view the Brecht Estate were lucky to get a showing of this rather dated exercise in Second World War propaganda. (To my knowledge there hasn't been one since.) I sensed Weigel depress something with her foot underneath the desk. It was evidently a bell in the outer office, because presently a secretary entered and stood by the door. My audience with her was clearly at an end. The whole experience had been a little like being turned down for a visa at a hostile embassy.

On the plane I wondered if the rights to *Arturo Ui* would now be withdrawn, but the production went ahead. The Berliner Ensemble proved very co-operative. They sent us tapes of their music, a fabulous Hans Eisler score, and I had no hesitation in lifting a few of their ideas. I continued to admire their work, but found it impossible to remain in awe of an institution where any sort of irreverence was out of order. The production at the Citizens' would have a comparatively minute budget and only three weeks to rehearse, but I was now confident that there was more than one way to mount the show. What we had which they didn't was an inspired Leonard Rossiter as the Hitler figure, giving a performance as resourceful, as terrifying and, it must be said, five times as funny as his brilliant Berlin counterpart, Ekkehart Schall.

The third foreign company to come to London couldn't have been in greater contrast to its predecessors: *West Side Story*, with the original

Broadway cast. This was theatre in the tradition that I had absorbed from the best of American films, forged in the face of the usual pressure of time and money, yet defying these constraints with a combination of abundant talent and feverish hard work. I found it a miracle of a show and a triumphant vindication of popular theatre. This story of young Americans at the bottom of the social heap asserting their right to a better life was virtually a hymn to individual aspiration, and would never have done in East Berlin. Nor for that matter in England. The idea of a British musical in which the *Romeo and Juliet* story was re-enacted in terms of rival gangs of Teddy Boys would have been smirked into oblivion. Working-class British youth was simply not credited with that degree of emotional seriousness or fervour. Kenneth Tynan was later to define what he called 'high definition performance', and *West Side Story* was the perfect exemplar. I was seeing what Broadway did best, theatre passionately conceived but executed pragmatically so that there wasn't a moment wasted or misjudged. What mattered was that everything *worked*. There can be drawbacks to this approach – it depends on who and how many are doing the arbitrating – but with *West Side Story* everything worked. I hadn't had such a good time since . . . well, since I'd seen another Broadway cast do *Kiss Me Kate* seven years before at the Coliseum.

These three companies, so apparently incompatible in approach, descended on London like a series of painted cloths each of which, as it filled the stage, eclipsed the one before. Artistic assumptions have a way of annihilating the competition, and while I was watching I was in thrall to all three. Listening to Bach, Puccini hardly seems possible. All were influential. The Russian and German companies demonstrated what subsidy could achieve, and brought our own National Theatre a little closer. *West Side Story* showed what energy and human resource could be liberated by the democratic idea, and fed the new wave of British films.

In the early years of an artistic career it often seems that nothing you are attempting yourself will ever match the work you admire from afar in others. You feel yourself in bondage to talents not your own, taking in but not giving out. Insecurity about yourself becomes compounded by what may be a genuine lack of opportunity. Then one day, like that subtle but absolute moment when the balance alters in a pair of scales, it is now your turn to achieve things and someone else's to be impressed. This much-desired moment also involves loss, because it means you will cease to be smitten by the work of others with quite the same perfect fervour. You have done your breathing in – now is the time to breathe out. All through the fifties I was breathing in, and I've barely touched on the most potent influence on me, the medium of my adolescent ambitions, the movies. I was constantly going to the National Film Theatre to catch up on early Lubitschs and Capras, or to see *Scarface*, or a great silent epic like *Greed*. Some of the best new work I saw at the Academy in Oxford Street, often in the morning on the first day of the screening before the critics had told me too much about them – films like the nihilistic *Wages of Fear*, or *Seven Samurai*, or the first of a string of Bergmans, *Sawdust and Tinsel*. These films, though they hypnotised me, made me ache with discontent, less as an actor than as the director I'd once hoped to be.

In the theatre my ambition was in line with the profession I already practised, and was therefore more realistic. There were two figures who could instantly ignite it. One was Olivier, whose every new appearance generated a special sense of anticipation. What would he be up to this time? The other was a critic, Kenneth Tynan, who, in his weekly endorsements and dismissals in *The Observer* might have been reading my mind. I was certainly reading his as I swung open the paper each Sunday and turned straight to his column, this eloquent, witty spokesman for a British theatre in the making. Ken was that rare thing, a critic of strong and sometimes withering opinions who remained a fan. Talent was what he revered more than his own opinion about it, though that was important too, and a source of evident satisfaction to him. Unlike his rival, Harold Hobson of the *Sunday Times*, about whose likes and dislikes there was usually an air of calculation and who always seemed to be looking over his shoulder in case his standing was under attack from an unexpected quarter, Ken asked something very straightforward from the theatre – the opportunity to feel passionately. When this happened, he wrote the best love letters of any critic alive or dead. He liked to mix socially with theatre people and I would often see him at some party, always in the company of one or two pretty women and sometimes with a New York celebrity tagging along. He and his party stayed only as long as the occasion held his interest. Then they were off, with Ken breathing disdainful smoke over the gathering from a cigarette held with calculated affectation between his middle fingers. Once or twice I attempted to engage him in conversation, but my qualifications weren't up to scratch at that time, and first his attention wandered, then he did – to someone more interesting across the room. In spite of this rudeness, posing as honesty and endemic in the young and fashionable, I would have given anything for a good notice from him, because as a critic he was incorruptible.

That year, 1958, was also to see me make my debut in movies, if the product coming out of Pinewood Studios at that time could be so described. 'Slowlies' would have been a better word. The Rank Organisation had fallen into the hands of an accountant, John Davis, who gave the green light only to projects of certifiable dullness and predictability. This happens on a regular basis in British cultural life, when the managerial class decides that the talent is getting uppity and takes over their prerogatives. Shirley's new job at Pinewood was as secretary to one of Davis's lieutenants, Connery Chappell, who had a sumptuous office behind a soundproof door, intended no doubt to prevent any good ideas getting in rather than secrets getting out. Shirley soon became acquainted with some of the actual filmmakers, grumbling and conspiring in lesser offices throughout the studio. One of these was Jack Lee, who was making a comedy about life aboard a passenger ship called *The Captain's Table*. She asked if there might be a part for her actor boyfriend. In due course I was offered a day's work playing a steward. It was a speaking part with one short scene, and I was told to turn up first thing in the morning and report to Make-Up, which I did, yawning nervously after an uneasy night's sleep. It may be because I appeared in a few of them that all the Pinewood films of this period strike me as being steeped in this early-morning anxiety; every listless shot looks as if it was probably the first set-up of the day. That zest, of which British films had proved themselves capable, under Alexander Korda or Michael Balcon at Ealing or in the productions of Powell and Pressburger, is entirely absent.

My face now painted a bright orange and kitted out in a white steward's jacket, I was escorted to a small windowless dressing room and told to wait there until called to the set. Hours passed and it was lunchtime. That afternoon, back in solitary confinement, I heard the beginnings of a thunderstorm overhead, and felt my spirits droop still further. At 5.30 they perked up a little, because it looked as if I would be needed for another day and would therefore earn a further £25. Suddenly the door swung open and the third assistant bounded into the room. 'Quick!' he urged me, 'Jack thinks there's just time to get your scene in the can, but you have to hurry!' The rain was now pelting down, and to get to the soundstage from the dressing room block there was a distance to traverse of about ten yards along a duckboard ramp. Thinking a rain-soaked steward might look out of place on a sunny cruise ship I made a dash for it, slipped on the ramp and knocked myself unconscious. The exasperated third assistant found me dazed and soaking wet, sitting in a puddle of freezing water. He dragged me back to the Wardrobe, where a kindly lady refitted me in clean, dry clothes, and when I eventually arrived on the set, Jack Lee greeted me affably and we went straight for a take. We did another one for luck and that was that. *The Captain's Table* is still occasionally shown on television, so my pop-eyed and somewhat concussed performance, all in mid-shot, has not been lost to the world.

On TV you can also catch another day's work I had on *Operation Amsterdam*, a sluggish wartime thriller, in which I play a young officer on the bridge of a destroyer. My dialogue runs along the lines of 'Cocoa, sir?' Then a pause while the Captain looks through his binoculars. 'Any sign of Jerry yet, sir?' The only direction I received was 'Stop blinking.' My pleasantest day's work was on an atrocious film starring Frankie Vaughan called *Heart of a Man*, directed by the veteran Herbert Wilcox. My scene was at a race meeting, and I wore a grey top hat. We did numerous takes and before each the director threw me a new line which I had to incorporate into the dialogue I'd already learnt. It was like a sort of test, which I must have passed because after the last take he said, 'You're good! Write home and tell your mother.' I was delighted, and indeed did so, but this welcome encouragement lost most of its meaning when the film was released and I discovered my scene had been cut in its entirety.

In the summer I had two engagements which raised me a little above the level of jobbing actor. The first was a small but excellent part in a Granada TV production of *The Browning Version*. The author, Terence Rattigan, attended our final run-through in London and smiled approvingly, then we caught the train to Manchester, where the show was to be broadcast live. The day of the transmission I became thirty years of age. Next morning I was back in London and catching a plane to Dublin, no longer, I now realised, a young man. I was responding to an offer to play the lead, Mirabel, in Congreve's *The Way of the World* at the Gate Theatre, where a few years before Micheál MacLiammóir and Hilton Edwards had enjoyed an illustrious reign and discovered the young Orson Welles. I had no idea how they had got my name or why they had chosen me, but it became clearer when I was introduced to my leading lady at the first day's rehearsal. This was an actress who had gained a reputation in Dublin reinterpreting all the roles made famous over the years by the great Dame Edith Evans. There was one hurdle she had yet to clear: Millamant in *The Way of the World*, a part in which Dame Edith had triumphed in the 1920s, and which my own leading lady would have had a better shot at round about the same time. Millamant is meant to be eighteen. It dawned on me why I had got the job. Only a leading man imported from abroad would be ignorant of the situation to which he was committing himself. The fact that none of the other men in the company envied me my role didn't temper their indignation that it had gone to an outsider from across the water. I had stumbled into a hornets' nest, and it was called Ireland. Only one man seemed glad to see me and that was Lord Longford, the eccentric Anglo-Irish peer who ran the theatre. This he did rather in the manner of an eighteenth-century owner of a big house who maintained a company of players for his own amusement. He was particularly interested in period costume, of which he had a vast and rather lurid collection, and I seemed to spend as much time in the wardrobe trying on things for his consideration as I did rehearsing.

Away from the theatre I found myself glad to be in Dublin. Like Edinburgh, it was a great European city which had had the good luck to be bypassed by the Industrial Revolution, and I spent hours exploring its endless wealth of Georgian squares and terraces. I had found myself a room on the top floor of a run-down but splendid neoclassical building which had been converted into a primitive hotel. Each morning I would descend to the deserted breakfast room and sip my tea whilst the proprietor, a gaunt man in his fifties, stood by my table and engaged me in genteel conversation. Whatever the topic under discussion and wherever it rambled, his talk, like a horse on the homeward journey, would always trot towards the same stable, the situation in Northern Ireland. Every day he would conclude our conversation with an identical catchphrase, uttered with a sad wag of the head and an undertow of threat, 'Ah, that border in the North! That border in the North!' I had the distinct impression that because I came from London I was partly responsible for it. Ulster was not yet in the headlines, and we knew little about the injustices meted out to the Catholic minority, but later, when the Troubles erupted and went on year after year in seemingly unbreakable cycles of vindictive violence, I felt that in this breakfast room I had had a slight foretaste of why.

Nevertheless, after a number of these morning conversations and in spite of the way they always concluded, the proprietor and I became friends. One day he said to me, 'Mr Blakemore, are you interested in fine music at all?' I said I was. 'Because I have these friends who have this superb instrument, it has a sound like you wouldn't believe, truly magical, and they have the finest collection of recordings in Dublin. They'll be having one of their musical evenings this weekend, and I know they'd be delighted to have you attend.' On Sunday evening, dressed to suit the occasion I accompanied the proprietor to a flat in another Georgian house, and walked through a door into a short story by James Joyce. A group of middle-aged people were gathered in a small drawing room, twittering with Irish courtesy and nibbling politely at light refreshments scattered here and there on various tables. In the very centre of the room, in a spot that a solo violinist might have chosen to give a recital, stood a cabinet-sized wind-up gramophone in polished wood, some forty years old. I remember my grandmother had possessed a similar model in the thirties. For half an hour the guests eddied around the cabinet at a respectful distance as if it might contain a relic, making hushed, vivacious conversation, and at the same time disposing of the sandwiches. We were then asked to sit down and when the room had fallen silent, our host raised the mahogany lid of his machine with the solemnity of a conductor raising his baton to focus the attention of the orchestra. For the next hour we listened to a succession of reedy tenors and famed coloraturas interspersed with favourites like Ravel's 'Bolero'. The proprietor had been right: the quality of the sound was extraordinary. It had the same presence as those offstage noises at the Moscow Art. If you closed your eyes you could almost believe the tenor was there in the room with you, even if that night he was in the grip of a lacerated sore throat.

The Dubliners I was most taken with were the ones in the most ordinary of occupations – waiters, taxi-drivers, people serving in shops or behind a bar – because of the surprising eloquence of their everyday speech and the helpfulness of disposition that went with it. Problems arose when I met people who worked in a field where ideas played an important part, and this of course included the theatre, as well as literature and journalism. Here independence of mind was in permanent collision with the Catholic Church, and a degree of doublethink was more or less a condition of survival. This was a Catholicism at far remove from the subtle, accommodating grandeur of the Church in southern Europe, or even in England, but it was one I recognised. In Australia the priesthood had been largely Irish, and orders like the Christian and Marist Brothers had enormous influence in education. At our Protestant school we would hear horror stories of the harsh discipline and physical torments imposed by the brothers on their charges. In this largely Protestant British dominion the Church had adopted a fortress mentality, which the grim, utilitarian architecture of its institutional buildings seemed to reflect. In Australia, however, Catholics were in a minority; in Ireland they were not, and the Church's surveillance extended to all aspects of national life, particularly those two wellsprings of alternative authority, culture and sex. The population seemed to be cowed by religion, crossing themselves with anxious haste on the top of buses at the mere sight of a church. When, after a party one night, I became slightly intimate with a young woman, I found I had released such a confusion of lust and religious terror that to continue felt as inappropriate as trying to seduce a patient from the psychiatric wing.

One answer to the conflicts induced by this sort of social conditioning is drink, and again I was reminded of the puritanic Australia of my youth, where bouts of anaesthetic drunkenness had been elevated to a largely male ritual. Men drank to trivialise uncomfortable ambitions and to dull the sexual drive, or at any rate the guilt, without which it was easier to get on with it. They drank to annihilate the impossible distance between what is and what could be. One evening in Dublin I had gone for a walk along the banks of the Liffey, when I saw approaching me a very drunk man of about sixty. He might have been any one of the thousands of working men I had seen reeling out of Sydney pubs at closing time. Even from a distance of about fifty yards I knew I had been targeted, and when we met he extended his hand. I took it and his handshake became an insistent request for money for another drink. I shook my head and tried to withdraw my hand, but he had me held tight. He was swaying and staring fiercely at me out of the world of drink. Finally he marshalled his thoughts. 'All right, maybe I've had one or two,' he said, 'BUT I HAVE PURE THOUGHTS.'

This, of course, was not the whole story. While I was in Dublin I met many charming, hospitable and untroubled people and saw much that was beautiful. However, it was the part of the story which interested me because it threw such light upon aspects of my own country about which I had always felt uneasy. One of the peculiarities about being born a colonial is that to understand the place where you grew up you must return to those countries on the other side of the world from which it has so recently derived its identity. This may explain why so many Australians once on the move never quite know where they belong.

If countries can be described as neurotic then the Ireland of these years must surely be a candidate, oppressed over centuries from without by the British and from within by its own religion – a child who only sees his absent and detested father when he turns up to administer a beating, and whose mother terrorises him with threats of hellfire and the withdrawal of love. Only recently, it seems to me, has the country begun to free itself from its long, tormented dream, and done so with the easy grace I once responded to in its ordinary citizens. The Church, at last acknowledging its own need of contrition, may have helped a little.

# EIGHT

# Almost

In July my mother came to England, this time to stay. She had received a proposal of marriage. Her suitor was Lawrence Heyworth, whom she had met before the war when he had been running the Australian end of the Unilever organisation. Lawrence was then married to his first wife, Eileen, and she became firm friends with the couple, doubtless drawn to them by the fact that they were English. It was a time in Australia, particularly in the circle in which my mother moved, when English was another word for best. He was one of three brothers who had gone to work for Unilever and who had all eventually risen to become members of the board. One had even become chairman and had received a peerage. In his sixty-fifth year, the same year he was required to retire from Unilever, Lawrence suffered two severe blows, the first his wife's death from cancer and the second a bad heart attack. However, wanting to make something of the remainder of his life and remembering his friendship with my mother, he had taken himself to Sydney and proposed marriage. She took some time making up her mind. She was fond of Lawrence, but no more. What probably decided her was that she would be on the same side of the world as her son, and also, I suspect, that by marrying she would relieve a struggling actor with an uncertain future of any financial burden attached to her old age. She was marrying for love but directed at the inappropriate person.

I took an optimistic but unconsidered view of this development, but then it is difficult giving serious thought to the intimate life of parents. One is happy to accept whatever they decide, but not necessarily to think it through with them. Lawrence's money was certainly a consideration. The three brothers, all of whom, though married, were childless, had agreed to lump their fortunes together in a charitable bequest bearing their name, leaving their widows without capital but well provided for. As she moved into her sixties, this at least would give her peace of mind. Lawrence lived in a big modern house overlooking the golf course at Quaybrook in Sussex, which he and his first wife had built in the thirties. They had been a cultivated couple, and the house their architect had designed was light and airy, and advanced for its time with an uncluttered interior and some good contemporary pictures on the walls. Shirley and I were asked down for the weekend, and made suitable noises as we admired the views and studied the big Victor Pasmore over the fireplace. Yet I had my misgivings. For one thing, while always hospitable, Lawrence could not be other than suspicious of me and I knew he would have preferred it if this stepson had not come attached to the bargain. Owning art was one thing; having an artist, and an underemployed one, as a relative was another. He also had an air of anxiety that I hadn't noticed some years before when he and his wife had made such an urbane couple. Of most concern was the society my mother would soon be moving into – business executives, stockbrokers, retired air vice-marshals and their wives, braying approval of each other over drinks on a Sunday morning. However, they were duly married in St Columba's Church off Sloane Square, with immediate family attending. The peer signed the register, jokily giving his occupation as 'Soap Maker', and we all laughed, then went off somewhere to have a drink. During the ceremony, though, as my mother stood there, I had noticed the telltale family response to stress, the wobbling knee.

I was still living in Carlyle Square, halfway up the King's Road, on its way to becoming the Yellow Brick Road to the Swinging Sixties. Already, like a first bud, a dress shop had opened with such an utterly new look that curiosity drew me inside. There I set eyes on Mary Quant for the first time, looking like an art student. She and her husband were arranging a display of stock. They smiled faintly, displaying a manner which was also new: a cool though not unfriendly indifference to whether you liked or loathed a look they clearly believed in. This same cool was evident further down the road at the Royal Court, where they spoke bravely of 'the right to fail' and where, of all the theatres in England, I most longed to be offered a job. I saw all their shows, and studied the actors of my age, some of whom, like Nigel Davenport, I'd been with in rep, trying to work out why they were there and I wasn't.

One actor in particular was playing just the sort of parts that I thought would have suited me. He lived further along the King's Road, and when he first joined the company I would often see him on his way to rehearsals in the morning, rather grey-faced and stooped with that preoccupied look of a young actor desperate to make his mark that I recognised when I accidentally caught sight of myself in a plate-glass window. This was Robert Stephens, and not long afterwards he made his mark resoundingly in *Epitaph to George Dillon*. In the weeks that followed, as he strode past Carlyle Square I saw his step lighten, his carriage improve and eventually that same pink look crept into his cheeks which I had once observed in John Osborne. When would it be my turn?

I had gone to a general audition at the Royal Court, but it had proved a gruesome experience and led nowhere. About fifty young men had been told to report to the stage door at four o'clock one afternoon. We were asked to form a kind of queue as we waited for our turn onstage, but the wings were so cramped and the line so long that it extended upstairs and out into the alley. A stage manager – I think it may have been Peter Gill – pushed amiably through the crowd in the opposite direction, giving each candidate a speech to read. When my turn came, I was pretty much bundled into a pool of light, stage centre. I had no idea who I was auditioning for until someone spoke out of the darkness. He didn't introduce himself but I immediately recognised the languid, unimpressed tones first adopted by Tony Richardson and now becoming the house style of the young Court directors. Like someone assessing an ambush, I guessed there were three or four of them out there. Afterwards, I realised that I hadn't done too badly (I'd made someone laugh), but I was bewildered how a theatre that claimed to be so anti-Establishment could have permitted such a poorly organised meat-market. These young graduates, so assured of the right to judge me, were my own age. One wondered if their avowed intent to change the country was simply a means of re-placing one elite with another. Joan Littlewood's auditions, I was told, were even more humiliating, particularly if you betrayed the least hint that you were other than working class.

Theatre and contradiction go hand in hand. If you wanted to be properly treated as an actor you had to go to a small West End management like Jack Minster's. He'd probably be seeing you for a commercial farce you'd shudder to contemplate spending a year of your

Australian photographer Alec Murray took these
pictures in his Eaton Square flat, 1951
1. The drama student looks to the future
2. My mother, coerced into a Freudian composition,
tries to keep an open mind

3. The photograph that finished my career as a publicist. Morton Gottlieb, Robert Morley, Nancy Stubbs the children's nurse with Annabel and Sheridan, and me, 1949
4. With my minder Fred, ashore in Port Said, 1950

5. On the RADA roof with the Americans, Theodore J. Flicker and Jack Salamanca, 1951

6. *Almost a Honeymoon* in rep, playing the sort of part in which I was doomed to excel. Ted Fellows plays my valet, 1954

7. *Meet a Body,* in which I briefly sniff success, Bristol, 1956

8. Tyrone Guthrie splendidly in charge
9. Olivier as Titus Andronicus

10. In the Stratford Green Room, Priscilla Morgan, Albert Finney and
Vanessa Redgrave, 1959
11. As Snout, with Charles Laughton (Bottom) and Peter Woodthorpe (Flute), 1959
12. As Dumain in *All's Well That Ends Well*, 1959

13. Just married. It's 9 o'clock in the morning and I'm off to rehearsals, 1960
14. Holofernes in *Love's Labour's Lost* with James Ottaway (Sir Nathaniel), 1962
15. Sir Toby Belch up to no good in the Middle Temple Hall, 1964
16. Badger in *Toad of Toad Hall* (the performance owed much to the prime minister Harold Macmillan), 1962

17. My father prepares his fishing tackle while I watch, 1940
18. My American grandmother. Her house on Sundays was a refuge from
The King's School
19. In the school uniform with little to smile about

20. Joe Melia and Zena Walker, incomparable in *A Day in the Death of Joe Egg*, 1967

life in, but at least he would sit you down in a chair opposite his desk, give you a cup of tea and a digestive biscuit, then have five minutes conversation on general topics before going on to discuss terms.

In the autumn, with the odd film and TV job to keep me going, I had the spare time to push ahead with the play I had started the year before. Despite some encouraging noises from a theatre in Australia, nothing had come of my first effort, *Gum Beach*. I hoped that this new one, the subject of which was British nostalgia for the war years, had a better chance and might even be the sort of thing that would interest the Royal Court. One morning I was staring at the typewriter when I heard the thump of a parcel falling through the letterbox downstairs. Any distraction from the contemplation of my entitlement to be a writer was welcome, so I ran to the front door to investigate. The parcel was for me and came with rows of unfamiliar US stamps. Inside was a hardback copy of a novel of some five hundred pages, and on the shiny slip cover I read 'The Lost Country by J. R. Salamanca'. Jack had inscribed it and enclosed a press cutting advertising the book with lengthy quotes from journals as important as the *New York Times* and the *Washington Post*. I could hardly believe what I was reading – so many superlatives, so much praise. All the critics were in accord: this was a first book by a major writer. I was excited and extraordinarily moved. The book I now held in my hand I had watched coming into being, on a kitchen table, on a desk by a bedroom window on a succession of winter mornings, a snail's trail of words stubbornly making its way across sheets of yellow paper. No one had commissioned it, or even asked for it to happen. How could they? It existed only as an impulse inside someone's head. Yet, after seven long years, the snail had completed its journey. It was home.

The welcome one gives to the success of one's friends can certainly be genuine, but once one becomes established in the arts it is rarely without a degree of ambiguity. In the last analysis you are both competing for a limited supply of attention. But in this instance what I felt was without qualification, and I look back at the person I was at that moment with warmth. I had believed in this man and had been right to do so. Two things happened. I plunged straight into Jack's book, a rapturous evocation of a boy's growing up in the American South and of his eventual loss of innocence, and I set to work on my own play with renewed courage. Rivalry plays a part in all our lives, but sometimes example does the trick with more grace.

I had other reasons to feel optimistic: I had made some interesting new friends. In a side-street behind the Knightsbridge tube there was a restaurant called The Stockpot, which was managed by an American actor, Gary Thorne, and his pretty actress wife Patti. They provided wholesome, cheap food and a youthful welcome, and had attracted as regulars a group aspiring to careers in the arts and the media. Leading the pack were the gay Avery twins, Wilf and Sam, both painters, and identical in their appearance and rather gnomic opinions, one of them finishing the sentence the other had begun. Blurring into one, they became the Gertrude Stein figure for what was the closest London had yet offered me in the way of bohemian café life. Providing you didn't question their judgement – difficult at times – the twins were a generous and protective pair, and threw parties at their flat in the New King's Road, where among the guests you would occasionally be surprised by a famous face, like the novelist Angus Wilson. There was one member of the group with whom I felt an immediate affinity. This was a writer, until recently a teacher, who had just won a BBC competition for a one-hour television play. His name was Peter Nichols, and he reminded me a bit of a young Fred Astaire in library-frame glasses. He was always humming to himself and, like Astaire, had a sort of musical restlessness.

Two things in particular singled him out. The first was that not only was he funny but he had a need, a hunger, to find what was comic in any given situation. You could sense him nosing around in the conversation, sniffing it out. The second was that he was a wonderful listener, looking at you with an absorbed stare as you embarked on some opinion or indiscretion. This is often a characteristic of writers, and it is flattering but dangerous. Afterwards, left to reflect on what was said and with politeness no longer a problem, they are as likely to ridicule with greater vehemence what they had first appeared to accept. This was certainly true of Peter, though not during our time at The Stockpot when we were very much of a mind. Our backgrounds had been very different in all but one thing. At an early age we had both been overwhelmed by the American cinema, and to embrace its vigour, technical dazzle and underlying democratic assumptions was in some way to turn away from England and the influence of things British. This we had both done. Peter was a clever mimic and Gary Cooper in *Mr Deeds Goes to Town* and Charles Laughton in *Mutiny on the Bounty* often joined us at our table over dinner. Simple-minded these black-and-white dreams may have been, but we had once believed them and it was impossible not to hold them in some affection. Another influence on Peter as a child had been the variety shows he had seen at the Bristol Hippodrome, and those same star comedians had also toured Australia, and come to the Sydney Tivoli. Out of these early, pristine enthusiasms would one day come the string of successes we had together, making ironic use of aspects of popular entertainment – *A Day in the Death of Joe Egg*, *The National Health*, *Forget-Me-Not Lane* and *Privates on Parade*.

I introduced Peter to Shirley, and since he was without a girlfriend at the time, the three of us were frequently in each other's company. I gave him my play to read, and he gave me his. It was called *Walk on the Grass*, and was about a young man in Bristol, struggling to free himself from the constraints of lower-middle-class life. It was clearly autobiographical, and like many of his later plays it contained funny, sharp portraits that drew directly on his own relatives. However, because he knew in his bones what had made these people what they were, his characterisations had the sympathy of anything truthfully observed. In comparison, my own play dealt with a reality more guessed at than experienced. There was much indignant rhetoric and characters whose main function was to serve the narrative, but it had one thing going for it – it told a good story, with a cliffhanging curtain line at the end of Act One. Robert Morley also read it, and his verdict was to the point: 'A great improvement on your first one, and if you write a third, someone might actually be fool enough to put it on.'

In November I was invited to audition for the forthcoming season at Stratford-upon-Avon. It was something I had half-expected since the *Titus* tour, when Paddy Donnell, the general manager, had hinted that there might be an entire season for me if they could find the right line of parts. In due course my new agents, Fraser and Dunlop, received an offer about which I was both excited and dubious. On the credit side, 1959 was the centenary year of the Shakespeare Memorial Theatre, and promised to be the most illustrious in its long history. More great stars were under contract than perhaps had ever been seen in one company: Laurence Olivier, Charles Laughton, Paul Robeson, Edith Evans, Sam Wanamaker and, among the young lions, Albert Finney, Ian Holm, Mary Ure, Zoe Caldwell, and the as yet undiscovered Vanessa Redgrave. Other leading parts would be played by gifted actors like Robert Hardy, Cyril Luckham and Anthony Nichols. The plays would be directed by Glen Byam Shaw, whose final year as Artistic Director this was, and Tony Richardson and the Director Designate, Peter Hall, both in their twenties though already renowned. The fourth director was someone I'd been hearing about ever since I'd come to England, Tyrone Guthrie. Two of his productions at the Old Vic had been among the most exciting things I'd seen since I'd arrived in London. One was *Tamburlaine the Great*, the first production of Marlowe's play in centuries, and a whirlwind of inventive spectacle and soaring rhetoric. Breathtaking was an inadequate word to describe the excitements that followed one upon another. At the end the tyrant, now decayed but unrepentant in old age, unrolled at his feet a huge map almost the size of the stage floor and stumbled across it on his stick, retracing the path of his conquests. The other production was *Troilus and Cressida*, which Guthrie staged in a period that evoked the central experience of his generation, the First World War. The generals on both sides, resplendent in ridiculous uniforms and bleating of honour, were donkeys. Thersites was a disgusted war correspondent with notebook and box camera, and what we saw of battle was squalid horror. A line of soldiers with fixed bayonets rose out of the trench of the orchestra pit and vanished in the upstage smoke. The last image was Pandarus, looking like Proust's Baron de Charlus, sitting on his luggage bearing the labels of the grand hotels of Europe as he waits to make his getaway from the ruined city, and crooning his malediction over the audience and all mankind that concludes: 'I'll . . . bequeath you my diseases.'

With such talents the 1959 season promised in the truest sense of the word to be fabulous. The problem, however, was the parts I'd been offered. I was not in *Othello*; it would be my play out, and I would eventually be grateful for those free evenings. I would have little to do in Olivier's *Coriolanus*, and less in Laughton's *King Lear*, in both of which I had speaking parts but not of the kind with which you could hope to make your mark. Much more promising was one of the mechanicals in *A Midsummer Night's Dream*, Snout the tinker, again with Laughton as Bottom. The show with the chance of making the engagement worthwhile was *All's Well That Ends Well*, to be directed by Guthrie. There were two parts, First and Second Lord, which were both rewarding, and I had been offered First Lord with the caution that it was not quite as good as its companion part which had already gone to Paul Hardwick. When I read the play in my grandmother's portable *Collected Works* (like my grandfather's typewriter part of my luggage since I'd been in England), I was puzzled, since First Lord was certainly the longer part and seemed to me to be the better. However, if I took the job to serve what might prove to be another period of apprenticeship, and I felt I'd got beyond that, it would mean abandoning London and a burgeoning career in television for the best part of a year. In addition the money was awful – £16 a week, only a pound more than I'd been earning at the Birmingham Rep. When my agent questioned the salary, Paddy Donnell replied, 'But we see Michael being with us for at least two seasons going from strength to strength. We keep salaries low in the first year so we can offer a really substantial rise in the second.' Paddy was Irish and so was this logic, but at least the company seemed keen to have me. Later that week, and still fretting about a decision I had yet to make, I was at the Buckstone Club discussing my dilemma with a friend over lunch. At the adjoining table was Kenneth Griffiths, whom I knew slightly. I had just explained that the only substantial part on offer was in *All's Well*. He interposed, 'And did I hear you say that Guthrie's directing it?' I nodded. 'Then do it,' he said. 'Don't think about it. Just do it! You'll have an experience you'll never forget.' This was the kind of thing that almost every actor who'd ever worked with Tyrone Guthrie said about him. Maybe I'd be going to Stratford after all.

First I had a visit to make, and that was to my mother and her husband in Sussex. From her telephone calls I guessed that something was seriously amiss. I arrived to find Lawrence looking much older and between the two of them a perceptible chill. That weekend they were having a large cocktail party, ostensibly to introduce my mother to Lawrence's circle of friends, and this she managed competently, if through gritted teeth. It was not until she was driving me to the station the following day that she allowed herself to speak candidly. She'd been to see Lawrence's doctor and had learnt that after his heart attack he'd begun to display early signs of senile dementia. Now the condition was escalating rapidly. The family had kept all this to themselves. Getting himself to Australia and proposing marriage had been the last achievement of a man whose grasp on the world was failing. Though financially secure, he was now becoming anxious about money, and had refused to give my mother any more to run the house than he had previously given his housekeeper – £4 10s a week. She had been too trusting, or perhaps too proud, to suggest anything in the way of a pre-nuptial agreement, and in money matters was entirely at his mercy. It was an appalling situation and I understood when she said she had seriously considered packing a bag and doing a bunk back to Australia. The worst thing was being shut up in this big house, sur-rounded by the possessions of another marriage, and with no com-pany except this ailing man whom she was beginning to both pity and detest. She had come to the decision that somehow she had to sell the house and buy a flat in London, where Lawrence would be nearer to the help he would need as his condition worsened, and she would have the support of her own friends. All I could do was agree.

The most important person with whom I had to discuss Stratford was Shirley. I knew she would not stand in the way of a job important to my career, and I'd now decided that this was probably such an offer. It would be the longest we'd ever been apart, about nine months, and though we didn't speak of it, both of us knew we might not survive the separation. We could, of course, have married; other actors had managed on less than £16 a week, and with young child-ren, but it was not a life I envied. And what was the point when I would be on call at the theatre day and night? She knew me too well not to be able to read my mind, and it was she who suggested what I thought I wanted: another separation, free of commitment, until I was back in London. Then we'd see. The weeks leading up to my depar-ture were fragile with sadness, which we papered over with the prac-ticalities of subletting my room at Carlyle Square (a tenant was to hand, Peter Nichols), excursions to Stratford to find accommodation (an attic flat in St Gregory's Road) and sorting out what I'd take and what I'd leave. Then suddenly, one day, like string snapping, I was off.

The first day of any rehearsal period is always tense, but a first day in a large classical company, at least a third of the members of which will be young men desperate to make their mark, but with limited opportunities to do so, is doubly so – a mêlée of apprehensive faces wondering what the months ahead will bring. Most of us did not know each other, but we all recognised Guthrie, taller than any of us and dressed as he would be throughout the rehearsal period in a navy polo-necked sweater beginning to go at the elbows, grey flannel bags and canvas plimsolls. With his short haircut and trimmed moustache he looked a bit like an Arctic explorer in retirement, or a brigadier with a peculiar hobby like needlework. He'd been in Canada when

*All's Well* was being cast and from there had nominated most of the leads, but filling the smaller parts and walk-ons was something he'd had to leave to others. Since this nether end of the company always played an important part in any Guthrie production, he was running his eye over us now, assessing the hand he'd been dealt, and not looking all that pleased about it.

The morning was taken up with formalities. Glen Byam Shaw introduced Doctor Guthrie to us, attaching, I thought, a certain irony to the appellation favoured by the director himself. I had a feeling he was a little jealous of him. Many of the actors whose careers Guthrie had fostered were now knights and dames, an honour not accorded him, so he had made perhaps mischievous use of the recent doctorate. It was a distinction that suited him, not quite official, a little to one side. Each actor was then issued with the text in the red pocket Cambridge Edition. I turned idly to my part, and could hardly believe what I was seeing. In the Cambridge, as opposed to my grandmother's rice-paper Oxford Edition, the First Lord was the Second Lord and the Second Lord was the First. I now realised what Paddy Donnell had meant when he said my part was the lesser of the two. Over the lunch hour I felt as miserable as if I'd woken up and found myself shanghaied and aboard a clipper ship bound for China. I faced the prospect that the entire season would be a waste of time.

That afternoon we assumed there'd be a reading of the play which would at least give me the chance of familiarising myself with my new part (I'd already learnt the other one), but Guthrie had other ideas. 'We won't have a reading,' he announced in his foghorn, slightly camp tones. 'It bores those with little parts and embarrasses those with big ones,' and he began at once getting the production on its feet. We had soon reached the First Court Scene in which all the young lords, those with speaking parts and those without, attend the sick King. Guthrie had already directed *All's Well* for the Canadian Stratford, the success of which had prompted this present English production, so he had a blueprint to follow. However, for a director the business of repeating a success can sometimes be a little unnerving, as his memory of a relatively perfect past collides with the stumbling and uncertain present. The horde of young men playing attendant lords shuffled around the stage with the tentativeness of sheep as Guthrie struggled to marshal them into one position, then another. 'Stand up straight!' he ordered. 'You're meant to be soldiers!' With my nose in the little red volume trying to articulate a text I hadn't begun to think about, and weighed down further with my private misery, I must have looked a particular offender. Suddenly, without warning, I received an almighty thwack between the shoulder blades and heard him bellow into my ear, 'STAND UP STRAIGHT!' Was this what Kenneth Griffiths had meant by an experience you'll never forget?

I returned to my new attic flat that evening extremely depressed. There is something absolute about the highs and the lows of an actor's life that makes the latter seem for the moment insuperable. What was it about me that attracted the hostility of the directors I most wanted to impress? Douglas Seale, for instance. Then I remembered how I'd solved that problem. Perhaps this called for the same remedy: learn and prepare the part in its entirety, so that when we next went through the play I would have something to show for myself. I sat down and opened the text. Though not as good a part as Second Lord, First Lord, I realised, had distinct possibilities. Guthrie's production was the first of a number of *All's Wells* to be placed in an autumnal, Edwardian setting, *circa* 1910 (others by John Barton and Trevor Nunn would follow), and I began to see my character as an earnest, ramrod-backed Regular Army officer, good-natured, perhaps a little stupid, but with a certain dandyish preoccupation with his uniforms. Maybe he should have a monocle. In the First Court Scene he has two lines to the ailing sovereign after the young lords have learnt that they are off to the war:

'Tis our hope, Sir, after well-ordered service
To return, and find Your Grace in health.

And I suddenly saw a way of doing them. "'Tis our hope, Sir, after well-ordered service' (fractional pause while he thinks what to say, then a vigorous expression of the blindingly obvious) 'to *return*' (followed by a loyal and enthusiastic afterthought) 'and find Your Grace in health!' I tried it out to myself and it made me laugh. Then I continued through the part and found all sorts of other things that could support this idea. By the time I went to bed I was almost happy.

When we next came to the First Court Scene I was no longer carrying the little red book and my carriage had improved. I said my lines to the King. The director stopped me. 'Good! But do it again and this time take three paces forward before you speak.' I liked that; it would give the First Lord time to agonise over what he was about to say. I did what he asked and out of sight to my right I heard Guthrie's laugh, a kind of muffled whinny. It was a sound I would become particularly attuned to during that rehearsal period, what a fresh fish must be to a performing dolphin. In this same scene the leading man, Bertram, makes his first entrance. He is a stranger to the Court and is in the surprising company of the garishly dressed rogue, Parolles. Guthrie had directed that everyone turn to look at this ill-matched pair; then I had to approach the young man and, in an exchange of whispers, get his name so that I could present him to the King. 'It is the Count Rousillon, my good Lord, young Bertram,' I was meant to say, but Guthrie stopped me. 'You don't know him, so don't quite catch his name the first time. Have to ask him twice.' I thought I could improve on this idea. My second question would be more a look over Bertram's shoulder to the person in the loud check suit a pace or two behind, as if to say, 'And who on earth is that?' I heard the whinny. '*Much* better,' he purred.

This brief moment, like so many of Guthrie's other touches throughout the production, was not just an overlay of comic business on a classic text that didn't require it. It clarified the storytelling. Two new people had come on stage, and the audience now knew that both were important and that their relationship was an odd one. They were curious about them before either had said a word. And a similar curiosity Guthrie was now extending to every one of us in the company. He had the reputation of treating walk-ons like stars and stars like walk-ons, which in the case of *All's Well* wasn't altogether true, since he treated the great Edith Evans, playing the Countess, with affection and just let her get on with it. Stars, however, had largely fulfilled their potential, and Guthrie was interested in people who had yet to do so. That's what rehearsals were for, to realise the potential of the cast, and that, ultimately was what theatre was for, to realise the potential in an audience. He was forever encouraging that spark and on the lookout for it in places where others wouldn't have bothered. In his famous production of *The Three Estates* at the Edinburgh Festival many of the cast were amateurs, but you would never have known it. In our show he would take a young actor who was perhaps timid or physically awkward and give him things to do which turned a liability into an asset. Dedication to this remarkable man spread from one member of the company to another.

There was, however, nothing soft about his benevolence. If an actor didn't give of his best he was in trouble and there could be no excuses.

'Rise above it!' was his famous injunction to anyone who came to him worried, depressed or just plain ill. This is perhaps what he'd been saying to me on that first day. Now I was being rewarded for having done so. Throughout rehearsals he kept giving me things to do, creating moments for my part, which I would then try to improve on or refine. A good role was turning into a marvellous one.

There was a nice little scene between the First Lord and the Second Lord (Paul Hardwick) that had not so far been staged. The army have gone campaigning and the two men are discussing the problems of their young fellow officer and friend, Bertram. Paul and I were called to the rehearsal room. 'I see this scene taking place after a good dinner in the Mess,' said Guthrie. 'It's a hot night and here are the two of you walking up and down under the stars, smoking good cigars. Now fuck off somewhere and work something out, while I get on with the next bit.' It was not yet customary, as it would soon become, to use obscenities casually in ordinary conversation, so Guthrie's use of them at unexpected moments and in unexpected places was funny and rather startling, as if they had emerged from the mouth of a bishop. Paul and I duly found ourselves an empty corridor and, smoking our pencils, we started to walk the scene. I soon found I had some thoughts about it – what the important moments were and how we could choreograph our back-and-forth walk to underline them. I wondered if Paul would object to my taking the initiative but he seemed happy to have someone else do the thinking. We reported back to the rehearsal room, showed the director what we'd done, and it went into the production just as we'd rehearsed it in the corridor. Thus, whether by design or accident, Guthrie gave me my first taste of direction. Word must have got around, because during the rest of the season, the younger actors would sometimes ask me to help them prepare their audition pieces.

Not since *Titus* had I gone to work in the morning with quite such enthusiasm, the more so because I now had a decent part to play. I hardly ever left the rehearsal room, even when I wasn't needed, because what was going on there was so interesting. When critics discussed a Guthrie production it was either to praise its sweeping theatricality or to tut-tut over some defiantly perverse comic touch. What was rarely acknowledged was his thrilling but invisible work on the spoken text. One afternoon I watched him rehearse a scene between Helena (Zoe Caldwell) and the ailing King (Robert Hardy), in which the young woman with healing powers earns the trust of her royal patient. It couldn't have been more simply staged; the King was in a bath chair with Helena sitting beside him. While the scene progressed, Guthrie, puffing on the inevitable cigarette, paced back and forth, not looking at the actors, but absolutely concentrated on what they were saying. Every so often he would bring the scene to a halt with a click of the fingers to suggest a stress or a better way of phrasing, but these interruptions were so deft they barely impeded the flow of the work. One small detail built upon another, and the scene was soon vibrant with impulses and shades of meaning that you would never have guessed were there.

In the playing of Shakespeare he placed great importance on correct breathing, and encouraged his actors to train themselves to be able to deliver three or four lines of verse on the one breath. 'Always observe the rhythm of the line, but don't take a breath until you've completed the sense of what you're saying,' he'd advise. This, of course, is exactly what we do in life, especially if we are passionate about what we want to say. He knew that complex verse, or prose for that matter, is more easily comprehended when the delivery matches the swiftness of the thinking behind it. What I loved about his remarks in rehearsals was that they were always about the connection between theatre and life. Another thing he said that afternoon was, 'The most thrilling sound you will ever hear in an auditorium is that moment when a great opera singer, having just completed a long and complex phrase of wonderful music, suddenly takes a breath!' He didn't say so, but he might have added that this is the same intake that a newborn infant makes as it reaches for life. It was also a sound I heard every night in *Titus* as Olivier was about to embark on, 'I am the sea . . .', but then, of course, Olivier's early successes in Shakespeare had been with this director at the Old Vic before the war.

Guthrie's most extraordinary use of breath in *All's Well* came at the end of the play, when, in the presence of the entire Court, Helena lifts her veil and reveals her identity as wife to the feckless but now penitent Bertram. For everyone on stage it is an awesome moment. Guthrie asked each of us, when the unveiling took place, to not so much breathe out as just let the breath slip from our bodies in astonishment. Had one person done as he had asked it would probably have gone unheard, but with twenty or more people the whisper it produced was uncanny. You could sense the goose-bumps rising all over the auditorium. This was one of those moments when the situation on stage is so strong it elicits a similar response from everyone present, but what most characterised his crowd scenes was that they were composed not of a crowd but of individuals. As groups of people eddied and flowed there was always something interesting or contrary going on in their midst. In a serious situation there might be one person who found it funny; or someone would suddenly break free from the pack and dart across stage to join a friend with whom he wanted to discuss what was happening. This sense of volatile humanity was perfect for Shakespeare's great comedy of reconciliation.

*All's Well That Ends Well* was probably Guthrie's last great British production. Increasingly he committed his energies to bringing classical theatre to the New World and rather lost touch with a changing England. His Canadian playhouse was now a triumphant success, and he was just about to found another in the United States. How these two theatres came into being typifies this extraordinary man. The first began with a long-distance telephone call from some civic-minded residents of a small town in Ontario who thought that their Stratford ought, like the one in England, to have a theatre. At the time, this sleepy little backwater might just as well have been Timbuktu, and any other famous director would have fobbed them off with a few polite words and hung up. Guthrie, however, got on a plane, met the town worthies and said yes. In his first season, with the theatre yet to be built, the plays were staged in a circus tent. He had appealed to an old friend, Alec Guinness, to come to Canada for peanuts and help with the launch, and together they did a *Richard III* under canvas. Within a couple of years he had supervised the building of a thrust stage, the first since the Elizabethans, housed in a theatre complex able to construct its own scenery, make its own costumes and provide office space for an administrative team. It was as self-sufficient as an ocean liner afloat on the Canadian expanse and people who had never been to the theatre in their lives travelled hundreds of miles every night to see what it offered.

That accomplished, he decided to provide North America with another cultural oasis. He took a map and looked for the populated area that was farthest in all directions from any theatrical amenity. It turned out to be Minneapolis, midway between Chicago and Toronto. This time it was Guthrie who approached the civic authorities, and before long, on a prime site, construction had started on another complex of comparable scale to Stratford. This theatre was to bear his name. Only someone of inspirational stature could have accomplished all this, igniting the zeal not only of theatre people, but of lawyers, business leaders and town clerks, to whom the prospect of building a theatre dedicated to classical drama in the middle of the American plains would normally have seemed hopelessly quixotic. And it could only have been done by someone who was indifferent to the usual ambitions and career prospects that govern the lives of most people in the theatre.

Ingmar Bergman has written that, ideally, he wanted to make films the way the great cathedrals of Europe had been built, by artists and craftsmen of all sorts, for whom coming to work in the morning was itself a kind of worship: stonemasons and carpenters happy to express themselves in a comic gargoyle or a carved rafter so high up that only God would see it. Something of this spirit began to attach itself to the rehearsals of *All's Well*, which, increasingly, came to seem a metaphor for something else, something of more significance. What that something was none of us quite knew and Guthrie was not such a fool as to attempt to put it into words. He was a briskly unsentimental man and never let us lose sight of the fact that we had a show to get right. He once remarked, 'No one is irreplaceable, and the sooner we all learn that the better.' But there was something building in the company, a good faith, which absorbed personal ambitions and discontents and put them to better use. The theatre, which can so often be trivial or bogus, has something going for it which the great solo arts do not. Literature and painting testify to what individuals can achieve, and to what other individuals responding to them can feel, but the theatre is about what can be done within a group, and then what an even larger group can collectively experience. At its best it always expresses hope, no matter what the play itself may have to say. Maybe that's what our rehearsals were a metaphor for: hope.

On our first night it was as if we had two things to present to our audience; a new production of Shakespeare's play, obviously, but also a demonstration of the spirit that had gone into its making. Were we saying that ends are indistinguishable from means? If so, in a mostly expedient world, this was a radical assertion. It was Guthrie's ability to conjure up such possibilities that made him the unique director he was. The first night was everything we hoped it would be, and was followed the next morning by a rapturous set of notices. In *The Guardian*,

Philip Hope Wallace described Paul Hardwick and me as 'brilliant'. I should have written Kenneth Griffiths a letter to thank him.

On the morning of that first night, trying to settle my nerves with a brisk walk, I had run into the Doctor in the street. 'Come to lunch tomorrow,' he said. 'It'll be just you and Dame Edith.' Excited but a little mystified, I turned up at the appointed time. The Guthries had rented a couple of rooms in the rambling Elizabethan house owned by the company's singing teacher, Denne Gilkes. It was right in the middle of town, just off the High Street, but you would never have guessed because you approached the house down a narrow, inconspicuous alley between shop fronts. This opened magically onto a small Tudor courtyard with a big tree in the middle. Denne, a delightful woman in her seventies, lived downstairs with half a dozen cats, the Guthries lived on the first floor, and elsewhere in the building in another set of rooms lodged the twenty-two-year-old Vanessa Redgrave. The house was bohemian and extremely romantic, if in need of a sweep, with odd staircases and corridors going off in all directions.

Guthrie and his wife, Judith, who was almost as tall as her husband, were waiting for me. As a couple they had a reputation for eccentricity. During a previous production at Stratford, they had lived on a barge moored on the River Avon. People walking along the banks in the early morning would see the two of them, stark naked, stepping off the boat and sinking below the water in pursuit of their daily ablutions. With her slightly anguished well-bred manner you wouldn't have been surprised to find Judith in a leaking stately home, sitting in a Sheraton chair, reading a socialist tract with a bucket beside her to collect the drips. Edith Evans, beautifully dressed and rather girlish for someone of seventy-two, had already arrived, and we sat in one small room, drinking sherry, until bidden into an adjoining small room to have lunch. This we ate off our knees on paper plates, the sort of meal one might have expected at the height of the Blitz, a lettuce leaf, a slice of spam and here and there a raisin. It was as odd an occasion as anything in Ireland. Eventually Dame Edith departed, and I was left to chat to the Doctor. We talked about the theatre in general and I tried to be confident and assertive. 'Before the theatre can do anything else it must first of all entertain,' I said, and he looked at me as if seriously considering the point. Wondering if this sounded a little philistine, I hastily added a rider, 'Granted that there are many ways of defining the word "entertain".' Later the conversation became more personal and I lowered my guard a little to express some anxiety about my professional future. His reply was laconic and brief, but it was the most encouraging thing that anyone had yet said to me: 'You'll be all right.'

There was, I think, a two-fold reason why Guthrie took an interest in me. The first was that I was an Australian and the New World was the present focus of his artistic energies. The other was that he recognised in me that British archetype from between the wars, the public school rebel. The unhappiness he had experienced as a boy at Wellington, I, in a kind of colonial time-warp, endured thirty years later at the King's School, and ever since I had been having that same unending debate with a background I might reject but was too marked by ever to escape. Ironically, what Guthrie found interesting in me, my own generation of British directors didn't. Most were grammar school boys whose wits and determination had got them to Oxbridge. Neither the rarified torments nor the self-regard attached to public school life meant anything to them, though, as Peter Hall would soon teach me, the totemic importance of Cambridge was another matter. In the theatre, a new elite was busy supplanting another, erecting new barriers even as they tore down the old ones. Intellectually, I was all for change. Emotionally, part of me was stranded in a second-hand British past.

Actors assess the directors for whom they work almost entirely by what happens in the rehearsal room, but there is another side to the job, just as crucial, which is over by the time rehearsals start: namely, the selection of the team through whose talents the director will realise his production. This includes not just his cast, but a number of designers, and occasionally a composer. It is in this area that a young director can compensate for his lack of experience in the rehearsal room. He has his ear to the ground and is directly in touch with the new ideas through which his own generation is defining itself. Our next production, *A Midsummer Night's Dream*, directed by a Peter Hall two years younger than I was, amply demonstrated this, though I was not to realise it until the dress rehearsal revealed Lila de Nobili's designs and introduced Raymond Leppard's brilliant pastiche of Elizabethan music. The assumptions behind the production had suddenly come vividly to life. This was a *Dream* in which Theseus' court was a big sixteenth-century country house; the woods outside Athens were Warwickshire forest; and Bottom and his crew were rural artisans.

The text which so richly evokes the English countryside was matched in this production to the specifics of place and culture that it actually describes. Because of the post-war interest in social history, the late fifties became an auspicious time to mount revivals of classic texts. There was fresh attention given to the body of ideas and beliefs that Shakespeare and his audience had once shared and taken for granted, as well as to more down-to-earth matters, like precisely how many yards of fabric went into the making of an Elizabethan doublet and how exactly it was cut. Lila de Nobili's costumes drew heavily on the Hilliard miniatures in the Victoria and Albert Museum that had first been drawn to my attention by Miss Byrne at RADA. When Albert Finney, as Demetrius, stood beneath a stage tree, one foot crossed over another, it was like seeing the famous miniature of the young man dressed in black and white come to life.

On the first day of rehearsals, however, all this was a month away. What was of most interest was the presence amongst us of a famous actor and film star, Charles Laughton, whose Captain Bligh had been a frequent visitor to The Stockpot in one of Peter Nichols' best impersonations. As a child I had watched, wide-eyed, most of his famous movie performances, from Henry VIII to Quasimodo, and here he was in the flesh, more delicately proportioned than I'd expected, with a big head on a small, plump frame. He had elegant, dimpled hands with a little finger crooked, and a hesitant, blinking manner like some burrowing animal suddenly exposed to the world above ground. Our director was taller and slimmer than his star, but both men had the same round faces that a cartoonist might have rendered exclusively with circles and curves. They could have passed for father and son. As Snout the tinker, all my scenes were with Bottom, as were those of the other rude mechanicals, and we became slightly miffed when we realised that Peter's attention was going to be focused exclusively on Laughton. One couldn't help thinking how Guthrie would have rehearsed us. This was unfair. Any young director following in the footsteps of the Doctor would have suffered in comparison. Guthrie was so well established, with a catalogue of international achievements behind him that he could afford to seem above personal ambition and to enjoy exercising disinterested benevolence. Peter, though something of a wunderkind, had his greatest challenges ahead of him and had yet to consolidate on his early successes. These included *Waiting for Godot* at the Arts Theatre, a *Twelfth Night* and a *Love's Labour's Lost* at

Stratford (productions on the strength of which he had become Director Designate of the Shakespeare Memorial Theatre) and a show which I had particularly liked, Tennessee Williams' *Camino Real*, part of an audacious, if commercially unsuccessful, season he had staged at the Phoenix Theatre.

Was I envious of Peter? Most certainly. Still in his twenties, he seemed to have everything – a film-star wife, Leslie Caron, who was not only delightful but a high earner, and all he wanted in the way of toys – a new sports car to take him up and down from Stratford, and tight, boxy silk suits of Italian cut, extremely modish in 1959, to wear to rehearsals. Most of all he had what I conspicuously did not, a successful and fulfilling career. Was I suspicious of him? I was indeed, to the extent that he was a prime representative of an expanding elite in the world of British arts – young graduates from Oxford and Cambridge. They were everywhere, at the BBC, in theatre, film, opera and, as spokesmen for their own generation, in arts journalism. A young man could move straight from one of these two universities (the others didn't seem to count) into empowering jobs that involved hiring and firing other people more experienced and often more talented than they were. About some of them, like the *Beyond the Fringe* team, I was wildly approving, because there can be no argument about being funny; either you are or you aren't, and if you can be funny and intelligent so much the better. Directing plays is a different matter. Though there may be such a thing as a talent for directing, it is nowhere near as specific and recognisable as, say, musical ability or, indeed, a gift for acting or writing. Because a director works through others it is not always possible to tell if he is enlarging on their talents or merely hiding behind them. A clever operator can do so for years, and most actors I knew had worked for a priggish young man with a fresh degree and a few opinions whom they had had to rescue from his own ineptitude as the first night approached. The irony was that the first of these young Oxbridge directors, the figure who before the war had supplied the prototype, was Tyrone Guthrie.

Charles Laughton stood four square behind Peter's concept for the production. They had obviously discussed it at length. But it was also soon apparent that he had no interest in British hierarchies and divisions. Escaping them had been one of the reasons he had spent most of his professional life in the States. After the first day's reading he had invited the five of us playing the other mechanicals back to his hotel so that we could get to know each other better. It was a rather awkward meeting, with Charles eyeing and quizzing each of us suspiciously as he tried to sniff out what talent the group had to offer. About one thing, however, we were left in no doubt: he wanted to be not 'Mr Laughton', but one of us, Charles. In the rehearsal room during that first week he had a tentativeness and an insecurity surprising in an actor of his renown. Either he had no stage technique or repudiated acquiring any because it didn't serve the sort of acting which interested him. He had little sense of voice projection and even moving from one position on stage to another seemed to present a multitude of problems. Peter deferred constantly to his anxieties with the result that rehearsals tended to go round in circles as Charles considered and rejected first one staging notion then another. The rest of us could do little but stand around wondering when the director and star would make up their minds. It was, however, too easy to be impatient with Laughton as some of the company were becoming. His remarkable film work spoke for itself; if this was the way he arrived at his moments then, however exasperating, he deserved to be indulged.

One morning, not having made much progress, we had taken a break and were chatting together over our mugs of coffee. I had embarked on an anecdote about my travails in weekly rep when I noticed a certain restlessness in Peter; he was concerned that I might be boring his star. By then I was getting to know Charles quite well, thought otherwise and continued. I had not yet reached the end of my story before Peter cut in, 'All right, Michael! We all know what an old pro you are.' I said nothing but was instantly seething. Implicit in this quip was the intolerable assumption that I had somehow *chosen* to work in weekly rep, that it represented my level. I felt as angry as a soldier from the trenches being reprimanded by a junior staff officer for having mud on his boots. Charles, who was extraordinarily sensitive to such situations, understood what was going on, and his gaze, all blinks and embarrassment, flicked back and forth between us like an agitated bat.

I wanted to like Peter; I wanted to believe in him. After all, it was in my interests to do so if I was going to be at Stratford for two years, but it was sometimes difficult. He was so obsessed with pedigree. First, there were the stars, then there were the workaday actors, then there were the walk-ons, and he allotted his attention to each accordingly. Though he was mostly civil and informal, there was no way you could get beyond the wall of his priorities, and whatever category he first found you in was the category in which you would find yourself pegged. Even his ideas had to have the imprimatur of Cambridge. Peter was in the process of articulating a theory of verse speaking that he had inherited from the Cambridge don George Rylands. The fact that one line of verse ended and below another began meant that every line ending had to be religiously marked, by an intake of breath preferably, and other places where it was permissible or forbidden to breathe were similarly prescribed. It was almost as if the layout of the text on the page had the authority of a musical score – precise instructions as to how the words should be spoken. Get these right and everything else would follow. However, the theory could not account, for instance, for the power and insight of the Russian film of *Hamlet* in the mid-sixties, in which none of the above rules applied. And it did little to address the first concern of the performer, or indeed the audience – what do the words actually *mean*, not just in sense but in feeling? This was something that could not be arrived at schematically, but was a shifting melt of the text, of the personality of the actor and of the times in which he happened to be living. The following year Peter would go into print in the *Sunday Times*, stating his intention of revolutionising the speaking of Shakespearean verse. This was not particularly gracious to a generation of splendid actors who thought they were managing quite well already, and who in today's theatre have yet to be replaced. They had learnt their skills, as had previous generations, not from Academia but from the leading actors of their youth, under whose spell it had been their turn to fall. This oral tradition is not perhaps conclusive evidence of the way Shakespeare's words may originally have been spoken. It is, however, the *only* evidence, as much later on Peter was to observe himself.

As rehearsals continued on the *Dream*, I was dismayed to find myself concluding that, of the two directors I had worked for during the season, it was the older man, now departed for North America, who was the radical, and the younger, the one on whom I depended for a future, who was the reactionary. At least I was getting on with Charles Laughton. For all the mechanicals, including Charles, the breakthrough at rehearsals came with the play scene in the last act. Charles took his cue from Theseus' lines: 'I will hear that play / For never anything can be amiss / When simpleness and duty tender it,' and brought to the comic desperation of the scene an innocence which was touching as well as funny. My part, Snout, has to act the role of a brick wall, through the chinks of which the lovers, Pyramus and Thisbe, will whisper their endearments. I thought it might be fun to play him as someone totally averse to appearing in public, to whom the mere thought of acting in a play was a nightmare. When Bottom addresses him, 'And thou, O Wall, O sweet, O lovely Wall,' I thought Snout should become crucified with self-consciousness. Charles picked up on this and played the repeat of the line for all it was worth, whilst I squirmed and bent one ankle sideways in painful embarrassment. It seemed to work well for both of us. Later, at the costume parade I found that in the play scene my costume was to be augmented with a number of painted plastic bricks attached to my shoulders and balanced on my head. These were quite unreal and fairly unfunny, so I asked if instead I could have a couple of real bricks, to be held one in each hand.

On the night of the dress rehearsal these props were waiting for me on the prop table, two beautiful battered red bricks that might have passed for the genuine Tudor article. On my entrance as the Wall, I carried them with me, and, just as we had rehearsed, stood stock-still, until an impatient nod from Peter Quince launches Wall into his opening speech. I'd decided to play my first two lines with the panicky speed of a runaway horse. 'In this same interlude it doth befall / That I, one Snout by name, present a wall,' and, on impulse, at the end of the couplet, I slammed the brick in my left hand on top of the brick in my right, thus, and almost by accident, constructing a wall two bricks high. This primitive engineering was accompanied by a startling percussive thwack! as one brick impacted on another. In the dark auditorium a handful of the company provided a scattered audience and I heard their surprised laughter. One person clapped. I was onto something. By the time of the next run-through I had refined the business by dusting the brick in my right hand with talcum powder, so that the impacting bricks now released a small cloud of brick dust. At every performance thereafter the business got a round of applause.

I've dwelt on this small moment only to show how such things happen, out of invention, certainly, but also because of the empathy between performers and by happy accident. The process is organic, one thing growing out of another day by day, and like all growth, it is risky because sometimes it doesn't happen. It is the very opposite of rigidly following a concept. Every production of a classic is like new blooms in an old garden, and these fresh and sometimes surprising shoots are the reason for revisiting a play you already know; otherwise one may as well stay at home and enjoy the garden in ground plan, all too often the better idea. For the actor, the playing of small parts, providing they are good ones, which First Lord and Snout undoubtedly were, can be excellent training. The playing demands detail and precision because there are very limited opportunities to warm up and none of the second chances that come with leading roles.

Our first preview of the *Dream* was not a happy experience. Charles seemed disconcerted by a set in which he was not yet at home, and by the presence of the audience, these guests who had arrived a little ahead of the party. He blinked his way through the evening as if the stage lights were headlamps in which he had the misfortune to be caught, and we were too nervous to help him. The four young lovers, who included Vanessa Redgrave in what should have been perfect casting as Helena, ran to and from each other with dogged energy but generating hardly a laugh. Two weeks before they had seemed to be on their way to a comic triumph. With Ian Holm (Puck) and Robert Hardy (Oberon) they had found a space somewhere in the building, and, as Paul Hardwick and I had done, made something of their own of their long scene of changing affections in the forest. When they unveiled their work in the rehearsal room we all felt some excitement. As actors will, they had gone hunting for the attractive qualities in the scene, its comedy and humanity, but in this instance they were the right ones. The playing was deft and they had blocked the scene with considerable invention. But Peter was not yet sufficiently experienced to take the actors that extra step beyond that which they had already achieved. His method was simply to say 'No' to the things he was offered which he didn't like. With each repetition of the scene, more of the steam seemed to go out of it. Soon Peter began to say 'No,' and before long the lovers were back where they had begun.

The morning after the first preview a gloomy company met in the rehearsal room for a post-mortem. In my estimation what the production lacked was focus and detail, a situation which could only be corrected by attending to specific moments and getting them right, one by one. However, Peter had another approach. He had set up a blackboard at the end of the room which he had divided into five vertical columns representing the five acts of the play. He now took three pieces of chalk, each a different colour, and drew three lines sideways through the five acts. These up-and-down lines graphed the three strands of the narrative – the worlds of the lovers and the court; of the fairy kingdom; and of the rude mechanicals. He explained that the graphs rose and fell in accordance with the importance of the story-line in each act, and that we could learn from this. I wondered in which Cambridge tome he had located this arcane aid. From the point of view of the company he might just as well have been charting the week's weather. Priscilla Morgan, who was playing Hermia, caught my eye from across the room and we exchanged one of those looks between actors that a director is lucky if he does not catch. The first night would have been a lost cause had not the evening ended well with the play scene when Charles' performance suddenly caught fire, and the following morning our notices were mixed. However, it would be wrong to suppose that it was a bad production; in its basic assumptions it was excellent, and later in the run, when the actors had had the chance to shape and refine their material, it would become the most enjoyable play in the repertoire with at least two outstanding performances from Charles and Ian Holm. I have described Peter Hall as I perceived him at the time, making no allowances for a lack of skills which it would be only a matter of time before he had gone some way to acquire. Nor did I have any appreciation of his extraordinary brilliance as an entrepreneur and later in his career as advocate for the theatre at large. However, I doubt if we would ever have liked each other, approaching the theatre, indeed approaching England, from such opposing directions.

The business that season at Stratford was phenomenal, and we in the company soon took it for granted that every performance we gave would be to standing-room only. As would be the case thirteen years later at the National, Peter Hall was in line for the most successful and well-endowed theatre in the land. There had been a Shakespeare Festival at Stratford since David Garrick's day, but when first Sir Barry Jackson, then Anthony Quayle took over the direction of the theatre after the Second War, it achieved a new zenith. The organisation had extensive real estate, enormous financial reserves, a guaranteed audience and a pool of star talent, both established and new to the scene, longing to be invited to work there. The following year Peter Hall was to embark on some audacious new policies, creating a permanent London base for the company where modern plays could be included in the repertoire, and offering contracts to his actors that extended over years, not months. For all of this he deserves credit. However, coincidental with these innovations, the Shakespeare Memorial Theatre, on the basis of its prior achievements, was granted a Royal Charter and was obliged to change its name. In the process someone mislaid its history. Something new, the Royal Shakespeare Company, had apparently been 'founded'. If so, no company has had surer foundations.

As an institution, on the other hand, the Shakespeare Memorial Theatre of 1959 might have been designed to engender discontent in most of those it had hired to perform. The poster for the season demonstrated how rigidly the acting company was divided by billing. One accepted that the country at large was still split along class lines, but what was a serious theatre doing mimicking such divisions? First, there was Top Billing in large letters, then in much smaller letters Middle Billing, the uneasy territory in which I resided, and finally in letters so tiny you could hardly read them, Bottom Billing. Sometimes on the noticeboard invitations to social events would be posted which read 'Top and Middle Billing only', or 'Top Billing only'. Because we spent so much time at the theatre, rehearsing all day and playing at night, it became a natural breeding ground for all manner of grievances and slights. One of the reasons that we had been so grateful to Guthrie was that he had briefly delivered us from this sort of littleness, and from the point of view of company morale his production was the high point of the season.

In such an environment you need a friend, someone with whom you can turn discontent into laughter, and I had found a lovely one, the twenty-two-year-old Vanessa Redgrave. We were both at about the same level in the company – Vanessa's only important parts were Helena in the *Dream* and Virgilia in *Coriolanus*, and she was walking on in her other two shows – so already we had something in common. Coming from a famous theatrical family, though not yet famous herself, she had an appealing modesty that acknowledged she had a way to go and in the meantime didn't expect any special favours. People who, from the day they are born, have grown up immersed in the world of the theatre are often the least theatrical, and the impression Vanessa gave at this time was that of a well-brought-up young woman determined to do her best following in the family's professional footsteps. With her openness of expression and the ready laugh of someone who can accept teasing, she was very lovely, though perhaps still too coltish to be described as beautiful. I was vastly attracted to her but in a protective way that I thought precluded anything beyond companionship.

Soon I was a regular visitor at the big studio she occupied in Denne Gilkes' Elizabethan house, with a kitchen off to one side and up a few steps, a small bedroom. Here I could bellyache about Peter Hall and she could fret bravely about the trouble she was having with Helena, a part which, on the face of it, she had been born to play. When the company departed for an outing as we did one Sunday to play baseball at a US Air Force base where nuclear bombers were stationed, Vanessa and I would usually find ourselves sharing the same bus seat. On this occasion, as we entered the base I made bleak fun of the sign over the gate, 'Peace is our profession', and later gleefully reported back on a conversation I had had with a pilot's wife who was providing refreshments for the company. She was a neat, blonde woman who might have stepped out of an advertisement in the *Saturday Evening Post*. I had just asked her in a fairly mild way, 'Do any of you ever question the morality of what you might be asked to do?', and for a second she seemed nonplussed. Then, as if the penny had dropped, she responded brightly, 'Oh, the morals at the base are *very* good!' Vanessa took a fairly dim view of this sort of seditious mockery which I often employed simply to get a rise out of her or provoke her laughter. By and large she found the world a promising place and with her natural optimism was wary of anyone who could be construed as a malcontent.

We enjoyed our argument, but my rather frayed radicalism was not to her taste. In the interests of truth I had patched it with far too many qualifications and Vanessa was not interested in anything as mealy-mouthed as truth. As I was yet to learn, she yearned for something with much more life to it, belief, and in a few years' time it would be belief that lit up her acting from within and set her on a path of recklessly courageous political activism. Typically, as the 1959 General Election approached, it was I who railed against the Tories, but on polling day it was Vanessa who told me she was taking a Green Line bus to London to cast her vote, though she refused to divulge who for. If we didn't always agree, I was finding more and more about her to admire. She had a range of skills that wouldn't have disgraced a Jane Austen heroine; she spoke French and Italian, played a musical instrument, and one afternoon I found her at work by the window on an accomplished watercolour of the garden below. She also possessed a more up-to-date talent in a well-bred young woman: the ability at a moment's notice to rustle up an elegant meal for two or three of us in the company who just happened to have dropped by. Vanessa was one of those people who have the admirable, if sometimes abused, quality of being willing to give more than they get. I really liked her.

In the professional area my life appeared to be on the up-and-up. A well-regarded critic, J. C. Trewin, who had been following my progress since the Birmingham Rep, wrote a piece about the *Dream*, exclusively in praise of two performances, mine and Anthony Nichols' as Theseus. I now had a another success to put beside *All's Well*, and as far as my second year with the company was concerned, I was confident that I had more than fulfilled my side of the bargain. Indeed, I was becoming quite pleased with myself. My parts in the remaining two productions were negligible, but I thought I might be able to show a little more of my hand if I was given something interesting to understudy, so I approached Glen Byam Shaw and asked if I could cover either Gloucester in *Lear* or Menenius in *Coriolanus*. It was the first time in my life that I had ever lobbied for a part and it would prove a mistake. The condition of the actor is that he exists, literally, inside his work, and on the stage can never see himself as others see him. In my own career most of my successes, then and later, were in parts in which I was initially surprised to find myself cast. Acceptance of what comes one's way is a necessary part of the life and it helps to have a little of the fatalism that goes with it. Actors need faith, not a sense of what is politic, and when they bring will to bear on their careers they often invite trouble. A week later I learnt that I had been given not one but both roles to understudy and it was too late to protest that there is just so much a thirty-year-old actor can do to differentiate between the characterisation of two parts twice his age.

The next show to go into rehearsal was *Coriolanus*, again directed by Peter Hall, and on this occasion he would be on surer ground. Laurence Olivier was repeating a part he had first played at the Old Vic before the war and knew exactly what he wanted to do with it, whilst the roles of Volumnia and Menenius were in the assured hands of Edith Evans and Harry Andrews. This suited Peter's method of direction, which was to be a kind of editor intelligently sifting through what others put before him. It was popular with stars, who were happy to accept guidance if it was offered deferentially and on their terms. Again his choice of designers showed real flair. The American

Boris Aronson did the set, which consisted of levels, steps and a monumental doorway, all of which appeared to have been carved out of the face of a huge rock. It was honeycombed with entrances so that in an instant an empty stage could be populated by the Roman mob like bees emerging from a hive. In the centre, a lip projected some ten feet above stage level, and it was from here that Olivier embarked on the moment for which the production became famous. He had practised it over the end of a diving board in Los Angeles where he had just finished filming *Spartacus*. It is the end of the play, and Coriolanus has just been betrayed by his great rival, Aufidius. Cornered by his enemies on this upper level, he is about to meet his death when suddenly the wounded Coriolanus, having shouted his defiance, hurls himself at Aufidius below. His assailants reach for him and just manage to catch him by his ankles as he twists in mid-air. Swaying back and forth, head down, his arms dangling, he is finally dispatched. Olivier had in mind the ignominious fate of the dead Mussolini, suspended upside down for all to see after having been riddled with bullets. For any actor, let alone one in his early fifties, it was an extraordinarily daring manoeuvre, and at every performance, as he leapt into space, there was the sound of a packed audience catching its breath. An onerous responsibility resided with the four or five spear-carriers who had to catch him. Sometimes you would see one of the hands lose its grip and go sliding down an ankle to latch at the last moment onto the strap of his sandal. Vanessa and I, waiting for the curtain call, used to watch from the wings, and lay bets that this would be the night when the most famous actor in the world would be dropped on his head.

There is no doubt that Olivier took pride in such moments and went hunting for them as a way of putting his stamp on the great parts. However, this particular moment of acrobatics was well judged. *Coriolanus* is a play in which the climax is not a battle or a duel but a long scene in which a mother prevails over her son. On the page the death that follows seems almost perfunctory. It needs to be staged with a certain size to fill the sails of the drama as it comes into harbour. During rehearsals he kept largely to himself, but on one occasion he made a rather calculated visit to the canteen to mix with the troops. He sat amongst us with a cup of tea, and, like Coriolanus in the play, showed us his wounds: the scar on his lip where a camera had backed into him during *Henry V*, the mark on his leg where an arrow had passed straight through during the filming of the battle in *Richard III*, and a variety of other injuries. His most alarming story concerned a matinee of the famous double bill of *Oedipus Rex* and *The Critic*, when, as Mr Puff in the latter play, he made his final entrance descending on a rope from high above the stage. On this occasion, waiting in the flies thirty feet in the air, he had reached for the rope only to feel it give under his weight. Someone had forgotten to tie it off, and the rope went coiling to the floor below. Caught off balance, he managed to find something to cling on to, and was eventually lowered to safety. But he had nearly lost his life.

Coriolanus was a wonderful part for Olivier, and no actor will ever reveal more of the character's mordant humour. In some scenes his performance seemed to be paragraphed by laughter coming from the house. The great speeches, notably 'You common cry of curs,' were thrillingly done and had the piercing resonance of a brass instrument. However, I never felt I was looking into the depths of his personality as I had sometimes during *Titus*. He also seemed a rather different man and some of the iron detachment of the character he was playing carried over into his behaviour in the rehearsal room. Once, when a group of us, playing rather unlikely Roman elders, waited with him to make an entrance, one we'd already rehearsed five or six times, two of the young men stifled a yawn. Olivier turned to them and muttered, 'Not enjoying this line of work, boys?' The sly menace of the line was undisguised. He had much on his mind at this time, his marriage to Vivien Leigh to conclude, another to Joan Plowright to plan, and he was just about to start work on the film of *The Entertainer*. Also, a National Theatre was at last on the horizon and I think he accepted that getting the crown for himself and making it happen, as well as sorting out his private life, would take all the steel in his nature. At one point he was playing Coriolanus in Stratford by night and shooting *The Entertainer* in Blackpool by day. He would be picked up by an ambulance after the show and would try to get what sleep he could during the overnight journey.

On the press night, the actor's moment of truth, I set off from my dressing room to make my first entrance, and ran into Olivier in the corridor that led to the stage. He was standing there having a final drag on a cigarette before the night's push. It made an odd picture, this man accoutred as a Roman general with a consoling smoke held between thumb and forefinger. He caught sight of me, threw his eyes up in a gesture of resignation, then stubbed out the cigarette on an ashtray attached to the wall and shouldered his way through the swing door. Within fifteen minutes of curtain-up Coriolanus would be in the midst of battle, and I thought, as I had so often on first nights, about the similarity between the lot of a company of actors and a column of troops as they wait, pulses racing, for the moment when they will be pitched willy-nilly into the action. The dangers are not comparable, but the nerves can be. In this instance the stage warrior wore lipstick and had shaved not only his legs but his arms and his chest to give a better suggestion of the young Roman hero. In his quick-change cubicle in the wings, Olivier had an enormous bottle of scent, half a pint of 'Miss Dior', with which he would douse himself, when, dripping in stage blood and sweating, he returned from hand-to-hand combat with Aufidius. Here he could inspect himself in an arrangement of mirrors, turning his face from side to side and tugging fastidiously at the back of his wig. Ahead of him that night was possible humiliation but hardly death, though neither are pleasant to anticipate. At such moments, acting can seem the oddest activity in the world no matter who is doing it, about as dignified as a fantasy played out with props and costumes in a massage parlour. Then suddenly – and this was about to happen – it is redeemed by passion, skill and imagination. But it is always touch-and-go, which is perhaps why sensible people are wary of the actor's calling and why the theatre cannot, and should not, ever be entirely respectable.

Respectability was waiting for us after the curtain came down, at the party which Olivier was giving at the Welcombe, a grand hotel a mile or two out of town. There he sat at his table, our host, this pleasant, greying man in a dinner jacket, surveying his guests through heavy, black-framed spectacles. He might have been a surgeon or a successful solicitor celebrating a wedding anniversary. This was his second performance of the evening in what might be described as an audacious double bill. Could this be the same man we had just seen challenging the Roman mob, and was he taking surreptitious pleasure in provoking the question? Vivien Leigh had come up for the first night and sat beside him, the last occasion most of us would see them together. In their company was an awesomely glamorous and recently widowed Lauren Bacall. I wanted to ask her to dance but my courage failed. Invitations to the party had not been extended to everyone in the company, but at least the guest list hadn't been decided solely on the basis of billing. I was delighted to be included and had no trouble taking a different view of the event from those who had not. My fortunes within the company were on the rise and so, inevitably, was my feeling that this was just as it should be. I met Peter Hall in the loo and we stood side by side, facing the porcelain in our black ties, and chatted and shook ourselves like the best of friends.

Was Vanessa at the party? I don't remember, but if an invitation had been denied her, she would have been, as usual, a good sport. Increasingly we were in each other's company, and I was now going back to her studio after the performance on a regular basis to find a Dubonnet poured, music on the record player and supper under way in the kitchen. It was obvious we were moving towards an affair, but notwithstanding my feeling for her, I wondered about the wisdom of it. For a start she was relatively inexperienced and I put a high value on what we already had. I didn't want to run even a slight risk of being the person who introduced her to harm. And there was another reason. I had formed an attachment to someone outside the theatre. It was not an unimportant relationship but it was a circumscribed one. The young woman already had a boyfriend with whom she had no wish to break up, despite his habitual neglect of her for sporting events in the company of other men. His carelessness had cost him her fidelity. We could see each other only intermittently but we had become close, meeting each other's roaming hungers. It seemed the very opposite of my friendship with Vanessa, but I hadn't yet recognised her formidable thirst for life, its pain as much as its pleasure, and her intention to take huge, reckless draughts of it. She wanted an affair that season and I was there. So one started; with some uncertainty at first, but Vanessa was unfazed.

In this tangle of spluttering fuses there was another waiting to be ignited. Since first-person pain is usually third-person farce, a better metaphor might be that a third banana skin had been added to the pile. One morning at the height of summer I found a letter from Shirley waiting for me at the stage door. The look of her artless handwriting on the envelope was enough to release a flood of opposed feelings, first a sense of invasion, then remorse, love and a growing apprehension about what the letter might contain. I opened it as I walked into the rehearsal room. The tone was sober and final. There was something about another person but she wanted to come to Stratford so that she could tell me about it personally and suggested the coming weekend. That Saturday I was expecting someone who would be a subdued and mournful match to her letter, but the Shirley who arrived was smiling, bursting with health in a cotton dress with brown limbs on display and as beautiful as I had ever known her. It seemed there was indeed another man whom she liked and who had asked her to marry him. She wanted from me the freedom to make up her mind and I gave it to her. We then went on, as if neither had spoken, to have another of those weekends that I remembered from towns and cities all over the British Isles, when she had taken me by the hand and led me out of some grim, brick street to the green hills about which I knew nothing but which were always only a step beyond the boundaries of the town, the beautiful country outside places like Sheffield and Chesterfield. That Sunday we packed a picnic and climbed the sunny Stratford hills and talked and laughed continuously just as we had done before, in all but one respect. Through every familiar thing we did, the thought 'Never again' tolled like a bell. It's no wonder that these decisions people have to make in the first half of their lives are so suffused in anguish; from the perspective of our imperious genes they are the most important choices of our lives. I saw Shirley onto the train on Sunday night and returned to my flat, overwhelmed with grief and an undefined sense that I had somehow betrayed not only her life but my own. The following weekend it was I who took the train to see her. We decided that at the end of the season, when I returned to London, we would get married. I had stopped and fatefully looked back. Would it have been better for both our sakes if I had not, and was it the fate of even the most perfect couple to become to each other both the worst and the best thing to have happened, the worst because it represents the denial of other possibilities, the best because without it we would never have been the recipient of this particular gift of love? Expecting answers to these questions is pointless though that doesn't prevent people spending a lifetime asking them.

In the meantime, and until the end of the season, other possibilities were still open to me. I told Vanessa about Shirley and she took a surprisingly realistic view of it. Maybe she regarded it as a challenge, but her response was not what I expected. She wanted the affair to continue and for that matter so did I. Thereafter, at each meeting I watched a little more of the woman emerge from the person I had thought of as a girl. It was as unsettling as it was exciting, like suddenly having to acknowledge unexpected talent in a colleague and I found I was constantly revising my view of her. Our affair had acquired a frisson of danger, like that moment on horseback when a canter slides into a gallop. It would not be long before the gallop became a bolt.

Of necessity we were seeing less of each other. *King Lear* was in rehearsal, and just as *Othello* had been my play out, this would be Vanessa's. My part was negligible, the Knight to Lear, but I was in a great many scenes and also had a big understudy to attend to, so all day long I was in the rehearsal room. The director was Glen Byam Shaw and he was conscientious but not much more. He reminded me a little of Anthony Eden, Prime Minister at the time of Suez – the same anguished charm deployed simultaneously to elicit sympathy and get his own way. He was a great respecter of billing. At an evening rehearsal that involved just four of us, Charles Laughton, Anthony Nichols, me and a young Ian Holm, playing the Fool and only recently promoted to top billing, Glen in one sentence referred to Laughton as 'Charles' when speaking to Ian, and a moment later 'Mr Laughton' when speaking to me. As usual on such occasions, Charles' eyes went walkabout with unease. At the end of the rehearsal we all stood chatting and I noticed Glen regarding me with his Eden smile fixedly in place. 'Goodnight, Michael,' he said evenly, and then when I didn't budge, repeated it. This time I understood and did what was expected of me – left, so that the three actors in top billing could go to Glen's office and accept a whisky from him. I was snorting with indignation. It was a ludicrous way to run a theatre and I couldn't wait to confront Vanessa with this latest example of English surrealism.

Charles struggled valiantly with his Lear but he could never really manage the big rhetorical moments, during the storm or when he curses his ungrateful daughters. He simply didn't have the voice. However, there was one scene that I doubt if I shall ever see better played and this was with the blinded Gloucester when Lear expatiates on his newly acquired insight into the world's darkness. Charles played it with an understanding and a simplicity that almost trans-cended acting. I sat watching him in the rehearsal room, spellbound, and if I was asked to nominate one thing in that entire season that approached the condition of art, it would be this scene that morning. I told him afterwards how wonderful it was and he looked at me side-ways with characteristic Laughton suspicion and asked, 'Are you com-plimenting me or Shakespeare?' 'Both,' I answered, amused, which seemed to be an acceptable response. I was getting quite fond of him and grateful for his support; reports often reached me of how Charles had been lauding my performance in the *Dream* to someone or other. During the run of *King Lear* I would stand beside him in the darkness of the wings waiting for us both to go on, while he sighed, huffed, puffed and occasionally groaned to dramatise the enormity of the task waiting for him. His first hurdle was mounting the small rostrum from which we made our entrance and, being rather unsteady on his feet, he liked me to give him a hand up. At the end of the season he inscribed an illustration of himself in the role of Lear which read: 'To Michael with affectionate remembrance for the strong and gentle help.' I still have it. The following year he would be dead from cancer of the spine. I knew Charles would not have made a good patient so it was a relief when finally his obituary appeared. Like many talented men at the end of their lives, I think he fretted that he had not always made the best use of his gifts, and coming to Stratford in 1959 had been a way of making amends. For all his insecurities as an actor and the occasionally absurd drama he generated around them, his talent was remarkably centred. He knew what he could do. At one matinee of *Lear* he lost his words right in the middle of his very first speech. Charles had better uses for his energy than for the panic and embarrassment another actor might have felt. He turned to the prompt corner and asked with the same directness you would expect in the rehearsal room, 'Yes?' The alarmed stage manager threw him a line and Charles replied with perfect audibility, 'No, further back.' The performance then continued serenely on its way.

One afternoon word swept through the company that Guthrie was coming to Stratford to revisit his production, and we were asked to gather in the rehearsal room a few minutes before the half-hour call. When he entered, this tall bird of a man – half eagle, half ostrich – the company gave him a protracted round of applause to which he responded with a show of benevolent impatience. His golden reign early in the season now seemed an age away, like archaeological remains, built over two or three times by later and lesser societies. Curiously that same night Olivier was also coming to see the show. The prospect of performing before these two men made me extremely nervous as I think it did the entire company and the performance that night was not one of our best. In the middle of the show and on this one occasion only, the eye-glass I wore suddenly popped from my eye, and though I managed to catch it in a gloved hand, the experience was almost as disturbing as losing an eyeball. I came off the stage with my self-possession in tatters.

A friend of Paul Hardwick's was in the audience that night and reported afterwards that these two great men of the theatre sat in seats across an aisle from each other and exchanged not a single word. One had heard rumours about the differences between them. Though they had shared some great successes together at the Old Vic in the thirties, most notably *Henry V*, by the end of the war the honeymoon was long over. When Olivier and Ralph Richardson, now film stars, took over the running of the Vic, Guthrie was elbowed out. In turn, Olivier was to be peremptorily sacked when he was on the Australian tour. In their autobiographies each writes guardedly about the other, Guthrie with perhaps the greater generosity. He describes himself as flattered when he sees the film of *Henry V* and realises that it has incorporated many of the ideas of his stage production. Olivier cannot conceal his resentment when, having asked Guthrie's opinion of his movie, he received the curt reply, 'Think it's vulgar.' This falling out between collaborators who early on in their careers have helped each other to success is not unusual in the theatre. The intensity of such partnerships defines them as fragile. However, at that time it bewildered me that these two men to whom I had so much reason to be grateful should remain unreconciled.

Later that evening I discussed this with Vanessa, but she had lived all her life with the feuds that are the bleaker side of theatrical success and took them as a matter of course. And a third glass of Dubonnet, for some reason at that time our favoured tipple, soon put the matter in perspective. Of much more importance to my own life was the realisation that I was falling in love with her. Her face, luminously sculpted out of the darkness, had turned into something perfect. Yet, where once we had met every day, at rehearsal or during the performance, now we were seeing each other only by arrangement. With all five plays now safely in the repertoire we had reached that point in the season when the understudy casts of each production were expected to show their work one afternoon to the director. First up for me was *Coriolanus* and I was extremely busy. We only had a few days to prepare, but with Albert Finney covering the name part there was a shared feeling that we might be able to achieve something a little out of the ordinary, and rehearsals became as focused as if we were preparing for an examination. This was close to the truth. Assessing us with a view to employment the following season would be Peter Hall and a young Cambridge academic, John Barton, whom Peter had invited to join next year's company as one of the season's directors. There was scepticism among the actors, which I certainly shared, about being judged by someone who, whatever his potential, had never before worked in the professional theatre. And was it true that Peter had said that any actor would be a better one for having gone to Cambridge? This is what Stephanie Bidmead, a member of the company, had told me. It worried me that such things made me so angry.

On the Sunday before we had to show our hand, Albert invited me to lunch at the small cottage he had rented not far from the theatre, so that we could run our lines. He had cooked an enormous cottage pie, not quite haute cuisine but solidly nutritious, which we consumed as we took each other through the text, and by the end of the afternoon we were both well prepared. The run-through the following day might have been a first night there was such a static of nerves and expectation backstage. Albert, extremely jumpy, came on for his first entrance with an eye as wild as a stallion's, but he soon demonstrated the leading actor's ability to transmute fear into something more useful like anger or recklessness and both were ideal for the part. After a disappointing season, *Coriolanus* offered him a challenge similar to *Henry V* and he played it with the same directness and banked-down rage that was characteristic of his best work. Before long, when the film of *Saturday Night and Sunday Morning* appeared, it would make him a star. His Coriolanus didn't have the skill or the strategic cunning of Olivier's, but it was just as powerful and gained by being played by someone more the right age. For all of us the show that afternoon became a genuine event.

Afterwards, as we made our way to the rehearsal room to receive our notes, we passed a succession of those surprised smiles that break out in a theatre when a run-through has unexpectedly come to life. Peter and John Barton were waiting for us with faces creased in approval so we thought we were in for a pat on the back. When everyone had gathered and found a chair, Peter rose and a thoughtful pause ensued. Then he spoken with the deliberation of someone giving important dictation. 'Considering the three great geniuses who perform in this production in the evenings you all did very well. No, honestly, you really did.' This was not quite what we had expected to hear. All of us admired the performers he had just extolled, Laurence Olivier, Edith

Evans and Harry Andrews, but they were irrelevant to what had just taken place. Besides, the principals had rehearsed for four weeks; we had got a show together in as many days! I couldn't believe the condescension of this opening remark or the fact that he was blind to its ineptness. And 'genius' was not a word to throw around like confetti, particularly if the use of it evoked other aspects of national grovelling.

We were then told that Peter would counsel each of us privately and he removed himself to an arrangement of two chairs and a table at the far end of the room while we gathered at the other end waiting our turn. I watched as a nodding Albert submitted to a smug purr of words and wondered if Peter was not a man I actually hated. My turn came and as soon as I sat down I knew he hadn't cared for my performance. I was so exasperated I couldn't listen and to this day have little idea what he said. And here is the first irony: Peter was probably right in his judgement. My part, Menenius, is a patrician, and in his first scene he successfully placates an unruly Roman mob. He can be played two ways, as a shrewd operator who knows how to woo and manipulate the plebeians in the interests of his own class, or as a reasonable and rather charismatic man adept at marshalling arguments that support social order. This latter could be described as the Tory approach, and dramatically it is the less interesting of the two. And yet in spite of my professed beliefs, in spite of the things about England I was in the habit of deriding, it was to this second approach that I had been instinctively drawn and to which Peter probably objected. My acting self knew something about me that my everyday self would have denied: namely, that to the extent that I wanted some for myself, I respected authority. Even if at the moment I couldn't afford to admit it because the prospect was so remote, I wanted to be a director. That was why, far more than others in the company, I was outraged by what I perceived as ineptitude in someone who was already doing the job. My passionate espousal of someone like Guthrie was similarly excessive because it is in the nature of such figures to be unique and it is absurd to demand their qualities in lesser people.

There was nothing exciting about the rehearsals of *King Lear*, which followed on *Coriolanus*. It was the usual understudy drudgery under the working lights, with few of us appropriately cast. I had some ideas about Gloucester but was now acutely aware that this was a part I could never be seriously considered for at my present age. The run-through, when we came to it, could be described as lacking in credibility. Summer had slid into a damp autumn and the flux of the seasons was a mirror to my fortunes. A couple of months ago I was the actor who had made a surprise success of his two roles. Now I was the company member who had been disappointing in his understudies. In the inward-looking world of a theatrical company, where triumph lasts as long as the weather, the change in nuance was palpable and I could sense it in the glances of the administrative staff who took their cue from above.

And where was Vanessa when I needed her? We rarely saw each other at the theatre. *King Lear* dominated the repertoire, and whenever it was playing she was off to London. Her studio didn't have a telephone so the only way I could catch her was to drop in, and she was never there. One evening, before an *All's Well* performance, I arrived on her doorstep just as she was leaving for work. She seemed startled to see me as if I had somehow interrupted her train of thought but she was quick to offer me a cup of tea. I watched her as she boiled the water and prepared the tray. There was a worst-case scenario that I thought remote but best to get out of the way. Was there someone else? Her answer to the question I had so casually framed was, in an instant, to turn us both into different people and to make everything else in my life a matter of neglect. She had confessed to another lover. Now she was no longer remote but tremulously present, both excited and confused as if, had the circumstances been different, I would have been the person to whom she turned to share her secret. As it was, she would tell me very little, not his name nor what he did, only that it wouldn't last because he was a visitor to the country and would be leaving in a month. Anger and indignation were not options open to me. My own conduct precluded them. It could even be said that I had been her instructor in duplicity. We talked on, hushed and horribly focused. She didn't want us to break up but she did want me to give her this month of freedom. Morally checkmated, I could only agree, astonished by Vanessa and lost in admiration for someone who could cause me so much pain.

Obsessive love is a little like having one's life permanently scored with a soundtrack of soaring, agonised music. It goes on all day and all night, arresting thought, preventing sleep. For weeks I listened to nothing else, somnambulating through the rest of my life. Perhaps this unqualified absorption in another human being was precisely the thing I had been searching for. If so, it was unfortunate that the cost of finding it was to mislay myself, because the person I now presented to Vanessa had little in common with the one to whom she had first been drawn. I became an open invitation to her cruelty. Other sorts of misery flourished at the theatre where rumours about next year's season – who was in, who was out – had become the sole preoccupation of the building. I anticipated rejection; it had a sort of tidal inevitability and I hated being amongst others also steeling themselves against the approach of hurt. Even more insufferable was the self-satisfaction of those few who knew they were coming back. The social cohesion within the company was rotting, and those rehearsals of *All's Well That Ends Well* might as well never have happened. Even the play's title had become a mockery. One night Paul Hardwick said to me, 'Haven't you heard? Guthrie's fallen ill. He's had some sort of stroke. It's in the family, apparently. He had these aunts who've gone blind with it.'

The story now rushes to a conclusion. Fret about a problem long enough and you can usually conjure up an answer. One night, of their own accord, the scattered pieces of the puzzle had slid neatly together: Leslie Caron was in Hollywood filming, Peter was not rehearsing and was often in London. It was obvious. Vanessa's lover was my enemy, the ultimate betrayal! I wanted to howl my indignation and misery at her but part of me knew that, in finding her out, I had evened the ground between us. I had recovered my old self and the means to fight back. The shape of her liaison was now clear. When Leslie Caron returned it would be over, and Vanessa would be on her own. Nursing our different hurts we circled towards each other again, but warily. In the matter of giving pain we had become quick learners and there was no going back to a better time. However, as the year drew to an end and that 'better time' became framed in the past, it became clear to both of us that for a while we had been genuinely happy. We had been careless with it and now we had regret to share.

Peter did not want me back the following season. Intent on further pain, I insisted on a meeting. The professional discussion was along predictable lines – the two parts brilliant, the understudies disappointing. What I had really come for was to assess what the connection was between the professional and the private. Did Peter know about me and Vanessa? Did he realise I knew about him? Did he care one way or another? There was no way of telling from his smooth flow of words. For the damage he had done to my private life I would gladly have killed him, but I couldn't blame him. In his shoes would I have behaved any better? Professionally it was a different matter, because what no artist can ever forget, or probably forgive, is an assault on his belief in himself. The meeting concluded with a surge of affability from Peter. 'Don't worry, Michael. I'm sure we'll work together again one day. People change. *You'll* change!' This was a proposition both of us would make the mistake of believing thirteen years later at the National Theatre.

So the season ended with a double loss. I had had setbacks before, but this was a new sort of bruising, internal and longer lasting. I didn't yet have the wit to realise that I had also been delivered from something. What good would it have done me artistically to go on working with a director with whose approach I was so at variance? And for that matter, why should Peter want to have someone around whose scepticism was so undisguised? It was true I loved Vanessa, but had we managed to make a go of it, our careers would soon have forced us apart. Within a year or two her soaring Rosalind in a great production of *As You Like It* by Michael Elliott would make her a true stage star and world fame in movies would follow. I had not yet even begun on the work for which I was best suited and would soon have declined into one of those figures who suckle on the fringe of someone else's celebrity. You find them around stars, often kind and amusing people, who one way or another earn their keep, but it was not a life I could have endured.

Fortunately, unhappiness on a day-to-day basis is no more consistent than its opposite, for most of us anyway, and the end of the season was not without its lively moments. An American company recorded a TV version of the *Dream* and I acted as spokesman and barrack-room lawyer for the lower half of the company and succeeded in getting us properly paid. Ian Holm decided to throw a party to celebrate his conspicuously successful year, and one night in the green room I saw him with a list in his hand, tiptoeing among the company whispering invitations to the selected few. Neither I nor Vanessa were invited (her season had ultimately been no more of a triumph than mine) so we decided to get a bottle of wine and have a party of our own. Recovering our old complicity for a while was worth a hundred invitations. On the last Sunday evening the company staged a kind of end-of-term revue in front of the entire staff of the theatre. Everyone was there, either performing or in the audience. Dame Edith Evans coaxed Albert Finney into a duet of 'Drink to Me Only with Thine Eyes' which, unfathomably, she intended as a tribute to the retiring Glen Byam Shaw. I wrote two sketches, one for Vanessa about a Spartacus-like uprising among the company's spear-carriers, and another for Zoe Caldwell and myself in which two heavily accented Australian academics make a solemn entrance, carrying the *Complete Works*, and argue the case that Shakespeare hailed originally from the Antipodes.

'Course he did! Came from Wagga. His dad was an abo.'

'Y' sure?'

'Whady' expect with a name like that?'

Close textual analysis provides the final proof.

'Here, whad'd I tell you? *Hamlet*, Act 5, Scene 2! "Enter *two grave diggers*." '

# NINE

# A World Elsewhere

My mother had succeeded in making the move from Sussex to London. In advance of her husband's arrival, she had gone to furnish and prepare a big flat they had acquired in Queensgate Gardens, off Cromwell Road. After Stratford I stayed with her for a couple of weeks to lend a hand. The house in the country had fetched a good price, so fortunately money was no problem though not much pleasure went into the spending of it. The flat was in one of those imposing but rather pompous nineteenth-century buildings which elsewhere in this part of London house Middle Eastern Embassies. The size of the rooms and the high ceilings gave it a chilly formality, but it had the space to provide Lawrence with a bedroom and a study to himself and to accommodate help as his condition worsened. He was declining rapidly, but I was too sympathetic to my mother's predicament to fully appreciate the horror of what he was going through as each day a little bit more of himself went missing. It would not be long before he would be unable to grasp even the nature of his own financial security. He no longer understood what investments were and became convinced that all he had in the world was the small change in his pocket. He would come to my mother, stricken, to break the news that the only thing that stood between them and penury was the £2 7s 6d that he held in his hand. All around the flat, under his mattress, at the back of a cupboard, inside a stud box, my mother would find small sums of cash he had hoarded against the day when they would be thrown out onto the streets. For a man who had spent a lifetime ensuring a comfortable retirement and whose rise to the board room had been precisely calibrated by increases in income from year to year, it was the bleakest irony. Eventually, after wandering from room to room in an ever more hopeless search for himself, he could no longer be cared for at the flat and was put to bed in a nursing home where he died six months later. My mother found herself provided for but the estates accumulated by the three childless brothers now waited on the demise of their widows before going to a charity memorialising their name. She had asked if she could acquire a flat of her own but the surviving brother had refused.

Shirley was not in London when I returned from Stratford. As so often happened when I was out of the way she had landed on her feet with a splendid job as PA to the Director of the York Festival, ministering to the musicians and performers who would be gathering for the event the following summer. Notwithstanding Stratford, my own employment prospects also showed promise. I had had two offers. The first had been a small role in the new Terence Rattigan play, *Ross*, starring Alec Guinness and going into the Haymarket; but what took immediate precedence was the second offer. Tyrone Guthrie had miraculously recovered from his illness and was to stage a new *Hamlet* in London with Christopher Plummer. He wanted me to play Osric and understudy the one part the words of which no actor would resent learning by heart, Hamlet. Everything about the offer was auspicious. Guinness, another Guthrie protégé, had got his start when the director had asked him to play Osric at the Old Vic in the thirties. Actors are reassured by such magical connections and I accepted the job with alacrity.

Before taking up her post Shirley had gone off on a skiing holiday over Christmas and, with a job to look forward to myself, I went out briefly to join her. We hadn't seen each other since the previous summer. She knew nothing of Vanessa, nor for the moment did I intend to tell her. However, she was quick to intuit that something traumatic had happened and probably on more than a professional level. I don't remember whether it was then or later that she released me from any obligations I had undertaken or promises given when I had last seen her in the summer. She wanted us to marry, yes, but only if I was still sure I wanted to. Had she recognised a degree of female guile in her visit to Stratford, and, if we were to have a life together, was it that she wanted it to begin on an uncompromised footing? Whatever it was, nothing else she might have said could have drawn me closer to her than this offer of liberty. Most of us see the person we're involved with as the most important supporting part in the starring vehicle of our own lives. Far fewer are able to see the well- being of the person they love in a way genuinely apart from their own self-interest, and I knew how rare this was. Shirley recognised the self-centredness of my ambition, was in no doubt about my philandering impulses and probably didn't care much for either. But her first instinct was to understand rather than to condemn. One thinks of the notoriously unfaithful H. G. Wells weeping like a desolate child at the funeral of his wife. A lover could be replaced but not the one merciful witness to the folly of one's life.

On the ski slopes of Seefeld over Christmas there was gridlock and the mountain might just as well have been an ant heap. One Sunday, which in the Church calendar marked the Massacre of the Innocents, I stood queuing for the ski-lift in blinding sunlight for almost an hour. At last on top of the mountain, I began a cautious traverse across the steep incline of packed, soiled snow, keeping a lookout for the weekend skiers from Munich who were dive-bombing around me with the aggression of hornets. From over the slope immediately above me I heard, but did not see, something approaching at speed. I looked in the direction of this reckless hiss and suddenly there he was, a stocky man, his eyes staring at mine alert with apprehension as he came rocketing towards me. He was braking hard and over the sloping ice the shuddering metal edges of his skis came at me sideways. The few seconds left before impact seemed to stretch like elastic as I waited with impotent fury for the inevitable collision. Then we were both twenty-five yards further down the hill, a tangle of limbs, skis and groans. He had now disengaged himself and was staggering to his feet, quite unashamedly relieved that he had been the one to escape injury. Like someone fleeing the site of an accident, one of my skis had already set off down the mountain and I could see it travelling at astonishing speed faraway down the valley. The other was still attached to my foot but at a very odd angle, and there was something the matter with my knee. I stretched a hand forward to assess the damage and felt only the contours of a joint; the kneecap was missing. My first thought was that Osric was out the window, my second was that I would never, ever, under any circumstances, go bloody skiing again. I tried to adjust my position and from the very back of my leg, like a bolt leaving a crossbow, the kneecap thwacked back into its proper position. I was still unable to move much so someone went for help and I was left perched on the side of a mountain cursing my luck.

In surprisingly little time two skiers arrived, one at the front and the other at the rear of a big aluminium pod into which they lifted me with the dispassionate efficiency of medical orderlies in a war zone. This was doubtless a busy Sunday for them. My descent was so breathtaking in its speed and skill, the skiers with the pod between them negotiating the slopes like a single, strange skiing animal, that I actually began to enjoy the experience of rescue. At the bottom we glided past that same queue standing by their skis and dressed in luridly coloured kit, in which, an hour before, I had been waiting. They stared at me curiously and without sympathy, as if there was a chance my accident had reduced the odds of something similar happening to them. I was the day's sacrificial victim to the mountain god of broken bones. My next stop was with one of his local high priests, a doctor who made a living out of needless injury. His surgery was so ramshackle and his equipment so out of date that I wondered if, in terms of medical care, I had drawn the short straw. Every time he walked to the X-ray machine to take a picture his floorboards bent and creaked so much that I was convinced his plate would come out looking like a Turner. He was a man in his fifties and his manner had just a hint of amusement, as if his patients had only themselves to blame for the predicament in which they found themselves. It was impossible not to wonder what had occupied him during the war. However, he appeared to know what he was doing and after studying the surprisingly graphic X-rays, told me that there were no bones broken in my now grotesquely swollen leg. I would be on crutches for a while, then a stick and in four weeks time might be better. The relief was enormous. After all, an Osric with a limp was not out of the question.

Shirley had already departed to take up her new job. I had a few days of holiday left and hung about the Austrian guesthouse willing myself to get better. On my last day I was sitting on the balcony staring at my knee, when somebody brought me a telegram. It was from my agent. Tyrone Guthrie had fallen ill again, and the production of *Hamlet* was off.

Back in London, I hobbled around the West End looking for work. Occasionally I passed the Haymarket Theatre where the Rattigan play was settling in for a long run and studied photographs of the actor to whom my part had gone. One morning I auditioned for Orson Welles on a stick but had the feeling that he didn't accept my explanation for it but put it down to the sort of gross affectation he might, in his younger days, have tried on himself. It would have been further bad luck had I got the job because the Welles production proved to be another casualty of the season and never went into rehearsal. In other areas the news was better. Now that my mother's future was secure, she offered to buy me a flat out of some money she had in her own name. Given that this somewhat compromised her personal independence it was very generous. The other good news was that the Salamancas were back in London. They had rented an apartment in a mansion block in Church Row, Hampstead, and I was a frequent visitor. One day they mentioned that the flat next door was empty and for sale. We acquired the key and went to have a look. It was curious leaving a ground plan through one door and opening onto its mirror image through another. Both flats existed side by side as symmetrically as a leaf. Each had a fair-sized room at the front overlooking the handsome eighteenth-century buildings opposite, then a long, dark corridor leading to kitchen and bathroom at the rear, with interesting views over the roofs of Hampstead. The differences were firstly that the flat we were in was so dilapidated and filthy it looked as if it had been unoccupied for a century, and secondly that the bedrooms off the corridor had no view, but looked into the gloom of the building's internal well. I wondered if these factors would be reflected in the asking price. It was 1960 and we were still a year or two away from the coming London property boom, but I was still astonished when the agent told us the asking price, £2,700. Even in those days it was a snip. Shirley came down one weekend to inspect and was as excited about its possibilities as I was. In no time the deal was done and for the first time in my life I owned a patch of England.

I knew exactly what I wanted to do with it. Peter Heath, with whom I'd shared the Carlyle Square flat, was now a painter and had moved in with a South African art student called Sandy whom he planned to marry. They lived in a couple of rooms elsewhere in Chelsea and one evening they invited Shirley and me to dinner. They had very little money, but Sandy and her art-school friends had found a way of doing up a place that was so fresh and affordable that it would become first fashionable, and then, for twenty or thirty years, the staple of cheap and cheerful interior design. An auctioneers in South Kensington called Coe's used to ship down from the North of England old pine furniture which had already been stewed in a bath of caustic so that it could be the more easily repainted. For £5 or £6 you could get a bow-fronted chest of drawers or a Georgian corner cupboard, which with some sandpaper, beeswax and a little effort came up glowing like honey. Also at auction or to be found in junk shops, for similar sums of money, were Victorian armchairs and sofas, filthy with dust and grime, but with their springs in order. Once you'd stripped them of their fussy, soiled fabrics and lugubrious varnish and reupholstered them yourself in a vivid, plain velvet, you had something surprisingly elegant to sit on. In street markets old brass oil lamps, still in working order, could be picked up for a couple of pounds. Arrange these objects in a room, painted entirely white, and you had a certain look which was not only novel but at the time irresistible. Perhaps it was that its vaguely Scandinavian simplicity suggested the coming egalitarianism of the sixties, when young couples who did their own housework would sit down to dinner parties in pretty kitchens with dressers and not worry too much if their children were scratching the furniture. A plain pine table, well proportioned and with a bit of history to it, seemed to provide a link with the way most people had always gone about their lives. Interior design is essentially the promotion of an idea, usually elitist, but this one was attractive in another way and remarkably tenacious. Years would pass before the absurdity of living in Camden Town and pretending you were cooking in a country cottage became apparent to harassed parents trying to raise children in the television age.

There were other things in the air I was learning about. Also visiting London was another American friend from RADA, Ted Flicker, trying to set up an English production of his off-Broadway success *The Premise*. This was an evening of a new American form, improvisational theatre, which would have its most successful manifestation in the work of Elaine May and Mike Nichols. After RADA, Ted, never one to settle for being a mere employee, had headed west to become actor-manager of his own dinner-theatre (another recent innovation), and for most of the fifties had been working from the moment he woke up till the moment he went to bed. His one day off had been Sunday and he told me he had found an interesting way to relax, smoking marijuana. There was now apparently a freemasonry of users throughout the States, codenamed Vipers, and their ranks were swelling. I shared the general perception of the time that all drugs were perilous, and when Ted assured me that pot was no more harmful than tobacco and asked me if I'd like to try some, I primly refused.

Later, one of the actresses he'd brought over from America espoused something else I hadn't heard of, the contraceptive pill. 'It's going to change everything,' she said.

My own career was not really going anywhere. I was keeping afloat financially with bits of television or a special week at a rep near London, but these were becoming gross interruptions of what was now my real obsession – work on the flat. It was not yet habitable so I was still living in Carlyle Square where my room had come to resemble a furniture depository, as the various bargains I had discovered were delivered and piled one upon another, waiting upon the time when they could be transported to North London. At one end of the room I was reupholstering a Victorian chaise longue, with two armchairs waiting to be done, and stacked against one wall were some pine pieces reeking of caustic, including a big eighteenth-century bookcase splitting a bit as it dried out. Shops selling stripped-pine furniture didn't exist at that time. You either acquired it at auction or bought it three or four layers deep in paint at second-hand furniture shops and laboriously stripped it yourself. I was particularly proud of a Georgian chest, a phenomenal bargain at £2 10s, on which I then expended about a month of labour trying to remove two centuries of paint.

I didn't have the money to refurbish the entire flat so I decided to do the rooms at both ends and the corridor connecting them but leave the three spare bedrooms just as they were. After years in bed-sitters and tiny flats, having so much space was a wonder, and I walked from room to room with as much pleasure as if I had just acquired Blenheim. I had a bright idea for the corridor, which had a dado halfway up the wall running its entire length. In Sydney, the Macquarie Gallery had displayed their pictures against walls covered in plain hessian. In an otherwise white hall I thought this might be just the thing. Hessian wallpapers were yet to be manufactured, so I bought yards and yards of sacking from a hardware shop and cut the material into appropriate lengths. These I soaked in the bath in a weak solution of wallpaper glue. Then, the same way you can dry handkerchiefs in the bathroom by stretching them out wet against a tiled wall, these huge sheets of sopping hessian were hoisted into place between the dado and the picture rail. Once they were clinging they could be shifted about to get rid of bubbles or wrinkles and to straighten out the joins. A few days later, now dry and taut, they looked as if they had been ironed to the walls. As I write, some forty years later, the sacking is still in place along that corridor waiting upon the time when someone else will come along with another bright idea, tear it all off and start again.

, I was not alone in being possessed by the nesting instinct. A number of my friends seemed to be getting married, including Peter Nichols, who brought his bride along to meet me when I was still at Carlyle Square. Peter had spent so many years lamenting his sexual prospects that I wasn't prepared for the startlingly attractive woman who came squeezing past the bookcase and the chaise longue. Thelma had cheek-bones and a mouth that one could imagine under a big hat in Peru, a lovely skin, a rounded body and the chatty appetite for life of an excited child. In the past I had seen Peter looking at Shirley as if from the outside of a locked cake shop. Now it was my turn. With her broad Bristol accent and lack of any shyness, her shrieks of laughter, I took to her at once, but, not for the last time, wondered how one was expected to order one's life in a world which contained so many desirable women. As the new wife of a good friend she was surely out of bounds (and in this case would remain so), but the problem of desire was one to which I could see no solution. We had grown up being told it was there to be resisted. But why? What was desire *for* if not to acted upon? Trying to work this out as the sexual revolution got under way would have its complications.

The flat in Hampstead, or enough of it, was now ready for its owner to take up residence and I spent my first night sleeping on the floor on a mattress in the front room, listening to the street sounds in this new part of London and watching patches of light, as yet unimpeded by curtains, shift back and forth across the ceiling. The Salamancas, next door, had been following the progress of the flat and the way it was absorbing far more of my energies than my nominal career. This was also making me uneasy. Spending the best part of six months renovating a new home was a harmless enough activity but it was hardly an exceptional one. I knew a number of actors, good ones, too, who, finding themselves neglected by the business, had tried something else part-time – antiques, carpentry, and, in one case, modest property speculation. Suddenly they had what their profession had denied them, a grasp on the world, and afterwards it was very hard to return to acting with the old dedication. This was not yet my case, but I could see it happening. Do anything long enough and you develop skills. I could now spot bargains in junk shops the minute I walked in the door. I knew how to renovate, say, a Victorian armchair, how then to sell it and buy something twice as good. I was on my way to being able to make some money at it. One evening, as Jack poured me a bourbon next door, he repeated what he had said to me eight years before at drama school, 'You should be writing,' and Mimi chimed in, 'There are so many interesting things you could do with your talents instead of just getting by as an actor.' Jack's second novel, *Lilith*, had just been published to excellent reviews and had been bought for the movies. In a month's time I would be thirty-two years old.

In fact, something had been brewing in my mind during those months that I had been applying paint-stripper and tacking fabric to the wormy frames of Victorian chairs. I was fairly disenchanted with the theatre, but how could I reject out of hand experiences as extraordinary as *Titus* and *All's Well*? I'd had eight years as an actor and frequent encounters with mediocrity, but also, from time to time, with magical excellence. In a season such as the one I had recently spent at Stratford, you were likely to come up against both. The story of such a season, of a company of actors cloistered together for the best part of a year, would be an ideal way of demonstrating the political dimension of artistic endeavour when it involves a group and how the professional and personal areas impinge and become interdependent. There had been many novels about the theatre but mostly written by people whose experience was literary, and whose presentation of the performer was always as a mysterious and often foolish exotic. Of the books I had read, only Colette's *The Vagabond*, which is about a dancer, gave a true sense of performance as work, as a way of earning a living. I felt that now I might be well placed to attempt a novel treating the life of an actor in a similar way, from the inside on a day-to-day basis, and that the Stratford season could provide me with a starting point and a ground plan. Had I at last found my subject, something of my own, waiting there to be done? One morning I unpacked my grandfather's typewriter and made a start. I would begin and end the book with that punctuation mark of an actor's life, a spell out of work. Indeed, it would be in a succession of such spells that the novel, little by little, came into being.

Shirley had been coming down from York most weekends to inspect the building works and join me in the hunt for bargains. We found a dining-room table for £3 in a shop in the Finchley Road called, inexplicably, the Earl's Court Repair Shop, run by two elderly but powerfully built Poles. They would move about the premises, wearing berets, with huge pieces of furniture balanced on their heads. The interior of their shop was as surreal as its name, with furniture stacked one piece upon another as high as the ceiling and the Poles moving about within it like troglodytes. If you searched among its caves and dusty ravines, it was a treasure trove.

Shirley's new job was proving even more interesting than she'd hoped. The director of the York Festival was the art historian Hans Hess, and he and his wife Lilli had rather taken her under their wing. Hans was a small, attractive man in his sixties, with a stringent intellect, no inhibitions about speaking his mind, and a lively interest in sex. He was a contemporary of Bertolt Brecht and between the wars had been part of the Berliner push of Marxist artists and intellectuals. Hitler had driven him to England, where, when war broke out, he was promptly interned, in spite of being Jewish and demonstrably anti-fascist. Now, in a flat in York, the Hesses were attempting to live the sort of life they'd left behind in Berlin, and on another weekend I took the train to meet them. That night they were having to dinner the conductor Walter Goehr, whom they would address throughout the evening as 'Maestro' with a very un-English mixture of exactitude and flattery. Shirley was already at home in this milieu, where the conversation moved between three languages and as many cultures and I was little more than a silent observer. Over time Hans became a good friend and we would engage in intent discussions in which I would sometimes, and very tentatively, question his political certainties, usually to have my wrist slapped. One day he delivered his verdict on me to Shirley. 'Michael has the best untrained mind I know,' he announced, but whether this was a compliment or a lament I was never quite sure. In any case I thought: what is a trained mind other than one well-versed and submissive to a discipline at least part of which will one day be shown to be in error? Like Hans' Marxism, in fact. Nevertheless, with his splendid candour and considerable learning, he was a man I admired.

At Easter Shirley had almost a week off and we began to get the feel of what life would be like in our new home. We had time to cook, potter about and discuss what we would do with the as-yet uncolonised bedrooms. That Sunday we tagged on to the anti-nuclear Aldermaston March as it passed the Albert Memorial and, in the company of people who had been on the move for two days, walked the modest distance to Trafalgar Square. For some reason I was wearing a suit, maybe we'd been somewhere else beforehand, and a middle-aged man with a military moustache heckled me from the footpath as we turned into Knightsbridge. Apparently the rabble I was keeping company with – bohemian women pushing prams and young men in ragged duffle coats – could be disregarded but not someone correctly dressed. We exchanged genial insults. The week almost over, I showed Shirley the pages I'd written. She'd always been the best friend of my writing and she said just enough to make me want to continue. It was that Easter that our son, Conrad, was conceived.

Shirley's job at York didn't finish until the end of the summer, so we decided we would get married on a Saturday in July. A few days before, and out of the blue, I landed a leading part in an interesting television play. It was called *Vitriol*, and was about labour conditions in a Northern mill town at the beginning of the twentieth century, one of a series of dramas from the Manchester School which Granada was producing and of which the best-known example is probably *Hobson's Choice*. The production had a good director, Herbert Wise, and an excellent cast which included George Devine as the mill owner and Barry Foster as the rebel worker. Since my offer had come at very short notice it was obvious I was a replacement for someone who had dropped out, but I wasn't so foolish as to be bothered by that. The role was a meaty one: a corrupt doctor who misrepresents medical data unfavourable to the interest of the mill. These days a similar play would probably be about Big Tobacco. The members of the cast tended to tip-toe around their colleague and star George Devine, who at the time was the artistic director of the prestigious Royal Court Theatre. We knew (and he knew, too) that he was a potential employer, and at those times when he wasn't rehearsing he tended to withdraw behind a veil of pipe smoke and his inevitable copy of *The Times*.

One morning, when he had been called to do a scene, Barry Foster inadvertently bumped into the chair George had just vacated and his newspaper slid to the floor. At the tea break Barry approached me with an expression of sly amusement. 'You know what old George's got inside his *Times*?' he said. 'A copy of *Playboy*.' This knowledge didn't help George's status as guru but it certainly humanised him, and by the time we'd arrived in Manchester to record the play George was as nervous as the rest of us and thoroughly one of the company. At that time a TV play was recorded by filming the television image of the show in real time, just as if it was being performed on stage. For the cast this meant no retakes or second chances. The countdown on the studio floor had a colder terror than a first night because it was impossible to visualise, let alone negotiate, with your audience. The floor manager signalled 'Go' with a silent stab of his forefinger and the show was off and running, as actors and technicians dragging their cables scrambled from one set to another, like soldiers in a battle securing a succession of positions. There was enough adrenalin pumping through the studio to service an Olympic Games and no one was exempt from the pressure. One of the factors that contributed to the health of the Royal Court was that the executive shared in the hazards of the people who had to perform, and George, who was not a particularly subtle actor though a powerful one, was always popping up in productions there. This may also have been a way of augmenting the miserable salary he paid himself. If you wanted to do work that meant something, you took it for granted that it would usually be for very little money.

Because *Vitriol* had only just gone into rehearsal on the day of the wedding and I had to go to work, we made an appointment first thing in the morning at the Hampstead Registry Office. Jack and Mimi were there, Peter Nichols and my mother, and even at the early hour of 8.30 there was a photographer on hand, waiting to take his first picture of the day. Shirley was glowing in a new dress and I was in my best suit. Then, with Peter supplying a jokey commentary, we went on to a brief wedding breakfast at a Greek caff in Kilburn High Street not far from the rehearsal room. That evening, this same group and a few other close friends met again for a proper celebration, for which Mimi and Shirley had spent the rest of the day preparing. There was still sunlight along Church Row, coming into the bay window sideways, and the new flat looked as fresh and lustrous as a petal. Shirley had brought with her a recording on an Archive 78 of Ralph Kirkpatrick playing the Goldberg Variations which she had heard live the week before at the York Festival. This was now playing on my new £38 Bush portable, one of those pieces of equipment which, with ever increasing refinment and prices to match, would soon become obligatory in every household in the land. During the fifties I had neither a player nor a TV set, only a battered wireless the size of a carrier bag. Now I was listening to that transcendent music with a rush of gratitude; none of the technical wizardry to come would have made these sounds, to which Shirley had introduced me, more beautiful. All through the sixties we would listen to our Bach and Mozart, be moved by it, and equate that with virtue. I glanced across the room at Shirley, observing her lovely profile as she attended to the needs of our guests with the gravity of a child, and was glad that after so long a journey we had reached this point together, that I was with her in this flat, among friends, a fortunate man. Then I had to leave the party for five minutes to buy more mineral water at the off-licence around the corner. As I entered, a woman was leaving. She was not merely attractive; that I could have dealt with. She was one of those rare ones who speak directly to the blood, for whom you neglect appointments, betray friendships and willingly go to hell. I watched her through the open door as she slid into a waiting car and was driven away. For a moment I was engulfed in hopelessness. Would there be no end to it? And were other people made in the same wretched mould that I appeared to be? I collected my purchases and returned to the party. 'I know you're going to have flings,' said Shirley a day or two later, 'That's all right, but just don't tell me about them. Because I don't want to know.'

With *Vitriol* behind me, I returned to my book. I'd only done a couple of chapters but the overall plan was taking firmer shape. In my mind I'd demolished the existing theatre at Stratford-upon-Avon, and to the site transported the Bristol Old Vic. Then I picked up the entire town and relocated it in Yorkshire on the North Sea and renamed it Braddington. The characters were undergoing similar metamorphoses. The young Oxbridge director was no longer Peter Hall, but an amalgam of a number of directors of his generation including, rather unfairly, Tony Richardson, with whom I'd never work but about whom I knew the gossip, and whom, of course, Vanessa would one day marry. When we eventually met I was rather attracted to him – like Hall an undoubted operator, but at least passionate about the changes he wanted to see in the way the English lived. The documentary film he made with Karel Reisz, *We Are the Lambeth Boys*, was at the beginning of a movement which would have a spectacular culmination in the Beatles – to give working-class kids as strong a presence in British life as that taken for granted by their middle-class contemporaries.

The central character in a *roman-à-clef* has to be the writer, but the minute I'd given myself the face and stature of a friend in Australia he became someone else, a person I could see from the outside and push about. Mary McCarthy had once said that no one ever wrote honestly about sex, and since I wanted to deal with the irreconcilables of sexual behaviour as they affected my leading character, I decided to have a shot at proving her wrong. The book is tame compared to others that would soon follow, but among its first readers there were some who were brought up short by its candour. Even Simon Gray, the playwright, told me years later that there were one or two things that had shocked him. I suppose I tried so hard to be honest that the tone is sometimes almost chilly in its detachment. As to the role played by Vanessa in my life, it was the thing that made the book necessary and propelled it into existence and for this I am in her debt. However, she as a person quickly vanished beneath a variety of disguises. I called her Amanda after a good friend at drama school, but gave her the appearance of another American girl at RADA, a slight brunette whom I barely knew, and thereafter the character followed her own course. She was never to approach Vanessa's emotional boldness and generosity of spirit. By the time I had finished the book, after six years of innumerable stops and starts, that commonplace of fiction applied: there was not a character, nor indeed an incident, which directly reflected my own life.

And what of Vanessa? After Stratford she found a flat that happened to be in the same part of London as my mother's and it was only too easy for us to see each other, though now with a certain wariness as if our proper lives were on hold. Then one day we conspired in acrimony and had the final row that was waiting to happen. Even so, neither of us could quite let go. Weeks would go by, then she would ring or I would. Just days before I was due to be married, she telephoned me late at night to tell me that a man she'd become involved with had proved a brute and was threatening to come round to her flat and beat her up. I believed her because I wanted to and charged across London in a black taxi. The man did not appear (unless it was me she had been describing), so I stayed on in his stead. Three or four weeks later, now married, I was the one to ring her, and we met for lunch in a pub, then went back to her flat. This would be the last time. The situation we had created for ourselves might have been devised to breed romantic torment. More than that, a new life was soon to be part of the equation. We dressed, sat on the bed clutching hands and exchanging stoic endearments, then I left. And that was that.

Few of my close friends, unless they were American, had somewhere to live as capacious as I had, and I was happy to share my good fortune. The Nicholses, also soon to become parents, couldn't afford to live in London and our flat became their metropolitan base. Peter was now becoming a well-regarded television playwright, but a promising reputation did not pay bills, and he was turning out work in conditions of some anxiety. Discussions about his plays with his agent, Peggy Ramsay, or with interested TV companies necessitated frequent visits to London and our door was open. He and Thelma were entertaining guests and I now valued Peter as the funniest of my friends. We were both struggling for a secure footing in fickle professions, and laughter was one way of reaching some kind of parity with those on whom we depended for work. Peter's hunger to exercise his comic talent was irrepressible. It had become habitual for him to structure the events of each day into a narrative, complete with dialogue and extraordinarily accurate impressions of the people he had been dealing with. These he would then perform for Thelma to hoots of laughter (no marriage ever had better cement) and to anyone else who happened to be present. Pompous TV executives, egotistical directors and actors, all had their come-uppance as they made an appearance in Peter's ongoing saga. It was empowering laughter, to which I made my own contributions, and I came to depend on it. Having a professional writer in the house also helped me with my own writing, particularly one whose disciplines were such that he became distressed if he went a day without working. After breakfast and the usual joke, indulged by our wives, about which of us was entitled to the last of the coffee pot, Peter would go roaming about the flat, humming intently to himself, a sure sign that he was edgy to get back to his typewriter. I would then follow to mine.

It was on one of these visits that Peter became severely ill with a collapsed lung. He had developed acute chest pains so we took him to the local hospital, the Royal Free, where they put him to bed for a month. This was not the large modern complex that exists today, but an antiquated Victorian building that had originally been a plague hospital during the Crimean War. It had high Gothic windows and narrow wards of immense length, in which the wounded in *Gone With the Wind* would not have been surprised to find themselves stacked. With a baby on the way and his work on hold, it was a depressing prospect for Peter, and also for Thelma, who was now in the awkward position of being dependent on friends. Shirley, with great thoughtfulness, made it as easy as she could, and Thelma stayed with us, and within walking distance of Peter, for the duration of his illness.

This bad luck was not quite what it seemed at the time. Eight years later, a hospital not unlike the Royal Free would be on stage at the National Theatre as the set for the play that Peter wrote and I directed, *The National Health*.

If we were proving good friends of the Nicholses, equally they were good friends to us. The following year Peter would be instrumental in getting me a lead in his television play *The Reception*, and later on a memorable job as dialogue coach to the Dave Clark Five in John Boorman's first feature *Catch Us If You Can*, the script of which he had written. They were introducing us to their friends, including Robert Bolt, then at the height of his success as a playwright, and we attended the first night of *A Man for All Seasons*. Bolt offered to read the first few chapters of my novel and wrote me a long and helpful letter. One excellent suggestion was to reverse the first two sentences of Chapter One. However, as important to me as advice was this gift of time from a man who, on the face of it, had absolutely nothing to gain. An ex-teacher, he smoked a pipe and was a shade pedantic, but gifted certainly and transparently decent. What he lacked was Peter's unforgiving stare, and as a playwright would soon be undone by the movies and his own good nature, buried under the sand-dune of money that came shifting towards him after *Lawrence of Arabia*.

Peter and Bob shared the same agent, Peggy Ramsay. She remains the only one of her profession ever to have left behind a reputation comparable to that of the famous clients she represented. There have been books, plays and films about her. Like most powerful personalities who achieve positions of great influence, she had a good side, which was very good, and a bad side, which was also not negligible. My first encounter was emphatically with the good. Since Stratford I had been looking around for some way of taking more charge of my own career. It had occurred to me that if I could find a play I liked, it might be possible to mount a production at an outer-London theatre like the Lyric, Hammersmith. I mentioned this to Peter and he suggested I pay a visit to Peggy. It was not like meeting a stranger; she was one of Peter's most frequent impersonations, and I knew how she crossed and uncrossed her legs, how she bucked about provocatively in the chair behind her desk, running her hand through her hair to reveal the underside of an upper arm, and all the while maintaining a mesmerising flow of indiscretions about her clients and other important people. What Peter hadn't quite conveyed was how attractive Peggy was, and how indifferent to this fact she seemed to be; nor the way you sometimes caught her looking at you, a look curious, possibly sympathetic, but also hooded and quite dangerous. She was stylishly dressed, but in a way that suggested she had thrown her clothes over her head thinking of something else. At one point during our meeting she jumped to her feet, darted across the room to the big ebony chaise longue on which lay various piles of scripts and retrieved one for me to consider. Though Peggy gave me her full attention, I was not yet important enough to interrupt incoming calls (I'm not sure anyone was), and every so often the phone would ring. The use of expletives in everyday conversation was just becoming fashionable and Peggy was in the vanguard. She would lift the receiver to her ear so that it timed precisely with the neat summing up of what she had just been saying to me, and announce into the mouthpiece, 'Yes, he's an absolute *shit*, dear! ... Hello?' or 'Good heavens, a load of *fucking rubbish*! ... Hello?' Her 'hellos' were always sweetness itself, as if she was expecting a call from a maiden aunt. I left her presence feeling much better than when I went in. Like Bob Bolt, she had paid me the compliment of taking me seriously and at that time it meant a great deal, given the strangled yawns and inattention that were usually my lot.

To the favourites among her clients, Peggy was the best agent in the world because she fostered in them the two things a writer must have – a belief in his abilities and the determination to get the work done. She was not, however, a particularly good agent for Peter because she mistrusted his talent. A witty woman, but not a humorous one, she didn't believe that a comic vision, no matter how truthful, was compatible with important playwriting. She had been much influenced by French theatre of the thirties and the immediate post-war period, and those prim Gallic divisions between classic and boulevard theatre, between tragedy and comedy, were still part of her thinking. These were distinctions that later in plays like *A Day in the Death of Joe Egg* Peter and I would do everything we could to blur. We embraced theatrical energy from whatever source we could find it and the whole idea was to ambush an audience with the emotion they least expected. This was not to Peggy's taste. Her idea of a serious playwright was Edward Bond, to whom she wrote in response to his unremitting *Lear*, 'My dear, you are a master.' She was to be far more shocked by Peter's bold use of his own experience as the parent of a hopelessly disabled child than by Bond's fictive and doctrinaire blindings and mutilations. Indeed, after the first performance of *Joe Egg* at the Glasgow Citizens' Theatre, she persuaded Michael Codron not to bring it to London because it was unsuitably painful. This speaks well for the integrity with which she held to her opinions, but not to her efficacy as an agent.

Another idea she brought with her from the forties was that writers should avoid the conventional life, and her suspicion was aroused if a playwright had a wife and small children somewhere in the background. It was the pram in the hall theory once again. A client like David Mercer, who got drunk and blacked the eye of his current live-in girlfriend, was, one felt, more what she expected from talent: people prepared to play dice with their lives. The exemplar, Joe Orton, whose plays were as classically formulated as any Frenchman's, was of course her client, and somehow couldn't have been anyone else's. For the writers she loved, she was as passionately attached as a tigress to her cubs, and you got between them at your own risk. This was bad news for directors, who need to bond with the writers whose plays they direct. Close friendships are not useful in the theatre, she liked to assert in defiance of much evidence to the contrary (and conveniently exempting her relations with her own clients), and she was not beyond doing her best to see they didn't come about. But her mischief sprang from passion on a grand scale. Even to her mistakes she brought a kind of emotional integrity. Few people commit their lives to their work as she did, as if it were self-evident that there was no other possible way of living. She made ever-increasing sums of money but seemed to regard the spending of it as too trivial to waste time on. In my later dealings with her, when I had established myself as a director, I found myself flagrantly betrayed on one or two occasions, which surprised me because she always gave the impression we were friends. I had to spell out my objections with some force before she would concede that vigorously pursuing her clients' interests did not excuse breaking undertakings she had made to me. She made sweet-natured amends, but rather like a secretly unrepentant child.

For an agent with such a varied and radical list of clients, Peggy could sometimes be surprisingly conventional. I once directed a *Cherry Orchard* in which I tried to present the merchant, Lopakhin, according to Chekhov's explicit instructions: not as the villain of the piece, but as a self-made man who was also gentle, courteous and neatly dressed in a black tailcoat – rather like the playwright himself, in fact, with whom his character shares a similar background, father a village shopkeeper and grandfather a serf. Peggy would have none of this. She saw Lopakhin as a cunning parvenu intent on gobbling up the estate of the unsuspecting gentry. This was the usual English interpretation, and I had seen it in a production not long after I had arrived in London. The merchant had a heavy North Country accent and had worn a tweed ginger suit, whilst the blameless brother and sister who were to lose their estate crooned their way through the evening like the sad and superior people they were. This reading of the play is akin to the view that Shakespeare couldn't possibly have written the work attributed to him because he was too low-born, and I was amazed to hear Peggy advocating it. I wrote to her, giving the opposing view with supporting quotes in Chekhov's own words, and in one of her wild, handwritten replies she conceded graciously, and a few days later sent me a book as a present, Chekhov's *Collected Letters*. To be fair to her, I think her position had less to do with snobbery than with her view that a degree of unscrupulous manoeuvring was part and parcel of all human exchanges.

As winter approached I had an offer that was both good news and bad. It came to me through Cyril Luckham, a leading actor in the Stratford company, who had liked my work and had promised to do what he could to help when we returned to London. He was about to appear in a new play, *Strip the Willow*, by a young playwright, Beverley Cross, and he had suggested me for a part. It was a comedy in the Ustinov manner which derived its humour by contrasting the behaviour of the British, the Americans and the Russians in a given situation. The problem with this play was the situation – the aftermath of a nuclear strike on Britain, when humorous contrasts of any sort would be rather beside the point. A proper treatment of this subject would have to wait until Peter Watkins' BBC film *The War Game*, later in the sixties, which no one saw because it was so horrific that the government had it suppressed. Meanwhile, we had this play. The curtain rose to reveal a charming gazebo standing in English parkland. An attractive young woman, who will spend the evening in a bikini, makes her entrance. Both girl and gazebo, we learn, have been spared in the destruction. So have a few other Englishmen ranging from the posh to the common. It is not long before foreign nationals arrive by air, first the Americans and then the Russians. The play had some funny lines and some strong scenes, but I was dismayed by its failure to even begin to comprehend the awesomeness of its subject. The part I would be reading for was a young American sergeant, a kind of James Stewart figure, which I knew I could play in my sleep, and indeed had already done so, but awake, in the Ustinov play at the Birmingham Rep.

Never had I set out for an audition feeling less nervous. It was a show I really didn't want to be part of. On the other hand, I needed the work and this would be what was called a first-class production, which, after a short tour, was expected to come into the West End. At the stage door I was given a scene between the sergeant and the young woman which I studied sitting on the steps leading down to the stage, and in spite of myself became quite interested in its possibilities. When my turn came I sighed, ambled into the lights, gave the most relaxed and probably best reading of my life, and was offered the part on the spot. I then returned home quite depressed. *Strip the Willow* was to prove as important as any job in my career, though it would take me six odd years before I realised it. Like one of those miraculous billiard shots where one collision leads to another, then to another and another until, like magic, almost every ball in play seems to be gliding towards a pocket, it was the first in a series of interconnected engagements which would lead to a new career and a startling change in my professional fortunes.

Once actors begin to inhabit their material they soon lose sight of any objective reservations they may have had, and making it work overrides all other considerations. My best scenes were with our brilliant young leading lady, who, the gossip had it, would soon be a major star, and who had this plain yet oddly distinctive name, Maggie Smith. Not many days were to pass before we spotted in each other's eye that complicit glint by which performers with a bent for comedy recognise each other, and rehearsals began to skip. We were both quite inventive, and soon the director, Val May, settled back, grinning, and let us get on with it. The young author was also on hand and had such winning enthusiasm for what was going on, and was so besotted with the talent and, one suspected, the person of his leading lady, that one wanted to do everything one could to please him. We dress-rehearsed one wintry day in Cambridge, and with the imminence of a first public performance, my misgivings about the play returned. Through the interminable, yawning waits of the process, working against the clock as the 7.30 curtain approached, Maggie walked nervously back and forth from her dressing room to the stage, shivering in her bikini and with goose-bumps showing through her orange body make-up. Beverley, who as author had most at stake, was in and out of Maggie's dressing room, ostensibly to give assurance, but looking as if he needed some himself. After the show there was a small celebration at which we all assured each other that it had gone very well. In part this was perfectly true, but as a whole I knew the show was doomed. We played a few other dates and finished up in outer London in the cavernous Golders Green Hippodrome. As a last throw the management decided to invite the London critics in the hope that a couple of good reviews would secure them a West End theatre. Tynan came, said the only things he could say and the notice went up. Yet I did not regret the engagement. I had been properly paid for a month and had had the experience of looking into the huge, blue eyes of an incomparable comedienne, and watching, as the lines went back and forth between us, spontaneous adjustments of timing and intent shifting about in their depth. For Maggie, too, *Strip the Willow* would have an outcome long postponed, but as important to her as mine was to me. Years later, having married Robert Stephens and had her children, she would be reunited with Beverley Cross in Canada, both of them now divorced, and have a second long and successful marriage.

I returned to my novel and the first obstacle was to persuade myself all over again that I wasn't wasting my time. The Salamancas had gone back to America, and missing Jack's support, I sent him the first few chapters for an opinion. He must have liked them because I had a letter back saying that he'd sent them on to his editor at Simon and Schuster, Robert Gottlieb, celebrated for his work on *Catch-22*. I didn't know it, but he was interested in the theatre and those involved in it and would soon marry a young actress, Maria Tucci. For whatever auspicious reason, one morning an airmail letter from him fell through the front door. It was brief, erratically typed (obviously by himself) but miraculously to the point. He'd liked what he'd read and his last sentence was, 'If you finish it we'll probably publish it.' My spirits soared, cruised, then fell back a little. I now had no choice but to drag the book like a cart through mud, stopping and starting while I earned myself a living, until I'd brought the thing to a finish. This was encouragement too exceptional to abuse.

By the beginning of 1961, with Shirley's pregnancy well advanced, another delivery was much closer to hand. We were about to become parents. It had been something she wanted so I had wanted it too, but as the moment approached I looked in vain inside myself for something resembling a paternal instinct. I knew Shirley would make a success of parenthood but would I? As an only child of divorced parents I wondered if it was something that I had never properly learnt, the way a chick needs to be encouraged to fly or a cub to hunt. My mother once confided something shocking to me. After I'd been born – following a labour needlessly induced by a disciplinarian midwife who liked things to happen on the day they were meant to, and so appalling that she vowed never to have another – my father had told her that a man finds a woman physically repulsive for at least a year after she's given birth. He had a number of views which increasingly, as I grew up, I rejected, sometimes with vehemence, and it was not until much later in England, when I encountered in Mary McCarthy's novel *The Group* a description of a young American doctor, my father's contemporary, whose ideas were a match to his, that it occurred to me that my father had not, after all, invented himself. The late twenties and early thirties were a bad time for medicine, tainted like so many things by the authoritarian political systems of the day. Notions of eugenics and behavioural engineering were fashionable, and mothers, including my own, were instructed never to respond to a crying baby by picking it up. The infant had to learn from the start that it was sub-servient to another's will. Eating, sleeping, bowel movements, all were to be a matter of strict regimentation. My father, I realised, was as much the product and victim of the times he lived in as he was spokes-man for his own beliefs. One generation on, so perhaps was I. Though intellectually I had rejected his ethos, how was I to know to what extent my emotional life had been distorted by my childhood experi-ence of it?

Did my resistance to domesticity, my panting after other women and my confusion, embarrassment even, about the role I would soon be required to play, have its roots in these early years? Shirley guessed at these thoughts which I'd hoped I was keeping to myself, and did everything she could to show me that the door to our marriage had no lock. We were starting our life together with our honeymoon, if we'd ever had such a thing, already eight years behind us in Santander, and there were few discoveries about each other left to be made. This, of course, had its benefits as well as its drawbacks. We were quite without the rancour of couples who were in the process of finding disappointment in marriage, and over the years we had built up an intuitive consideration one for the other that I knew to be uncommon. We had days of sharp happiness, exploring together our new terrain, Hampstead Heath, when Shirley would become my instructor, pointing to a particular tree, a patch of sky or a scuffle of wildlife that I was too busy talking to notice. Or we would spend a weekend absorbed in some improvement to the flat, with the volume up on the baroque music, and me in charge, trying to impose some male notion of perfection onto imperfect bricks and mortar, while Shirley assumed the role of subtly insolent Number Two. There were times when the Bach we were listening to seemed a mirror of the harmony between us. Trouble, the little we had, always arrived with other people. And now another person was on the way and coming to stay on a permanent basis.

One Sunday night in January, Shirley suddenly decided the time had come to make marmalade. In a junk shop a few weeks before, she had found one of those huge brass cooking pots used in the preparation of jams and she'd filled up a store cupboard with dozens and dozens of oranges. Heavily pregnant, she lugged the brass pot onto the stove and set about cutting all the fruit into pieces. Then she lined up rows of empty glass jars to receive the finished preserve. Some hours later, at the moment when she had sealed the last jar with cellophane and an elastic band, her waters broke and the baby was on the way. I called an ambulance and together we went to the hospital, where I delivered her into the hands of the nurses and the disturbing female mysteries of labour. This was long before either a father or a camera had been allowed to be present at a birth. I was ushered out of Shirley's presence and told to go home and wait for a phone call in the morning. Shivering under my raincoat and too confused to feel much beyond numb anxiety, I walked back up Haverstock Hill, an unemployed actor of uncertain prospects, wondering if life at last had him in its sights and was closing in. At the flat I fell into a deep, drug-like sleep, and it took the persistent ringing of the telephone the next morning to wake me. Guiltily I scrambled to take the call, trying to make myself sound alert and awake. What was I about to hear? The news began to penetrate. Mother and child were fine and I was the father of a son.

I returned down the hill, wondering what I would feel when I got there. Shirley was holding the baby, and I saw at once that she had come through the experience well. My son I approached mainly with curiosity, about the grip of his minute fingers and his look of intense preoccupation as he grew by the second in the crook of his mother's arm. He resembled neither of us, but reminded me, slightly to my alarm, of Shirley's mother. A few days later the three of us were together under the same roof. Shirley had prepared everything as well as she had for her jam-making, and I watched with a degree of awe as she went about this, the greatest and most solemn adventure of her life. It was something she intended to do well and to do on her own. She let me be a bystander, sympathetic, occasionally helpful but not centrally involved. This was generous and possibly rather shrewd. I became interested. Each morning, as soon as I was awake, I would tiptoe into Conrad's room and look into his cot, only to find him already waiting for me, each day a little more confident in his enthusiastic if inept struggle to engage with the world. One day, as I leant over him, something happened that astonished me quite as much as if he had suddenly spoken a complete sentence. As our two faces met, his was transformed by something quite new, a broad smile. It expressed need, joy, impossible longing, but what touched and amused me most was its unqualified assumption that I was glad to see him. At that moment I became a father. He had been programmed to smile on a particular morning, and I had been programmed to respond, and all my anxieties about having a paternal instinct were neither here nor there. As a young man I wasn't remotely interested in children. Half a century later I can barely imagine my life without the existence of a son and two daughters. Despite often overwhelming evidence to the contrary, despite the visible dangers and cruelties of existence, if you are a certain sort of person there are some steps you simply have to take on trust, one foot following another like a blind man on a zebra crossing. Breaking with my background had been one such step. This had been another.

Alas, overwhelming evidence to the contrary would soon manifest itself in the lives of our close friends, the Nicholses. They were now living in Devon, in a rented flat, spectacularly sited in the hills that rise up steeply from the town of Dartmouth. Like many people in the arts, they had the knack of finding interesting accommodation whatever the state of their finances. Having found the right place to live, Thelma now decided to have her baby at home. However, the hospital was a distance away and difficult to reach, and the doctor attending her was young and fearfully inexperienced. The labour lasted a terrible forty-eight hours. Somehow both mother and child came through and eventually the new family came to stay with us in London. The flat became a place of cloth nappies and feeding times. Peter and I made rueful jokes about being demoted to supporting parts, but seeing the two infants side by side it soon became apparent that all was not as it should be. The Nicholses' daughter Abigail, though she looked physically robust, seemed much less advanced than our son, and was subject from time to time to tiny seizures. They decided to seek advice, and embarked on a dismal round of doctors and specialists as worse news followed upon bad. Their baby had been so damaged during the protracted labour that she was virtually without a mind; she would never talk, or make significant movements, or register the world around her. In the words of one of the specialists, she was a vegetable. There was also the possibility that Thelma would not be able to have other children. As bad luck it seemed absolute, and Shirley and I felt like soldiers on the battlefield who see their friends falling around them and can only wonder afterwards, 'Why them, not us?' It was a situation beyond amelioration. Or so it seemed then. By the time Abigail had died in a home some ten years later, Thelma would have gone on to have three healthy children, and Peter would have written a play out of the experience of his first-born which I would direct, and which would make the reputations and alter the fortunes of us both. Only Abigail herself appears to have derived nothing from her short life beyond tremors of distant, pointless pain.

People can be damaged by events, but their fundamental natures usually remain intact. In the summer we took Conrad, now aged six months, to visit the Nicholses in Devon, and we found that they had adapted to their situation by deploying Peter's salient and quite irrepressible attribute, his comic intelligence. He had invented a fantasy life of high achievement for their daughter in which nothing was beyond her, from mastering quantum physics to running the four-minute mile. The labour of caring for her was punctuated by these inventions, which allowed her parents to give their mute child a voice. These jokes could hardly be described as unkind since Abigail was in no position to hear them and they helped time to pass with less pain. When *A Day in the Death of Joe Egg* eventually reached the stage, with this behaviour faithfully rendered, other parents of afflicted children told us that they, too, had used laughter to help them cope. But until then it had been secret laughter because they assumed that outsiders, not comprehending its uses, would have been shocked. This was initially true of the play itself, which was perceived by those who first read it to be a sick comedy in questionable taste. On the contrary, it was a robustly healthy comedy about what people do in an honourable fight to stay afloat. It became part of a movement which would help to release the disabled from the ghetto of sickly compassion in which up to then they had been largely confined, and it did what plays are supposed to do but rarely manage – it modified public consciousness.

Surprisingly, this holiday with the Nicholses was an extremely happy one, and was the apex of our friendship. The weather was continuously sunny and they took pains introducing us to the beauties of their part of Devon, the intricate coastline where we swam, and the walks following the tops of wooded hills or along the byways of the pretty town below. We chatted and laughed incessantly. It was only when we took our children to a public place, a beach perhaps or a café, and we noticed a passer-by glance into Abigail's carrycot then quickly look away or, worse, persist in a shameless stare, that an uncomfortable vision of the Nicholses' future impinged on our present. Abigail was already quite heavy and had to be taken everywhere. Thelma, perhaps unable to have further children, was prompted by all her instincts to cling to the one she'd got. Peter was a writer confined by his work to the house. The prospects didn't bear thinking about. Yet neither of them ever complained. Maybe they felt too vulnerable even to risk it. Thelma, who had been to art school and was an excellent painter, took up her brush again, and Peter pressed on with his writing. His television work was moving into a new area of excellence. There was *The Reception*, about a wedding in Bristol, the play in which he was instrumental in getting me cast as the bridegroom. Two that followed later, both beautifully filmed by Christopher Morahan, were *Hearts and Flowers*, about a funeral, and *The Gorge*, about a family outing to the Avon Gorge. They showed the funny particularity of characters whose lives most writers at the time would have considered too ordinary to dramatise. Provincial life came over as quirky and poignant as it is in early Fellini movies.

Since *Strip the Willow*, its director, Val May, had been pestering me to join him at the Bristol Old Vic, where he was to assume the artistic directorship in the autumn. I say 'pester' because Val always began these approaches by saying, 'I want you for your comedy,' and it is always irritating being solicited in terms of what someone perceives as your limitations. Besides, I wasn't sure I wanted to pack up and once again leave London, even if it meant joining a theatre with the reputation of this one. I was nervous, too, about going back to a city which six years before, when I was single, had meant so much to me. Val persisted and dangled a tempting programme of plays in front of me, including a new Tennessee Williams and a comedy, *The Flanders Mare*, which had already been a hit in Paris. Eventually I was persuaded, but failed to ensure that the parts we had discussed were listed in the contract. Shirley and I made a day trip to Bristol in search of accommodation and found an amazing flat in a street of Georgian houses called The Paragon, perched on the cliffs high above the river. We found a tenant for our London property and started sorting out what to take and what to leave. A few weeks before we were due to depart, Val May telephoned again, this time to tell me that, alas, I wouldn't be playing in the Tennessee Williams play. He was quite candid about the reason; an actor he had been trying to work with for years, John Franklyn Robbins, had suddenly become available, and Val needed a really good part to tempt him to join the company. It would not have been too late to withdraw from the engagement, although it would have been difficult to untangle the lets and sublets I'd agreed. There was also the matter of the actors' strike against the television companies which was just about to begin, and it was unlikely that there would be much work in London for the rest of the year. It seemed I had to grit my teeth and accept the situation.

The reader will now have a reasonably comprehensive idea of what miserable places theatrical companies can sometimes be, and I don't intend to dwell on the awfulness of this particular season. Trouble usually begins at the top and from my point of view had already begun, with the manipulative use of the casting prerogative. This would continue throughout the season. John Franklyn Robbins, an excellent actor, but at that time an extremely ambitious one, having successfully commandeered one of my parts, thought it quite reasonable to lobby vigorously for the others, and relations between us grew chilly. The company was led by Harry H. Corbett, who, as a character comedian, would soon achieve national fame in the TV series *Steptoe and Son*. However, that season he was seriously over-parted, and he did not have the leading actor's instinct to keep himself a little above the factions which quickly develop in unhappy companies, but instead actively encouraged them. The most beautiful theatre in the land was also the draughtiest and dampest backstage, and as winter approached the aggrieved actors, when not rehearsing, would sit a little apart from each other, buttoned up in overcoats on upright chairs like patients waiting their turn in the corridor of an East European hospital.

The winter of 1961 was a record one. Heavy snow clogged the entire country, and in the heights of Clifton, where we lived, it became impossible to push a pram or even walk with safety on the sheets of ice that covered the sloping footpaths. Magnificent views over the Avon, now obscured by foul weather, did not compensate for the fact that all we had in the way of warmth were four tiny electric bar-heaters, one for each room. We ate our meals and read our books under layers of clothing. Conrad had just come home from the hospital after a hernia operation, and, guided by some unerring instinct, lay on his back quite motionless for four days while his wound healed. He seemed to have made a good recovery when suddenly he had an allergic reaction to some aspect of the procedure and broke out in eczema from head to toe. One night after the curtain came down on our perfectly dreadful Christmas pantomime, I did the mountain climb to Clifton through miles of icy slush – all the bus services had been cancelled – and fell into bed with a high temperature. A day later Shirley became infected and also collapsed. Conrad was now so exhausted by the misery of his itchy, blistering skin that his crying was reduced to a bewildered little moan. We were running out of food and the flat had no telephone. Shirley and I, already very sick, now became quite frightened; it was a bad situation which had the possibility of getting much worse.

However, as we moved further into the New Year, the snow melted, our health improved and, with the conclusion of the pantomime, my contract came to an end. I had no wish to stay, nor did the management want me to. For the hell of it I barged into their upstairs offices and ranted and roared about the rotten way they were running their theatre. I thought I had nothing to lose, but wondered afterwards if I was becoming that doubtful animal about whom word spreads quickly through the business, the 'difficult actor'. I had developed such a clear idea of the right and the wrong way of putting on plays that keeping my mouth shut was becoming increasingly difficult. I left Bristol quite unaware that a second collision had taken place in that miraculous billiards shot, and that another ball was now in motion. On it was written the name of Denis Carey, himself once a distinguished artistic director of the Bristol Old Vic, and in the season just passed, visiting director of the one show in which I had managed to retain an excellent part, *The Flanders Mare*. This was a play about the marriage of Henry VIII to the woman of the title, Anne of Cleves, and my role was that of the minister charged with overseeing the union. The best scene was on the wedding night when the monarch, his bride and his minister all sit on the canopied double bed and pass the time playing cards. Denis and I got on well, and later in the year he would make me an offer which would bring me one step closer to the career I was beginning to despair would ever come my way.

There are few other professions where the sun can suddenly shine at midnight (which may explain why so many of us persist in it), and back in London a quite incredible surprise was waiting. Tyrone Guthrie was to direct a new American play, starring my first employer, Robert Morley, and Broadway's Ruth Gordon, and there was an excellent supporting part that was now on offer to me. It was called *A Time to Laugh*, a rather lame title until restored to its biblical context in the Book of Ecclesiastes, and Guthrie had been drawn to it by his interest in the nature of faith. He had already directed Paddy Chayevsky's *The Tenth Man*, about Judaism, and here was a play by a Catholic writer, sceptical about many aspects of his religion, but ultimately submissive to it. To my knowledge, Guthrie held to no set of religious convictions himself, but his grandfather had been a bishop and an influential one (his statue stands in Princes Street, Edinburgh), and there was always a little of the evangelist in the way this director could fire the altruism of the people among whom he worked. Ruth Gordon's part was that of a rich and featherbrained American woman, a kind of ostentatious Roman Catholic groupie, who lives on a Caribbean island in a house in which luxury and piety uneasily co-exist. Among her guests, the chief catch is an amusing and worldly bishop, which was the Morley part. Mine was that of the scandalised young priest employed as his secretary. It delighted me that twelve years on I should be appearing on a West End stage with my old mentor, and that we would have a number of scenes together. The producers were Robert himself, in partnership with Robin Fox, so he had more than his reputation as an actor riding on it.

We gathered one morning to read the play on the stage of the Phoenix Theatre and the first thing I noticed was that Guthrie was far from well. He had a sinus infection which would plague him throughout rehearsals. It is always intimidating doing a reading with an empty auditorium yawning over your shoulder, the like of which the muttering actors will soon be obliged to fill. I glanced across at my colleagues in the other supporting roles, all reputable actors but only one North American, and wondered if we were not missing the tune of the dialogue. English actors had yet to achieve that ease with the American idiom which many possess now. Likewise, the model of the set, standing on a table to one side, was not what I had expected. It was a Gothic fantasy, as playful as the Brighton Pavilion and extremely European, suggesting a play by Jean Anouilh or perhaps Christopher Fry. I had been anticipating something more along the lines of a lavish ranch house in which had been incorporated such bizarre additions as stained-glass windows, a grotto and a chapel bell. I had never visited America, but felt I could make a pretty good guess at it from the experience of my own country, and like most Australian actors, had few problems with US accents.

Once we started rehearsals, the vestigial director in me went back into his box. To begin with, it was impossible to be detached in the face of Ruth Gordon's extraordinary professionalism. She had come with all her lines learnt and her thoughts about the part in place, and could easily have given a performance at the end of the first week, indeed was doing so. She and Guthrie, whom she referred to as 'Coach', had already had a great success together in *The Matchmaker*, and they held each other in mutual esteem. Our other great star was rather more dilatory, though he, too, held the Doctor in affectionate regard and had played Professor Higgins in *Pygmalion* for him at the Old Vic before the war. Robert regarded learning lines as a tedious chore, best postponed till the last moment. He was also rather mischievous, and one morning he inveigled me to the stalls bar for a private rehearsal, where he set about changing the blocking of our first scene, rather, it must be said, in favour of himself. Bits of text he disliked would also mysteriously go missing. In some cases, Guthrie allowed these alterations, in others held his ground, and although rehearsals never became acrimonious, I began to understand his wariness about working with West End stars. Because it was their presence that attracted an audience, they had an economic clout which in any confrontation could reduce the director's authority to a fiction. On the principle that attack is the best defence, Guthrie had adopted a no-nonsense attitude to his star performers which was often resented. Ten years later at the National, after one or two drinks too many, Olivier would say to me, 'A director is a butler. He shows the actors on stage.' This was perhaps half a joke, but only half. Part of him believed it, and in the West End of those days there were a number of excellent butlers happy to do what was required of them.

At the beginning of the third week Robert and I were asked to run our first scene. He still knew barely a word, and the prompter and I did our best to ease him through it. 'Onward!' said Guthrie when we had eventually limped to a humiliating conclusion. This was reprimand enough. In the wings Robert turned to me, flushed and embarrassed, but there was little I could say to comfort him. He had left himself wide open. Suddenly he announced to no one in particular, and with much more emphasis than was called for, 'I *like* acting! I've *always* liked acting!' Then, having convinced himself that this was the case, went off to have a good lunch. However, he'd got the message, and by the end of the week was perfect on his lines. He would soon be giving the best performance in the show. By this time I was no longer mesmerised by Ruth Gordon's technical brilliance, and was beginning to realise something. Ruth realised it, too, when she encountered our first audience, out of town, in Oxford. She was seriously miscast. The part required someone like Billie Burke, the thirties movie actress who could be both foolish and likeable. Ruth Gordon was essentially smart, and her comedy style was knowing and loaded with New York savvy, none of which, on this occasion, fitted what she had to say. At the curtain call our reception was apathetic, and when we gathered in the stalls bar afterwards, I knew we were in trouble the moment I set eyes on Robin Fox. From the bottom half of his face came compliments and smiling encouragement; the top half expressed the shock of someone who's just seen his house burn to the ground. He and Robert had their own money in the show. Panic on the road is more a Broadway phenomenon than a West End one, and Ruth had brought it over in her luggage. That week the rest of the cast knew that there were intense discussions taking place in hotel rooms; what we didn't know was that Ruth was insisting on withdrawing from the show, and that it wasn't until Robin Fox, until recently an important agent, reminded her of the terms of her contract, and hinted at the legal action that might ensue if she neglected to observe them, that she relented. At the end of the week Guthrie called a company meeting. There was work to be done, he told us, but he still believed in the play and we were on course for the Piccadilly Theatre. Thereafter we all relaxed a bit.

Our next date was Brighton. This was where Laurence Olivier lived, and on the Wednesday night he came to see the show. He had just launched the National Theatre and I longed to be a member of his company, so I was extremely nervous. On one of my entrances the director had given me a child's bucket and spade, which the young priest has employed collecting shells on a walk by the seashore. As I came down a short flight of steps, I tripped and the bucket full of shells went flying over the banister. When something goes wrong on stage, the difficulty is finding the time and presence of mind to correct it without interrupting the headlong momentum of the play. Now, on my knees and continuing the dialogue, I reached with my free hand through the uprights of the banister in an effort to retrieve the bucket but it was too big to pass back through. Now desperate for time, I contorted myself to reach over the top of the handrail and collect the bucket in the hand that also held the spade. The audience found this hilarious but I was in too great a state to realise why. After the curtain had come down an actor friend, who had been in the audience, came backstage to see me: 'What a wonderful Guthrie touch that was, when you couldn't get your bucket through the banister.' In a sense he was quite right. Had it happened in rehearsal, Guthrie would have leapt at it with a cry of 'Keep it in! Keep it in!' Such accidents as this, if a director has a sharp enough eye, are pure gold, particularly in comedy, because they are moments of self-evident truth. They really happened, and an audience will always recognise their veracity. An accident of a different sort happened at the mid-week matinee. Ruth Gordon had a nosebleed in one of her long scenes and in trying to control it with a small handkerchief, smeared her entire face with blood. The play continued its remorseless progress, but this was a reality with which no fiction could compete, and the audience sat there like people at a funeral.

We opened in London to a lukewarm press and were told we would be coming off in a fortnight. Robert remained his splendid magnanimous self, and you would never have guessed he was in a flop which had also cost him a bundle. It was, I thought, his best stage performance since *Edward, My Son*, with passages of direct address that he handled with the immense presence I'd admired in Australia. He enjoyed speaking to the audience; he was the host at the party and it was his way of welcoming his guests. I'd also become quite accomplished in my part, and occasionally had the pleasure of actually impressing him. That pop-eyed look when you managed to elicit his interest still had its rewards for me. Among the company I'd made good friends with Cleo Laine, who was widening her professional options by playing a non-singing part, and in whom I recognised another giggler. She and John Dankworth introduced me to their friends who came to see the performance, including Doris Lessing, whose *Play with a Tiger* would be one of my first productions at the Glasgow Citizens' Theatre. I even managed to flog the Dankworths a Victorian chaise longue I'd done up and now wanted to dispose of, because I'd found something I preferred in Bristol. *A Time to Laugh* was a show about which I had no regrets, and in any case, I had another job to look forward to. Denis Carey had offered me Toby Belch in *Twelfth Night* at the Regent's Park Open Air Theatre.

I had now been in a Guthrie triumph and a Guthrie flop, but my regard for him was undiminished. This, I suppose, could hardly have been otherwise, given the interest he had shown in me, though I don't believe I was ever misty-eyed about his talent. His best productions were incomparable, but the play I had just appeared in could have been better done, and I knew the theatre to which I instinctively belonged was moving in another direction. Even about the artistic precepts that had fired his pioneering work in North America, I had a few doubts. Could an imported production style, including a way of speaking, be imposed on another culture and take root? What made him so potent a force wherever he touched down on the globe was his generosity of spirit. Like a whirlwind, he whipped self-interest and vanity out of the temple, and reminded you what theatre should and occasionally could be. He gave of himself in a multitude of ways, never bothering with image building or the creation of his own epitaph. Throw yourself into your work and all that would follow.

Seven years later, when I was a director myself, I tried to woo him to do a production with us in Glasgow. I thought I had a chance because he had begun his directing career with the Scottish National Players, the precursor of the Citizens' Theatre. We corresponded, and his replies, always handwritten and from all over the place, were prompt and to the point. Eventually one arrived which said 'Yes,' and suggested dates. I was able to meet him in London to make the final arrangements, and the venue he proposed reflected his rather prim disapproval of undue expense and ostentation – Lyons Corner House off Piccadilly Circus. We sat there, chatting affably over a pot of tea, but with this curious new reality to deal with: I was a young director for whom the world was opening up, and he was an old one with his greatest achievements behind him. It was like sitting in a draught, which neither party can do much about because you don't quite understand where it's coming from. When he arrived in Glasgow, I was just about to go to New York to direct *Joe Egg*, but I was there to escort him to a reception given by the theatre's board. He still wore the plimsolls I remembered from rehearsals of *All's Well*, but now out of necessity, because his great height had taken a toll on his feet and ordinary shoes were painful. He was no longer Doctor Guthrie but Sir Tyrone, having at last received the knighthood which had been for so long overdue. Our chairman became extremely flustered on meeting the great man and began introducing him as 'Sir Guthrie'. During his rehearsal period I was away in America, but returned in time for the final performance. The play he had chosen was Bridie's *The Anatomist*, principally because it afforded good parts to the actors he had worked with in his youth, now veterans. In the cast were old friends like James Gibson and Jean Taylor Smith. It had dated and the production was not exceptional, but as an adieu to colleagues among whom he had first been able to exercise his powers, it was an affecting occasion.

Towards the end of his life, with his health uncertain (chain smoking his way through years of rehearsals can't have helped), I think he had wearied of the theatre. That exceptional energy with which he transcended its temporal and temporary nature was turning to ash. The toll on his wife Judith was even more severe as she followed him dutifully around the world, from one company of actors to another, watching each mirage of achievement fade in the quest for a new one. The only place that afforded them some sense of continuity and of family life was their house in Ireland 'Anna-ma-kerrig', and here Guthrie ruled over the village with the same resourcefulness that he brought to his productions. One of the most distressing problems facing the small community was the departure of its young people. There was no work for them locally, so they were all leaving for the city. Guthrie proposed a solution: build a jam factory. This would encourage the growing of local produce and provide the necessary jobs. To raise the capital for the venture, he set out on a well-paid but gruelling lecture tour of the States. Alas, unlike Paul Newman's pasta sauces, the jams failed to find a market, but one can scarcely imagine a more selfless undertaking.

When he died, seated in his chair, opening the mail that arrived every morning from all around the world, his gardener is reported to have said, 'A mighty oak is fallen.' His memorial service in London was held on a perfect still summer's day in St Paul's Church, Covent Garden. As the congregation approached the entrance, we were confronted by an enormous tree lying on its side, which had mysteriously toppled over during the night. As a coincidence it was sublime. The service played to a packed house and can accurately be described as joyous. Alec Guinness gave an address which provoked the sort of laughter you sometimes hear in a theatre but rarely in a church. He described how, as a guest in Ireland, he had watched Guthrie entertain some elderly aunts, all nearly blind, with a game of cards. He had made an entire pack out of sheets of cardboard, and the players sat there, holding their gigantic cards in splayed fingers and squinting to assess their hand. Everyone present that day knew that here was something to celebrate, a life better lived than most. Afterwards, Judith Guthrie waited in the sunlight to say a few words to each of us as we filed by. Within weeks she, too, had died.

In Peter Hall's *Diaries*, that extremely partial account of his early years at the National Theatre, in which I and Jonathan Miller feature as chief villains, there are a number of things that angered me, but none more so than his savaging of Tyrone Guthrie, both his work and his character, in his entry for 19 December 1976. A few pages back Peter has just discussed, in glowing terms, the opening of his production of *Tamburlaine*, which I remember as being over-stuffed and inert. Was he trying to forestall any unfavourable comparison with Guthrie's legendary production of the early fifties?

This rediscovery of *Tamburlaine* was only one of Guthrie's many remarkable firsts. In his 1933 season at the Old Vic, he threw out nineteenth-century decorative design and instead brought in an architect to erect a modernist structure, which was to serve all the Shakespeare productions that year, and allow them to be staged as simply as they had been at the Globe. For the first time he introduced other dramatists to the Vic's repertoire – Wilde, Congreve and Chekhov – and his production of *The Cherry Orchard* was the first in English to suggest that comedy played as big a part in the author's intentions as tragedy. These changes so affronted the Vic's usual audience and the more reactionary critics that it would be three years before he was asked to work there again. He would then do what no other director had attempted, and use a Freudian key to unlock the concealed sexual impulses in *Othello* and *Hamlet*. Later, at Stratford, Ontario, his

*Oedipus Rex* with James Mason would be the first modern production of a Greek play to use full masks in the way they had been used twenty-four centuries before.

After Lilian Baylis' death he was asked to assume her mantle at the Old Vic, and stayed at his post from 1936 to 1945, struggling to keep together an unwieldy organisation consisting of a theatre company at the Old Vic, and at Sadler's Wells opera and ballet companies, through six years of war. When he was bombed out of the Vic, he reopened for business in Liverpool before returning to London to a temporary home in the West End at the New Theatre. As both artistic director and financial administrator, the workload was enormous, but by the time of his last season, in which Laurence Olivier entered the history books with *Richard III*, he had helped nurture and advance the most notable generation of British actors of the last century, and with them built up a passionate audience for classical drama. A National Theatre was no longer a pious dream but something within reach, and any director who has earned a living in the subsidised theatre is in Guthrie's debt.

On the subject of Tyrone Guthrie, let Alec Guinness have the last word. This is a comment that he wrote for the dust jacket of Guthrie's autobiography, *A Life in the Theatre*: 'He is not only a great man of the theatre – an unpredictable and sometimes wayward genius and adventurer – but a great man in himself. The omissions [in his book] are typical of the man – his innumerable acts of kindness to young and old, his generosity, and the fact that so many of us owe him, largely, our careers.'

# TEN

# Ladders and Snakes

The Regent's Park Open Air Theatre had been founded in 1930 by the actor-manager Robert Atkins, who devoted the rest of his life to it. In its early days it had attracted young actors of the calibre of Jack Hawkins and Vivien Leigh, but as Atkins aged and his vitality declined so did that of his theatre, and by the time it closed in 1960 it had become the butt of jokey theatrical anecdotes. Now, two years later, it was reopening with two much younger men at the helm. One was David Conville, with whom I'd been friends since RADA, and who had been one of those ex-public-school actors whom the Principal, Sir Kenneth Barnes, thought added a certain tone to the Academy. He was to be the management and his artistic director was to be David William, another Oxbridge director, but one about whom the word was good. The problem always in the Park was the English weather, and Atkins had erected a large tent adjacent to the theatre in which performances could continue in the event of rain. David Conville decided instead to offer audiences free seats on another night, and use the tent to provide upmarket refreshments. He asked Clement Freud, then a modish restaurateur, to take charge, and soon excellent light dinners and good wines became available.

They called themselves the New Shakespeare Company, and their first production, the obvious choice for the Park, was *A Midsummer Night's Dream*, in which David William played Oberon as well as directing. The critics sat up. They had not expected a show as well mounted, nor as vital and intelligent. At the head of a gifted young company was the TV star and ex-RSC actor Patrick Wymark, playing Bottom. The press were unanimous that something fresh and lively had arrived on the London scene. I was to join the company for the second production of the season, *Twelfth Night*. Why Denis Carey had cast me as Sir Toby Belch I had no idea, when there were two other parts for which I considered myself far more suited, Malvolio and Aguecheek. However, the role was an excellent one, with more to say than anyone else in the play. I took a week off and went down to stay with the Nicholses in Devon, where I would have the peace to come to grips with the text and do some learning. Like most people, I had thought of Sir Toby as a sort of lesser cousin to Falstaff, with the same pot belly and grey hair. I soon discovered there were no references either to his girth or his age. If he was uncle to the young Olivia he was more likely to be forty than sixty. He drank and caroused like Falstaff, but so do many younger men. I remembered once, at a theatrical gathering, seeing a lean and very drunk Trevor Howard (this was in his hell-raising days) grinding his teeth against the effect of too much alcohol and then, without warning, letting out a kind of whoop, loud and very aggressive, which for a moment or two brought the party to a complete halt. Even a convivial drunk can put the sober on their guard.

I was beginning to notice other interesting things about Sir Toby. Like many idle people, particularly if they are short of cash, he was very prickly about his social position. Also, though amusing, he was not a particularly pleasant man. He was intent on relieving Aguecheek of his money, and his idea of a practical joke usually involved cruelty. It began to dawn on me that I had seen this Englishman many times, wearing a club tie and cavalry-twill trousers. You found him in saloon bars, in the foyers of station hotels and on the balconies of yacht clubs all over the country, speaking in a loud drawl, rarely paying for his round, and all the while looking restlessly to left and right for some action. We weren't doing a production in modern dress, so none of this could I make literal use of, but it seemed a promising way to go, particularly in a part which would otherwise be a stretch for me. I wanted him to be extremely funny, obviously, but never cosy.

This at once raised a problem because Denis Carey, though an able director, had a distinct inclination towards the cosy. He was best known for his productions of two Julian Slade musicals, *Salad Days* and *Free As Air* – sweet-natured, tinkling West End successes, against which the tide of theatrical fashion had now turned. Like Dougie Seale, he was a small, rather attractive man, but he lacked Dougie's quickness of mind and abrasive directness. Instead, he conducted rehearsals with the whimsical gravity sometimes employed by schoolmasters to charm their charges whilst setting themselves above them. His notes could be as oblique and exasperating as crossword-puzzle clues, though there were some actors who claimed to find a certain poetic guidance in such indirectness. Not, however, Peter Nichols, who had been in the Bristol Old Vic company when Denis staged a version of Dostoevsky's *Crime and Punishment*. At the interval on the first night, an urgent message came over the backstage tannoy system: the director wanted to see the full company on stage at once. The cast trooped down from their dressing rooms and gathered behind the lowered curtain, wondering what the matter was. After a long wait, Denis made his entrance, staring at the floor and apparently lost in thought. A silence ensued, during which he stared gnomically, first at one actor, then at another. 'Just remember,' he suddenly announced, 'there's a body upstairs!' and in a flash he had skipped away into the wings. Peter was not among those who nodded reflectively as they turned away and returned to their dressing rooms. He was too busy laughing.

Notwithstanding his feyness, Denis ran a strict rehearsal room, and had various devices for keeping his actors on the wrong foot. One was to call a full run-through at a time when the company least expected one, and each of his actors would go home afterwards so suicidal about his own performance that mutiny of any sort became the last thing on his mind. Whether Denis was buying my reading of Sir Toby I wasn't at all sure. In the play there is a scene late at night when the upstart Malvolio upbraids the revellers for keeping the household awake. Sir Toby responds and has a line, 'Art any more than a steward?' that I wanted to inform with the incredulity and gathering rage of someone who realises through a haze of drink that he is being reprimanded by a social inferior. Denis smelt the possibility of offence in this reading, of something a little too real, and he asked me to say the line foppishly. 'Throw it away – "Art any more than a steward" – make light of it,' he said. I did as directed, but felt that the show had lost a good moment. I cheered up the following week when David William came to see one of our last run-throughs, and, even without my preferred reading, saw what I was up to and encouraged me to go further with it.

Before performing in the Park, we had two weeks as part of the Ludlow Festival, playing the comedy out of doors in the magnificent, if sombre, ruins of Ludlow Castle. I had been looking forward to being in Housman country and to seeing a little of Shropshire for myself, but the landscape had other ideas. From the moment I arrived I had appalling hay fever, sneezing all day long and wheezing through the night. It was one of those clear, extremely hot English Junes that come along about every ten years, and the air was a soup of grass pollens. We had to dress-rehearse under a blazing sun, and particularly for the comic actors it was hard, exposed work that left our costumes drenched in sweat. By the opening night I was exhausted and struggled in vain to muster the energy for the performance I believed I could give, but it proved a wretchedly disappointing evening for me. I could find only one positive and very curious thing to say about it. As the moment of my first entrance approached, and with it a wave of intense nerves, my sneezing stopped. The antidote to severe allergic reaction is an injection of adrenalin, and I had just manufactured my own dose. For the rest of the run I would sneeze all day, stop just before I stepped on stage, then start again two and a half hours later as I returned to my dressing room.

By the time we had returned to London, the grasses had stopped pollinating and the huge cloud of toxins which had hung over the British Isles had been dispersed by the winds. Also, I had become well practised in my role. This London first night would be an important one for me, appearing before the metropolitan critics in my best part so far, and I had carefully psyched myself up for it. In the Park it was a cool, still summer night, perfect for comedy, and by the time the sky had faded to an urban pearl, and the stage lights had begun to assert themselves against the darkness that came seeping through the trees, I knew we were home. The laughter coming from the canvas deckchairs was clean and spontaneous. There is no more delicious feeling for an actor than being at his best on an opening night, and knowing that the audience is his. Afterwards the company gathered in Clement Freud's refreshment marquee, where I joined Shirley and had too many glasses of mulled claret as I accepted compliments from the two Davids and from others who had been present in what turned out to be quite a distinguished audience.

That night I slept badly, acting the part all over again in my head, and woke early, hollow with misgiving about what was waiting for us in the daily papers. I threw on some clothes, walked fast to the tube station with a pocket full of coins, then stood on the corner, hunting through the crackling pages as if my life depended on it, while people circled round me on their way down to the Underground and to less ridiculous jobs. By and large the notices were favourable, if here and there condescending to the venue and to a production from the director of *Salad Days*. I had a paragraph to myself in *The Times*, which described my approach to the part in some detail and concluded, 'This lightens and speeds up the scenes in which he is involved considerably, to the general advantage of the production.' This pleased me, but I wasn't sure it would please Denis. What gave me most satisfaction was J. C. Trewin in the *Birmingham Post*, who had been following my progress ever since my days with Sir Barry Jackson. He had already reviewed the production in general terms during its run in Ludlow; now he devoted almost his entire notice to this fresh take on Sir Toby Belch. However, in spite of my pleasure in this recognition, what struck me even then, as it would throughout my career when I turned to the papers after a first night, was the odd dislocation between the actual event of which I had been part and this later summation in a column of newsprint. Whether the review was good or bad, it was only with the very best critic that you felt the two were ever a match. More often it was as if the show had talked in one language and was now being judged in another.

There is a price to pay for first nights, even successful ones – the hangover the next day that follows an excess of exhilaration, and what made the company feel even more depleted on this occasion was the matinee we were obliged to play that afternoon. This would not be to an audience of sympathetic supporters on a balmy night, but to rows of highly visible schoolchildren, shifting in their deckchairs in the glare of the afternoon. I struggled through the show as best I could, determined to get an hour's sleep before the evening performance, which would be attended by a handful of important second-night critics. Among them was Alan Brien, whose column I resented for its arrogance; so, of course, I was particularly keen to impress him. I had cut out one of his more outrageous assertions and pasted it on the back of our lavatory door. Brien had written, 'In the history of the drama it has always been the critics who have breathed fresh life into old embers,' a clear case of the cart getting up on its back wheels and proclaiming itself the horse. I had already made up my mind that he would hate my performance, but I intended to put up a fight. First, however, I needed a nap, and before that, something to eat.

We had been told that on matinee days, between the shows Clement Freud would provide food for the actors at a reduced price, so we duly made our way to his tent, the women in the flimsy, much-washed gowns in which they made up, the men stripped down to all but the rudiments of their costumes. We'd taken off our wigs and various hairpieces and, now with white patches on our pancaked faces, looked like a huddle of burn victims. None of us were recognisable in the parts we had just played, but stood there in our ragged motley with the passivity of refugees. Eventually someone noticed us and told us to move to the rear of the tent, sit down and wait. Clement and his staff of comely young women were at the other end, preparing food with no particular urgency for the paying customers expected that evening. A quarter of an hour passed, then half an hour, then three-quarters, until, finally, on behalf of the group I called across the tent for a little attention. A girl approached, said someone would be with us shortly and went away again. Fifteen minutes later I again had to speak up, and this time the same girl sulkily took our orders. A further twenty minutes passed. I glanced at my watch; the time for my nap had already passed. When the girl came our way next, I yelled at her. She glanced at me, then went straight as an arrow to her boss and they muttered together. Clement Freud threw down a cloth, then came striding through the tent, metaphorically rolling up his sleeves as he came to sort us out. I was his target. In very loud tones, as if he was addressing the ringleader of grumbling servants in a country house, he proceeded to tick me off. In comparison, it was behaviour towards the actors that made Polonius look like the President of Equity, and I completely and quite uncontrollably lost my temper. This has happened to me only four times in my career, and these detonations have been so unexpected and so huge that they have surprised me quite as much as their targets, or anyone who happened to be standing by. Clement Freud was now confronting a maniac, and he had the good sense to say nothing more and retreat. Otherwise I might very well have killed him.

I was taken back to the men's dressing room, trembling with rage and in a kind of despair. Those few remaining reserves of energy that I had been hoarding for the evening performance had gone up in one plume of black smoke. Comedy is all about superfluous energy, those impulses that have nowhere else to go but into enjoyable mischief, and I had not a quantum of playfulness left. David Conville looked into the dressing room briefly before the performance. Earlier in the week we had had an altercation about billing, and I saw him looking at me now with the sort of pained regret that he might have extended to a member of his golf club who had broken the dress code for the second Sunday in succession. I went on stage trying to remember what it was that had worked so well the night before. Eventually we reached the scene between Malvolio and the night revellers. This was something I *could* play. I focused hard on Clement Freud and out came the line, 'ART ANY MORE THAN A *STEWARD*!?' with every bit of rage and contempt I could muster. It was a moment of which Olivier himself would have been proud.

At the interval I was just about to stretch out on the floor for ten minutes' rest when the stage manager leant through the door: 'Everyone outside, please. Denis has called a full company meeting.' I got to my feet, my fatigue now qualified by a certain bleak alertness; I thought I knew what this might be about. We gathered on the concrete outside the dressing room block, and waited there in the illumination of the weak exterior light. A silent Denis stood opposite us, swaying slightly, with a dark mass of leaves and branches rising up behind him, and beyond, the distant, shallow buzz of the audience at intermission, milling about in the tent. He had been drinking since midafternoon, and his expression was ominous. We waited for him to speak and when at last he did so, it was exclusively to attack me – about my performance, my behaviour and my row with Clement Freud. For some reason he skirted around the line reading, the one thing about which as director, he had some reason to complain. I listened with my expression an exhausted blank as he abused me with growing ferocity, and in the process revealed more and more about himself. On display were his bruised vanity, his prickly concern for his own authority and his rage at a worthwhile career which seemed to be passing. Without drink, these were feelings that he would probably have kept to himself, and in any case I understood them. What I considered disgraceful was using his authority as a director to impose this state of mind on one of his cast in the middle of an important performance. It was a big part and more than half of it still lay ahead of me. I wondered if I might be approaching another explosion, but I had run out of rage, too. Instead, I went back to my place at the dressing table and gave in to the only emotion I had left. I wept.

The rest of the performance was a washout, for me personally and for the show. At one point I caught a momentary glimpse of Alan Brien, sitting in the middle block of seats on an aisle. He was not just yawning; he was stretching. And yet, if nothing else, the evening had vindicated my contested reading. I had been quick to see Malvolio in Clement Freud, but from Denis Carey's point of view I was something of a Malvolio myself, and in his own performance of Toby Belch during the interval I had triggered just those depths of indignation about which, originally, we had been in dispute.

The following evening, as with most backstage dramas, the blow-up was all but forgotten, or rather the slightly embarrassed principals did our best to pretend it was. After the performance, Clement Freud sidled up to me in the tent and murmured, 'Sorry about yesterday. One always seems to be rude to the wrong people.' This was gracious of him, even if it left unanswered the question of who were the right people to be rude to. In any case, my mind had now turned to more important things. David William had asked me to play Holofernes in the final production of the season, *Love's Labour's Lost*. Suddenly the billiard balls had collided once more and were off in a new direction. I didn't know the play, and it took me a while to pick my way through its thicket of verbal conceits. The part of the schoolmaster, Holofernes, with his Latin tags and ludicrous vocabulary, is at a first reading almost incomprehensible. However, as soon as I'd worked out exactly what he was saying, I began to perceive beneath the fallen leaves of sixteenth-century verbiage the outline of a marvellous and surprisingly modern comic part. In the play, word games are an expression of the young lovers' abundant vitality. Holofernes turns these games on their head in a display of cramped, immensely self-regarding pedantry. It was curiously liberating to discover that long ago an enduring type had been so hilariously skewered. The Establishment club had just opened, and I had been going there to watch emerging performers like John Bird and Barry Humphries. Now it seemed that Holofernes was reaching out over the arc of centuries to shake the hand of Peter Cook.

On one of my visits to the Establishment I watched the great Lenny Bruce perform. The first remarkable thing about him was that he was in no hurry. That show-business imperative to please and to have an effect simply wasn't there. It was up to us, the audience, to make up our minds whether or not we found him amusing. Soon, and almost by stealth, he led us into one lethal booby trap of laughter after another. On one side of the stage there was a low screen about five feet high. Lenny went behind it so that all we could see of him was his head. For a while he said nothing, and there was a little nervous tittering. Then, without the least change of expression, he told us that he was now doing the most disgusting thing ever done on stage. The only thing to look at was his face, and that was as blank as a mask. He had once more lapsed into a prolonged silence. The audience, now abandoned to its own conjectures, began to laugh. The laughter grew and grew as the silence stretched into minutes. Eventually the house became quite hysterical. It was a perfect illustration of one of the attributes of theatre: that so much of what we take from it comes from our own heads. Later in the evening Lenny's material swerved onto the subject of cancer, a disease of which, at the time, discussion – certainly in comic terms – was still somewhat taboo. Suddenly a middle-aged man in the audience leapt to his feet and, in an assertive South Kensington bellow, said, 'Right! That's it! *Cancer!* Come on, Muriel! *Cancer! Cancer!*' He had grabbed Muriel by the arm and they were now both leaving the theatre, Muriel, I thought, with some reluctance. This was what Lenny Bruce could do; make you pick through the trash-can of your own mind and confront the contents. It induced either delight or blind fury.

I had found a clue to the playing of Holofernes on television. The historian A. J. P. Taylor had been giving a series of lectures, immensely accomplished and informative displays, straight to camera, without the benefit of notes or cue-cards of any kind. Without suggesting that this estimable man was a Holofernes, there was something about him (suggested perhaps by that tell-tale third initial) – a scowling acceptance of his own importance – which I found very funny. He could be my starting point. Another clue to the part came from my schooldays. In the play Holofernes is accompanied everywhere by the curate, Sir Nathaniel. They make an odd but perfect pair, the schoolmaster loftily holding forth and the curate all ears and grovelling encouragement. At the King's School I had had just such a friend, a withdrawn boy called Pfeifer, as keenly interested in military history as I was in the arts and cinema. Since we were at an institution where all prestige derived from sport, Pfeifer and I existed very much on the sidelines of school life. I'm not sure that in another environment we would have been drawn to each other, but at the King's School we were bonded by real need. I did most of the talking, he did the listening, and we were always in each other's company, trailing along the riverbank, or walking past a sports field, quite indifferent to the strenuous activity nearby, in which we were supposed to be taking an enthusiastic interest.

By the end of the first week's rehearsal of *Love's Labour's Lost* I knew it was going to be one of those exceptional experiences that can make the life of an actor not merely endurable but privileged. We were a group of mainly young performers considered to have promise and on the cusp of something more, and we were embarking on one of those Shakespearean comedies with such an even distribution of wonderful parts that morale in the company is almost a given. Guiding us we had a director who might have been born to do this play, whose own love of language, playfulness and sense of honour had a shining mirror in the text. We were all quick to recognise that, in a certain way, he owned it, and we were happy to put ourselves in his hands. David William was then in his mid-thirties, an actor-director with, on first acquaintance, a haughty, rather prancing manner like an over-bred horse, which left you unprepared for the humour and firm benevolence with which he ran a rehearsal room. It was a pleasure to come to work because you knew you were going to get justice. His authority had the transparency which comes not from egotism, but from a passionate concern for the greater good, something which any group of people will quickly sniff out and respond to. He never hesitated to intervene when he felt that mistakes were being made, or when a scene could be improved, but he also had the modesty, when rehearsals were going well, to simply watch and become, in Guthrie's phrase 'an ideal audience of one'. (This same definition of the job I later heard from another great director, Peter Stein.) I have attributed to David qualities which were certainly his, but which this particular play, and this set of circumstances nourished and brought splendidly into play. A truly successful production is the consequence of so many imponderables – the right text with the right cast and the right director and designer, and, as important, coming at the right moment. Its success can never be entirely a matter of analysis. What one can say about exceptional productions is that they are occasions when, rather mysteriously, everyone becomes free to work at their optimum.

Any rehearsal period has its ups and downs, and we were not exempt. The show took its worst nose-dive when we left the comfort of our indoor rehearsal space and had to start shouting our lines into the leafy reaches of Regent's Park. How could we expect an audience to give us the close attention the play demanded when jet planes flew overhead, and one gust of wind rattling through the trees was enough to obliterate half a page of text? At the dress rehearsal our labour of love seemed, if not lost, then hopelessly mislaid as we struggled in unfamiliar costumes to attain focus beneath swaying boughs, which, like bored members of an audience, seemed to be having a conversation among themselves. Even David William's confidence occasionally faltered. He was coming to the end of a season which had made considerable demands on his stamina, and both he and David Conville knew that they had the artistic credentials of their new company riding on this last production. The learning curve of people in the theatre, performers and backstage staff alike, as a first night draws near, must be one of the steepest in the world, and the difference between a dress rehearsal and the public performance one day later can sometimes seem little short of miraculous. Our first night was to be one of those miracles. By the time I had made my first entrance with Sir Nathaniel, a wonderful performance by James Ottaway, I could already smell success in the moist air. We were jumping onto an already moving vehicle, and just the look of these two new passengers, the one tall and beaky, the other round-faced and short, provoked laughter. For its last half-hour the production was airborne.

The following morning, early, I was back at the tube, buying the newspapers. As with *Twelfth Night* our notices were mixed, but with this crucial difference: those that were on our side were ecstatic. 'No need now for open-air charity,' ran Herbert Kretzmer's headline. Above Bernard Levin's review it read, 'A labour of love and joy beyond all praise,' and he went on to say, 'I cannot recall more than half-a-dozen occasions at the theatre in my life which were productive of so much unalloyed delight.' His notice was an unqualified rave. The actors received high praise, though, justly, most acclaim went to the director. David read it that morning on a plane taking him on a well-deserved holiday, and, as he told us later, to his great embarrassment, burst into tears. Over the next ten days the remaining press continued to endorse us. *The Spectator* put us on their cover with a deft Quentin Blake illustration of the cast beneath the trees of the open-air stage, and inside Bamber Gascoigne's notice was a rival to Levin's. Let me quote from it, not only because of the satisfaction it obviously gave me, but because it was one of those occasions when artistic intent and a critic's perception of it prove a true match:

'Regent's Park seems hardly a promising place in which to make a theatrical reputation, but this summer David William has triumphantly done so. His production of *A Midsummer Night's Dream*, which opened the season was sylvan magic. And now his *Love's Labour's Lost* is almost equally delightful and very much more surprising, since the jungle of punning verbiage in this early comedy is virtually impossible to appreciate on the printed page. Mr William takes a firm grasp on the quips and quiddities of the prose characters and on the elaborate "taffeta phrases, silken terms precise, three-piled hyperboles, spruce affectation and figures pedantical" of the courtly lovers; and he lets no phrase pass until he has found and revealed its meaning. Even more important, he has helped his actors to find solid characterisations behind every bout of verbal horseplay in the text. To the reader the part of Holofernes may seem a mere indulgence in a string of scholastic jokes, but as played by Michael Blakemore this proudly pompous pedant is a character of infinite subtlety. He knows that scholarship, however brilliant (and his is not), will always be an inferior accomplishment in this courtly world, and his reaction is to become a raging intellectual snob.'

To our surprise we had become a genuine London hit, and a highbrow one. Dame Edith Sitwell had brought a party to see us, and at the curtain call of a mid-week matinee I spotted Evelyn Waugh sitting bolt upright in his deckchair. We heard a West End management was interested in a transfer, which would have been entirely possible, given the excellence of our designers, Henry Barden and David Walker. However, David William was still on holiday and David Conville, with bills to pay, was cautious. I longed for some executive involvement in this theatre company of which, otherwise, I was so happy to be a part. Both men were my good friends, but I wondered if they lacked a quality which I believed I had, one neither admirable nor particularly interesting, but important if you work in the theatre: an instinct to strike while the iron is hot. I had a vision of where this company might go – in the summer, as at present, a season in the Park, but then around Christmas, a winter season in a proper theatre, capitalising on the hits of the previous summer, and perhaps previewing shows for the forthcoming one. With luck and a subsidy, the company could emerge as a third force between Stratford and the Old Vic. If the company confined its work to the Park, its hopes of being taken seriously would always be compromised by a factor unrelated to the quality of the work – the English weather.

This thinking was prophetic. We had opened *Love's Labour's Lost* towards the end of August. September saw an early onset of bad weather, with cold winds and a constant drizzle of rain. Most evenings we were arriving at the theatre uncertain whether we would be able to perform. Our public dwindled to a handful of stoic supporters swathed in blankets, some even nursing hot-water bottles, and the cast shivered among the dripping trees. This exquisite production became an abandoned toy, left out in the rain, and by the time we closed, the New Shakespeare Theatre, which with better luck would have made lots of money, had fallen slightly into the red. And yet, even today, the Park is a memory that can still move me. The rain that fell on us was the same English rain that had once fallen on performances at the Globe, and attested to what is always true about theatrical enterprise – its riskiness and the quixotic gallantry that is sometimes needed to sustain it. In the open air all performances begin badly. Broad daylight is not kind to actors and their pretences, and the dramatic propositions they bring on with them can seem ludicrously simplistic in a setting of indubitably real trees and open sky. You wonder if disbelief will ever be suspended. Then, slowly, the darkness falls, and the surrounding world begins to close down to that small patch of illuminated grass. The see-saw of credibility begins at last to tilt in favour of the players, as they extract a single strand of drama from that which surrounds them, and is now receding into the shadows – the world's chaos. I can remember waiting to make an entrance through a tunnel of leaves, smelling the humid vegetation around me and the soft earth underfoot, and sensing what one never does indoors, night stealing across the length of Britain and releasing its provocative energies. The last hour of a good production in the open air can have a power all its own, as, against the odds, the idea of theatre slyly raises its banner.

I was out of work again but, with a file of good notices on record, I hoped it would not be for too long. One of the curiosities of an actor's life is that a success or the winning of an award, far from being the beginning of something, is more often the end of something, a sort of culmination, and it is often followed by a long spell of neglect. I thought the phone would ring. It didn't, and I had no choice but to return to my novel. Unfortunately, the tortoise sustains himself with a different set of disciplines than does the hare, and starting to write again was not easy. I would work in the mornings, but by mid-afternoon the urge to get up from the typewriter and go banging out of the front door in search of life at first hand would usually get the better of me. Shirley was out of the house experimenting with a series of jobs that would eventually lead to teachers' training college. Conrad's daytime hours were now in the charge of a succession of au pairs (two duds for every success), the present one being a sweet, conscientious French girl called Danielle, who giggled a lot and who would become a lasting friend. It was all too easy to give in to one's restlessness, and I now had a particular reason for doing so; I had embarked on an affair. Her name was Dona Martyn, and we had worked together in the Regent's Park company. As an actress she had a quality that suggested Europe rather than England, and she was beginning to gain a reputation with striking performances in Sartre and Strindberg. Her rare good looks and air of enigma were a little reminiscent of Arletty, the French film star, and I was soon spellbound.

The married sexual ethic I, and others, espoused at that time derived, I suppose, from the upper classes, ameliorated by Bloomsbury's cult of friendship. Essentially it said that you always protected the marriage and the children, but otherwise could do what you liked, and it applied, at least theoretically, to both sexes. This was not entirely a licence for licence; certain rules governed our infidelity. It had to mean something, to be special, and such opportunities were not necessarily plentiful. When they came along you were entitled to embrace them – but somehow without hurting or humiliating anyone else. As a moral formulation it was pretty optimistic, especially since so few of us had the piles of money, the possessions and the real estate which helped considerably to focus the minds of upper-class adulterers when one of their marriages came under serious threat.

The unfaithful husband of the sixties considered his wife his best friend, a contradictory proposition, but which, where Shirley was concerned, I honestly believed to be the case. Perhaps it was guilt on my part, or gratitude for her tolerance, or the fact that I was released from demanding of her things it was unfair to expect after ten years together, but we rarely fought, often laughed, and were gentle and attentive to one another. The exemplar of this sort of behaviour was Kingsley Amis, who, though devoted to his family, was as ambitious and determined in his affairs as he was in the writing of his books. For him, and for most of us, the remnants of morality that we clung to in the name of love – concern for our children, loyalty to our wives – would be blown away in the storms and last chances of middle age. In any case, the burgeoning sexual revolution of the sixties, which we thought of as giving us its blessing, would soon move in a very different direction, as more and more women perceived themselves to be short-changed in the arrangement and had a revolution of their own. Heterosexual liberty is now for the unattached and beautiful young, armed with condoms and with a death's head in their minds. What has followed for social groups A and B is a life of serial monogamy, with marital continuity and its implications for children considered an irrelevance. On the housing estates there is sexual anarchy and drugs. Whether there is more happiness and less misery, more or less goodwill between the sexes, is an open question.

This was not my first foray outside marriage. There had been another, important enough for me to have pursued it with some recklessness, but both of us were already attached, and concerned with preserving those attachments. Now I had become involved with someone single, whose spare time matched my own. It began as an affair with no demands on either side, if you discount a sharp and growing hunger for the next meeting, but inevitably it began to grow concealed roots as I became more deeply absorbed in her beauty, her delicate intelligence and her strange story. As a child her schooling had been interrupted by illness, and she had spent her adolescence travelling the Continent as the companion of a young Portuguese aristocrat she had met in a Swiss sanatorium. A political radical and opponent of the Salazar regime, he had contacts all over Europe with the artistic and intellectual world, and Dona had spent her teens mixing with some of the famous names of the day. What she lacked in formal education she made up for with her own reading and an increasingly cultivated taste in music and the visual arts. With winter approaching, warmly enclosed within the walls of her two attic rooms near Regent's Park, and with no need of a life beyond them, it felt sometimes as if I was becoming a participant in a short story, one, say, by Thomas Mann, having a life only within these spaces, the way a character in fiction is confined to the existence he has on the page. This intense intimacy blinded me to the possibilities of future pain, and all I could wonder at was my incredible luck.

An offer of work brought me back into the world, and from a familiar source. David Conville had acquired the rights to A. A. Milne's dramatisation of *The Wind in the Willows*, a Christmas annual in London, and he had asked David William to direct an entirely new production. There would be sets and costumes by Peter Rice, fresh orchestrations for an augmented orchestra, and, most radical of all, someone other than Richard Goolden to play Mole. This elderly actor had appeared in the first performance in the twenties, and had had a leasehold on the part ever since. What the two Davids hoped for was a revitalisation of the material, but this would have to wait until Alan Bennett's version some years later at the National. The Milne script, though excellent in its way, and renamed *Toad of Toad Hall*, was too shop-worn to support an innovative production. Our show was nevertheless a success. Peter Woodthorpe played Toad, rather like Oscar Wilde on the run, and I was Badger. As a child, the original book had never meant much to me, though in Anglophile Australia we were expected to enjoy strolling though its lush Edwardian prose. Moles, water rats and weasels weren't, I thought, quite a match for kangaroos, wombats and flying foxes, an opinion shared by another Australian, the drama critic of the *Daily Telegraph*, who alone gave the National Theatre's later production a poor review. The editor was so outraged by this affront to the memory of the English nursery that he fired him.

Despite a similar cultural confusion, I saw that Badger was an excellent part, and I knew at once how to play him. I dropped my voice an octave into a lugubrious upper-class drawl, and made him a cousin of the then Prime Minister, Harold Macmillan. With the co-operation of the wigmaker I also invented a Badger make-up for which Sir Kenneth Barnes, had he still been alive, would have given me the highest marks, and which was so effective that it was copied in all later productions. Once again I had a set of excellent notices to paste into my book, and the new National Theatre, which would be staging its first production at the Old Vic later in the year, sent along someone to have a look. It was an enjoyable engagement, with a large cast of improbably bewhiskered animals crowding the wings, one or two extremely pretty, and you had to be careful not to stand on their tails. We did two performances a day, and in the centrally heated Comedy Theatre, muffled up in a heavy costume, I would become extremely dehydrated, so on my way to work I would buy six big navel oranges from a barrow near Piccadilly Circus, and between the performances, like a rugby player at half-time, consume the lot.

It was the beginning of 1963, and the decade was already acquiring the definition, the sense of itself, which one imagined people must have felt as they lived through the twenties. England was changing fast, and most people under forty rejoiced. At the very least we were all curious about what was going on, and wanted to understand it. The sixties could never mean for me what the fifties had meant. I was now thirty-four, with a family, under a roof of my own, and a career to fight for, but I was an enthusiastic bystander, and cheered on those younger than me at the head of the parade. One afternoon, when the Hampstead-bound tube had stopped at Camden Town, the doors opened and a rush of kids in neat school uniforms tumbled into the compartment. They were a lively mix of black and white children, but what I realised was so new about them was that they were all piping away in identical London accents. Up till then a black face went with a Caribbean sound, but these children were all *English*. I wondered, with a trace of borrowed pride, if on this small island of all places, once the hub of imperial dominion, the inequities of racial difference might one day be resolved.

That year the music of the Beatles began to take up residence in all our heads. They sang with the same fraudulent American accents of earlier British bands, but this time it didn't seem to matter. In their own way their sound was as authentic as Louis Armstrong. It wasn't only the music; it was their clothes and their haircuts. Previously, popular British culture, even when it was being cheeky, tipped its hat towards the posh. The Teddy Boys of the fifties derived their gear from the post-war Edwardian cut first made fashionable in Savile Row, and less rebellious working-class youth, hoping to look smart, would go to the chain store 'Burton, the Tailor of Taste', where Mayfair styles were sedulously and crudely aped. Now such imitative behaviour was starting to shift in the opposite direction. This Liverpool band had a silhouette all their own, and it was a shape that suggested the future. In the theatre such changes were well under way, including the symbolic importance of dress. When Laurence Olivier, in a dinner jacket, opened the doors of the National Theatre with his inaugural production of *Hamlet* at the Old Vic, his two young associate directors, John Dexter and William Gaskill, attended dressed not in black tie but, like Bertolt Brecht, in black leather.

What was changing everybody's lives up and down the social scale, as uniformly as if the country had been dipped in bleach, was quality television. The programmes were so good, the medium so novel, that we put our books to one side and avidly turned to the box. For a while TV seemed to presage something quite wonderful, McLuhan's 'global village', where values and ideas would become accessible to all and where folly would be exposed before it became mischief. There were nights when the entire population seemed to be staying indoors to watch, say, *That Was the Week That Was* or a drama like *Cathy, Come Home*, and the following day such programmes would be discussed excitedly by strangers at bus stops. I was riveted by the documentary material, particularly the archive film, of which we had seen so little. It seemed to provide a strange insight into the recent historical past – what it was actually *like* to be there – unavailable in a book, or not in quite the same way. In news and current affairs a generation of articulate and principled journalists were all over the place, showing you what was happening on the spot and explaining why. Throughout the sixties the Vietnam War unfolded on British TV with far greater explication and foreboding than it did on the screens of the country that was waging it. Early on we knew about the carve-up of North and South at Geneva, and the broken undertaking to allow an election. As it was happening we knew about the 'advisors' being sent in by Kennedy, and the puppet governments being installed in Saigon. There was one report that has always stayed with me because the passage of time was to endorse everything it said. The journalist – it may have been James Mossman – was seen in an idyllic Cambodia, which its leader, Prince Sihanouk, had been juggling desperately to keep out of the war. We were told its history, shown its beauty and the tranquil routine of its daily life, then offered an uncanny forecast of what the future held for it. The Wooden Horse was being constructed plank by plank before our eyes.

This was quality television because we believed it to be so. Forty years later, the expression has become almost a contradiction in terms. The brilliance of some of the programmes is not in dispute. The problem is the passivity with which they are experienced. I remember the Cambodian broadcast, but what of the thousands of hours between then and now that have disappeared so completely from my mind that I might just as well have been staring at the wall? Like other aspects of the sixties, the high hopes we once had for television as a factor in society now seem simple-minded; and there was one event on the box in 1963, a truly indelible memory, which both demonstrated the power of TV and sowed an early seed of doubt.

It's often said that people can always tell you where they were when they learnt that President Kennedy had been shot. I certainly remember where I was, sitting at home looking at a black-and-white television screen. I was watching the BBC's current affairs programme, *Tonight*, that I turned on as a matter of course on weekday evenings at seven. It had an excellent team of investigative correspondents, who spoke to us not in the old BBC standard English, but in their own robust regional accents. There was the very Welsh John Morgan, and Fyfe Robertson with his tweed hat, beard and Scottish burr. The anchorman on the programme was the genial Cliff Michelmore, whose geniality that night was about to be tested to the limit. He was midway through one of his pieces to camera when he stopped abruptly, and there were a few very long seconds of unaccustomed silence. When he spoke it was to tell us that the programme was to be interrupted for a news bulletin. We went to the familiar picture of the newsreader sitting at his desk, and we learnt that shots had been fired at President Kennedy's motorcade as it drove through Dallas. Then we were back with Cliff Michelmore attempting to pick up where he left off. Again he stopped. This time the picture changed to the BBC emblem of a slowly revolving globe, which stayed there on the screen for what seemed minutes in total silence. With a jolt we returned to Cliff Michelmore in the studio. He said nothing, but his face was lifted and his gaze was to one side like an alerted animal, as he tried to ascertain what was going on and what was expected of him. Then another jolt as the newsroom reappeared on the screen. The President, said the newsreader, had been seriously wounded and was being rushed to hospital. As I listened with my mouth open, a hand holding a piece of paper, no more, just a hand, came in from the left of frame and froze. The newsreader noticed it, took the piece of paper and the hand withdrew. He opened it, and as his eyes ran along the lines he went from one shade of grey to one much paler. Then he controlled himself, raised his head and told us calmly that the President was dead.

The picture returned to the silent, revolving world, then cut to a mute Cliff Michelmore, still standing on the same spot in the studio, then cut back again to the world. Suddenly the screen was filled with noise. The programme that was to follow *Tonight* was a comedy series called *The Harry Worth Show* and its opening credits played over a long tracking shot, accompanied by rowdy comic music, of the comedian in his bowler hat leaving the door of his house and parading along the street. Someone had made the hopelessly inappropriate decision to bring the programme forward. It was like the band striking up to cover some ghastly accident on stage. The news of the assassination, spinning the world like a top, had momentarily undone a huge, confident organisation. By the following day the BBC was once again its familiar, monumental self, and at little notice succeeded in putting together a special edition of *That Was the Week That Was* paying eloquent tribute to the dead President. However, what we had caught a glimpse of was something else – a group of frantic people, trying, like any other, to cope with the sudden arrival of a new era of misgiving and violence.

Over the following days, seen once, twice, three times on successive news bulletins, the black-and-white images arrived by satellite, but with the technology in its infancy they came to our screens with a glare to them as if bounced off the chromium bumper of one of those cars in the motorcade. One clip, I remember, was of Jacqueline Kennedy running away from the camera towards the hospital where her husband's body lay, then stopping and looking back over her shoulder like someone in a Greek play. Every time you turned on the set there she was, looking back at her pursuing Furies. We were watching an incomplete but utterly mesmerising reality coming into existence, squared off within the confines of a television screen, in which the past, reorganised in dislocated, dramatic fragments, could be recalled at will. The assassination was the first of those news stories, which only seem to come out of America, in which the revelations and twists are so incessant, one capping another, so startling and improbable, that it's almost as if the medium itself had invented a new form of storytelling to appease its voracious audience. We were not merely told that Ruby had killed Oswald, we saw it with our own eyes. Yet, once one had recovered from the shock, every new development seemed to conceal as much as it revealed. The more we learnt the less we knew. The repeating images began to develop a lurid, parallel life of their own. As truth they were smoke, and television, far from showing us a way out of the maze, left us where we had always been, stranded at the centre.

In the spring I had a letter from Bill Gaskill, an associate director at the National Theatre, offering me a place in the new company. With some reluctance I felt I had to turn it down. The parts were much on a level with those I'd been offered at Stratford four years before, and I was at a stage in my career where the first consideration had to be the part I was being asked to play rather than the context in which I would be playing it. I accepted instead David Conville's second season in the Park, reunited with James Ottaway in another comic double, Dogberry and Verges in *Much Ado About Nothing*. However, the new

National was where I hoped one day to be. Its work promised to be a synthesis of the great tradition of British acting, embodied in its artistic director, in collision with the more searching, abrasive values of the Royal Court, and indeed Gaskill's production later in the year of *The Recruiting Officer* exemplified this marriage to perfection. It had the textual rigour and spare visual elegance that one associated with his previous address in Sloane Square, but it was performed by a cast almost every one of whom was or would become a star – Olivier, Maggie Smith, Robert Stephens, Colin Blakely and Lynn Redgrave among them. Likewise, his fellow associate, John Dexter, had not only the best cast he could have hoped for in *Hobson's Choice* – Michael Redgrave, Joan Plowright and Frank Finlay – but also every penny of the budget he required for his spectacular staging of *The Royal Hunt of the Sun*. At last a British theatre had the resources to rehearse for six or seven weeks, to give proper importance to stage design, and to hold on to an ensemble of exceptional actors for as long as two or three years. Whatever intellectual structure directors and designers brought to the work it was always complemented, and to an extent qualified, by that rendering of recognisable human behaviour which is always and only in the gift of talented actors. As a result some of these early productions at the National were, among their other qualities, thrilling entertainment – what Tynan was to describe as 'high definition performance'.

There was no need to argue solemnly that the theatre was important. Like Joan Littlewood's *Oh, What a Lovely War* at Stratford East that same year, it was blindingly obvious. To many of us this new era at the Old Vic seemed to be the beginning of something wonderful. I wonder now if, like a great success in an individual career, it, too, was not a culmination, an end of something, which the departure of the two actor-managers, first George Devine at the Court and later Olivier at the National, would only serve to underline. Since theatre endlessly renews itself, other forms of excellence have followed, though increasingly in smaller spaces and for more specialised audiences. But at the Old Vic at that time what John Osborne and I had once enthused about as we stood chatting in the Charing Cross Road, and what Guthrie had spent his life working towards, seemed to have arrived – uncompromised excellence intended for everybody.

*Much Ado About Nothing* was to be the first production of the new season at the Park. It was lavishly mounted with the façade of a great

Tudor house seen amongst the trees, and with the actors attired in beautifully rendered Elizabethan costumes, the work of Henry Barden and David Walker, the same design team responsible for *Love's Labour's Lost*. David William, who again was directing, had assembled an excellent cast, led by Denis Quilley as Benedict. I had seen this first-rate actor playing the lead in the British premiere of the Bernstein musical *Candide*, and now he was showing himself to be accomplished in Shakespeare. It bothered me that neither the Old Vic nor Stratford had ever considered him for their companies, because actors of his quick skills and immediate masculine presence are as rare as they are valuable, particularly in the classics. He had prospered in the theatre because in addition to these attributes he had a good singing voice and had slipped easily into leading roles in a number of musicals. However, this was a time in the English theatre when someone like Denis was as likely to be penalised as admired for having a range of abilities. This struck me as absurd, and a decade later at the National I brought him into the company and persuaded Olivier to let me cast him as the elder brother in *Long Day's Journey into Night*. This was to be the first of a number of exceptional performances he gave at the National during the last thirty years of his life.

I mention this because it's relevant to the kind of theatre that by 1963 I had come to believe in. I agreed with the poet Louis MacNeice, who in his essay 'In Defence of Vulgarity' says that the plays he likes best are 'a sort of mixture *à la* Shakespeare – comic relief sticking out in the middle of tragedy, rant, jokes for the groundlings and slapstick'. MacNeice confesses to liking a tune, and being more interested in the subject of art than in style. 'I am all against the rarefying effects of good taste,' he writes. Temperamentally, this was my position, but, more than that, I believed that the democratic nature of public performance, depending on an audience composed randomly of anyone prepared to roll up and buy a ticket, more or less imposed it on the medium. When the aspiration and the exclusiveness of high art were countered with the vigour and craft of entertainment, then the pretensions of the one and the sentimentality of the other were both under mutual surveillance, and it was somewhere there, in the middle of this collision that you were likely to find a healthy – a Shakespearean – kind of theatre.

We opened *Much Ado* at the height of summer, and at the interval it was still broad daylight. The audience lingered in Clement Freud's tent gulping down his mulled claret as if they were at a garden party, and as the second half began streams of people were still making their way back to their deckchairs. This was during my first scene. No one was listening and it was impossible not to curse the Park and long for a proper theatre where the audience sat down, shut up and listened. It still proved a successful first night, if without quite the surprise and excitement the company had engendered the previous year. That second season there were only two productions, not three, the second being a revival of the *Dream*, in which I played with no great distinction the role of Theseus. It, too, was a popular success, the weather held, and by the last performance the New Shakespeare Company was in the black. It was no one's fault that in the minds of the public and the press the Regent's Park season was regressing to what it had always been, a regular summer attraction like the Chelsea Flower Show or the concerts at Kenwood.

Once the *Dream* was playing I had my mornings free and I returned to work on my novel. On matinee days it became my habit to pick up the 74 bus at Camden Town, get off when it reached the outskirts of Regent's Park, then walk the half-mile or so across the fields to the theatre. With my mind still operating in writer mode the stroll was an opportunity to mull over what I had done that morning and think about what should come next. The book was about at the halfway point. One day, staring down at the summer grass as I went on my way, a detailed outline of what had yet to be written started unrolling in front of me in an effortless ribbon of narrative. It was like looking down a long corridor and seeing a succession of doors open of their own accord one after another, until there in the far distance was a frame of sky. I became very excited, firstly because of the strangeness of the experience itself, but also because I now knew for certain that this was a task I would accomplish. It was like being handed a child's colouring book; all I had to do was pick up the crayons.

That summer the Profumo Affair was reaching its climax, and I would take a bundle of newspapers to the theatre to devour in waits between scenes. Not since Suez had the governance of Britain shown itself in a more disgraceful light as the Tory Party, the judiciary and the police closed ranks in a witch-hunt. Stephen Ward, an osteopath, had been made the scapegoat for the dishonesty and sexual misconduct of others better placed and his present trial had the same whiff of prurient hypocrisy that had once brought down Oscar Wilde. At one point the judge, ever even-handed, referred to the defendant as 'this filthy fellow'. It was the Establishment putting the boot in, and on the other side of the road the rest of Britain stood watching with passive fascination. I followed this vicious paperchase up and down columns of newsprint to its shocking conclusion: the photograph of Stephen Ward, unconscious on a stretcher, being taken away to his death after attempting an overdose. A blanket was thrown over the limp body, and his face, in a last concession to the demands of his notoriety, lolled sideways towards the camera. Poor Stephen Ward; with his half-smile and rather obvious good looks he might have been a West End actor of the day. He had become skilled at mimicking the manners of the upper-class end of his clientele, and may even have convinced himself that he had become one of them. But when push came to shove all the telephones remained on the hook. It was a very English death.

I was out of work again, but writing, and going to the typewriter each morning with a new resolve. The rest of my life, however, was far from orderly. A battered pocket diary for that year, which optimistically has 'Engagements 1963' impressed in faded gilt on the front cover, records few of any consequence. The handwriting is ragged, almost demoralised, though it firms up a little when I record the titles of the films I plan to catch at the National Film Theatre, among them a season of Von Stroheim and some Max Linder silent comedies. In the space for 14th October I have written '*Income Tax:* Income £930 6s 8d. Expenses £550 18s od.' These figures I had reached with the help of an accountant, my first, Sam Kershen of Kershen, Fairfax & Co. He was a stocky, rather severe man, whose manner may have derived from the hours he spent on the Bench as a Justice of the Peace, and he ran a tight ship at his offices up a flight of stairs in a Georgian house off Baker Street, frequently barking at the cowed young men who worked there as juniors. Towards me he was friendly, if perhaps a shade so sympathetic it approached pity. One day he said, 'For handling your affairs to April '63 we will be charging you £27 10s. I should tell you that's the least the firm has ever charged one of its clients.' I murmured how grateful I was. Sam leant forward over his desk, a puzzled smile leading the way for what he was about to say. 'Forgive me for asking this,' he said, 'but how do you actually manage to *live?*' My voice became even more of a mutter: well, I had a flat without a mortgage, and, oh yes, my mother had once helped me with an electricity bill. Sam managed to resist wagging his head, but he sighed.

I didn't resent his question, but it had taken me aback, because I thought I'd been doing quite well. Very few of the people I worked with seemed to earn much money, but in the England of those days you were still allowed to believe that there were other things by which you could be judged. That was what I most liked about my adopted country. I might be inconvenienced by lack of money, but never intimidated. That intimidation is now worldwide.

How, actually, did I manage? There were the seasons in the Park, for which I received top salary of £25 a week. There was *Toad of Toad Hall* at Christmas, when I could expect an additional £10. In between there were odd parts on television bringing in £100 or £200. At least I had what the juniors in Sam's office certainly didn't, my freedom; rather too much of it, perhaps. It was around this time that my love affair slid into its second year. It had become the passionate focus of all that energy and spare time left over from two unrealised careers, and it was sending out tendrils like an exotic flower confined in a hothouse. By now it had breached the walls of her flat, and involved lunches together, visits to the cinema and even a few days in Cornwall when Shirley was visiting her family. Other people entered the circle, friends of hers with whom it was obvious she had the right to share the truth of her life. What I had recklessly and selfishly begun I now hoped to control by an exercise of virtue, trying to acknowledge and balance the rights of both women. Had I thought about it, I would have realised that this was an area where there can be no such thing as fairness, only struggle. A particular dilemma for me became her search for a new place to live. I wanted to be what help I could, but felt uneasy with the implications of our afternoons spent inspecting properties together. I was perhaps more deeply involved with her, more mesmerised, than I had ever been, with times between us that were so complete and playful that they seemed entirely good. But could I bring myself to leave home? I hungered for love, but apparently it was deep affection I trusted. And there was one vestige of traditional morality that I clung to: adults should not abandon their children.

Somehow or other I knew this had to be put into words. I made two attempts a couple of months apart. On both occasions she let me have my say, but simply refused to engage with me, as if discussion of the matter was somehow beneath us. The subject of my intentions grew to resemble a sharp religious or political difference between two intimates, who finally skirt around it altogether. The subject, however, was still there, like a sharp object in a dark room. Shirley had once asked me never to tell her of my adulteries, though I doubt whether she had ever envisaged anything quite like this. Now the only circumstances in which I could have told her, even if she'd wanted it, were afterwards, when it was over. But on winter afternoons when we lay in the crumpled bed, and I watched the smoky light guttering to darkness outside the windows, I knew this was something I couldn't yet give up. Had she decided to finish it, that I could have accepted, even welcomed as pain that in the long run this would have been best for both of us. What I couldn't do was make the break myself. One day, perhaps, but not yet. Incredulously I watched my life drifting toward something that one read in the papers about other people: I was starting to have a double life. Each new development in the affair, even the most innocent, such as the luscious cakes which we had discovered in a nearby Viennese patisserie and which we wolfed down with the smell of fresh coffee in our nostrils, led to a complementary discovery about myself. I was capable of steely secrecy; I could live with deceit. In my twenties I had thought of myself as a fairly blameless person, but in my thirties I was reaching less comfortable conclusions about the species of which I was a representative, and in the evenings I was taking these discoveries back with me to the Hampstead flat.

As Christmas approached so did *Toad of Toad Hall*, and David Conville, who would this year be directing, offered me my old part. I was grateful for the work, but a little depressed by what seemed a step back in time. A greater concession to the past was the reinstatement of the seventy-five-year-old Richard Goolden in the role he had first played in the twenties, Mr Mole. Richard was a type you found everywhere in the arts in England at that time, the ex-public-school eccentric. He so identified with the furry little creature from *The Wind in the Willows* that he had a plaque outside the front door of his Kensington flat which read 'Mole's House', and when he picked up the telephone would answer, 'Mr Mole speaking.' However, he was not soft, and had the survival instincts of his background together with a sharp sense of the nuances of class. Having won his old part back, he prevailed on David to cut mine. Richard took me aside. 'Last year,' he confided, 'it became "Badger of Badger Hall", and we can't have that,' thereby flattering and admonishing me at the same time. I was, of course, furious, but didn't care enough to walk out. The part was still a good one, and I checked that the barrow near Piccadilly Circus would still be able to supply me with navel oranges.

Many of the experiences I was having as an actor during this time were, in various disguises, making their way into my book. The most dramatic was Richard Goolden's close encounter with death. Our first performance of *Toad of Toad Hall* was given around noon to an audience of very young children. The climax of the piece was a battle between Toad's party and the villainous stoats and weasels. The combatants were armed with inflated bladders on sticks with which they could thwack one another without any danger of doing real harm. Richard, back in harness again and egged on by the squealing children, became overexcited, began thwacking far more aggressively than he had at rehearsals and must have lost his bearings. He began to skip backwards in triumph, unaware that only a few feet away was the dead drop of the orchestra pit. Hardly believing it and unable to do a thing about it we all saw him reach the edge of the stage and vanish. After a wait long enough to catch your breath and hold it, we heard two sounds in quick succession, the muffled thump of his body landing followed by the more percussive impact of his head. Everyone on stage stood stock-still, and the uniform squealing of the children fell away into a medley of plaintive treble enquiries. The conductor, with arms raised and frozen like a victim at Pompeii, began looking first down at the floor where Richard lay, then up at the actors, then down again, totally at a loss how to proceed. Soon David Conville was on stage and addressing the audience. 'Children, Mr Moley has had a little accident, but he's going to be perfectly all right, and you're not to worry. However, we'll have to bring the curtain down now, and I'd like you all to leave the auditorium. Thank you for coming, and we hope you had a lovely time.' As he spoke Richard, lying unconscious at the feet of the musicians, began a sonorous snoring.

The curtain came down and the stunned company retreated to their dressing rooms, speaking in whispers. There was no way, we felt, that the old actor could have escaped serious injury. Within the hour another audience would be gathering for the second performance. Some fifteen minutes passed before we were told that Richard, now conscious, was back in his dressing room and that a doctor was attending him. The next announcement was even more surprising: Richard would be doing the second show. This sounded utter folly. A man of seventy-five had fallen flat on his back from a height of nine feet. I knocked tentatively on his dressing-room door and heard a reasonably vigorous, 'Come in.' There he was, sitting beside his mirror in his Mole costume, wearing the same mildewed, furry balaclava he had first worn in the part over thirty years before. He had a crumpled cigarette to one side of his mouth. Tactfully, I wondered aloud if it was really wise to attempt the second show. He squinted to avoid the rising smoke, and shot me his practised twinkle. 'No bones broken. Why not?' he said. Mr Mole played that afternoon and at every performance, twice daily, during the run.

With the New Year came the prospect of another Regent's Park season, and David William asked me to his flat to discuss parts. The centrepiece was to be a spectacular *Henry V*, in which I was being offered Pistol. David was intent on a grandly heroic production of the play, which meant cutting much of Pistol's mordant commentary on the nature of war. The more I studied the text the more I became convinced that the drift of the times, and indeed my own convictions, were against any interpretation which even hinted at jingoism. The sixties brought us *Oh, What a Lovely War*, and, later the BBC's fine series on the same grim subject of the Great War. With some regret, because David had now become a close friend, I had to turn him down. However, the New Shakespeare Company had another project, unrelated to the Park, which they were able to offer me. This was a tour of *Twelfth Night*, in which David Conville suggested I reprise Sir Toby. This again would be a little like marking time for me, but there were aspects of the engagement which obliged me to take it very seriously. Firstly, the production would have an excellent director, Colin Graham, and an excellent cast, including Annette Crosbie as Viola, Stephen Moore as Aguecheek and twenty-four-year-old Michael Crawford as a stripling Feste. The tour would be going to interesting places, including two dates abroad, in Lisbon and Oporto. What clinched it for me was that its final destination would be as part of the City of London Festival, and we would be giving the play in the Middle Temple Hall, where, in front of Elizabeth I, *Twelfth Night* is supposed to have had its very first performance. We, too, would have a Royal audience, another Elizabeth, the Queen Mother. It seemed probable to me that this event would generate considerable interest and be widely reported. I needed a showcase production to get my career really moving, and who knows? it might even lead to a contract with the National. Once again my novel went into cold storage.

Even when an actor has already played a part, he is never exempt from the anxieties that attend the first days of rehearsal among people who for the moment are strangers. The cast, like a pack of dogs, newly acquainted, go sniffing around the rehearsal room, adjusting to and assessing each other whilst studiously appearing not to do so. The space itself takes a day or two to become inhabited. Then one morning eye-contact becomes as natural as breathing, and the day's work begins to find its rhythm. One of the director's jobs is to help everyone get to this point as soon as possible. Colin Graham and I were initially rather watchful of each other. I, naturally, wanted to retain things from my old performance that had worked for me. Colin, equally, was on the lookout for any old and unwanted baggage dragged in from another production. We came to the line 'Art any more than a steward?', and my reading was apparently to his taste. We both relaxed a little, and soon he was encouraging me to find other areas where this volatility might be useful. We opened in Belfast, at that time still more or less at peace with itself, and on the day of the first performance had two dress rehearsals, after the second of which I had to jump in a taxi, still in costume, and go to Ulster Television for a promotional interview, then back to the theatre for the first night. As a consequence by the time I went on stage I had lost my head of steam. I knew it as soon as I opened my mouth, and had to watch as Stephen Moore, playing Aguecheek, ran away with the evening. Like me, he had played his part before, very successfully, at the Old Vic, and early on we had picked each other out as rivals. It was a company with plenty of talent, and we were a competitive lot, particularly the men. I vowed that by the time we reached London the balance would have swung the other way, or at least be on a level.

The prospect of going on tour is not often one that actors relish. The reality, however, can be extremely enjoyable. You are suddenly cut free from what you thought you wanted to cling to – the tangle of your everyday life – and all your wearisome possessions are slimmed down to the contents of a suitcase. Each week brings new sights and new people, and introduces you to corners of the country that have been getting on surprisingly well without you, and will continue to do so after you leave. One of our most interesting dates was a private theatre, the Rosehill, built by the textile magnate Mickey Seccer, in the grounds of his Cumberland house. Mostly he invited musicians to perform there, but occasionally theatrical companies. It was a tiny stage, but we had a permanent set the configuration of which could be adjusted to almost any space. On stage throughout the performance, and dressed in Elizabethan costume, were a harpsichordist and a flautist, who played some lovely incidental music composed for the show by John Dankworth. It was like giving a play at a European court theatre two centuries before. At the end of the week our host threw a party for us and the chamber orchestra, who would be giving a concert that Sunday. Mickey Seccer presided over these occasions like a benevolent German princeling luxuriating in his largesse to art and artists. It was impossible to imagine, as this generous man moved among his guests, that ahead of him was a reversal of fortune of Shakespearean proportions. He would lose his house, see his theatre closed and spend his last days penniless in a basement flat in Bayswater.

Most of our dates were places like Oxford and Norwich which we were happy to visit; less so Darlington, particularly when we found hardly a ticket had been sold. The only advertising was a drab poster outside the theatre, and advance publicity had been non-existent. I thought the problem required a Robert Morley solution: if we could tempt enough people to see the show for nothing in the first half of the week, word of mouth might enable us to sell a few seats in the second half. Michael Crawford and I were the chief promoters of the plan, and, having cleared it with management, set about motivating the company into a sales force. We approached the personnel managers of all the big High Street shops – Boots, Marks and Spencer, etc. – and offered employees block bookings of free seats for the early part of the week. Whether it made much difference to the box office I can't remember, but at least we now had an audience to play to, and it was fun for those few days to be taking charge of one's life like Mickey Rooney and Judy Garland in an MGM musical. Our next stop was Portugal, where, thanks to the Gulbenkian Foundation who were funding the festival of which we were part, we stayed in excellent hotels and were much fussed over. Lisbon, like Sydney, was a city built around hills and water, but there the comparison ended. The vast sway of ancient tiled roofs over which you looked down on the distant estuary gave the city an organic unity, as if it had come into existence the way a beehive does or a colony of coral. I was surprised by it, this example of the beauty, even then receding, of old Europe dozing in the sun.

Back on tour in England I became engulfed in an invisible cloud of pollen and sneezed for the next two weeks. However, by the time we arrived in London and were readying ourselves for our three performances in the Middle Temple Hall, my pocket diary for 1964 records a propitious entry – 'Hay fever abating'. The big opportunity for which I think everyone in the company had been preparing was now upon us. Why then did it not feel like it? On the afternoon of our first night I asked David Conville why there were no posters or anything in the papers about us. 'No point,' he said. 'All the performances are sold out.'

'What about the critics? Who's coming?'

David looked a little embarrassed. 'You know what the City of London's like. With the Queen Mother attending and so forth the Festival people felt they didn't really need the Milton Shulmans and the Bernard Levins.

I was aghast. These were two of London's most influential critics. And what exactly did they *mean* by 'the Milton Shulmans and the Bernard Levins'?

'I think they may have invited *The Times*,' said David.

I went backstage in some despair. This *Twelfth Night* had received a wonderful press wherever it had played. After nine weeks on the road surely the cast and the production team were entitled to a proper London exposure: this was a show of which the New Shakespeare Company had reason to be proud. I put on my make-up trying not to waste my energies in anger.

However, if my intelligence accepted that the game was probably up, my body refused to believe it. I had spent so many months assuming this performance would be crucial that adrenalin was already programmed into the experience. Waiting in the shadows on a rickety bentwood chair to make my first entrance in a role I'd already played hundreds of times I experienced the worst nerves of my life. My heart pumped as if it was trying to escape from my chest, my mouth became bone-dry, and I felt such physical listlessness that half-a-dozen times I would rise from the chair only to sink back onto it with a sigh like a death rattle. I told myself that this was ludicrous, and so it was, but my physiology wasn't interested. Then, like boarding a moving train, I was suddenly on stage and talking loud and fast. Fifteen minutes later I was giving as good a performance as I'd ever given in the part. I even started to enjoy myself. It was strange and rather wonderful to raise one's eyes to the great oak ceiling of the Middle Temple Hall, damaged in the Blitz but now restored, and know that the words you were speaking had first resonated in this same space three and a half centuries before. It was England as it's supposed to be. So was the Queen Mother afterwards, to whom we were presented still in full costume and make-up. She looked delighted and a shade alarmed, as if she'd just stepped down from a ride on an elephant, so that was one good review of sorts. Then we all went home.

The following morning I bought my copy of *The Times*. They'd sent along their second-string critic and given him a meagre column to one side of the Arts page. At the top of the review it read, 'Sir Toby in High Spirits', but what was given in the headline was taken away in the body of the notice. Or appeared to be. I read, 'Mr Michael Blakemore's untrained performance . . . ' It was clear once I'd studied the context that 'untrained' should have read 'unstrained', but to the casual reader (that is to say, everyone except me) the damage was done. The following day they published a correction, apologising for the typographical error and adding that this was 'poor recompense for the pleasure he gave our critic'. This was gracious of them, though I doubt if that same casual reader would have spotted the apology let alone bothered to read it. I had one more rave review, from my accountant, a beaming Sam Kershen for whom I had arranged seats at the last performance. He was never again to question how I earned a living, though this remained a problem.

What to do, then? Well, one option open to me, at present the only option, was to get on with the bloody book.

# ELEVEN

# Home from Home

Shirley had not been in London for the performance in the Middle Temple Hall. She'd already seen the show at the Rosehill Theatre when she'd come to visit me in Cumberland, and now she was in France with Conrad at the invitation of Danielle, the ex-au pair with whom we had become friends. The intention was that I should join her in Arcachon for the last week of her stay. However, a better plan occurred to me: if I really intended to push ahead with the novel, why not do so in France, away from the distractions of the theatre and the city. By sub-letting the Hampstead flat we would have just about enough money to support a long stay abroad. Finding the right tenant would probably take some weeks, but I had the offer of a few scraps of work which would fill in the time and put a little more money in the bank. I did not seek it, but the delay suited me for a more covert reason; it would allow my affair to have what it had never had before, a few weeks of clear time. During the day I returned to work on the book undisturbed in the empty Hampstead flat, and in the evenings did those simple things which before had been difficult if not forbidden – having dinner together, going to the movies or to a play, sharing time without the awareness of time passing. It was like a window opening on other and better possibilities – what we might have been like with each other had things been different. Thinking ourselves free, we began assiduously weaving around us a new and invisible net of intimacy. As the time of my departure approached, with emotions pulling in all directions, I was almost unsure as to whom it was exactly that I was being unfaithful.

However, I was serious about the book and determined to see it through. I knew my agent was sceptical, and reasonably so; an unfinished

novel by someone who has never been published is not a project on
the outcome of which you'd bet money. I set off to France giving him
firm instructions to turn down all offers of work short of a season playing splendid parts at the National Theatre, and leave me undisturbed.

Arcachon is a pleasant town built around the shore of an immense
circular bay on the Atlantic coast of France. I was to fly to the nearest
city, Bordeaux, where Shirley and a friend of Danielle's, who had a car,
would pick me up. The meeting point was the railway station, a huge,
grimy cathedral consecrated to the miracle of nineteenth-century
transport, and stylistically quite at variance with its counterparts in
Britain. It was a lovely day in late August, not hot but with that enveloping warmth that confirms you are no longer in England. With
time to spare I entered the station to buy some postcards and collided
with another defining characteristic of mid-twentieth-century France
– the smell of their cigarettes. On my first trip out of England in 1950
I had travelled on the channel steamer to Dunkirk, and could hardly
believe the pungent reek of Gauloise smoke which hit us as the boat
prepared to dock. It announced a world as exotic and different as only
remote parts of the Far East can seem today. Waiting by Bordeaux
station I thought of that first visit to France, and of the person I had
been then, peering down from the deck to the quay in amazement,
where the mêlée of porters, dressed in their uniform blue smocks and
all smoking, shouted and gestured upwards to attract business.

The car approached, with Shirley and Conrad waving through the
windscreen. They were both sunburnt and looked happy and excited.
As we started on the journey to Arcachon I felt a rush of bewildering
pleasure to be with them again, but there was too much to catch up
on (and in my case conceal) for the words to come out in anything but
a jumble. Danielle had helped Shirley find a surprising place for us to
stay. An elderly woman, a friend of her family, lived in an imposing villa
on a sharp rise overlooking the bay. It was called 'Grand Paradis', and
at the bottom of its winding drive was a small gatehouse, 'Petit Paradis',
which we were allowed to occupy for a nominal rent. It was a very
pretty building, but on its way to vanishing in the thickets of a garden
that hadn't been tended for years. There was electricity, but no telephone, and you cooked with gas from a cylinder. A wood-burning
stove supplied hot water. In the perfect September weather which
would follow, one day upon another, it was nothing short of ideal. No
telephone rang with an all-important message; no television gave us

access to an indispensable programme. We had soon established an easy rhythm of work and leisure. I would write until a late lunchtime, then the three of us would set out to explore some new aspect of the town and the area. Inland we found country lanes where you could pick wild blackberries, warm with the sun, and eat them out of your hand as you continued on your walk. Abutting the harbour were Arcachon's celebrated sand hills, which rose up steeply like a miniature mountain range, and afforded long, tumbling descents down to the water's edge. Our most frequent trip was by launch to the oyster beds on the far side of the bay. As the vessel reached the mid-point of this journey it started to buck against a strong ocean tide intent on sweeping anything in its path out towards the distant white-flecked water which marked the open Atlantic. There was a frisson of danger in knowing that all that stood between you and the jaws of those huge, faraway rollers was the splutter and cough of the engine. I watched Conrad, now three and a half, as he took in these things – the spray from the slapping bow of the boat, the immensity of the sky and the surrounding sea – just as I had done at a similar age on the East Coast of Australia, both the child now and the child then mesmerised by the ocean, and not a little scared of it. I had never seen him look so well, or so gravely absorbed in where he was and what he was doing. This was probably true of us all. Once ashore, there was a further journey across the sandy isthmus to our final destination, the great, open beach of Cap Ferret. Here I found what I'd hardly dared hope for – waves, long lines of big, gentle waves to sweep me over and over again from the deep-blue water back to the sand.

In the evening we had dinners under a clear night sky, prepared by Shirley from produce she had bought that day in the market. Next morning I would settle down to work in a house protected from the heat by the engulfing vegetation, and flecked with broken sunlight like so many splinters of glass. Here I would have the experience, particular to the writing of books, of being equally in two places at once – the place where I was working and the place I was endeavouring to conjure up in my head. Two things distracted me. My thoughts kept darting back to London, and the person I had left there. I'd written letters but had received not even a coded reply. Then there was the other distraction. Hanging centre in the frame of the window beyond the pane was a big garden spider, which had made its home there. Each day it would be waiting for me, spreadeagled in its web and malevolently still, and I developed a growing hostility to it. Petit Paradis was good to its human inhabitants, but it was a true paradise for spiders. They were there in their thousands, spinning their webs over every bush and random shrub. The mist of insects floating through the undergrowth in the shafts of sunlight provided them with a continuous banquet, and they appeared to have no natural enemies except one another. And one morning, me. I rose from my table in the middle of my work, found a long twig, disengaged the spider in the window from its web and swung it on a strand of its own silk into the web of another spider. Immediately the resident creature appeared from its concealment behind a leaf, and the two faced each other. There was a moment of weird stillness; then in a simultaneous scramble they had engaged, and in a matter of seconds it was all over. Though the spider from the window was the larger of the two, it was he, not the resident spider, who was soon being turned over and over as his adversary, with the swift delicacy of a woman finishing her sewing and biting the thread, enveloped him in a cocoon of silk and dispatched him. This was an odd result, so I experimented with other sets of spiders, and the victor was always the one in whose web the contest had taken place. I was suddenly aware of a small figure standing slightly behind me. It was Conrad, watching. Something else had just been passed down the generations. As a child I, too, had watched my father in our garden at Rose Bay playing identical games with the more dangerous red-back spiders, making two fight, watching one perish. I returned to my work feeling that something disgraceful, and all too human, had just taken place.

Apart from this uncomfortable incident and the minor alarms about health and injury that inevitably attend the rearing of a small and spirited child, September passed in a succession of days of idyllic weather and a growing sense of effortless well-being. Until one morning a telegram arrived. It was from my agent. I had been offered a part in a television series, *Redcap*, about the military police, two weeks' work for £200. Would I please ring him? My peace of mind collapsed like a building that had always been unsafe. I was furious with my agent for disregarding what I'd asked of him, but another part of me thanked him for providing a reason to return to London, and to find answers to some questions that waited for me there.

The events that followed I remember with an almost melodramatic clarity and foreboding, but this may be something that was imposed

upon them later when it became clear they were the prelude to an unpleasant development in my life. The day of the telegram was extremely
hot. I abandoned my work and walked the mile to the post office to
make the international call. For a long time I stood outside the building
in the intense noon glare, the telegram in my hand, trying to decide
what to do. If I went to London I would be away two and a half weeks
at the most. Getting there and back would cost about £50, which
would leave me £150 in the bank to support my writing. Our flat was
let, but I could take a suitcase to my mother's, which would cost me
nothing. And surely it would be professionally useful to be on television
again and remind people of my existence. There were any number of
reasons why I should accept the job, but only one of them was honest.
I went inside the post office, which after the glare outside was like an
eclipse descending, rang my agent and told him I was on my way.

It just so happened that the previous day I had had some sort of
parental upset with Conrad, and in one of those unappeasable rages
of which small children are capable he had screamed at me, 'Go away!
Go back to London! We don't want you! Go away!' Now in the fearful recesses of his three-year-old mind he began to blame himself for
my imminent departure. Waiting on the station platform it became
impossible to console him, and as the train approached his crying
became quite desperate and terrified. I climbed aboard, and through a
moving window had to watch an increasingly anxious Shirley try to
calm our struggling and now hysterical child. On their way back to
the house, she would later tell me, his condition began to turn into an
asthmatic attack. She let them in through the front door only to find
trapped inside the house a large blackbird. It had evidently come down
the chimney, and was so distressed it went flapping wildly from room
to room unable to grasp that escape was now possible through an
open door or window. It took her half an hour to get rid of it. Then
she went to find a doctor for Conrad's asthma.

It was the beginning of October and much colder in London than
it had been in France. We rehearsed at Teddington Studios, to which I
travelled by bus, an hour's journey each way, so the working days were
long. *Redcap* turned out to be run-of-the-mill television, though professionally demanding, and each day found me more exhausted and
anxious than the part I was playing warranted. This was not conducive
to the real reason I had come back to London. In addition, my mother
was distressed by my numerous unexplained absences, some of them

overnight. She felt she was being asked to collude with her son against his wife, and we exchanged a few curt, inhibited words about it.

'But what am I meant to say if Shirley rings up and asks where you are?'

'Tell her the truth. Say you don't know.' I sensed she had had many conversations of this sort, but with my father. Could I be turning into him?

The day of the recording began early, with the usual listless, nervy drag through a camera rehearsal. That afternoon I had a succession of abdominal cramps, which I assumed to be diarrhoea, though there was something unfamiliar about the condition that I couldn't quite place. I was due to fly back to France in two days' time, so when the cramps continued the following day I hurried to a doctor, who diagnosed an infection and prescribed antibiotics. What I was actually experiencing was the onset of a chronic disease, ulcerative colitis, against which the pills would be useless.

The Arcachon I returned to might have been somewhere else entirely. In my absence the Atlantic had issued new instructions, and strong winds and chilly rain lashed the town. It was as if summer had simply fallen from the sky and lay smashed to bits in the puddles in the streets and along the windswept footpaths. At Petit Paradis all the spiders had gone, and the surrounding trees, which had once offered protection against the sun, now enclosed the house in dripping shadow. We tried to return to our old routine, but the morning's work was regularly interrupted by cramps, and in the afternoons, if we visited the ocean, the waves at Cap Ferret were so enormous and came thundering down so close to shore that it would have been dangerous even to attempt to paddle. I could hardly believe that a few weeks before I had surfed with such confidence and pleasure in the same sea, now a turbulent gnashing of gigantic teeth all along the coast as far as you could see.

I had soon run out of pills. Danielle arranged with a French doctor to supply me with a further course, but they didn't help. One morning, on one of my increasingly wearisome trips to the lavatory, I thought I spotted blood. It was time to get back to London and into the hands of doctors who could tell me precisely what was the matter. The Hampstead flat was still let, but for the remaining weeks of the lease my mother was able to accommodate us in the empty rooms once set aside for her husband, and it was in his study that I returned to my book. By now my doctor had referred me to St Mark's Hospital, which for more than a century had been specialising in bowel diseases, and they, too, decided my condition was an infection and prescribed another sort of antibiotic. This was probably more an expression of hope than a diagnosis, since dysentery can be cured but colitis can't. Each Wednesday afternoon I attended their clinic for an internal examination, grateful to the National Health Service and confirmed in my respect for the principle behind it, even if the implementation of that principle could sometimes be a bit rough-and-ready. About fifty of us gathered in the waiting room, people of all sorts and ages now equals in the democracy of illness. There wasn't a spare seat, and the few limp copies of *Radio Times* and *Woman's Own* had long gone into circulation. When your name was eventually called the medical staff, the more senior of whose faces you were lucky ever to see, launched into a cheerful and extremely brisk dialogue with your backside. I could only guess what was going on, but it felt as if I was being penetrated by a length of curtain rod which then became a telescope to spy and poke about inside. The examination took place in a curtained-off space about the size of a sleeping compartment on a Pullman train. Only a few feet away in both directions other patients were lying on their side with their legs curled up enduring similar indignities, and I could hear their grunting and wincing. However, it never lasted long. You were in and out in no time, with an appointment made for the following week.

After a month or so there was no improvement, so I was brought into the hospital to have a more comprehensive examination under a general anaesthetic by the senior consultant surgeon. This revealed nothing more than they already knew, so they concluded I had colitis, and the surgical department washed their hands of me. 'We're passing you on to the physiologists!' said the red-faced consultant, beaming, as if I was being promoted from the Second Eleven to the First. This was a much less frantic department, since there were fewer patients and they were dealing in palliative measures, not cures. There was time allowed for sympathetic discussions, and it was then that I learnt I would probably have the condition for life.

Mine, fortunately, was a comparatively mild case – the disease can be completely disabling – and I'd already gone some way to adapting to it. I was leading a fairly normal life, and had found some work which would allow me to continue to write. A couple of days a week

I was teaching at RADA. My subject was Technique, but since I wasn't sure a plausible system could be deduced from a craft so dependent on personality, I more or less made up my classes as I went along. It was fourteen years since I had been one of these aspirants myself. Now I was climbing the same staircase, entering the same spaces, but with my role reversed, and I soon learnt how quickly one comes to judgement about who is gifted and who is not. It seemed as self-evident as the good looks of some of the young women, and I began to see my own teachers, Miss Ecks, Miss Wye and Miss Zed, in a slightly more tolerant light. One student, a few years older than the others, stood out. This was Richard Wilson, who, in addition to a marked flair for comedy, had a wider concern with everything that was going on around him, and because of this had been co-opted as spokesman of his group. Such gifts are as important as any other in sustaining a career. Actors are always alert to good looks and theatrical facility in their contemporaries and rivals, but audiences are shrewder. They will recognise and reward attributes that have as much to do with character as talent. An enduring career is dependent on both.

The Nicholses had moved from Dartmouth back to their home town, Bristol, and when Peter succeeded in getting a production of his first stage play, *The Hooded Terror*, on at the Little Theatre, Shirley and I went down to see it and spend a few days with them at their new address. They had rented a roomy Victorian house on one of the hills high above the town in a part of Bristol not yet fashionable, but bound to become so because of its amazing views and abundance of unrenovated Georgian houses. Once Thelma learnt that she could have further children, they put Abigail into care, and were now the parents of a rudely healthy daughter and son. Peter had gained a well-earned reputation as a leading television playwright, and although a little more money would have helped, his career was in considerably better shape than mine. These improvements in his life, however, only seemed to point to what was still unforthcoming, and he was now given to much complaining. Some of it was specific, about the better luck of other writers, such as his friend and fellow Bristolian Charles Wood, who was earning large sums working in films. Some of it was more general, and expressed itself in affirmations of socialist doctrine.

By the mid-sixties the serious theatre had moved well to the left. By temperament I knew I was not a political creature, too impatient to be attracted to the work of committees, and too naive to accept the halting and qualified nature of political advances. I was also too sceptical to swallow whole any belief system. I had a few convictions, much the same as I have today, but they hardly amounted to a political position. The only belief I could claim to have acted upon was the one implicit in my choice of career: that the arts were important because they offered a challenge and a respite from the scramble for money and the constraints of group thinking. I certainly knew what I was against, capital punishment for one, and official secrecy for another, but was more cautious about what I was actually for, and this, I thought, was as it should be.

What I disliked on a day-to-day level about the Marxism of the sixties and the seventies was what it did to ordinary codes of behaviour. Since revolution was inevitable, and since revolution alone was the instrument of reaching a perfect society, all morality came down to a couple of simple questions: Are you for the revolution? And, if so, are you prepared to hurry it along? Anything else in the way of a moral code was further evidence of the flattering self-deception of the bourgeoisie. What this amounted to was a licence to disregard goodwill, and I encountered a number of squalid if petty examples, of which one is recorded in Peter Nichols' published *Diaries*. He was asked to a party given by John Osborne's agent, Robin Dalton. She was a friend of mine, whom I knew to be a generous and stylish hostess, and she had a lease on an elegant period house on the edge of Lord's Cricket Ground, where she did her entertaining. After the party, Peter offers a lift home in his car to another guest, a young Marxist academic, on his way to lecture in Eastern Europe. As they pull away the Marxist produces from under his coat a full bottle of whisky which he announces he has just stolen from his hostess. Peter is at first shocked by this abuse of hospitality. Later he thinks about it. Given Robin Dalton's 'unfair advantages' and the Marxist's arguments, 'Why not pinch her Scotch?'

An incident of a little more consequence concerns an approach made to me by an actor-friend who was active in the Workers' Revolutionary Party. This Trotskyite organisation was staging a fundraising rally at somewhere like Earl's Court or Wembley, and wanted to know whether I would direct one of the evening's pageants. This was 1969, and I was at a point in my career as a director when I was considered to be the hot new arrival, so I was not surprised to be approached, particularly as I had running at the Saville Theatre the first British production of Brecht's *Arturo Ui*. Since I wasn't remotely a Trotskyite there was no question of accepting their invitation. I made my excuses, wished them luck and forgot all about it. A month or so later someone at the National Theatre, where I was directing *The National Health*, drew my attention to a programme of the WRP's rally. There I was, conspicuously credited as one of the directors of the event. My name had been self-righteously stolen to ornament their programme. This was more than irritating. I was living in Britain on an Australian passport, and didn't want to be filed away in some cabinet at the Home Office as a supporter of an organisation I neither belonged to nor believed in. Both these examples are, of course, trivial when set against the many appalling things that have been done in the name of the future, but they are the first tiny steps along the same path. First Robin Dalton's Scotch. What next, her house? Her life?

Bristol, at the time of my visit to the Nicholses, was home to a number of gifted people trying to make their way in theatre, films and television. One was a documentary film-maker, John Boorman, who had made a name for himself at the BBC and was now looking for a way into features. He had been approached by a producer, David Deutsch, who had an idea for a film doing for the then popular Dave Clark Five what *A Hard Day's Night* had done for the Beatles. John, in turn, approached Peter to ask if he would collaborate on an original screenplay to provide a vehicle for the group. It was not the sort of work either man would have chosen, but it paid well and had the possibility of leading to other things. The problem for John was that he had never worked with actors, and as a maker of documentaries distrusted their skills. The Dave Clark Five weren't even actors, but musicians trying to act, and John would have to be their tutor as well as their director. He decided he needed someone to help him. With my few months as a teacher at RADA and a recommendation from Peter I became a likely candidate. David Deutsch prepared a generous contract, and for the first time in my professional life I was earning in excess of £100 a week.

My duties centred on Dave Clark himself. Peter and John had concocted a road movie, with the Dave Clark Five on the run through the West Country, parts of England not far from Bristol that they both knew well. The group would move from location to location getting into scrapes and bumping into new and amusing sets of people. They called their script *Catch Us If You Can* and it was contrived so that the livelier dialogue which carried most of the comedy could be distributed among a relay team of gifted supporting actors. However, Dave Clark was the romantic lead, he appeared in almost every scene, and there were times when he simply had to open his mouth. These times would be my responsibility, and I started preparing Dave some weeks ahead of the shoot. Each morning I would catch the tube to Southgate and walk to the suburban house where he had been brought up and in which he still lived with his family. He'd spent a little money on some improvements, notably a bar in the sitting room with a thatched roof and two cigarette lighters disguised as highwaymen's pistols, but it was a modest abode for a high-earning pop star. He still slept in the same small bedroom he'd had as a boy, but now decorated with an array of framed gold discs and other mementos of his considerable success.

My strategy with Dave was twofold: to help him with his part, but also to earn his trust. In a few weeks time we would be working against the clock and surrounded by the many distractions of a film shoot. I knew it would get me nowhere shouting for his attention. He had to volunteer it; he had to need me. This was my only authority. With all jobs there is a price to pay in the way they affect your character, and this was my first taste of the possibly corrupt and certainly calculated benevolence which directors need to acquire if they are to get their way without too many arguments. We worked through the script a little each day, and he was a willing student even if sustaining his interest sometimes required quick thinking. Dave was no actor, but with his youth and dark good looks I thought he might have some sort of presence on screen and I worked hard at getting him to listen properly. In life he had a veiled quality, and I thought it odd that there never seemed to be anyone else in the house whenever I visited. I'd heard that it was the others in the group who were the better musicians. Dave was leader of the band by virtue of his shrewdness and his skills as an operator. He played the drums in a centre position, and on television your eye went to his smile rather than anything he was doing with his hands.

I began to realise that my job on the film might turn out to be crucial, and was gratified when David Deutsch indicated that he thought so too. The night before the commencement of the shoot he included me in a dinner he gave for the director and the screenwriter. At the end of the meal I watched John Boorman as he drew on a very large cigar, in the circumstances remarkably cocky about whatever the morning might bring. It was hard not to envy him, slightly younger than I and embarking on the career that years ago in Australia I had dreamt about. And to an extent still did. Mainly, though, I was grateful to him, not just for the job, but for his clear offer of comradeship during the adventure that lay ahead for us both. The prospect of finding myself attached to a shoot from start to finish, and with something useful to do, was very exciting for me. Who knew where it could lead?

There is something primitive about the experience of being part of a film unit on location. Like a peasant farmer you rise in the morning before the sun is up, and cease your labours twelve hours later when the light begins to fail. Modern distinctions between work and leisure blur as the long day swings between periods of enforced idleness and those moments during a take when the attention of the entire group is like a single pair of eyes. You live the life of the film, mixing only with others similarly engaged, packing your bags when they do, then like a nomadic community settling down in the next new place. Whatever life you had before is put on hold. There is an assumption just as there was on the *Otranto* when I worked my passage to England, that one's health will stand up, and usually it does. The long hours, the intense chatter within this closed community in which privacy hardly exists, makes for the sort of robust and interactive life you see in wild-life films among our primate cousins in the jungle, and it is no surprise that some of the great lighting cameramen, like Jack Cardiff and Freddie Young, dominant figures in these temporary societies, retained their vigour and practise their skills well into old age. As week followed week, more or less satisfied with my place in the hierarchy, I shared in this corporate well-being, and one day I realised that without my having noticed, my colitis had gone. Very soon good health was something I once more took for granted.

I was working hard with Dave, dragging him away from his canvas chair and the noisy company of the other boys in the group so that we could retreat to some quiet corner and prepare for the upcoming scene, then finding a position for myself just before the camera rolled where he had a clear view of me willing him to do his best. At the end of a take, Dave's eyes would flick towards mine for an assessment, and I became adept at squeezing through the crew to whisper a suggestion and then as quickly extricating myself. John was quite indifferent to what another might have considered a threat to his authority, and encouraged me to intervene whenever I thought it necessary. He also seemed immune to the currents of scepticism and mischief that inevitably circle around a first-time director. We had a lighting cameraman who was playing obstructive games to get more control, and an openly malicious make-up man, who had once put Richard III's nose on top of Laurence Olivier's, and was now affronted that John had dared to question his usual procedures. Our leading lady was none too happy either – if she was to bring any sort of life to her scenes with Dave she felt she needed a little more of John's interest and understanding. Even I was a little concerned with his cavalier way with Peter Nichols' dialogue. He would sometimes arrive on set in the mornings carrying a battered script in which lines had been crossed out or amended with pencil scribbles of his own. The new speeches didn't strike me as funnier or sharper than those they replaced.

However, as the shoot progressed I began to perceive that John was striving for a kind of cinema very different from that in the minds of most of those around him. Even the films that Peter and I admired – obvious ones like *Citizen Kane* or *The Maltese Falcon* – though unquestionably movies not plays, were built around notions that derived from stage practice: the good scene, the well-delivered line. John was interested in something less direct, more elliptical, in suggestion rather than succinct explanation, and a few years later in his first Hollywood film, *Point Blank*, he would find a subject to vindicate this approach. But if I was learning something new on *Catch Us If You Can*, it must be said so was John. One morning after a take at a freezing, snowbound location in Somerset, he came to me in a state of some excitement. He was not a particularly articulate man, and had a habit when beginning a sentence of repeating the first couple of words over and over again, possibly as a way of getting a better hold on precisely what was in his mind.

'I've only just, er . . . I've only just, er . . . I've only just, er . . . I've only just, er, realised something!'

'What, John?'

'Actors, er . . . Actors, er . . . Actors, er, they can't see themselves!'

He had just hit upon something so self-evident that it is invariably overlooked, but which explains why performers are the way they are, and why they swoop between insecurity and voluble assertiveness. For other people work is something outside them – a meal to cook, a page to write on – and involves actions than can be seen and assessed by those doing them. But the performer labours down the mineshaft of his own self, inside his own body. He is entirely dependent on other people to tell him he is not wasting his time, in there where he can't see. And of those who hold up the mirror to the actor the first is the director. Thereafter, John became more attentive to the members of his cast and more interested in their skills, which he now realised they were deploying essentially blindfolded. His empathy with the profession was sealed when towards the end of the shoot he embarked on an affair with one of his young actresses. Again he sought me out one morning, his eyes alight.

'We did, er . . . We did, er . . . We did, er . . . We did it four times last night!' And in between had doubtless had sympathetic discussions about her part.

Throughout the shoot I was often surprised and admiring of the way John lived with risk. Professionally, he was constantly juggling with a contradiction. He wanted to make films, and to make them his way, certainly, but he didn't care if the film business knew he held it in contempt. The latter position was a kind of insurance policy taken out on the former, because he had no intention of letting the slippery world of movie-making get the better of him. He was going to use *it*, not the other way around. A few years later in Hollywood with *Point Blank* this was exactly what he did. With his big grin, pale eyes and wild hair he reminded me a little of a warrior, not averse to a scrap for its own sake, emerging from the Northern European forest to confront an effete adversary. He was also a warrior with a code, of which I was a beneficiary, and I wasn't surprised when he later made a film about the Knights of the Round Table.

As the weeks went by, Dave Clark was growing in confidence, but this had less to do with increased skill than with his familiarity (if not boredom) with the routines of film-making. It's all too easy on a shoot, with its long waits that culminate in nothing much more than a few apparently ordinary people muttering to each other for less than a minute in front of a spindly bit of machinery, to lose sight of what is actually going on: moments of time are being frozen for ever, moments which will eventually be enlarged to grotesque proportions on a screen, then stored in a can to be held against you for the rest of your life. Seasoned professionals are constantly reminding themselves of this, and of the need to remain alert and make an effort. As a novice Dave was losing sight of it, and this did not endear him to the rest of the unit. People like our designer, Sally Jacobs, or our excellent New

Zealand sound man resented having their conscientious procedures taken for granted or even challenged.

Our line producer, Alex Jacobs, was John's right-hand man on this film as he would be later in Hollywood. He was also Sally Jacobs' husband. One afternoon we were filming among the rolling hills of the Somerset countryside. It was early spring and the fields were dotted with newborn lambs bleating beside their mothers. On this pleasant day and in these pretty surroundings we were ticking off the remaining set-ups before we moved on to a new location. Around three o'clock, and with no explanation, the day seemed to be over, and we were told to pack up and go home. The very few who seemed to know why exuded a sense of tight-lipped crisis, and were saying nothing. 'Look over there,' someone said to me. On the brim of a distant Somerset hill were two tiny figures. Though faraway, mere dots against the low sun, their body language was unambiguous. One was very distressed, waving his arms about and shaking his fist at the sky. The other, clearly trying to give comfort, had an arm around the shoulder of his companion. They might have been Lear and Gloucester on the Cliffs of Dover. 'Who is it?' I asked, and soon received my answer. The story was going around the unit at the speed of a hurried walk. In Alex Jacobs' presence Dave Clark had said something derogatory about Sally Jacobs' costumes. Instantly Alex had punched him hard in the face. Dave, and his ballooning nose, were now in a car speeding towards London and emergency treatment from a Harley Street specialist, while an overwrought Alex was being taken for a long calming walk by the director.

That night we waited at the hotel for news. If Dave's face had been seriously damaged the shoot would have to stop, no one knew for how long. John was jumpy but clearly exhilarated by this explosion of real life in the middle of his film. 'I don't mind him hitting him, but why did he have to hit him in the face?' he said, though I suspect he thought it rather wonderful that Alex should feel something so strongly he was prepared to flatten the one person indispensable to the making of his own movie. News from London came through at about ten o'clock. Dave's nose was not broken, but it was extremely swollen, a condition that could only be ameliorated by injecting a needle straight into the nose cavity. With this procedure, and a little luck, he would be back on location the following afternoon for a few carefully selected shots. Unfortunately the treatment would be extremely uncomfortable. This last bit of information made its way around the unit with the swiftness of a man on the double.

The last week of the shoot brought us back to London and the magnetic field of our personal lives. Mine, from which the film had provided a respite, seemed particularly tangled. I knew it had to be resolved, but I had no idea how. In these final days I was still working with Dave on every scene, standing by during every take, and at the end of the day making sure he had the right pages for tomorrow's shoot. However, Dave, like a schoolboy who sees no point in trying since term will be up by the end of the week, had already gone on holiday. One afternoon, with two days to go, we were shooting a difficult scene around a dinner table. Dave hadn't learnt a word of it, and John for the first time showed real anger. Dave blushed. 'Sorry, John, but Michael forgot to gimme the pages last night.' This was not the case, and in front of the unit I said so. I could have waited; Dave was humiliated enough as it was, but after so many weeks together we were all operating on short fuses. For the remaining few days he avoided me, and rarely left the company of his group who had closed ranks around him. We didn't speak again even to say goodbye, so I never got the gold watch or whatever it was that he was planning to give me. I did, however, receive an expensive Parker pen from David Deutsch and a charming note. Best of all, when I eventually saw the film, I found I had been given an enormous up-front credit, 'Personal Assistant to the Director'. This was John's present to me, and he couldn't have thought of a better one.

The most dramatic and, in the event, ambiguous consequence of *Catch Us If You Can* was that it would facilitate a return to Australia. Among the excellent actors waiting their turn to give Dave the best possible support as the film progressed, the most dazzling was Robin Bailey. Elegant and charming he had played in any number of West End comedies, and was one of the first names you'd think of to take on a role for which Rex Harrison was unavailable. Indeed, he'd had a huge success in Australia playing Professor Higgins in *My Fair Lady*. He was as specifically gifted as someone with musical talent: that is to say, he had an infallible comic sense, and, among other things, was a brilliant mimic. He usually played 'posh', which he sounded and looked, and it was therefore surprising when he told you that he was the son of a Nottingham miner, with roots closer to D. H. Lawrence than Terence Rattigan. However, the British theatre in which Robin had succeeded expected social contortions from those it was prepared to favour, and even in the sixties there were many self-taught Eliza Dolittles watching their tongues at the tea party. As a chameleon Robin excelled, but the price was a certain highly strung confusion, because he was by nature an honest and sympathetic man. When we came to shoot his scenes he had such a way with Peter's dialogue that John was content just to point a camera at him, and let the script and the actor do the work. Between takes we got to know each other with that mercurial swiftness with which schoolchildren and actors, when pitched into an unfamiliar environment, can sniff out temperamental affinity. He told me his next job would take him to Australia as star and director of *A Severed Head*, J. B. Priestley's stage adaptation of the Iris Murdoch novel. There was one part still to be filled, that of the American psychoanalyst, Palmer Anderson, but Robin was reluctant to have it cast sight unseen by his Australian producers. Since I had the necessary qualification of being Australian he asked me if I'd be interested, and I, of course, said 'Yes'.

It was exactly fifteen years since I'd left Sydney, and, as with most expatriates, a selective memory of home was like a small, deliberately neglected savings account intended as a hedge against the possibility of one day having no choice but to return. I had a life in England, and by and large was happy with it. Nevertheless Robin's offer couldn't help but arouse my curiosity about exactly what I'd left behind, and how it would relate to a frieze of memory, in which blue skies and the friends of my youth were permanently in place. Sometimes these recollections felt so unreal, so remote, that it was almost as if I had dreamt them. And perhaps in the intervening years Australian society had changed in a way to match the physical beauty of the country. Perhaps it was a place where theatre now meant something, and where I could make a significant contribution. Perhaps I would go home and discover I wanted to live there. Perhaps, on the other hand, and quite as likely, I would hate it. The prospect had the same confused and secretive expectations as that of going to meet an old lover, with whom one had had a painful break-up many years before. I discussed the matter with Shirley. Ever since we'd known each other she'd been listening patiently whilst I unloaded my ambivalence about my homeland, and she knew that some time or another this was a journey I had to make, and possibly on my own. At that time there were no cheap fares to Australia, and I wouldn't be earning enough to travel comfortably with a family. Also – and this I kept to myself – I felt a perverse compunction to be even-handed in my two intimate relationships, and to leave both, rather than one or the other, behind. On my own, I thought, I might work things out.

And so one afternoon I boarded a plane for Sydney, and heard the buckle of the safety belt click into place like the fractional advance of some clock before it begins to strike. Just before take-off a Qantas air hostess leant over me. 'Care for a Minty?' she said, smiling in that artless, awkward way that went with sun-damaged skin and the cookery pages of the *Australian Woman's Weekly*. She was offering me one of the white, sticky sweets, wrapped in white, red and green paper, that had dragged on my teeth throughout childhood. Even before we had taken off Australia had engulfed me in a claustrophobic rush. I was back there, and wondering quite why. The country of my growing up had been such a distance from those other societies with which it had things in common, that ordinary products like confectionery, disinfectants, cough medicines and beverages had been fabricated locally, and were unique to the place. All it took to awake expatriates to the life they'd left behind was a string of these brand names: Bonnington's Irish Moss, Aeroplane Jelly, Bex Powders, Buckley's Canadiol Mixture. All day long in the thirties and forties these names had been repeated on commercial radio with jingles to match, and on a hot summer day, with windows open all the way down the street, you would hear the murmur of this litany of petty commerce rising and falling as you passed by each house, the tone invariably upbeat, the import one of resigned isolation, between one house and the next, between Australia and the rest of the world. Yet these everyday particulars had their own poetry. The Wintergarden cinema in Rose Bay, to which as a child I rushed with my ninepence every Saturday afternoon, was cleaned with a disinfectant the unique smell of which I still remember as the doorway to a limitless world of black-and-white amazement.

By 1965 the jumbo jet was still three years away, and we travelled in a thin silver tube, which had to refuel every four or five hours, first at Rome then at a scattering of airfields across Asia and down through the Far East. By the time we arrived in Sydney some thirty-five hours later I'd lost track how many times we'd landed and taken off. It was a very ragged group of people who waited to disembark. Further down the cabin I noticed three uniformed staff rather surreptitiously attending to an elderly passenger, the rumpled top of whose slumped grey head I could just see. He looked suspiciously inanimate. Suddenly there was an official striding through the plane spraying us all with insecticide, the living and possibly the dead alike, and looking very pleased about it. I found myself grunting with amused recognition: This is Australia – don't expect frills. However, it was impossible not to be excited when I stepped out of the plane into the early morning sun, and caught among the competing smells of tarmac and fuel the unmistakable scent of my own country.

For my first few days I was to stay in the Vaucluse house my father shared with his third wife, Joan, whom I had yet to meet. On the taxi journey from the airport I thought I should warn them of my imminent arrival, so I asked the driver to stop while I called from a public telephone. My father answered, and my first surprise was that he sounded Australian. He had always been so sarcastically insistent about points of syntactical correctness and what he had described as the 'King's English' that it never occurred to me he might have an accent. But why not? He had lived most of his life in Australia. I wondered if he would find me English. We pulled up outside the house, and he must have been waiting for the sound of the taxi, because he was suddenly there, coming through the door in the garden wall smiling and – something I had least expected – nervous. The father I had left behind, aged fifty-two, in his grey flannel suit and spotted bow tie, had been good-looking and authoritative. So to an extent was this man, but I wasn't prepared for the practical jokes age plays with the face. As a young man, first in the army during the Great War, then later at medical school, he had been an amateur boxer, and this, as he advanced to shake my hand, was what he reminded me of now: a boxer, with features skewed a bit and puffy from a losing bout, but rising cheerfully from the mat to fight on.

His present house was more modest than others he'd occupied, which held title to bold harbour views. You could look out of the window and say this was yours. My mother had told me he'd mellowed with his third marriage. Joan was a woman in her early fifties, who it soon became clear got along splendidly with my father by seeming to agree with everything he said. She was exactly what I remembered of Australian respectability, jolly and insular, and in this she differed from his other two wives who had a sort of restless cosmopolitanism you once found in fashionable pockets all over the British Empire.

Much later on, after my father died, I would recognise in Joan qualities of pluck and independence, but for now, I regarded her warily.

It was nine o'clock in the morning, and I'd been awake for the best part of three days, so I asked if I could take a nap. They'd prepared a bed for me in my father's dressing room, and on top of his chest of drawers I saw a small photograph of my mother when young. I found I was too stimulated to sleep, and instead lay there listening to my father moving about in the adjacent room. He had always been an active man setting about his spare-time activities – whether pruning trees in the garden or organising his tackle for a fishing expedition – with an edgy single-mindedness. He still moved swiftly but was much heavier on his feet, and I kept waiting for the intermittent thump of a footfall. I got up and found him on the point of leaving the house. He told me he was taking the car into town to buy something at the big hardware store, Nock and Kirby's (those words, Nock and Kirby's!). I proposed coming along for the ride. On an upper of excitement and a downer of jet lag, both extreme, I floated towards the city hardly believing what I was seeing and feeling – rows of buildings that hadn't changed by as much as a brick and extraordinary yet absolutely familiar views – as we breasted one hill after another on the main road to town. Strangest of all was that remembered rhythm of driving through Sydney, the car swinging down to one of the bays of the harbour then rising steeply towards another panorama. All this had once been my world, and it was like re-entering a dream.

The rest of that weekend I found waiting for me unchanged the life I had left behind. I had picked up a book after fifteen years, turned to the page where the corner had been turned down and started to read. On Sunday under a blue sky we drove along the coast to a place I knew well, Palm Beach. I swam in the lush familiar ocean and my father pleased himself by catching a wave which I missed, ran into women on the beach who a moment ago had been girls, and whose marriages, births and divorces had, for all I knew, taken place just where I had left them, on this same stretch of sand. In the grounds of the clubhouse, still the same, still complacently exclusive, we peeled fresh prawns, made slow conversation and drank chilled beer under a canopy of semi-tropical vegetation. The experience had the stasis and fascination of an archaeological dig, and as I felt Australia once again becoming my reality I had a small moment of panic. Was my hard-won English life already being bleached away in this dappled sunlight?

That night in the sitting room after dinner I took a closer look at the interior of my father's house. I'd already spotted the leather-bound set of the *Encyclopaedia Britannica*, the volumes stacked one above another in its mahogany stand, which had originally been acquired by my grandfather in the twenties. More recent acquisitions included the numerous volumes of Churchill's *History of the Second World War* lined up in the bookcase alongside his *History of the English-Speaking Peoples*. On the shelf by the window was Sir Arthur Bryant's *Our Island's Story*. It had been thirty years since my father had been in Britain. Did he know that it had changed? Would he be interested in learning how? And was it any business of mine to tell him? But how else could I explain changes in myself? He had always admired Churchill, and in fact rather resembled him – the same expression of tolerant amusement, the same predilection for bow ties. I admired Churchill, too – who couldn't? – but I thought him an uncomfortable hero for Australians, whose troops he had so disastrously deployed in the First World War, and whose entire country he had been prepared to abandon to the Japanese in the Second. But this was a discussion to put on hold, possibly for ever. And the truth was that in spite of some bigoted opinions – on the superiority of the Northern European countries, particularly Britain, for instance – he did not have an entirely closed mind, and frequently took the position you least expected of him. Most of his contemporaries supported the attempt of the Menzies government to involve Australia in the Vietnam War. My father opposed it. He was also contemptuous of the homophobia which was a given in Australian life at that time. This, and the fact that he could sometimes be very funny, made him an unpredictable adversary. Nevertheless, we were on opposite sides of the fence, and always had been, and some kind of struggle between our opposing views would probably ensue before I left. When I was growing up, in all such confrontations, except the last one, I had capitulated. There was no question of another retreat. I had too much at stake. That night when I went to bed I felt an ominously familiar grumbling in my lower gut. I had first noticed it on the plane, and it appeared to be getting worse.

I had arrived in Australia on a Friday, and on the Monday we started rehearsals of *A Severed Head*. I remember little of the first day's reading except that it was nervy and uncomfortable. I remained ill at ease for the rest of the week and couldn't understand why. Jet lag was not something much discussed at that time, but it forced me to think hard about the play in which I had agreed to appear. I had read the original novel, and enjoyed it as much for its evocation of a London winter along its smarter terraced streets as for anything it had to say. The dramatisation reduced the book to the bare bones of its narrative, a schematic tale of musical beds. Torn from its envelope of elegant prose it became, as the critic indifferent to Puccini's score said of *Tosca*, a shabby little shocker, with perhaps the word 'genteel' replacing 'shabby'. The moment when the leading character discovers the fraudulent American psychoanalyst in bed with his own sister had provided the West End theatre with its first glimpse of bare breasts, thereby adding a few months to the run. I began to realise that, beyond offering a snobbish identification with promiscuous upper-middle-class London, the play had nothing very useful to communicate to Australians. We would succeed to the extent that it worked as a comedy. Fortunately, Robin Bailey was wonderfully cast in the huge leading part, though with his additional responsibility as the play's director he was carrying a precarious workload. The part of his young mistress had gone to a pretty English actress, Jan Leeming, who would later return to her own country and became a well-known television newsreader for the BBC. I hoped I'd be okay as the American. Other big parts were assigned to good but somewhat miscast resident actors.

By the end of the first week's rehearsal I was staying in a place of my own, a flat belonging to a friend of my mother's who now lived just outside Sydney. She had made the generous offer that I occupy her pied-à-terre for a nominal rent. I accepted, but it was a mistake. The flat overpowered me with its past associations. She had been one of a number of single women, either unmarried or divorced, to whom my mother had looked for support after she separated from my father. A few of them worked, something which in their circle was as uncommon as divorce. They had odd nicknames – 'Googie' Edwards, 'Codge' Barrett, 'Nuttie' McKellar – and they made for a sympathetic and vivacious sisterhood, particularly where a child of divorce like myself was concerned. At the age of ten I was obsessed with horror stories, and would bury myself in quite demanding texts like Mary Shelley's *Frankenstein*. I was also a draughtsman and would spend many hours turning out lurid pen-and-ink drawings in which blood dripped from the fangs of vampires and monsters went wandering under a full moon. These women were humorous about my interests but they took them seriously, and on the last evening of the school holidays, when tearfully I had to contemplate returning to my detested boarding school, they would gather round and lavish kindness and attention upon me. At the time this seemed like a vote of confidence in the sort of person I was, not the one the school and my father intended I should become. Twenty-five years later, in the familiar spaces of this Edgecliff flat, the memory was one of oppressive unhappiness – and not only mine, theirs also, because beneath their laughter and encouragement I had a childish intuition of lives that had turned out to be not in tune with their expectations.

This is what I had least expected from Australia: that I would be catapulted back into the past and unable to escape it. I was beginning to see some of my old male friends, but the question that had once so exercised and bonded us – what would we make of our lives? – had now been answered. Each of us had made his choice; now it was a matter of seeing who'd made the best ones. They had worked hard and were now doctors, lawyers and stockbrokers, doing well but still with a way to go. They had wives and children, owned houses and cars and were already planning for the next stage of ownership, a beach house along the coast or a yacht to sail at the weekends. One's thirties are the make-or-break decade for professional success, and though they asked politely after the life I had been leading in England, they had no real interest in it. And why should they? Such knowledge was no help to them in the living of their own lives. In any case how could I begin to explain it? In my mind it was about different values: not necessarily superior ones, but alternatives. And here there was one predominant value – material success. My friends were not greedy or obsessed with money; on the contrary they were generous and unostentatious. But they accepted as a given that the one sure measure of success in life was the amount you were able to earn. Keats and Mozart were not in the equation. My salary in *A Severed Head* was the most I had ever earned in the theatre, but for the first time in my life I felt poor.

I still had much in common with these friends, a shared growing-up, and it remained vivid and irreplaceable, but I regarded it over a chasm of fifteen missing years, and their company always dragged me back to the person I wanted to leave behind. These days all one has to do is pick up the telephone to reassure oneself that there is an elsewhere. At that time I don't think I had ever made a single long-distance call between England and Australia. It was troublesome to organise and expensive. Instead, hungry for contact, I subscribed to the air-mail

edition of *The Observer*, printed on rice paper and delivered to one's
door by post on a Friday. As week followed week I waited for it with
increasing desperation, and was finally tearing open the paper seal as
if it was a wartime communiqué from a liberated country.

Being 12,000 miles away was not much help, either, in the sorting
out of my private life. On the contrary, distance lent an element of
romantic loss to my existing confusion. It was my lover I worried
about – beautiful, alone in London and increasingly idealised by separation. She was now working at the Royal Court in John Osborne's
new success, *A Patriot for Me*. I wrote her frequent, distressed letters,
and we made plans to meet for a holiday in Greece on my way back.
Her replies, with precious news of London, were original and often
funny, written in sentences spare as verse. They only served to
underline the prose of my present existence. To Shirley, feeling myself
tongue-tied and ashamed of it, I sent postcards and newspaper cut-
tings. I was losing all sense of what I really wanted and, torn between
two women and two countries, I knew I was heading for trouble, and
what that trouble was. My colitis had returned. And yet among my
Australian friends I took a secretive and contrary pride in this
personal chaos with which I had been juggling for three years. They
had submitted to the laws of our tribe, collectively monitoring each
other at each stage of the journey, through school, through university
and into marriage. My satisfaction was to have lived in a country
which allowed me to go to hell in whatever way I chose, and where
the limits I put on my life I had marked out myself.

As the first night approached other things demanded my attention.
A big shock was the set, which I first saw on the day of the dress
rehearsal. It was a composite affair in which various bedrooms revolved
into view on an upper level, then areas below to suggest drawing
rooms in Chester Square and Hereford Square. The management
had acquired the rights to use the London design, but they had
worked entirely from technical drawings. Mechanically the set was
fine, but it was decorated like a Bondi motel. Robin already had too
much to think about, so on his behalf I approached someone I knew
who ran an antique shop in Double Bay, and he lent us a few sticks of
period furniture which raised the tone a notch. Style being in short
supply, we were ever more dependent on the play's comedy. Here the
generosity of Australian audiences came to our rescue, and by our last
preview I thought we had a show. Afterwards, much relieved, Robin

and I went out to supper at a dimly lit restaurant in King's Cross and ate their speciality, Boeuf Stroganoff. Ambitious restaurants in Sydney were still aping heavy European haute cuisine. Robin had been particularly good that night, and the audience had given him an exceptional welcome. He settled back in his banquette. 'Well,' he said, 'it's nice to know that somewhere in the world one's name really means something.' I felt a superstitious chill. Australia was not a place where you could ever take anything for granted, not the weather, not the economy, not the venomous wildlife, and certainly not Australian critics.

However the press night that followed seemed to go reasonably well, though Robin, having peaked the night before, compensated by overplaying a little. Mimicking Broadway, the producers held a party to await the arrival of the notices. The most important paper, particularly for a show which pretended to a little class, was the *Sydney Morning Herald*. Its reviews were literate and well informed, if a little too insistent on proclaiming the reviewer's high standards, particularly where uppity overseas visitors were concerned. At last the *Herald* arrived, and with much ado it was thrust into Robin's hands; he was then hoisted onto a table and asked to read it aloud. On Broadway someone would have had the sense to skim through the notice before bringing it into the room, but this was like the set: imitating something and not getting it quite right. Almost the first words Robin had to read were 'ultimate tennis-flannelled fatuity'. The production it seemed had 'opened limply at the Philip Theatre'. The rest of the review went on to rubbish the play (it must be said in much the same terms as my own reservations) and afterwards attacked the production and Robin's own performance. He struggled through to the end as gallantly as he could, then got down from the table wondering how much time he could decently allow before he bolted from the room. We had other reviews which were better, and I, personally, didn't come out of it too badly, though the tone taken invariably supplied the subtext: 'Don't think you can pull the wool over *our* eyes.' I read that I was 'reasonably accomplished' and 'intermittently astute'. It was like being sprayed with insecticide at the airport.

Not entirely a flop, certainly no success, we were locked into a run of some months in Sydney, before going on to Melbourne for a four-week engagement, where, it was thought, we might be better received. Because of *My Fair Lady* Robin had his own following, and that provided us with an audience in the first few weeks. After that our business went into a gradual but remorseless decline. This was a mirror to my health, which like a dripping tap was growing a little worse and more difficult to disregard with each passing week. I'd soon reached the point where I needed to see a doctor, and my father arranged an appointment with a colleague in Macquarie Street, Sydney's equivalent of London's Harley Street. This hive of doctors and dentists I never visited as a child without a sense of alarm, but it had been a handsome thoroughfare sloping down to the harbour, with the Botanical Gardens on one side, and on the other, among the occasional tall buildings, a wealth of late Georgian colonial houses fronted with balconies stacked one above another on delicate neoclassical columns. Most of them had now been replaced by high-rise, but in one of the few that remained this specialist had his surgery. As I entered the waiting room he was seeing a devastated elderly couple to the door. Whatever he'd just told them, it wasn't good news. 'You just go for a walk in the Gardens,' he said. 'And come back in half an hour and tell me what you've decided.' His manner was brusque like a military doctor, and to an Australian it was only too familiar. Doctors, particularly consultants, occupied a lofty position in Australian society. They were the officers and the patients were the troops.

Since he knew my father, when my appointment came we began with a little small talk. I remarked what a beautiful house we were in, and expressed the hope that this building, at least, would be saved. 'No, it'll be coming down,' he said. 'You can't stop progress.' He then examined me. Afterwards he said, 'Well, you've got it, and there's not much we can do about it.' He told me there were some cortisone preparations on the market but he didn't think much of them. 'No, you'll just have to live with it. Mind you, if you stopped this life of yours racketing around hotel rooms, it might help.' Architecture and theatre, both, it seemed, were for the dustbin.

My father's surgery was next door in the BMA building, and I caught the lift to the sixth floor to give him an indignant account of the consultation. He was much amused, and told me that the doctor I had just seen suffered so badly from stomach ulcers that on two occasions he had haemorrhaged and almost died. Stomach ulcers were also a serious problem for my father. 'Maybe you should both stop this life of yours racketing around hospitals,' I said. 'Maybe,' he replied with good humour.

The Sydney Wasp ascendancy hadn't changed its ways by a jot in the time I'd been away. Never mind that the rest of the western world had been turned upside down by the sixties, the Australia I had been part of hadn't heard about it, and didn't want to know. The Royal Sydney Golf Club and its members might just as well have been submerged in embalming fluid. There were changes in the life of the city, highly visible ones, but predictably they were being dictated by money, and the most obvious and distressing was the destruction of old Sydney in the latest real-estate boom. The city centre I remembered of scattered colonial buildings, intriguing Victorian arcades, horseshoe theatres and majestic picture palaces was gone or going, and the developers now had their eyes on Sydney's wealth of nineteenth-century terraces. This was the architecture, encrusted, like New Orleans, in decorative ironwork, which so impressed and delighted later visitors from England like John Betjeman and Joyce Grenfell. In 1965 it was all under threat. Key players in the real-estate game were New Australian businessmen from Eastern Europe, forerunners of the entrepreneurs who have run amok in Russia since the end of the Cold War. Their superior energy and guile were helping to carve up Sydney, and rather than resisting this attack on the country's small but precious legacy of historical buildings, the local establishment gave every impression of going along with it. It's the misfortune of countries which begin as colonies to have decisions about their future made by people who have never had a childhood there. Once it had been the Foreign Office and English Governors who gave the orders. Further down the track it would be international corporations.

The city I grew up in had had a handful of clubs which had been founded in the previous century with a deferential nod in the direction of St James's and Pall Mall. My father's had been the Union Club, a handsome sandstone building in Bligh Street. In the sixties the membership acquiesced in a property deal in which the club was demolished and then rehoused over two floors of a brutally undistinguished high-rise. The elaborate, late-Victorian affair, the Australia Club, home to the legal profession, would soon go the same way. For a moment I thought the America Club in Macquarie Street might be pointing the way to a more imaginative solution. A huge development was in progress on the site, but it towered high above the old clubhouse, which had been left to nestle between four enormous supporting columns like something valuable stored beneath a sideboard. It turned out that this extremely expensive manoeuvre was temporary and intended for the convenience of the members. Once new premises were prepared for them in the concrete above, the old building below was to be demolished and replaced with office space. At the time this vandalism was happening globally, but it was particularly unforgivable in Australia, where connections to the past were so few and frail.

Soon, however, it would be brought to a stop, and in a manner without parallel in any other country. A union leader, Jack Mundy, persuaded his members to simply down tools when asked to demolish any building of significant worth. A system of green bans was put in place whereby architecture designated as having historical or cultural importance was protected from destruction. The strategy was a success because it was what most people wanted, and it was in line with Australia's radical past. The antipodean countries had been the first to give the vote to women, to have a minimum wage and an eight-hour day, the legacy of those early arrivals from Ireland, Scotland and the industrial North, who had left Britain in protest and often in chains. It was these people and others like them – immigrants who had been driven to the far side of the world by desperation, or convicts who had served their time and were now trying to make this strange new country their home – who had the right to call themselves Australians, because they had nowhere else to go. My tribe, the people who since the founding of the colony had been the deputies of Britain, administering it, manning its professions, looking for favours from the colonising power, had no need of a specifically Australian culture, because that sort of thing was already supplied from England. Unless it was the work of a painter of reputation, whose canvas you could hang on the wall like a framed and certified cheque, local artistic endeavour was considered a bit of a yawn and probably second-rate. Two figures represented the times: the Prime Minister, Sir Robert Menzies, and the Chief Justice, Sir Garfield Barwick, who would later play a key role in the dismissal of the Whitlam Government. In their own country they were regarded as hard-headed realists and sceptics, but once they set foot on English soil they shrank to fawning sentimentalists, whose coarse perception of culture was realised in a royal ceremonial or a parade of High Court judges in robes and bell-bottomed wigs. Menzies on film, quoting Marvell in a speech to the Queen – 'I did but see her passing by, / But I shall love her till I die'– remains one of Australia's most embarrassing moments.

Until I returned I'd never perceived the battle-line running through the middle of Australian society, or realised that I'd spent most of my life on the wrong side of it. I was following the route already taken by the novelist, Patrick White, with whom I shared a similar background and with whom I would one day become acquainted – going into European exile then returning to see my country with new eyes. Patrick believed that he and people like him were obliged to return and do what only artists can – lay down that second level of consciousness, a kind of lustre over the day-to-day apprehensions of survival, which will eventually transform a mere location into something better, a place. It would not be my journey, and my second departure would be decisive, but I would have a new respect for those for whom it was. When Patrick White received the Nobel Prize for Literature he accepted it on behalf of two people, himself and Jack Mundy. And probably a line of long-forgotten Jack Mundys, who had stood perplexed in the Australian sun, and struggled to make the best sense of it.

In 1965 a number of splendid buildings in Sydney were coming down, but one quite remarkable structure was going up – the Sydney Opera House. Jorn Utzon's visionary edifice was being built in three stages. The first and least dramatic had been the construction of the vast concrete base on which the various auditoria would rest. This had taken years and generated much local scepticism because to those without an understanding of the engineering, nothing very much seemed to be happening. Now, however, the second stage, the erection of the huge sails, was almost complete, and all Sydney could see with what a miracle they had been endowed. I went down to the site to have a closer look. The structure lacked its cladding of white tiles, but the scale and uniqueness of the thing were still astonishing. The following year Utzon planned to begin work on the third and final stage, the interiors, and here his intention was to contrast the mono-chromes of the outside of the building with a palette of specifically Australian colours, some derived from the bleached landscape but others reflecting the vividness of native blooms and bird life. As audiences proceeded from without to within they would experience a magical alteration.

Sydney owes its Opera House primarily to two men: the conductor Eugène Goossens and a Labour politician, Joe Cahill. In 1945 Goossens had been invited by the Australian Broadcasting Commission (the country's copycat version of the BBC) to conduct its Symphony

Orchestra. He became one of a number of English artists in the first half of the twentieth century to be captivated firstly by the beauty of Sydney and then by a vision of the sort of city it might become. Others were the sculptor Rayner Hoff, who saw in Australia the possibility of another pagan Greece, and the architect Leslie Wilkinson, whose mission was to bring the shapes of the Mediterranean, rather than those of the English suburbs, to the hills and bays of Sydney. Almost upon arrival Goossens started promoting the idea of an opera house – it was an essential amenity without which Sydney would never be the great city it deserved to be. He'd fallen a little in love with the place, or anyway with what it might become, and as a teenager I remember passing him on Bondi Beach, both of us traversing the water's edge from opposite directions. It was a morning of crystal beauty, and with his very white skin, little pot belly and hat, Goossens seemed charmingly out of place. He was looking about him at this panorama of Australians at play with a sharp-eyed, amused benevolence. He had quickly assumed the role of ambassador for the arts at large, and you saw him everywhere. He gave a talk about film music to the Sydney Film Society, which I attended, and he was often present at theatrical first nights in the company of his tall, handsome American wife. It was rumoured that this stylish couple were the centre of a fast set.

Joe Cahill was his complete opposite. A man in his sixties from a working-class Irish background, he'd spent most of his life in the slippery and compromised world of state politics. However, like that other Labour politician, Prime Minister Ben Chifley, who had brought Tyrone Guthrie to Australia at the end of the war to advise on a National Theatre, he had the imagination to sense that something was missing in Australia's idea of itself. As Premier of New South Wales he wanted to leave behind a beginning to that not yet articulated future, and in Goossens' passionate espousal of an opera house he thought he might have found the cause he was looking for. He knew that the task would take all his determination and guile. The Conservative Coalition of the Liberal and Country parties would, of course, oppose it, the one out of endemic philistinism, the other because opera in Sydney would mean nothing to rural constituents scattered far and wide across the state. There would also be problems on the left with his own party, who would question whether the funding would not be better spent on hospitals and schools. From its inception the building would inspire rancorous debate. Nevertheless, in 1954 a start was made on the project. The following year Bennelong Point, one of the prime sites of the harbour and up till then (all too typically) a tram depot, was approved as the location, and in 1956 an international competition to choose a design was held in Sydney.

In any such competition Jorn Utzon's proposal would have attracted attention. Not only was it unlike any opera house that had ever been built, it was blithely unconcerned with solutions to the multitude of engineering problems the design raised. Elsewhere in the world it would probably have been admired, discussed, then politely put to one side. Australia, with inspired recklessness, decided to run with it. Eero Saarinen, the Finnish-American architect, was not the only judge on the panel to cast his vote for Utzon, but it was probably his enthusiasm, backed by his international reputation, that won the day. Like the Scandinavian he was promoting, he knew about buildings seen against sky and reflected in water, and both men shared a scepticism about the doctrinaire insistence on box shapes among many of their modernist colleagues. 'There is also the whole question of how to relate buildings to earth and sky,' Saarinen had written. 'Is the sharp horizontal really the best answer? We must have an emotional reason as well as a logical end to everything we do.'

So Utzon's opera house with its great white wings seemed to have got off to a flying start. Its enemies, however, had other plans. That same year Goossens went on a trip to Europe. A few days before he was due to return the Director of the ABC, Charles Moses, received an anonymous tip-off that Customs were going to search Goossens' luggage on his arrival at the airport. He was a friend and ally of the conductor but this warning seemed so far-fetched he felt foolish passing it on. Goossens' luggage was duly searched, and officials found a number of what would today be described as sex toys, items now freely and legally available all over the world. In the Australia of the 1950s Goossens had broken the law, and the penalty was harsh: a fine of a few hundred pounds and a completely destroyed life. The story reached the papers with uncommon speed, and was soon around the world. Australians, who may not have known much about art, knew how to make the most of a good scandal, and Goossens became more of a household name as pervert than he had ever managed as musician. His days as a public figure were over. With his Australian dream in ruins, he resigned from his post and crept back to England, where he died eight years later.

The Opera House was under way, but in the face of increasingly polarised public opinion. The same year that Joe Cahill died, 1959, work commenced on the site. When I arrived six years later the Opera House, rising up beside the harbour, seemed to me to be the most significant thing that had happened to Sydney in my lifetime, and I was appalled by the virulence of the opposition to it. There was constant sniping in the press, and on the radio an announcer known only as 'Andrea' had a morning programme in which she never let a day pass without a malicious attack on the building. What particularly exercised its critics was the amount of money being spent on it, but since funding came, not from taxation, but from a special state lottery set up for the purpose, the cost was not a pressing issue. More ominously, opposition to the Opera House was being twinned to an altogether different cause – Australia's participation in the Vietnam War. Those who were against the Opera House were, by and large, for the war, and soon to be in favour of the Opera House was construed as being in some way unpatriotic. This notion was expressed with vivid grossness by a Country Party delegate, a Mr Mair. 'All the talk among café society by long-hairs and others about the spirit of the opera and mystique. Don't these people realise that there are a lot of people fighting a war? Don't they realise there's a nasty drought about?' Mr Mair continued that the only spirit he'd like to see at the Opera House 'was a few thousand gallons of petrol and a match'. These are sentiments, though less pithily expressed, that rank with Goering's 'When I hear the word culture I reach for my gun,' and they were not uncommon in the Australia of my growing-up.

Mr Mair was wrong in more ways than one. The 'café society' of the Eastern Suburbs were by no means united in their support of the Opera House, and I had a number of arguments with people I knew well who were against it, and for the war. By the eighties you would be hard pressed to find anyone who had not always been both peacenik and opera lover, but by that time the Opera House was up and running and an acknowledged success. More than any other single thing, it had changed the way the rest of the world perceived Australia, and in turn how Australians perceived themselves. Here was a landmark you didn't have to go abroad to see. Abroad had started coming to see you. Some have claimed equal iconic stature for that other spectacular structure, the Sydney Harbour Bridge, but the Bridge stands for sound British engineering at its grandest and economic development. The Opera House was about something more unusual, technological risk and spiritual aspiration. It was never about common sense and money, which is why some people hated it, though by now it must have paid for itself a hundred times over in the economic stimulus it brought to the city. From the beginning it teetered on the edge of folly, and was often given a push in that direction, but its foundations held. You could describe it as the world's first secular cathedral.

The troubles that the Opera House had experienced up until 1965 were as nothing to those that followed, when in the election later that year the Labour Government was replaced by the Conservative Coalition led by Robert Askin. There then ensued the most corrupt period of government New South Wales had ever known. Addressing his supporters on the night of his victory the new premier announced 'We're in the tuck shop now, boys,' and went on to prove it by accumulating at the time of his death some five million dollars in excess of his earnings over the previous twenty-five years. Joe Daniel Testa of the Chicago Mafia, sensing a business opportunity, paid his first visit to Sydney not long after Robert (later to be Sir Robert) Askin assumed power.

The Coalition had always made trouble for the Opera House, but now that it was on the way to completion they realised that the trick was to make it seem not Labour's achievement, but their own. Askin handed the problem over to his junior partner in the Country Party, Davis Hughes, who was now the Minister for Public Works. What remained to be done was stage three, the design of the interior spaces, and Hughes decided that Utzon, accused by his enemies, not least the Coalition, of scandalous cost overruns, had become dispensable. A new presiding intelligence would bring the building home to glory – Davis Hughes. His method of getting rid of Utzon was crude but effective. He simply cut off his money, both the funding for the work on the building to continue and the payment of his own fees, on which he depended for a living. Because there was no tax agreement between Denmark and Australia, Utzon's personal finances were in a perilous state. He was being taxed in both countries, leaving him less than ten per cent of his income to live on. Now even this pittance was denied him. Unable to proceed with his work, or even pay his bills, he had only one weapon with which to fight back, the threat of resignation. Impulsively he wrote such a letter, which, without hesitation, Hughes accepted. Utzon was out.

In 1966 he left Australia brutally hurt, vowing never to return, and with the balance of his fees still owing to him. The team of nineteen which he had so carefully assembled – three in Denmark and sixteen young architects recruited from all over Australia – was disbanded. A panel of four architects was now appointed where previously there had been one, and responsibility for completing the work eventually fell to someone from the Design Section of the Government Architect's Branch of Public Works. A typical Australian bureaucracy was soon in place, far surpassing in size Utzon's team. The new cost overruns made the previous expenditure look like parsimony. During the nine years Utzon worked on stages one and two of the project, he spent approximately fifteen million dollars. By the time stage three was completed the total cost had soared to an incredible hundred million. More than money had been lost. Davis Hughes had taken it upon himself to reallocate the uses of the various auditoria. The opera theatre became a concert hall, and state-of-the-art stage machinery already built and paid for at a cost of four and a half million dollars, was sold as scrap at a dollar a ton. Opera was relegated to the drama theatre, and drama to a small house intended only for experimental work. The Sydney Opera House had become effectively the Sydney Concert House.

Nevertheless, there it stands, this mutilated building, but one which when first encountered has a grandeur beyond all one's expectations. Its many auditoria are mainly full, and day and night people promenade around its base and make good use of the restaurants and amenities it has spawned along its approach. Had it not come into existence the nation would have been the loser, and it may be that remarkable buildings in other parts of the world (the Guggenheim in Bilbao is one) would not have had such an easy birth. Its story is the supreme Australian paradox. And at long last as I write some amends are being made to the man whose vision it was. There are plans to redesign the interiors so that they go some way to realising Utzon's intentions.

# TWELVE

# Boats against the Current

Eugène Goossens and Jorn Utzon had both found Australia a dangerous place, and now it was beginning to frighten me. As my health
continued to decline, so did any pleasure I had in being in Australia,
and soon it became impossible not to associate the one with the other.
Improbable fears assailed me: that the Vietnam War would escalate
and cut me off for ever from the Northern Hemisphere, that I would
never be able to resume my life in England. I was still getting a few
grains of nourishment each week from my rice-paper *Observer*, and in
one edition spotted a favourable notice of a book I was pretty certain
would never be available in Australia because it would be banned.
This was *Eros Denied* by Wayland Young, an eminently respectable
and well-researched history of sexual repression in Christian Europe.
I wrote off at once to Dona, asking her to send a copy to me. The book
never arrived. Instead I received a letter from the Australian Customs
who had confiscated it. I learnt that if I cared to fill in the enclosed
form the book would be presented to me as I boarded the plane for my
flight out of the country. And good riddance to both you and your filthy
reading matter, the letter might just as well have added. More and more
things about Australia were making me snort with anger. I'd forgotten
how thick and dull the financial pages of the *Sydney Morning Herald*
were, and how a sense of money pervaded the city, hanging there like
humidity between the swaying masts of the small craft moored in
every bay of the harbour, or along the leafy tunnel of Darling Point
Road. It was not money as in 'big money', signifying temptation or
extravagant folly, but 'cautious money', the thought of which was
meant to bring you to your senses and back into line. On the way to the
theatre each evening I passed a huge neon sign on top of a building,

staring over the city like a couple of red eyes. I'd no idea what it meant, CAGA FINANCE, but there it was, as blunt as a reprimand. Through this circumscribed world my doctor and lawyer contemporaries were prudently making their way, and though I continued to see them I had less and less to bring to the table. I was an actor in failing health appearing in a play no one thought much of. I wondered if they looked on me as one of those people, common to every generation, who, once bright with promise, are somehow marked to fall by the wayside.

This, I suspected, was becoming my father's view. He remained perfectly friendly, but his curiosity about me had gone, and I'd once again become what he'd long ago decided I was. One Sunday afternoon I went out to visit him at Vaucluse. He'd been gardening, and came into the house wearing a navy boiler suit – the same boiler suit that I'd seen in photographs of Churchill at leisure. He wore one of his spotted bow ties and offered me his expression of tolerant amusement, and I suddenly understood that the life of this realist was as much propped up by an element of fantasy as that of any of the scruffy bohemians and long-haired intellectuals about whom he liked to be so sardonically dismissive. I was far more comfortable with the adversarial father I already knew, the one who supported capital punishment, who had told me at the age of six that war provided the ultimate test of national character, and who had given me by way of a sex education, and without comment, a pamphlet of lurid coloured photographs showing the ravages of syphilis.

One day I was given a ride by a young taxi-driver who'd just returned from six months in England. He was articulate and hungry to talk, so we exchanged impressions. He'd found digs with a family who had a house in outer London, and what most impressed him about the way they lived was the string of complex relationships they maintained, firstly with members of their family, some living around the corner, others scattered across the city, then with all the other people who lived in their street. Returning to Sydney, he said, the first thing that struck him was its loneliness. Given the largely correct impression the world has of Australian friendliness, this was a curious observation to make. He hadn't meant it pejoratively. The pleasures of the bush and the beach are lonely ones, and probably the more intense for being so. It was simply a fact of Australian existence, and an unsurprising one in a country of such size, sparse population and so distant from its roots. Over the years I was often to encounter taxi-drivers like him, autodidacts and loners, who revved around Sydney for twelve hours at a stretch as they bit their lip and puzzled away at life.

The prosperous Eastern Suburbs I had explored as a boy, trailing on hot summer days up and down the slopes of Rose Bay, Bellevue Hill, Double Bay, or the long trek along Dover Road, then up again to Vaucluse, past a succession of closed garage doors and barking dogs, said very little about community, though volumes about wealth. The houses, no two alike, sat on their ledge of prime land behind a cover of lush vegetation, and looked down at the harbour as if from the shaded interior of a private enclosure at the race track. The two addresses my father occupied in the forties with his second wife, Sybil, were both strangely vacant places. Each had a spectacular outlook, but the splendours of Sydney are so ubiquitous that there are days when the city can seem like a feast laid out in front of a man who's already eaten. Their first house, on Dover Heights, was a modernist building with a flat roof and a huge picture window facing the sun as it set over the distant harbour bridge. In the afternoon great blocks of hot light pushed so far into the room that they bleached the spines of books on the opposite wall. The second house, at Parsely Bay, was random and architecturally undistinguished but it had a commanding location with a garden that dropped straight into the harbour. All day long there was the slow-motion drama of distant ships coming and going through the heads. At neither address did we have anything to do with the neighbours, nor except in one case even know their names. The exception was Miss Riley, an elderly spinster lady, whose greatest pleasure was reading. When she learnt that she was going blind, she got up one morning, made her way up to the huge cliffs facing the open ocean above Watson's Bay, climbed decorously through the fence, and jumped. My father spoke admiringly of her grit. What was so odd at that time about the Australian attitude to life, in spite of the kettle continuously on the boil for a cup of tea and a heart-to-heart, in spite of the noisy mateship of the pubs and the easy, sentimental way of life in which so many good things came for free, was that core of harshness that people like my father seemed to welcome and almost insist upon. You were on your own. And you'd better get used to it. That's what Miss Riley must have felt, and she acted accordingly.

Confused about my life and now quite seriously ill, all I could see in Australia were the things that weren't there. I was under few illusions about England, and there was much about it that I still disliked, but what it offered was choice. Among its innumerable tribes and categories I'd found one that suited me, the theatre. There I could live a life, whatever its travails and privations, with my energies properly engaged and my self-respect intact. In my own country there seemed to be no such secure harbour because, notwithstanding differences of class and education, it was culturally homogenous and you failed to fit in at your cost. While I waited with increasing desperation to return to the other side of the world I tried to impose some order on my life. There was the performance to give at night, and I was writing a little in the mornings in between visits to the bathroom. In the afternoons I went to a yoga class in the company of other odd and distressed people. In between I was flailing around. I pursued women grimly, as if I was an agent for the distant sexual revolution, but succeeded only when I was indifferent to the outcome. One piece of good news arrived in a letter from London: David William was going to the Glasgow Citizens' Theatre as Artistic Director, and he offered me not only an acting job but my first shot at directing. Yet, such was my state, that even this proposal wearied me. It would mean having to pack my bags again when all I wanted was to get back to London and stay put. In any case I wasn't free. I wrote back to say that I was about to go on tour to Melbourne for the second lap of *A Severed Head*.

In advance of my arrival I'd booked accommodation in a building with the promising name of Magnolia Court. This turned out to be an ugly new block of one-room flatlets, intended for short lets to theatre people and other professional wanderers. My room still smelt of wet cement and was sparsely equipped with the most basic of motel fittings. A few doors down in an identical concrete box was another touring theatrical from Britain, Stanley Baxter, who had been similarly duped by the lure of a huge tree with blossoms the size of saucepans. We crossed regularly in the dark corridor, and developed a line of mordant jokes about our bleak accommodation. It was in just such a place in Australia that Tony Hancock had killed himself. By this time I had become very pale through blood loss, and Stanley expressed concern. One morning he knocked on my door holding in his hands a small, dark bottle. 'Try this,' he said. 'It might help. "Dr Collis-Browne's Mixture".' This was a Victorian patent remedy for diarrhoea once readily available at chemists all over the Empire. I was so grateful for any show of concern that I was ridiculously moved.

We opened strongly at our new date. The show had become much more assured, and this was reflected in our press. In any case, Melbourne is a more culturally centred city than Sydney, which is split and spread by its expanses of water into any number of relatively self-contained suburbs, and where the semi-tropical climate militates against leaving the garden or the shore for an entertainment indoors. We were playing at the Comedy, a theatre which you might have mistaken for one in Shaftesbury Avenue and where, sixteen years before, Robert Morley had appeared in *Edward, My Son*. I was occupying Sophie Stewart's old dressing room, so there was an odd sense of having come full circle. But to what exactly? I was still just about getting through the show each night, though there were times when I was so enfeebled I could barely get up from my chair in the wings to make an entrance. However, acting draws on different energies from those that simply get you through the day, and with appreciative houses there were performances that I actively enjoyed. Two letters arrived for me at the stage door. One was further correspondence from David William, who had refused to give up and was proposing the same offer he had made in his first letter but in a later time slot. I felt chastised by the persistence of his faith in me, and wrote back at once to say that if I was well enough I'd be delighted to join him in Glasgow. The second letter was less welcome. Someone had told Peter Nichols at a party about my complex private life, and he was writing to demand why I had never told him about it. It was true that he was probably my closest friend in England, but he was also Shirley's friend, and it irritated me that he couldn't see the impossibility of confiding in him something I had yet to tell her. In any case, where had it got me?

I had some friends in Melbourne going back to the time of *Edward, My Son*. We looked each other up, but drinking too much together was something that no longer had much pleasure for me. To one of them, however, I owe a debt: a sardonically intelligent lawyer who had married well and now lived a comfortable and reformed life in Toorak. He was the one who had said to me before I set off for England, 'What do you bet? This time next year you'll be back doing medicine.' He was quick to gauge the state of my health, and the following afternoon at his insistence I was in the consulting room of an excellent specialist he'd been able to recommend. The doctor pulled down an eyelid and whistled. 'You should be in hospital. You're seriously anaemic,' he said, and that night I was, having a blood transfusion. Next morning I rang my father to tell him what had happened. There was a silence before he responded, a momentary one, but long enough to evoke the ailing boy with a string of middle-ear infections who had never been quite the son the father wanted. Instantly I recalled my childish distrust of him. Then we continued talking, and he offered sound advice.

I liked my new doctor, an alert, amused man only a few years older than I was. He had immediately put me on to the medicines that the Sydney specialist had ridiculed, and for the first time in months I felt I might recover. I also liked lying in my hospital bed in a cool room shaded from the humming Australian glare beyond the veranda, where I could give up on everything except the struggle to get better. I had hung in at the theatre night after night because I knew my understudy was too young and inexperienced to manage a satisfactory takeover, and I was reluctant to add to Robin's problems. Now the decision had been taken out of my hands, and the relief was enormous.

One morning I had a letter from my mother's brother, Jim Litchfield. He had heard that I was in hospital, and was proposing that I come to recuperate with him and his wife, Charmian, at Hazeldean, the family property in the Monaro district of New South Wales, where, among many thousands of sheep, he and my mother had grown up. Until the age of about eight I'd always spent Christmas there, and in 1934 almost a year of my life, when first my uncle and aunt, then afterwards my mother, went on trips overseas. The various parents took turns in minding the three children, me and my two cousins, of whom James, at seven, was the oldest, and Ann, at five, the youngest. I was in the middle. In the course of that year we were never apart, and we became more like siblings than cousins. I accepted my Uncle Jim's invitation with alacrity. The Monaro is high country midway between Melbourne and Sydney, and I travelled there in a small plane which swung over the peaks and ravines of the Snowy Mountains as it descended towards Cooma, the town some twelve miles' drive from the property. As a child I had always travelled on the overnight sleeper from Sydney, rocking about in the top bunk of a much decorated but poorly suspended Edwardian compartment. I invariably woke just before dawn, greatly excited, and lay peering at the strange ash-coloured landscape emerging out of the night – steep hills of rock face and gum trees, which would rear up, then slide away to nothing, or be suddenly obscured by a wash of white smoke from the engine. City life fell to one side like so much packaging. This, you knew for certain, was the real thing: Australia.

My uncle was waiting for me at the airport, and I was pleased to see a face I knew so well. During the time I'd lived in England he'd made numerous trips to London, and in the early days, perhaps to please my mother, had usually checked up on my welfare. As a student I'd been taken to dinner at the Devonshire Club in St James's, dull food in imposing surroundings, for which on both scores I had at the time no lack of appetite. When Charmian was with him we went to restaurants, and Shirley had once entertained them with some trepidation at Gardnor Mansions. We were now driving along a broad surfaced road, which I remembered as once being dirt, and had soon turned off onto the first of a number of gravelled tracks which through a string of gates and over ramps would lead eventually to the drive of Hazeldean. Anticipation welled up in me as we proceeded through instantly familiar paddocks and past isolated trees that I still recognised, and approached the house that I hadn't seen for a quarter of a century.

The original James Litchfield had first set eyes on this landscape in the early 1850s. He and his new wife, Ann, landed in New South Wales when they were respectively twenty-five and twenty-one years of age, and little is known about the background of this small farmer from Essex. Another uncle, stationed in England with the RAF during the Second War, tried to research the family, but found that the churches which might have housed the appropriate records had been on the flight path of German bombers making their way home and were destroyed when the planes dumped what cargo they had remaining. The two young people were evidently fairly respectable, since they arrived with a few sticks of furniture and some silver, probably wedding presents, and some letters of introduction. James also had a muzzle-loading shotgun, complete with powder horn, which is still in the family. His name, 'James', is engraved at the base of both barrels, but there are no markings or serial numbers to indicate a manufacturer. This would suggest a close association with the shooting world, but whether as gamekeeper or poacher is unclear. There has been speculation in the family that James may have been illegitimate, and, with limited expectations in England, had decided to try his luck in Australia. Another vestige of oral history has him quitting his farm in Essex because he'd become enraged with the local hunt, who routinely trampled his crops and ruined his hedges. Whatever it was, he put it behind him in Australia and landed a job as an under-manager for a man named William Bradley, a squatter who had grazing rights over a huge tract of Crown Land in the Monaro. Bradley was a well-liked employer, who often gave to the young men who worked for him small parcels of stock – sheep and cattle – which they were encouraged to cultivate on their own behalf. James worked for him for twelve years, raising a family of four sons and three daughters, and acquiring an intimate knowledge of the differences between grazing sheep in Australia and tilling English soil.

In 1861, to encourage small farming, the Robertson Land Act was introduced, which took land back from the squatters to make settlements of between 40 and 320 acres. The would-be farmer could choose his plot, and provided he built a house on it, in which he was required to sleep, the land was his for the asking. The figure of some 300 acres had been decided by civil servants in London, and was appropriate for English conditions. In Australia, where a single sheep needed at least an acre of land to feed itself, it was usually quite inadequate, and many settlers came to grief. Not so James Litchfield. He had noticed that whenever Bradley's sheep and cattle strayed, they always made their way over however many miles to the same spot. This was a place where water could be depended on, and it was here he made his selection. He built his house on the extreme corner of his rectangle of land, so that the bedrooms of his sons overlapped three adjoining plots. The family holding, which he had called Springwell, had now increased to over 1200 acres, and it prospered. Other farmers, who had chosen their land because of the view or because that year the grass happened to be green, were wiped out by the first drought, and every week at the land sales in Cooma their plots came up for auction. James was often in attendance. The patches of land that he began to acquire slowly converged into a gigantic quilt thrown over the bare rolling hills of the Monaro. Eventually he had accumulated a property of 80,000 acres. This he divided between his four grown sons, who then built houses of their own.

These, and other properties like them, were rambling late-Victorian affairs with touchingly inappropriate English names like Woodstock, or indeed Hazeldean, and they had many features in common. From a distance you would see not the house, but the perimeter of big pine trees planted to give shade and protection from the wind, rearing up like an oasis in a huge expanse of land and sky. Drawing nearer, you would approach the house up an avenue of more pine trees until suddenly there in front of you was an English garden, with hedges, lawns, European trees and neat beds of such things as snapdragons and hollyhocks. Plentiful bore water, dredged up by a windmill, kept the garden as unnaturally verdant as a Kent summer lasting all year long, and in all directions stretching away for miles and miles from this lush oddity was the straw-coloured country. You felt these gardens could be easily picked off by some giant fingernail of neglect or misfortune. Rural Australia's unpredictable rhythms, a good year or two followed by five or six of vindictive drought, meant that even the most successful grazier never took anything for granted, though the Monaro was gentler to these white intruders than other parts of the continent. These properties were largely self-sufficient, with vegetable gardens and fruit trees, and a dairy where cream was separated and butter made. Once a week a sheep was slaughtered to provide meat for the house and for the station-hands who lived with their families in nearby cottages. First the carcass would be hung in a big, shaded, open-air meat safe, proof against the ubiquitous flies, then cut into joints and chops and distributed. For recreation there would often be a tennis court, and in the evening a billiard room for the men and a grand piano for the women.

The Litchfield sons prospered, though one, later in life, became chronically depressed and retired from the land, and another had a scandalous relationship with his housekeeper and fled to Queensland. By and large, however, the family went forth and multiplied, and now after five generations there are between three and four hundred Litchfield descendants scattered across Eastern Australia. A few of us have made our way back to England. In the Cooma district telephone book there are some thirty Litchfields, as well as the names of the various husbands Litchfield women have married. What is true of all extended families, though it is more often obscured by geographical distance or the temporality of city life, is here laid out like some inscription across the landscape; a history of the endless, arbitrary ways people can advance themselves, or just get by, or become unravelled. In the early 1900s the first Hazeldean house burnt to the ground, so with wool booming my grandfather decided to have another built while he took off for Europe on the Grand Tour. The architectural plans describe it as 'Hazeldean Cottage', another nostalgic glance over the shoulder to England, but few cottages have seven or eight bed-rooms, servants' quarters, an office and a billiard room as this one did. On his overseas travels he acquired fancy elements for the new house, and shipped them back to his Australian builder. They included a terracotta roof from Italy, decorative tiles for the hall between the drawing room and the dining room, and stained glass for the veranda. This was the house where I lived with my cousins for the best part of 1934.

All houses have smells, which often vanish when they are altered or redecorated only to make a mysterious return some years later. This was the case with Hazeldean. By the mid-thirties, when the taste had turned against Victorian decoration, my uncle asked the architect, Leslie Wilkinson, to remodel the house for him along simpler lines. His solution was audacious. He simply clawed out the veranda and a couple of rooms from the middle of the house, so that it now had windows onto a three-sided courtyard. This was shaded by a vine-covered pergola and led down steps to the garden. The entire house was then given a wash of a muted apricot colour and became a Medi-terranean villa. Nevertheless, when I stepped through the front door into the foreshortened remains of the long dark corridor which had once run the length of the building, it was the old house that I smelt. The past in its unending detail had been waiting there to ambush me, and I was overwhelmed by it.

The life we had once led within these walls had been modelled, a little optimistically, on that of the English country house, with the hierarchical distinctions somewhat roughed up. There were servants about the place. The maids were young girls from Cooma, who woke you in the morning with a cup of tea and very thin slices of buttered bread sprinkled with sugar. There was a man and wife, the woman to cook and her husband to assume with only partial success the role of butler. Other people, the wife of a stockman perhaps, pottered about the house, cleaning, laying fires and talking a lot. The social lubricant between employers and employees, as between family members, was often humour, and in the early days on the land developing a sense of it was a practical necessity. The country was so yawningly empty, and there were too few people to start rubbing any of them up the wrong way. At Hazeldean there was a stockman, Tom Snowden, who had worked on the property all his life, and who in old age made himself useful doing odd jobs in the garden or around the house. He'd developed a very funny line in sly impudence, and enjoyed being the subject of Tom Snowden stories. He'd also developed a habit of sneaking into the office and pinching cigarettes from the silver cigarette box on top of the roll-top desk. My uncle's solution to this problem was one the ingenuity of which Tom himself would have grudgingly conceded. He wrote a note, put it on top of the cigarettes in the box and closed the lid. Anyone lifting the lid would have read 'TOM, YOU'RE FIRED'. Thereafter the cigarettes stopped disappearing, though Tom found other ways to embellish on his cheek.

With people they didn't know well, the Litchfields, particularly the Hazeldean side, were extremely reserved and quietly spoken. Among themselves, however, they never stopped laughing. The stern expressions would crack open, and there would be rows of teeth on display, in those days a bit yellowed by tobacco and an aversion to dentistry. They went sniffing like hounds after something to laugh at, and found it mainly among themselves. There was, for instance, my Great Aunt May at Springwell, who subscribed to the London society magazines, and had hundreds of copies of *The Tatler* and *The Bystander* stacked and tabulated under the billiard-room table. She spoke of the Births, Deaths and Marriages of English titled families as if they were living at a property ten miles over the next hill. She would say something like, 'I see the Duke of Rutland's younger son is engaged to be married to that charming Cavendish girl,' and the men would look up and nod absently before returning to their speculations about the prices they could expect to get at the forthcoming ram sale. Or there was Uncle Rowley, one of her sons and something of a black sheep, who turned up at her funeral drunk, having left for the city and gone into the film business. In the thirties he was still attempting the country life, and concurrently a love affair with a nightclub singer in Sydney. The telephone costs were enormous, so Rowley, when booking calls through the Cooma operator, passed himself off as his cousin Jim, and had his bills diverted to Hazeldean. On one occasion he took the sleeper to Sydney to visit his lady-love, and at one of the longer stops on the journey left the train at midnight to make a call from the station waiting room. So fervent were the exchanges of endearments that he didn't notice the train pulling away, and was left to rage on the platform with no belongings beyond the pyjamas he was wearing. Beneath these anecdotes, of course, other realities were always shifting – hints of breakdown or private nibbles of despair. But the stories served their purpose, which was firstly to make the most of company, and then, a subtler purpose, through laughter to provide a way of truth-telling which would neutralise resentments and aggressive impulses before they could make real trouble.

This laughter, as robust as appetite, was not something you'd normally expect to hear in a country house in England, though I've often heard something very like it at a table of theatre people eating together after a performance. It was only one of a number of such differences. The owners of Australian properties had a much more hands-on approach to the work involved, and at the end of the day would return to the house as dusty and spent as the men they employed. They had the same brown cheeks and white foreheads from wearing a hat all day under the unremitting sun, and the same heavy hands with the odd blackened nail or healing scar. They certainly had better grammar, but both spoke in cadences unmistakably Australian, even if there was never to be any doubt who was boss. After a long, hot bath these graziers would, as like as not, dress for dinner, the men in black tie, the women in long dresses, and afterwards play cards or read. There were many books on the shelves, and hot titles arrived regularly from Sydney. One I recall seeing at Hazeldean in the thirties was Spengler's *Decline of the West*, which stuck in my mind because it sounded so ominous and exciting.

Charmian, who had heard the car approaching from a distance, and had been waiting at the door to greet us, was now showing me to the same big room I had once shared with my cousins, since then improved by French doors leading out onto Professor Wilkinson's patio. In the late afternoon I took myself for a walk. There were a few changes in the garden; formal beds had given way to more lawn, and the big pines and elms were even more of a presence. The house standing in its green surround had a more comfortable look, as if the landscape had at long last conceded its right to be there. I had had some indelible childhood memories of this place, but I was still taken aback and disturbed by its power over me. With adult eyes I could also see that objectively it was extremely beautiful: the house on its slight rise looking towards the bare, distant hills streaked yellow by the last of the sun. Dawn and dusk are the times when Australia escapes the monotony of the glaring hours in between, and becomes a country of subtle and magical shifts. On a patch of land near the drive, densely overgrown with elm suckers, the Monaro magpies had commenced their warbling, an intensely musical though random sound unique to this species, like something improvised by a crazed xylophonist. As children the beginning and end of our days had been marked by their song. In the front paddock a flock of galahs was feeding in the grass, and as I approached rose as one like a flying carpet, revealing first the grey of back feathers then, as the carpet banked, the sunset pink of breast. Was it any wonder there had never been any space in my head for English birds? They had been pre-empted by feathered creatures four times their size that screeched, gargled and rattled like castanets, and in the case of the kookaburra made a sound like a skeleton laughing. Similarly, it was blossoms dry as parchment, the flannel flower, the paper daisy and the bottle brush, that had most engaged my young mind.

I continued on my way, past the wood pile and the yapping welcome of the sheepdogs tethered to their kennels, and on to the wool shed standing against the sky like a corrugated iron church. Here the sheep were shorn, so it was indeed a place where thanksgiving was in order. Each year the shearers would arrive like a band of gypsies and for a week the big shed would hum with noise and enormous effort. The wool-presser, who was part Chinese, had a sister who worked in a Cadbury's factory, and he always came bearing huge boxes of chocolates for all the children on the property. Then, as suddenly, it was over; the shearers and the wool-classer in his white coat were gone, and in the still, empty space of the shed, pungent with the smell of wool, all that moved was the dust in the shafts of sunlight coming down from the high windows above. I was now at the foot of Hazeldean Hill, rising up to one side of the house, and I decided to make the ascent up the irregular steps provided by stones and coarse tussocks of grass. From the top the layout of Hazeldean with its garden, outbuildings and surrounding trees looked as precise as an island seen from the air. You could turn a full 360 degrees, from the Snowy Mountains in the far distance still capped with the last of the winter snows to the swell of hills opposite, rolling through mists to the faraway coast, then round again to the mountains, and not see another building. They were probably there somewhere, but lost in the fold of a hill or behind a grove of trees.

As children we had climbed to this spot many times. In fact there wasn't a square yard of land within walking distance of the house with which I didn't feel acquainted. Like cattle in a field who will begin the morning in one corner then during the course of the day shift ground until they have utilised all the possibilities of their space, the three of us trailed all over the property until so many paths had criss-crossed that we had woven in our minds a tapestry in which there wasn't a stone or a tree trunk unaccounted for. This made for another difference between us and those glossy sepia children photographed with their mothers in the pages of *Country Life* and *The Bystander*. We might have passed for the privileged English young our parents hoped they were rearing after our baths in the evening, or when we were being prepared for some special event, and Ann wore a dress with smocking and James and I took care to part our hair on one side and brush it across the head, never back (the 'brushback' was for larrikins). We were also in character on wet afternoons when we would be allowed into the drawing room, given a chocolate and told to play cards or look at a book. Or when our governess, Miss Graves, a sweet young woman, whom we called first 'Gravey' then 'Dot' after her many readings of our favourite bedtime story *Dot and the Kangaroo*, taught us how to write spidery letters to our parents faraway overseas.

The time when we were truly ourselves, however, and it was most of the time, was when we were running wild. The outdoors was a constant invitation. There were blue-tongued lizards a foot long to be found under big stones, which we would roll over, leaping clear with a squeal in case we had disturbed a poisonous snake. There were feral cats to hunt and kill with our fox terrier, Peter, and bright-green frogs in the garden pond to plug with James's air gun. During the day we never wore shoes, and our soles became so thick and tough that one evening we found a needle and thread and scandalised the cook by going into her parlour off the kitchen and sewing patterns across the bottoms of our feet. It was almost as if we had heard a spectral whisper from those aboriginal children that had preceded us, and who had been driven from this part of the country so long ago they weren't even remembered. Like all small children left to themselves, we had lively excremental lives. Away from the house we would pee together, James and I crossing swords with our streams, whilst Ann crouched with her knickers around her knees feeling somewhat disadvantaged. Or we would all squat in a circle, as focused as bridge players, as we strained to leave our mark on the terrain, jumping up afterwards to inspect our achievement before hunting for the right handful of grass with which to wipe ourselves.

We didn't differentiate between the beauty of what lay around us and its cruelty, and the special event of our week was the slaughter of the sheep. This took place on a wooden platform with a hoist above, surrounded by earth turned black with the blood of previous killings, and always at sundown after the flies had gone. We arrived early so as not to miss anything, and sat on the wood fence swinging our legs and waiting as the western sky behind us turned as red as the blood that would soon be spilt. Nearby was a cramped triangular pen in which four constrained sheep made small adjustments to each other, but without acknowledgement, like people in an overcrowded lift. I remember thinking how strange it was that of these living animals one – but which neither the sheep nor we knew – would soon be dead. Then the stockman arrived, made his choice, and we watched as the sheep with hopeless passivity yielded to the knife going through its fleecy throat as easily as through sponge cake. As the blood gushed and the kicking stopped we children would follow from one second to the next the enthralling enigma of death. There followed the lesser dramas of seeing the sheep skinned and gutted, when our thoughts would turn from the killing of the sheep to the prospect of eating it. We would keep a special eye out for the liver; if it was tunnelled with fluke there would be no lamb's fry for dinner that week.

We mixed with other children, to almost all of whom we were related, whenever there was something like a tennis party or a big picnic at one of the other properties, and it often involved long drives over primitive roads. Here we could resume conversations with cousins who had also been chasing cats and watching sheep killed, and go exploring a less familiar terrain. The long day came to an end, and we returned home, one car on an empty road through a night as black as space. Sometimes a ghostly wallaby would leap across our headlights, or a dead gum tree would rear up at a turning to remind us that though our own kind were few and scattered, we were not alone in that vastness. Christmas at Springwell was usually a large gathering of the family. We were joined by our second cousins, the Allens and the Wilkinsons, and in the evening eleven soiled and exhausted children took a bath together in the enormous Victorian tub. We were arranged as in a racing eight, with the oldest nearest the taps and the youngest cousin, little Johnny, barely two, at the far end. The cleansing proceeded in an orderly if noisy fashion until one of us noticed that we had been joined in the bath by a twelfth presence, one of little Johnny's turds. The squeals of indignation and glee could be heard all over the house as dripping children leapt from the tub pointing at the intruder, and leaving its perpetrator sitting there alone in the water, his face crumpling into a mask of bewilderment and grief. In the community of children no one could remember an event as outrageous and exhilarating, and we discussed it amongst ourselves for weeks. The tale had soon acquired mythic status, a seismic event never to be forgotten by someone who was actually there. Little Johnny is now a man in his seventies, but if I tell my cousin James that I'm going to visit him, he will as like as not say something to the effect, 'If he invites you to take a bath with him, don't accept.' And we will both laugh helplessly.

I climbed down Hazeldean Hill with this lost world swimming in my head and my gut in turmoil, and hurried to my room to hide my distress. In other circumstances I might have welcomed this rush from the past, but my illness turned it into a kind of judgement: one half of my life already over, and what lay ahead in jeopardy. My uncle knew the uncertain prognosis of the disease, and was a model of sympathetic tact, and yet it was impossible not to feel in some way admonished by this figure from my childhood; by this family of Jims and Jameses who alternated their names to distinguish the generations. They had made the very best of the life they had been offered, and they worked at something the value of which no one could dispute. Of all the Litchfields, my uncle had managed his inheritance with the most vision and prudence, diversifying into cattle as a hedge against wool, and like his grandfather discreetly accumulating new acres. Like most country people he was conservative, but with a small, unprejudiced 'c', an informed and thoughtful man, who had begun reflecting on Australia's racism and its relations with its near neighbours in South-East Asia long before many of his contemporaries even considered it an issue.

I stayed with them about a week, writing a little in the mornings, walking a little in the afternoons, willing myself to get better. The show was finishing in Melbourne, and I had told Robin that I would try to rejoin them at their next date, Newcastle, a big mining town north of Sydney. My uncle drove me to the airport. It occurred to me as we bumped down the road away from the house that, instead of once crossing the seas in a callow search for the English Gentleman, I need have looked no further than the man sitting beside me. With his unemphatic courtesy and plain good manners, his shotguns and fishing rods from St James's, his English tailor in Conduit Street, he had held to the code from a distance of 12,000 miles with rather more rigour than others I had met closer to what Australians once called 'home'. He was the last of a breed, and one that may have impeded Australia's growing sense of itself, but there were things to regret in its passing. He and my mother typified this Anglo-Australian world. They had been extremely close all their lives and had largely identical opinions. After her husband died she flew out every two years to stay at Hazeldean, and for six weeks you would hear a continuous murmur of conversation and laughter from this ageing brother and sister as they moved through the rooms of the house in which they'd grown up. And in one respect they were both unmistakably Australian – their attachment, keenly felt but rarely expressed, to a stretch of hilly country that resembled nothing but itself.

As soon as I'd made-up, dressed and gone down to the stage I knew I'd come back too soon. By the curtain my nausea had returned, with it, the ominous dissolving sensation in my lower gut. I had no choice but to tell Robin that I had just given my last performance in the show. Next day I caught the train back to Sydney feeling the sickest I had ever felt. I still had the key to the Edgecliff flat, and getting there and through the front door used up the last of my strength. Not caring if I never got up, I crawled into bed. I had lain in the empty flat perhaps an hour, as mute and helpless as a sick animal, when I heard the sound of a lock turning and a door opening. It was Googie Edwards, the friend of my mother who had allowed me the use of this apartment. She now lived in Dural, just outside Sydney, but had happened to be in town for the day and, thinking I was in Newcastle, had dropped in to collect a suitcase. Once again, and by chance, my childhood had come to my rescue. I was soon bundled into her car and on my way to a large comfortable bed in her sunny spare room at Dural. She was a woman I had known all my life, and with whom I was completely at ease. Nevertheless there were things I couldn't discuss with her. All my thoughts were now on Greece, and the person who would be waiting for me there. Like my uncle, she had met Shirley and liked her, so keeping my betrayal to myself seemed the least I could do. Googie never asked the questions which were hanging in the air, though if she'd done so I doubt if I would have been able to answer them. Guilt and deep confusion about the choices ahead of me had me tongue-tied. In addition to all the practical things she was doing for me, this discretion on her part was an expression of love, and after some days I felt the tide of my well-being once again begin to turn.

In a week's time I would be leaving Australia, but I had one more appointment to keep with my past. My father and his wife Joan were about to spend a long weekend at Bawley Point, a beach about 200 miles south of Sydney, and they asked me if I would like to join them. It was impossible to say no. I had had two Edens in my childhood, and this had been the other one. Bawley Point itself was a bare stony peninsula that extended into the Pacific like a huge finger pointing to whatever lay beyond and out of sight. On either side of it were necklaces of deserted beaches, each suspended from headlands or cliffs, and with bush growing right down to the sand. This stretch of coast was Crown Land and couldn't be built on, but somehow two houses had gone up at Bawley Beach when no one was looking. One was a small privately owned cottage and opposite, across a dirt road, a country boarding house, a typical one-storey structure with a corrugated-iron roof and a veranda running around the outside. It was extremely primitive; the water supply came from tanks which collected rain from the roof, there was no electricity, and the sanitary arrangements consisted of a seat and a bucket housed in a small shed to one side of the veranda. None of this mattered much to guests, who spent most of the day in and around the ocean.

This boarding house had become the secret of a group of friends, mainly professional people, who would book the entire place for the two or three summer weeks over Christmas. They were mainly doctors and all keen fishermen. There was my father, an anaesthetist and his wife, Harry and Jean Daley, and a prosperous radiologist with one of those fancy names you often found among upper-middle-class Australians born around the turn of the century, Bouverie Anderson Stewart. He had a brand new Cadillac imported from America, a rarity at the time, a wife and two children about the age of my cousins, Peter and Primrose. Others included a lawyer, an academic and, for a short stay on his way to somewhere else, the chairman of a bank. My parents were divorced by the late thirties, and the first time I went to Bawley Point was because my mother was again in England. In lieu of alimony my father had given her a trip overseas. When she returned they remained on self-consciously good terms, and in the school holidays I was passed back and forth between them. I quite liked my new stepmother, and soon accepted that this was where I would now be spending my Christmases. Hazeldean had given me my strongest sense of family; Bawley was to show me what the word community meant. By now, and if allowed to be, I was a talkative and precocious child, and something of a performer, qualities about which my father would normally have been suspicious. However, at Bawley there was equality between the generations, and the children of the house were there not to be brought up correctly but to be enjoyed. Peter and Primrose called the adults by their first names, something I was not allowed to do, though I no longer had to jump to my feet and call the men 'sir'. In the evenings we would gather on the veranda for drinks, Schweppes' lime juice for us, the same for the adults but with gin added, and I would entertain the gathering with conjuring tricks, at which I was becoming surprisingly accomplished. Nothing pleased me more than persuading some patient grown-up to watch a new trick, and seeing their expression change from suppressed yawning to real astonishment.

My father was seeing me through the eyes of his friends, and raised no objections to what he saw. It was a good time for him. He was becoming one of Sydney's leading eye surgeons, and was enjoying the best early years of his second marriage. It also became a good time for me, because for the first time in my life I began to feel some affection for him. When I was small he had not been a particularly harsh parent; half a dozen times I had been spanked, and I had been repeatedly corrected at an age when it had been pointless to do so. What frightened me, even in the earliest years, were his ideas. More than his spanks it was his *belief* in spanking that disturbed me, like his belief in discipline, in the pre-eminence of sport in a boy's life, in the military virtues. I felt I was being marshalled to fulfil an ideal for which I was ill-equipped and, more to the point, had absolutely no inclination. Throughout my childhood a shadowy but constant presence was the memory of the First World War. It was there on school boards honouring the Fallen and in war memorials dispersed throughout the city and in every country town. Most of all it was there in the minds of the men who fought it, and on Anzac Day, when we were released from school to see the parade, the collective experience gathered over the centre of the city like oppressive weather. From lunchtime on, the streets would be crowded with drunk, dull-eyed men, still wearing their medals across their civilian suits from the march that morning, who seemed to have been marked by an experience so grim and particular that it excluded anyone who had not shared it.

The Australian Imperial Forces had been an army entirely of volunteers, and in my father's circle not to have joined up was an omission that those who did would remember for the rest of their lives – men like Dr Hill, for instance, who had lost a leg in France fighting for Britain and the Empire. I had once joined the Hill children in the stern of a dinghy as their father tried to row us across Wamberall Lake. He was wearing shorts, and his stump kicked back and forth in the air as he fought with little success to balance himself correctly on the oars. We watched in helpless silence as his bitterness grew and he no longer bothered to disguise it. To my father the Great War was some huge, terrible game, which the human race had always been obliged to play, and which would recur every generation or so to test the mettle of its young men. That's why dangerous, competitive sports were so important. They prepared you. Even at the age of six I wanted out. Later, in adolescence, it was his ideas that continued to divide us. As a companion he could be urbane and amusing, but what was I to make of his insistence on the superiority of the Northern European peoples, of science over the arts, or of his belief in authoritarian government and in eugenics.

Fortunately, at Bawley Point the pleasure of the sea was our only ideology. My father stopped shaving and spent most of the day in his fishing gear. This included a dilapidated trilby hat and an old blazer made for him in London in the twenties, which, though ragged and full of holes and with its pockets stuffed with tackle, was still quite dashing. Among Australian men he had a certain elegance, and something else of which I was aware but would only identify later – an attractiveness to women. I was often with him all day long, setting off first thing in the morning on one of our long expeditions along the coast, him carrying his rod and smelly canvas bag, packed with subtle and mysterious hooks and lures and disgusting fragments of bait, me trotting along beside him while I maintained an uninterrupted stream of bright chatter. 'No questions before eleven o'clock, remember?' he would say, and I, enjoying the tease, would hold my tongue for about ten seconds. He fished from the beaches but more often from the adjacent rocks, where great washes of spray from the breaking swell would reach up like hands grabbing at us. While he stood for hours, one leg crossed over the other, attached to that limitless moving ocean by one taut thread, I would explore the varieties of life in the rock pools, waiting there in those undisturbed depths as still as the pebbles at the bottom. Then without warning the surface of the pool would be broken by the propulsion of an octopus, and a crab which had been

357

sunning itself just above the level of the water was no longer there. It was like the slash of a concealed razor. Now it was over, the pond was still again, and the wait had resumed. The whole coast was like that, as far as the eye could see: a beautiful, agonised waiting. The childish longing I had often felt at Hazeldean I felt here – a pride in this Australian wilderness but with it a need to somehow render it, to give it meaning the way other parts of the world had meaning, the Wild West or Darkest Africa. Crouched on a slab of rock I would score it with scraps of song, or try to imagine stories that would help furnish its majestic vacancy.

In the middle of the day we lunched off whatever my father had caught, a blackfish or a bream; it depended on what was biting. He gutted and scaled the fish, and we collected driftwood to make a fire, which he had the knack of igniting even in falling rain. That afternoon we would return the way we had come, leaving a second set of footprints, a large and a small, along a beach which was otherwise empty of any sign of human presence. In the early evening we would all gather on the veranda and, as darkness approached, light the feeble oil lamps, until the bush night with all its sounds had wreathed like smoke along the corridors and into all the rooms and sent us off to bed. I would lie beneath a mosquito net, hearing the distant grumbling of the surf, and when I closed my eyes would see as vividly as if they were projected on a screen those same lines of breaking waves that had absorbed me all day.

Bawley Point was not without its special events. There was the night when we went shark fishing and in pitch darkness hooked a big grey nurse off the point, the reel whining as the shark ran with the hook. After half an hour of give and take the huge creature was coaxed towards the beach and landed in the shallows. In the light of a torch beam, fourteen feet of shark writhed against the sand, as the wash of the surf came and went around it, and the children were cautioned to stand well clear of its ferocious rows of teeth and whipping tail. One year at dusk a small bush fire approached the boarding house, and we were all sent out with buckets of water and wet sacks to beat it back. At the foot of a burnt tree I saw red beading along a length of bark and embers glowing in the grey ash as brilliant as neon. Some of our greatest excitements were to do with food. On one of the nearby beaches there were small clams, which we called pippies, and which you located at the waterline by twisting your foot in the wet sand.

On one day of the holiday all the guests at the boarding house set off to collect a sackful, from which we made an enormous pot of pippy soup. We ate so much we would be satiated until the next feast twelve months hence.

By my third visit, Christmas at Bawley Point had become the highlight of my year, and I decided to give my father a present which would symbolise my changed relationship with him. What I had in mind was something I had seen at the local stationers in Sydney, a long tapering fountain pen, which, like a quill in an inkpot, sat upright in a stand set in a little block of marble. When I went with my pocket money to purchase it I found it had temporarily sold out. My mother agreed to buy a replacement for me when one arrived and post it on to me. Christmas Day was approaching and the pen had still not appeared. I went to my father and asked if I could make a long-distance call to my mother. He wanted to know why, so I let the matter drop and decided to wait another couple of days. Still the pen had not arrived. I went to my father again and requested the call. This time he was irritated and insisted on an explanation. I knew, of course, what he was thinking: I'd gone soft and was missing my mother. I repeated my request with that stubborn dullness behind which children often disguise their secrets, and he got quite angry. I was mortified to be so misunderstood, and also to see the re-emergence of the father I did not like. I ran from the room, and kept running until I'd found a big blackberry bush behind which I could hide and give way to the baffled, choking sobs that racked me for the next twenty minutes.

The car journey that always began these holidays at Bawley takes you from Sydney, down the Bulli Pass and along the coastal road, a splendid drive with the ocean appearing intermittently on one side, and on the other green dairy country rising up towards the mountains. I would sit on the broad front seat between my father and Sybil, and look down on three pairs of knees in shorts, two very large ones and mine in the middle, as skinny and pointed as two white pencils. This stretch of road was at the centre of my universe. Now, some twenty-five years later, I was travelling it again, but sitting in the back, this time with Joan and my father in front, and thinking about it in a very different way. A huge map of the world had come into my mind. Down towards the bottom and off to one side, and about as far away from Europe and America as it was possible to be, was Australia. On its eastern seaboard there was a section of road along which the car

I was in was moving, but so minuscule was it, so fractional its journey, it might as well not have been there at all. What a strange, arbitrary thing it was, I thought, to be an Australian; to have been born and grown up in this place. There had been as many reasons for coming here in the first instance as the people who came, but most of these reasons had one thing in common: discontent. Either the discontent that had driven them from their own countries, or the discontent with what they found waiting for them when they arrived. I began wondering if these migrations to the New World didn't represent a kind of natural selection of the restless. Were the genes that had brought my forebears here operating in me only the other way round – sending me back to what they had once abandoned?

The first Blakemore to arrive in Australia was a sea captain, William. He was born in Leicester, and had lost his mother when he was young. His father married again to a woman the boy came to detest, and in desperation he ran away to sea. Eventually he became Master of his own ship, and traded among the Spice Islands of the Far East. On a trip to Sydney he met a Miss Riley, a young Protestant woman from Ulster, who agreed to marry him but only on the condition that he gave up the sea. The new husband found a position with a mining company, working long hours by day, and in the evenings studied for a degree in engineering. With a family to raise, these were difficult years, but eventually he prospered, and his eldest son, George, my grandfather, grew up to become a mining engineer himself. As a young man George went to work at Broken Hill in the outback of New South Wales. This huge concern was being run by an American, John Howell, for whom the Board had headhunted overseas. He had brought with him his wife, Elizabeth, née Adams, whose great-grandfather had been the American President, John Quincy Adams, and their daughter, Dura Maud. At Broken Hill the young mining engineer wooed and won the well-connected young woman. They married and had the first of their three sons, my father, Conrad.

George Blakemore's career flourished, and before long his work was taking him all over the world. My father was removed from the King's School (which I would one day hate but which he loved) and sent to board first at an American military academy then later at a school in Switzerland, but he didn't think much of either. Eventually the family returned to Sydney, and bought a house in the western suburb of Strathfield, which at the time was considered a desirable area, not because of its proximity to the water but because it was a polite remove from it. It was a one-storey turn-of-the-century building, with closed-in veranda and the usual sprigs of decorative cast iron, and it was here when they were in their sixties and seventies that I came to know my grandparents. The house was much larger than it looked from the front because of the layout, which resembled a London mansion flat, a very long dark corridor with rooms going off on either side. There were two reasons why I looked forward to my visits. The first was that I was devoted to my American grandmother, and the second was all the rooms in the house and the amazing things they contained. In the drawing room, heavily shaded as if we were in the tropics, with its slowly rotating overhead fan and heavy Edwardian furniture, was the clutter of objects my grandparents had collected on their travels. There were oil paintings from Italy in which all the colours and even the gilt frames seemed to be drifting towards a tobacco brown. There was a chaste nude in white marble on a stand by the sofa, and in the corner a glassed-in cabinet displaying ornate, spindly pieces of china and a small mosaic picture of St Petersburg which they had picked up on their way through Russia on the Trans-Siberian Railway.

The things which were specifically my grandfather's told very different stories from those which were my grandmother's. In the dining room over the sideboard were two enormous bas-reliefs, a round and an oval, executed in solid silver and framed in red velvet. They were as crowded with incident as a pair of Florentine doors, and at the centre of one of them St George in armour slew a writhing dragon. What they actually celebrated was the quelling of two miners' strikes, in which apparently my grandfather had played a key role. They were gifts of appreciation from the silver-mining concern he had worked for, so it was no surprise that they presented a possibly one-sided view of the dispute. The harshness of industrial relations in the early 1900s was also suggested by the swordstick that was kept in a cupboard in his bedroom. As he walked the streets of the mining towns during times of unrest he had always carried it with him to see off assailants. If such a one approached and, thinking the swordstick to be a mere cane, seized it, George, with a twist of the wrist, would unlock the mechanism and withdraw three feet of Toledo steel. These were unforgiving times, and given the conditions under which the miners were expected to work, not surprisingly so. On one occasion, so my grandmother told me, a scab worker was cornered by a mob of miners' wives. They withdrew the long hatpins which fastened their hats to their buns of hair, and spiked the man to death. As a boy of about ten, I can remember my grandfather lecturing me, 'Michael, you either work, work, work until you've made something decent of yourself, or you spend your life digging up the streets with a pick and shovel. Make up your mind. There's nothing in between.' One of the pleasant surprises of my life has been discovering that there is. My grandfather prided himself on his iron self-control. At one time the house was odorous with dozens of scented boxes of Havana cigars, which were his particular indulgence. One day the doctor advised him that his health was in danger. 'I stopped that very day,' he again lectured me, 'not the following day, or the day after, or the day after that. No cigars from that moment on. There's no other way to do it!' The smell of sandalwood vanished from the house.

When we arrived for our Sunday afternoon visits, my grandfather was often behind the closed door of his reading room. This was a square space with bookshelves and cupboards on all four sides, and at its dead centre a big upright armchair with a moving arm to support an open book. Immediately above was an electric light. The only other rooms I knew that had a single armchair right in the middle and unsubtle lighting were the dentist's and the executioner's, so it had an ominous feel to it, particularly since, unless the bulb was lit, it was permanently in the dark. There was a window, but my grandfather had built himself a workroom only a foot away, which obscured even a hint of natural light. Seated in his reading chair for hours on end he pursued his quest to determine who was the greater military comman-der, Wellington or Napoleon. On his shelves he had the standard works on the Peninsular War by Oman and Napier, which he would read and re-read, leaving the margins of the pages heavily annotated in pencil with many underlinings and exclamation marks.

The highlight of these Sunday visits was my grandmother's after-noon tea, or rather, in the American manner, afternoon coffee. This was always freshly ground, then mixed with an entire egg before being brought slowly to the boil. The resulting liquid had the clarity of coloured glass, and when served with cream was uniquely delicious. At four o'clock sharp my grandmother's maid, Beth, a jolly woman with her hair in a bun and still dressed in the style of 1910, would wheel a trolley into the drawing room, rattling with ornate china and superfluous bits and pieces of silver like sugar tongs. On board would be neat chicken mayonnaise sandwiches, at a time when both chicken and homemade mayonnaise were considered delicacies, and a big sponge cake. Now came the moment for my grandfather's entrance. He would walk into the room removing his pince-nez with a somewhat distracted air, dressed as usual in a tie and starched white collar with rounded points, waistcoat with fob watch and a loose jacket of grey alpaca, and take his customary seat. He did not so much converse as insert from time to time a very long and emphatic paragraph into the conversation before once again retreating from it and leaving the women to peck about amongst life's trivia. Yet he wasn't a frightening man. You sensed that most of his battles were with himself. Or someone like Napoleon.

Towards the end of his life he occupied himself by prospecting for gold in the Far East, visiting the places that had once been his father's ports of call, in Sumatra, Java, Bali and Malaya. He would return from these undertakings with stories of twenty-course dinners with wily Chinese businessmen, and presents of silk batik and beautifully carved wooden busts of bare-breasted girls with flowered headdresses. I have one of these, but of a young man with elaborate turban and polished shoulders. He frequently came back much richer. But he was uninterested in money, and everything he made in one venture he would gamble on the next. My father told me he had made and lost three fortunes capitalising gold mines, but to the family's regret the final swing of the pendulum was in the wrong direction.

After he died, my grandmother, to keep a teenaged boy amused, allowed me the run of his private domain. The big workroom was piled high with interesting junk – rows of glass jars containing mineral specimens or semi-precious stones, discarded equipment like the crystal wireless set, battered photographic gear and mysterious tripods and brass gadgets to do with his engineering. To compensate for a penny-pinching youth, small articles which most people would buy one at a time, he bought by the gross, and in one drawer of his rolltop desk you would find box after box of new pencils, in another a hundred rubber erasers and in others nothing but pipe cleaners or elastic bands. What interested me most were his stacks of old magazines. Throughout my growing up I drew and sketched obsessively, and now in copies of the radical Australian weekly *The Bulletin*, going back forty years, I found political cartoons by the famous pen-and-ink artist, Phil May. In one entitled 'The Widow's Mite' the elderly

Queen Victoria was ridiculed for her meanness, and in another an octopus with the head of a Chinese coolie warned the workers of Australia against the encroaching Yellow Peril. Even more lurid were the wash drawings of the First World War French cartoonist, Louis Raemaker, which I found in another pile. These showed Germany as a kind of King Kong figure wearing a spiked helmet and dragging by her hair the pale, ravished virgin of Belgium. In another the Kaiser and his feeble son, Prince Willi, conspired together like vampires. The venom of this dusty propaganda was as startling as finding a hoard of rat poison in one of the drawers of the roll-top desk. However, an even greater excitement awaited me in the reading room. At the rear of a cupboard and somewhat concealed behind some volumes of history, I came across a limited edition of some erotic etchings by Norman Lindsay. I had never seen anything like them, and had just reached the age to be overwhelmed by such images. For the first time my grandmother and I had become separated by a throbbing secret, though, from her point of view, not such a secret, because the next time I looked for the volume it was no longer there.

Judgemental my grandfather may occasionally have been, but my grandmother was the spirit of mercy itself. She was the foremost of those women who mediated between the life I had when I was young and the life I dreamt about. Proud of her Adams connection, she made me aware that, at whatever dilution, the blood of two American Presidents flowed through my veins, but her stories of her family – how one had been a diplomat, another a writer or a foreign correspondent – were told less to feed my self-importance than to remind me how wide the world was, and how full of possibilities. Her Americanness intrigued me, though it was unlike any America I had ever seen at the movies. She seemed to have no accent, though she spoke with a certain lilt that was neither English nor Australian. She was rather formal, and the last generation of women who, as they grew older, continued to dress in the style of their prime, and let fashion pass them by. In her case this meant ankle-length dresses in very fine dark materials, worn with loops of beads down to her waist made of such things as amber and cut agate. She wore very pointed delicate shoes that fastened across the front with one leather button. Her bedroom, which was big enough to have her own sitting area in the bay window, was full of gadgets made of silver and tortoiseshell, with which she buttoned her shoes or heated her curling tongs before arranging her long gold-grey tresses elaborately on top of her head. Her taste had a certain prettiness that I never thought of as being American until I paid my first visit to the East Coast, and Jack Salamanca took me on a visit to the Capitol Building in Washington. Its monumentality was familiar to me from photographs and films, but not its ornamental and rather delicate architectural detail. It was like looking at my grandmother's silver.

For a ten-year-old boy the most exciting of her things were the Red Indian artefacts she had brought with her to Australia: beaded moccasins, a pouch of soft doeskin and a pair of snowshoes. As a child during a Massachusetts winter she had seen a line of Indians trudging through the snow wearing just such shoes as these. However, the prize possession was the one you could just see through the open drawing-room door hanging halfway down the hall. This was a big oil painting executed on a rough triangle of deerskin of Chief Sitting Bull in full war regalia, which she had acquired on a visit to a reservation. She knew how much I coveted these relics of the Wild West, and all of them finished up decorating the walls of my bedroom in Ocean Street. What separated my grandmother from all my other relatives was her concern with the sort of person I actually was and what I should be doing with my life. Thus, at the age of fourteen, when I had been bowled over by James Cagney prancing through *Yankee Doodle Dandy* and the vivid picture the movie gave of backstage life, it was my grandmother who one afternoon put on one of her black Robin Hood-shaped hats, fastened it firmly in place with a hat pin, and set off to the cinema to buy a single ticket, and see for herself what all the fuss was about. When I left for England it was the present of her own *Complete Works of Shakespeare*, printed on rice paper and bound in red Moroccan leather in three small volumes, *Comedies*, *Histories* and *Tragedies*, that I took with me and used at drama school.

The week before the *Otranto* steamed out of Sydney Harbour my father rang to remind me of my obligation to go to Strathfield and pay her a last visit. It was a wasted call because this was something I would never have left undone. She came to the door, now frail and rather stooped, and did as she had done for as long as I could remember, took my face in both hands and gave me a prolonged and rather tense kiss, first on one cheek then the other. This was her one display of overt emotion, after which she reverted to her amiable, reserved Yankee self. I think she had always guessed that this moment of departure would one day come. When I was young it never occurred to me that she might have harboured some regrets about a life which had passed by so far from her birthplace, not that she ever gave so much as a hint that this might be the case. I've wondered since if she felt that her own story could only be brought to a proper completion through the lives of the grandchildren to whom she gave so much of the best sort of love.

There were changes at Bawley Point, but it was such a perfect spring day when we arrived that I was hardly aware of them. The dirt road which turned off the highway was the same, and so was the dry concrete weir which, as we drove across it, had always marked the end of the journey. It had been built above the lagoon to maintain the road in times of flood. As we caught our first sight of the ocean I noticed that there were some new bungalows set back a little from the beach, among them ones recently built by my father and the Daleys. Their construction was too rudimentary to be described as ugly, but as an alternative to the old boarding house, and notwithstanding electricity and plumbing, I couldn't help feeling they were a pointer in the wrong direction. One of the unique features of this beach had been an area of natural parkland, a large semicircle clear of scrub which stretched back from the ocean and which was dominated by a number of very tall, straight gum trees. They were evenly spaced, and from the boarding house you could look through them and beyond, as if they were the supports of some huge, shady veranda, to a dazzle of sand and the utter blue and white of the breaking ocean. This had been preserved, and after lunch on the second day I sat with my father in the garden of his new bungalow taking it in. As with Hazeldean, I had not misremembered it. By any measure this Australia of towering gums and shattered sunlight lying around the ground in pieces, and, all of it, horizon and soaring sky, held in the palm of a still, warm day, was spectacularly beautiful.

The conversation turned to my father's days at Sydney University studying medicine. He told me how one professor always took his new students to see the incurables in the Hydatids Ward, and he went on to review for me the lifecycle of the hydatids larva – how it reached the ground in the droppings of sheep, infected the water supply of unsuspecting country people, entered their bloodstream and lodged in the brain, where it developed the fatal cyst. Animals then ate the corpse, and the cycle went into its next round. The ward, it seemed, was the professor's crash course in life's realities. I listened to him as

I had all through my growing-up, in silence, nodding my head in feigned agreement as I struggled for ideas that might counter or at least qualify the argument. I rarely found them, and of course he was right, as far as it goes – but that 'as far as it goes' seemed too uncertain a thing for me to come to its defence. Even on this perfect day everything around us supported what he was saying – the bull ants a few yards from our feet dragging their ferocious stings sluggishly across their nest, the tiger sharks out there beneath those blue waters perpetually on the hunt, and the bush around us rustling with the most venomous wildlife on the planet. It had a compensating beauty, this world always in flux and predicated on death, but you needed to be very watchful as you passed through it. My father's answer to the hazards of life was straightforward. First of all you had to be tough-minded enough to see it for what it really was, and even take satisfaction in its mercilessness. Then you had to get a profession to hold it at arm's length, and to protect you from the pitfalls of your own foolishness. Of these professions the best was undoubtedly medicine, because it had truth written all over it. With these arguments, baited with humour and a paralysing scepticism, he had once gone fishing for me, but somehow I had wriggled off the hook and instead gone swimming after 'as far as it goes'. I didn't yet have much to show for it.

That evening we left our new box to have drinks with the Daleys, Harry and Jean, seventy-five yards down the road in their new box. Like all my father's contemporaries they were now grey and tamed, but they had always been a sympathetic couple, my favourite among his friends, and were less changed than some of the more aggressive and imposing figures I remembered coming to Bawley to fish. Their conversation turned on local matters and acquaintances they shared with my father, things about which I had little to contribute, and I sat there as silent as I had been that afternoon. Harry Daley made an effort to include me. 'But what do you *do* with yourself all the time in London, Mike?' he asked with genuine incredulity, as if life began and ended with trips to a seaside cottage. Had I liked him less I might have huffed with impatience and listed for him all the interesting ways corrupt old England had allowed me to divert myself. Instead I held my tongue and gave a self-deprecatory shrug, but my memory of the boarding house and the life there we had all lived was becoming tarnished by the moment.

That night the weather changed. Rain pelted down and turned the roof of our bungalow into a drum. In the morning and all that day there was a thin drizzle, which at first was not unpleasant because it evoked another memory, that of the fresh, arousing scent of dripping bush. My father was busy gardening. This was the purpose of his visit, to prepare the garden for the summer, and he and his under-gardener, Joan, gave me a wave as I set out for a walk with a broken umbrella. I knew that to the north of the boarding house the coast was still protected and exactly as I remembered it, a perfect wilderness of ocean and bush. To the south, however, the local authorities had yielded to the case for development, and cottages now split out along the point and the foreshore of the next beach along. I decided to take a look. Bawley Point was too barren and stony to have supported the growth of any trees, and it was this bareness that gave it its character. Now along its entire length it had been divided into rectangular plots on which people had been allowed to build just about whatever they wanted. There was no overall plan or architectural idea, just a succession of cheap, unrelated and occasionally eccentric dwellings. Without a tree in sight it was as if the point had been engulfed in gigantic litter. I walked on grimly, making for the far end of the point where I could look out to sea and at least have my back to this desecration. Because it was completely exposed, this was where the waves were always their biggest, and as children we had often come out here to scare ourselves with the power of the ocean. As long as I gazed seaward nothing had changed and it was as if no time had passed. The huge waves still approached in sets, one behind the other, cloaked and silent like the advance of some doomed offensive. They still reared up and hurled themselves at the point with thunderous despair. The difference now was that they had something to despair about.

The next day the rain was heavier. I had brought no gear for this sort of weather, and was running out of dry clothes. Ahead of me was the prospect of a day indoors. But what would I do with myself? There was a small set of bookshelves but it contained no books, only a dog-eared collection of maps, a road manual and a woman's magazine with the cover torn off. There was no paper to write on, no picture on the walls, no small, interesting thing to pick up and examine. The prospect of boredom can sometimes induce something very like panic. Then a sound rescued me. A car was approaching, had stopped, and voices were being raised in conversation. By the time I reached the front door the car was driving away. 'Who was that?' I asked Joan, who stood there in the rain with clippers in her hands looking a less enthusiastic gardener than the day before. 'Only the Daleys,' she replied, 'They asked if we wanted to go for a drive but we told them we were busy in the garden.' I went back indoors, already sick and now beginning to feel angry. I might just as well have been sent to my room and forgotten about. In three days I would be leaving Australia. Was this the best use of my time, and what was I doing in this house anyway, with a parent for whom apparently I barely existed and with a woman I hardly knew? Over lunch something was obviously written on my face because Joan said, 'This can't be much fun for Mike, Rad. Do you think we should leave tomorrow?' His response was tetchy: 'I've still got those fruit trees to attend to.' Joan smiled brightly at both of us. 'Oh yes! I'd forgotten.'

Incredibly, the rainfall increased, and by nightfall there were gales, snapping the branches off trees and driving the downpour horizontally as if buckets of water were being hurled at the windows. In the morning we found that the telephone had gone dead. Now there really was something for me to panic about. I had a plane to catch the day after tomorrow, and twenty-four hours after that an appointment to keep in Athens. What if flooding were to make the road impassable? How could I contact the airline to postpone my flight? It was becoming imperative that I get back to Sydney. But of course, I'd forgotten; there were fruit trees to tend. Joan had now given up on gardening, but not my father. I looked out of the window, and there he was in an old rubber mackintosh and sodden hat, trudging back and forth in the pelting rain, as he ministered to his frail young trees. I had to get out of the house. The broken umbrella would be useless in the wind, so I climbed back into clothes not yet dry and reconciled myself to getting wetter. My feet were the problem. I had brought with me sandals and a pair of shoes, but the sandals had disintegrated in the wet on my walk to the point, and the shoes were a handsome pair that nine years before I had saved up for and had had made for me by a London shoemaker. With care they had another nine years of life ahead of them. I was too desperate to bother. I put them on, leaned into the wind and stepped into the first puddle.

The Australian weather, like the continent itself, is not so much hostile to its human inhabitants as profoundly indifferent. It follows its own rhythms and stupendous whims with as little concern as a dog extends to its fleas. This storm, going on and on regardless, constantly raising the stakes, awed and belittled me as much as one of those sullen bush fires, ten miles across, that casually incinerate houses on their way to some other purpose. The ocean was an angry chaos and the land more water than clay. I pushed on through the wet, along sodden beaches pockmarked by rain and through tunnels of dripping gums, glumly exhilarated by phenomena that so perfectly matched my mood, like some anguished nineteenth-century romantic. My shoes were sopping, the shiny leather now dark and lustreless, and they squelched so much I took a perverse pleasure in wading through water. Once they'd got me to Sydney I'd leave them behind, shapeless and with the toes turned up like discarded shoes in a strip cartoon, one more thing that Australia had ruined.

Then in the morning the storm was over and there was the sun again. Coming out of the bush you could sense, if not hear, the murmur of innumerable rivulets and streams taking away the fallen rain and returning it to the sea. We packed the car and started down the dirt road that led to the highway. 'What we do,' said Joan, 'is drive straight through to Sydney.' Then, with one of her big smiles and a glance at her husband, she added, 'But we always stop at Nowra for an ice cream.' This was all right by me; the sooner I was back the better. My spirits began to rise until I looked through the windscreen, and they dipped to an even lower level. We had turned a corner to confront the weir now operating in full flood mode. The water that eddied across it looked about a metre deep. 'Can we get through that?' I asked weakly. 'We'll soon see,' replied my father as he drove the car forward. Water began to come in under the door, and I was certain I knew what was going to happen next: the engine would splutter, cut out completely, and we would be stranded for two days until the water level fell. Then, miraculously, we were beyond the deepest point, and the car was rising clear of the water. I began breathing again, and felt my fury retreating. We drove on for half a mile and turned another corner. Across our path and completely blocking the road lay an uprooted gum tree, and in what had once been its upper branches was a tangle of telephone wire. This explained the dead phone. There was no way the three of us could move the tree. 'You two wait here,' said my father. 'I'll walk back and get an axe.'

I sat in the car with Joan, trying to resist the tirade of indignation that I would readily have given way to had the person sitting beside me been a friend. All I said was, 'I've got a plane to catch,' but Joan rose to it sharply as if I was holding her responsible. 'You know what Rad's like! You won't change him!' We skirted round further criticism, each wanting to speak but, given our relationship, feeling that it would be improper to do so. Joan was no longer smiling; she looked sour and preoccupied. At one point she said, 'Rad's sixty-eight. I'm only fifty-one. I've got the rest of my life to think about.' I realised that like his other wives and all his children she, too, was a little frightened of him.

Much sooner than I'd expected, my father came walking round the corner carrying an axe, which he'd borrowed from a neighbour. He told us that on the return journey he'd encountered another victim of circumstance looking to save itself, a black snake that had sought refuge on the dry ledge that ran along the lip of the weir. With great care he'd stepped over it. Did he guess that in however restrained a manner we'd been talking about him? I doubt it, and if he did I don't think he cared one way or another about what these two dependants had to say. I asked what I could do to help and he said, 'You're not well enough. Just stay where you are.' So I sat in the car and watched him take the axe to the tree, sever it into manageable sections and drag them clear of the road. Here was something else I hadn't mis-remembered; he was a formidable man. Of all the right-wing virtues self-reliance was the most unassailable. He returned to the car and we drove on, now running an hour and a half late. We would not be in Sydney till four. We made our one, brief stop at Nowra for three ice-cream cones, and arrived at last at the outskirts of the city, all of us hungry, and, to a greater or lesser extent, irritable. I was explosive.

Dropping me off at my flat would have entailed a diversion of not more than five minutes, but it was not part of the routine, and as usual he drove straight on to the Vaucluse house. We disembarked from the car. 'Mike might like something to eat before he goes,' said my father, and Joan snapped back, 'I'm not putting on an apron now! I've got far too much to do!' and went into the house banging the door. It was the only time I'd ever seen her stand up to him. My father raised his eyebrows and smiled. I said I'd better be off. He got my bag from the boot and I followed him to the gate. For the farewell he'd assumed his expression of amused tolerance, of realistic benevolence, the Churchill look. What was it saying to me – that the visit to Bawley had been a success? That I'd be seeing him again in a week or two? That I wasn't leaving Australia the following day, possibly, and with any luck, for ever? Nothing in the last few days had quite so angered me. I walked up to the bus stop in New South Head Road and sat waiting for the bus.

The morning of my departure was the first day of true Australian summer. The houses and trees along the route sat there stunned by sunshine, shuddering occasionally when heat off the tar in the street rose and distorted their image. I was leaving one winter for the beginning of another, and the thing I had been most looking forward to, surfing along the coast on a day like this, I had hardly done at all. The plane was waiting for me a hundred yards from the terminal. I walked through the intense glare coming off the tarmac, aware of the peculiarity of Australian light, how it conceals nothing, exposes everything, the good and the bad without differentiation. Sometimes the candour of that light was almost insupportable. At the foot of the steps leading into the plane, a flight attendant stopped me and asked me to wait. Presently from the distant terminal there emerged two men in lumpy double-breasted suits and wide-brimmed felt hats who began walking towards us, taking their time. They had a small package which they handed to me. Were they smirking? It was hard to tell. I signed a customs declaration and began the ascent to the plane with my copy of *Eros Denied*. Australia had been saved from corruption, and I was now at liberty to pollute myself any way I pleased. At the top I looked back at the departing figures in their blue serge suits, and shook their dust from my feet.

This rejection of my own country was, however, fraught with ironies. The first was that Australia had been changing under my nose, and I had been too locked in my own past to notice. All over the country people younger than I were writing their first play or novel, planning their first film, and in the decade to come would transform the standing of the arts in their country. The seventies would become Australia's sixties, and the components of the Australian psyche would be re-ordered in surprising ways. The cultural soil in what were once colonies may sometimes be rich but it is always thin, and in times of change old ideas come up by the roots with one pull. Thus a country whose White Australia policy had once given bigotry the blessing of government, would shortly become one of the West's most viable multi-racial societies. Institutionalised homophobia would give way to exceptional sexual tolerance. Australia's natural beauty would soon be the concern and pride of everyone, with construction on cliffs and headlands prohibited and National Parkland zealously maintained. Even among the conservative elite with whom I'd grown up, those who weren't prepared to learn for themselves were soon instructed in change by their children who were taking lovers or coming out of the closet without a hint of apology, and choosing whatever sort of work appealed to them.

There was a greater irony. The England that I thought I now knew well, and to which I was so passionately intent on returning, was actually not a country at all, but one brief episode in that country's long history: namely, those two decades after the Second World War when the British, having been forced by adversity to bury their divisions, tried for a while, once the war was won, to find a more equitable way of living with one another. I had been caught up in this new spirit, and mistaken it for the national character, but even as the plane took me back it was beginning to fade. There had been other Englands biding their time and waiting for a chance to reassert themselves. There was, for instance, the England that Anthony Trollope returned to (also, coincidentally, after a trip to Australia), the commercial profligacy of which he describes in *The Way We Live Now*. Further back there was the England of the East India Company. Margaret Thatcher would soon be opening the door to both, and her Britain would make the materialism about which I complained in Australian society look like welfare. This was the point, because Australia hadn't taught itself to be what it was. It had had an instructor. All countries with empires have exported their greed and cruelty to their colonies – that is what the colony is for – and in its early days Australia had had a sharp experience of both. Even after nominal independence, it was still the offspring of a parent who shows little interest in its child, while insisting on emotional servility and an expensive present every birthday. The Second World War introduced a little reality into the relationship, though the lessons learnt would take a long time sinking in.

After the Fall of Singapore Churchill had been prepared to let Australia go to the Japanese, so that he could better prosecute the war in the Northern Hemisphere. An Australian Prime Minister, John Curtin, insisted on recalling three Australian Divisions from the Middle East, so that his own country could be defended. En route Churchill tried to have the troopships diverted to the battle raging on Crete. Curtin, in a display of national leadership without precedent, stood firm, and very grudgingly Churchill relented. 'Bad stock,' he complained to his physician, Lord Moran, about the citizens of a country he had never visited. The trouble was that for too long a number of influential Australians, infatuated by their British connections, had half agreed with him.

This then is my final argument with England: its carelessness about the country it brought into being, and the effect that once had on the people born there, including, me, my mother, my father and so many others of their generation, all of us fashioned square for a land of round holes. We had been pulled back and forth across the globe, in our minds if not by ships and planes, because we hungered for a somewhere that didn't depend for an identity on being part of some grander British fiction of Empire or Commonwealth. It was probably the Opera House that began the process that saved us from ourselves, and the recent Olympic Games in Sydney, a brilliantly planned and executed success, brought that change to its completion. Australia could at last relax. It was its own somewhere, and there were now some delicious ironies for all Australians to enjoy. The country about which fifty years ago an Englishman had said to me, 'Funny thing, Orstralia's a place I've never wanted to go,' was at the top of the list of destinations coveted by British travellers, and all over the British Isles schoolchildren from private schools to lowly comprehensives were imitating the upward inflections at the end of sentences coming from the young actors they followed most nights of the week in the Australian soap *Neighbours*.

As for my father, by the time of my next visit to Australia I'd had some success in the theatre, and with it my hostility to him and to my now transformed country melted away. I had realised that the son almost always wins the argument. If not through his own achievements, then by the father's death he has the last word. I still took exception to some of his views, though I was better able to enjoy their concise and witty exposition. As a doctor he was fortunate to have lived in the twentieth century, but never under the sort of government which might have encouraged him to put his more dangerous opinions into practice. Instead he led the life of a successful and conscientious eye surgeon, revered by patients to whom he showed real concern, and respected by his colleagues and students. There is an operating theatre in Sydney Hospital named after him. He was never any good at family life; nor are many men. The concerns of wives and children simply didn't engage him. But on a fishing expedition you couldn't hope for a more resourceful or amusing companion. I haven't yet acknowledged one strange thing about him, an undertow of melancholy. To those around him it could sometimes be very affecting. You became aware of the private battles he was fighting, with himself, with the consequence of his actions, with the stomach ulcers he'd had since his days as a student and which on two occasions had almost cost him his life. As for that gene for tunnel vision, it was to prove extremely useful in the career which was about to open up for me.

# THIRTEEN

# The End and a Beginning

Dona and I had our holiday in Greece and saw many wondrous sights, none more so than on our first morning – down a street between shadowy buildings, the distant Parthenon, like a miniature of itself, standing sunlit on its pedestal of rock as if the sprawl of modern Athens simply wasn't there. We ate fish in the open air at waterfront restaurants, and from Hydra watched a sunset in which a scatter of diminishing islands dissolved into the haze across the Aegean. Dona had paid her air fare from London and, reasonably, wanted us to see as much as we could. Indeed, in our letters we had discussed a breathless itinerary, on and off boats, in and out of hotels. But I was too unwell to be a good companion. Like a sick cat that crawls under the bed and doesn't reappear until it gets better, I simply wanted to find some tranquil spot and stay put. We had many good moments and no great rows, but the illusion that all lovers begin by sharing, that they are of a single mind, was moving into our past. We were approaching another stage on the journey men and women take together, one which marriage may have been invented partly to sustain, where resentments are not so easily brushed aside and where ultimatums are compromised by bluff. We were too passionately attached for it to end, nor would it do so for many years, but I was beginning to realise I could not leave the child and the marriage I already had. This did not mean my personal life had been resolved. That's probably a matter for the grave. But the pieces had been shifted, moved about a bit. Something different, and perhaps a little more honest, was coming into being.

I arrived back in Hampstead one afternoon in late autumn. Church Row was lit with low, creamy sunshine, as flattering as fresh paint, and looked as hospitable as one huge, beautifully proportioned Georgian room. England was where I now wanted to live, and this clear-cut decision would prove to be a passport to a new experience of it. It was as if somebody had just been waiting to say 'Come in.' Conrad, now almost six, opened the front door of the flat and stared at me in silence, wanting to smile but too shy to do so. This was the way, at the same age, I had greeted my mother on one of her returns from England. Without saying one word he took me by the hand and led me round the flat, pointing out all the things that had happened in my absence – a leg glued back on a Victorian armchair in the sitting room, a cupboard that Shirley had stripped back to the wood, a window pane replaced in the bathroom. These were the things that he must have decided would interest me.

I would have five weeks in London before I had to be off again to join David William in Glasgow – just time to finish my novel. My intention had been to conclude the book on a sombre note; talent is no guarantee of a career, and I'd known a number of gifted people whom the theatre had rejected or who had abandoned it in despair. This was to be the fate of my central character. But pessimism has its own glibness, and I wanted to acknowledge that one of the remarkable things about the business is that it is never too late for a door to open. An apter conclusion, one of hope but no promises, could be borrowed from what was about to happen to me. Had I ever told David William that my first ambition years ago in Australia had been to be a director? I can't remember. Perhaps David had spotted in the performances I had given in the Park some organisational instinct struggling to express itself. At any rate, inviting me to direct three plays was a generous act of faith that would change my life.

Over the next few weeks I worked steadily on the novel until I was about at the same place in that book that I am in this, the end in sight. I'd reached a sequence where the leading character goes for a walk on Hampstead Heath with the girl from whom he thinks he is about to part. It had been snowing the night before, so I decided to take a look at the Heath in its new clothes and found it doubly transformed, firstly by its white disguise, and secondly by my awareness that I was going to describe it on paper. I climbed up a hill and came upon a bench covered in snow as thick and even as a layer of cake, then scooped clear a space so I could sit on the bone-dry wood and observe the wintry life going on around me. I was amazed by how much activity there was; birds and squirrels were going about their business as if they had deadlines to meet. Then I went home and put it all into the book. A week later and it was done.

There was now something else I had to do: tell Shirley what I'd kept to myself for so long. She listened in silence, and remained very quiet during the few days left before my departure. Once I'd gone she became angrier than I'd ever known her to be, and there were some terrible telephone calls in which I became very frightened less for myself than for her and the child I could just hear in the background. She was more than entitled to her anger, but I knew it was also directed at herself for choosing not to see what had been in front of her eyes for so long. The storm had to play itself out and did so during the next few months. However, when I made a second move to Glasgow the following year, Shirley and Conrad were with me. And in that season Dona joined the Citizens' company to play a string of excellent parts.

I began the new engagement in my capacity as an actor, playing Casca in *Julius Caesar*. David William was directing the production, but he had also taken on the role of Cassius, and the workload had left him very exposed. One afternoon he and Michael Meacham, playing Brutus, were scheduled to rehearse the quarrel scene, and David asked me to sit out front, provide an independent eye and perhaps make a few suggestions. Almost automatically, as if I'd spent a career doing it, I became absorbed in what was happening in front of me. Though I empathised with the two actors, I had no wish to take their place. It was enough to let that amazing text, and what the performers were trying to do with it, wash through my head. I felt sharply focused, and yet at the same time free to let my thoughts slide sideways towards other possibilities of expression, other arrangements of staging. I don't recall much of what I said to my two companions that afternoon. What I can remember is the discovery I had made about myself, that this was work I was absolutely certain I could do well.

I limbered up with two productions in our studio theatre, Peter Weiss' Auschwitz documentary *The Investigation* and a two-hander *Chin Chin*, before moving on to my first production in the main house. This was David Halliwell's *Little Malcolm and His Struggle Against the Eunuchs*. One thing I liked about directing was that it was all-consuming; there were no ragged little bits of mind left over to fret about this or rebel against that. Though I had much to learn about the technicalities of design and lighting, this was compensated for by a steely confidence in my understanding of text and my usefulness to the people who would interpret it. I had been one of them too long not to identify with their odd sort of courage and the tenacity of their belief that somewhere there was work worth doing. Above all, unlike certain novice directors, they did not frighten me.

I once saw a TV interview with François Truffaut in which the film director was asked if he had much of a social life. None, he replied; he particularly disliked dinner parties. 'Why?' he was asked. 'Because I always want to direct them!' I knew exactly what he meant. It wasn't a question of wanting to dominate the table himself. It was simply an itch to impose a higher order on the proceedings, proposing a subject to discuss perhaps, then terminating a rambling monologue here, allowing a timid guest his say there, ensuring that the progress of the party was lively and to the point. This notion of directing as the imposition of a kind of harmony on a gathering of divergent talents, not only actors but designers, musicians and stage management, so that they can function at their optimum in service to a text is an attractive one and I believe accounts for at least half the job. Except on the extreme fringe, where zealots go roaming in search of their Ayatollah, the director as puppet-master is a fiction of critics. The more gifted his collaborators, the more his authority depends on consent, and I was now finding that earning it was a delicate, sometimes dangerous and exhilarating activity.

We rehearsed *Little Malcolm* on the stage of the Citizens' Theatre. Each morning I would check for mail in the front-of-house office, and then proceed through the auditorium to make a start on the day. There, waiting for me and wanly lit by a single worklight, was the platform on which our work would soon be exposed. Like a boxing ring between fights or a neglected tennis court, there was something almost forbidding about its dusty emptiness. On would come the actors from the green room, nursing mugs of tea and edgy at the prospect of a new day's push. Yet once we started to work impulses seemed to sprout out of the floor like crocuses. I was fortunate on two counts. The play I had been given to do was original and wildly funny. It dealt with the pretensions and the fantasies of power shared by a group of layabout art students in Huddersfield, who gather in the attic room of their leader, the baleful Little Malcolm. It was, if you like, *Look Back in Anger* performed by the National Front, and it was to speak volumes to our Scottish audience. My other stroke of luck was a cast it gives me pleasure to name: Richard Kane, Del Henney, Sebastian Breaks, Robin Humphries and Louise Breslin. I had a young designer working with me, Maurice Strike, fresh from art school, and with three productions to do as we liked with the two of us felt as liberated as children let loose in a toyshop. When we had an idea, without further thought it went on stage. The results were immensely energetic and probably quite vulgar, but then fortunately so was the play. From the flies we draped huge pages of text, everything from *Mein Kampf* to *Das Kapital* with columns from the popular press and the political weeklies thrown in. This was the ill-digested contents of Little Malcolm's mind. Dwarfed beneath these typographical banners was the grubby attic of the protagonist, and we took delicious pains with the arrangement of the variegated rubbish which would fully express its squalor.

My memory of the first night was of a theatre full of people pitching from side to side almost seasick with laughter, then at the end of the play, as the comedy had its revenge, sitting as still as their bolted-down seats. The Citizens' is one of those elegant and sly Victorian theatres where no part of the audience is entirely isolated from another. The horseshoe circle looks down on the stalls, the stalls look up to the boxes and the gallery looks down on the lot. The body language of an audience amused or moved sends a signal around the house at the speed of light, and that night they were one creature.

One of the advantages of Glasgow at this time was a number of intelligent and supportive critics, among them Christopher Small of the *Glasgow Herald*, Allen Wright of *The Scotsman* and Cordelia Oliver writing for the northern edition of *The Guardian*. They weren't exhausted by the cultural glut of London, and when they found something they liked they jumped up and down. On this occasion the reviews were ecstatic. Even more extraordinary was a letter I received from the Vice-Chairman: 'In my experience as a member of the Board this is the first occasion that we have minuted our appreciation of an outstanding performance.' Something remarkable was happening to me, like emerging from a kind of chrysalis, and I seemed to be imperceptibly trembling all day. Would a predator get me before I could unfold my wings? But the next show, *Who's Afraid of Virginia Woolf?*, which Michael Meacham directed and in which I played George, was received with matching rapture. It was the end of the season and David William was leaving. The Board offered Michael Meacham and me joint artistic direction.

However, I soon learnt that a little success is simply to exchange one sort of struggle for another. I had secured a footing on that small plateau at the top of the hill, but others had already arrived and there was rather more jostling than I had been expecting. On the ascent the approach had been steep but spacious, and more than once I had been offered a hand up. Now, from the very people to whom I owed my present position came a slap in the face. When the Board had interviewed me for the job, I'd stressed the importance of finding new writing if the theatre was to make a wider reputation for itself and attract the best talent. Ideally we needed something fresh and lively to get the forthcoming season off to the best possible start. Now, newly appointed, I believed I had discovered just such a play. Over the years the Glasgow Citizens' Theatre had been a staunch supporter of the work of Tennessee Williams, and to show his appreciation the playwright was now prepared to offer us the rights of a play not yet seen in Great Britain, *Sweet Bird of Youth*. I already had in mind a great star perfect for the role of the Princess – Vivien Leigh. But could she be persuaded to come to Scotland and work for a novice director? We could only try. Within days word came back that she was extremely interested. The *Titus* connection was presumably a factor, and I could only wonder in what unexpected ways the past wheels back to impinge upon the present. Opposite her, to play Chance Wayne, her gigolo lover, we found a charismatic and abrasively ambitious young actor, Steven Berkoff. The project promised to be an astounding coup for the new artistic directorship, and I already had thoughts about how it should be staged. Then word came down from the Board. They had read the play, found it unsuitable and would not permit a production at the Citizens' Theatre. This would have been a resigning matter had I already established some sort of track record, but to resign now would have been to kill a career before it had barely started.

There was someone on the Board to whom in other circumstances we would have immediately appealed. This was Michael Goldberg, whose family business was the big department store in Glasgow bearing his name. He was a humorous, intelligent man, to whom more than any other I owed my job, and he had actively supported the theatre over many years. It was through his efforts (and I suspect his money) that we now had a second auditorium, the studio space in which I had directed my first production. He even wrote plays himself, but secretly, which he would submit to the theatre under an assumed name. He always accepted their invariable rejection with good grace. However, he had one terror – that the organisation to which he devoted so much energy should become associated in the public mind with sexual impropriety or sensation. *Sweet Bird of Youth* with its paid-for sex, drugs, mutilations and undertow of gay lament, promised just such associations. In his extensive theatrical library he found an unfavourable notice of the New York production by Kenneth Tynan, which he offered as proof that the play was unworthy of its author. I admired Michael and was too much in his debt to express my bewilderment and anger, but I thought it a catastrophic decision. We gritted our teeth and set about making other plans.

Before the new season began there was a break of a couple of months so I was able to return to London. In the hope that it might improve my health and also allow me the time and seclusion to complete a fair copy of my novel, I took myself off to a health farm for a fortnight. While I was there Peter Nichols sent me the first draft of his new stage play. For some years we had been in the habit of discussing each other's work; I would send him instalments of my novel and he would give me his latest television play to read. I knew what he most wanted was a stage success, and I hoped that this would be it. The play was structured conventionally except for its brilliant beginning. On stage strides a schoolteacher and starts yelling at the audience as if they were his barely manageable class. This was a reworking of a sketch Peter had written at teachers' training college and, as well as being funny and scabrous, it could have served as a metaphor for the comic hopelessness of humanity. There follows a wonderful scene in which the teacher, Bri, comes home to his wife, Sheila, and gives her an account of his working day, complete with imitations, just as I had seen Peter give Thelma on innumerable occasions.

This couple, classless, mockingly intelligent, and getting on with their lives in a provincial city as best they could, had been seen on television but they were a new presence on the stage. Yet they were now all over England, talking, dressing and rearing their children in a new sort of way. The scene is interrupted by the ringing of a doorbell. Bri goes to answer it and returns pushing a wheelchair in which lolls his completely disabled child just returned from day-care. It's only then that you realise what the real subject of the play will be. Peter was toying with various titles for it, but the one he favoured was *A Day in the Death of Joe Egg*. Later that evening Bri and Sheila are visited by another married couple, for whom they don't appear to have much regard. The man is an aggressive do-gooder convinced that there is no cloud without a silver lining, and his wife a well-groomed but utterly conventional woman with a secret horror of disablement. It was with the arrival of these two that the play got into trouble. Because it observed the conventions of the well-made play, Peter could only tell the audience what they needed to know about the child's history by having Bri and Sheila unburden themselves in a string of confessional speeches to people they apparently disliked. The play shifted from vivid dramatisation to inert description, and ran into a road block of implausibility.

Peter had such an investment of work and feeling in the play that it was difficult knowing quite how to respond. I wrote to him making one good suggestion, and one bad and certainly tactless one – namely that he'd really written two plays, one about modern marriage and the other about disablement, and that the first had more going for it than the second. I hope my second suggestion made up a little for the first: he'd already established the convention of direct address in the first few minutes, so why be constrained by traditional playmaking elsewhere? Couldn't Bri and Sheila tell their story straight to the audience, about whom, unlike their visitors, there is always a presumption of sympathy and understanding? Was I perhaps remembering Robert Morley addressing the house to such effect in *Edward, My Son*? Or was it the Old Vic production of *The Skin of Our Teeth*, which twenty years before Peter had seen in Bristol and I had seen with the Oliviers in Sydney, and which we had often discussed?

Meanwhile there was the forthcoming season. We all returned to Glasgow, and despite the rebuff over *Sweet Bird of Youth*, got off to an excellent start. I directed two plays which had never been seen outside London, Doris Lessing's *Play with a Tiger*, and Hugh Leonard's adaptation of *Portrait of the Artist as a Young Man*, which he had called *Stephen D*. I then returned to being an actor. Since the success of *Who's Afraid of Virginia Woolf?* Michael Meacham and I had been looking for another project which he could direct and in which I could appear, and we thought we'd found it in John Osborne's *Inadmissible Evidence*. This turned out to be the most harrowing undertaking of my career, because until we started rehearsing I had not really grasped the sheer size of the role. The first twenty-five minutes of the evening is a frantic monologue in which the central character, Maitland, hardly pauses for breath. Then the play proper begins and he stays on stage for a further two and a half hours. With under three weeks to rehearse I had no idea how I would find the time to learn the lines. Public humiliation became a real possibility. I began working from the minute I woke up to the moment my head hit the pillow that night, and at one point had to ask for rehearsals to be cancelled so that I could stay in bed and catch up on my learning.

On the first night I left my dressing room for the stage numb with dread, and waited in the wings like a channel swimmer shivering on a beach with choppy water stretching as far as the horizon. However, somehow, some way, as actors always do, I reached the far shore, and the evening was deemed a success. In the life of the city our theatre was being talked about and welcomed. We had become hot, and just to feel *useful* was wonderful. The banner headline to the notice in the *Glasgow Herald* read 'Feat of Endurance by Michael Blakemore at the Citizens'' and it went on to smother me in praise. Glasgow, which had given me a new career as a director, was now providing a final accolade for the one I would shortly be abandoning, that of performer, and it enabled me to let it go without resentment or regret.

There remained the problem of finding that new play which would put the Citizens' at the front rank of British theatres. Through the post one day arrived the second draft of *A Day in the Death of Joe Egg*. It was now sitting on my knees in the back of a taxi home, and I was reading it in a state of staring excitement. Everything in the play was now in accord with its unconventional opening. The background to the child's disablement was conveyed to the audience directly in a string of taut comic sketches aimed at keeping them hopping from one foot to another as they were touched one moment and barking with laughter the next. The play no longer asked for sympathy. It acknowledged that there is just so much people can be expected to feel about another's woes. What it expected was razor-sharp alertness, and it insisted on it through its demonstrable talent. Direct address was used in a variety of contexts. Towards the end of the first act Sheila, alone on stage, tells the audience of a moment of hope she had once felt for her damaged child and how that tiny spark was extinguished. She leaves the stage on a note of heartbreaking bleakness, and you expect the curtain to come down. But to end the act Peter had contrived a startling *coup de théâtre*. The lights suddenly come up and the child actress, who so far we have only seen slumped unconscious in a wheelchair, suddenly bounds on stage with a skipping rope and announces in a cheerful piping voice that it is now time for an interval. In a flash, and only for a moment, we have been allowed a glimpse of the little girl who might have been.

If I loved what Peter had done, others apparently were less enamoured. The play had been rejected by managements in the West End, by the Royal Court and the Hampstead Theatre, in fact everyone to whom it had been sent. Posting it to me in Glasgow had been his last resort. My enthusiasm for the play did not blind me to what others had baulked at. It was still much longer than it needed to be, and any play tackling such a provocative subject had to be as lean as a greyhound if it was to keep ahead of an audience's misgivings. Even as I sat reading this new draft I could see precisely where the cuts could come and how material could be transposed so that Acts Two and Three became the second half of a two-act play. It fell into place with almost uncanny ease. Also there was no direct address for the visiting couple, who, notwithstanding their foolishness, were as entitled to explain themselves to the audience as anyone else on stage. I don't believe it is the function of a director to fool around with a playwright's work, but just occasionally in a career you can be so at one on a generational level, so sympathetically informed about his material, that you are able to see possibilities of which the author himself is as yet unaware. This potential, however, is always a quality of the play itself, which the director, prospecting for gold on someone else's land, has had the luck to spot.

I telephoned Peter that night and told him that if I could get it past the Board, the Citizens' Theatre would certainly present his play. I then passed on my concerns about Acts Two and Three. Peter sighed and, sounding weary but not resentful, said, 'You'll have to show me what to do, then. I've been working on it so long I can't see it any more.' So that is what we did. He came to stay with us in Glasgow during a week when I'd caught some kind of intestinal bug. I was in bed, the script propped up on my knees, with Peter sitting beside like a doctor taking notes in his pad. Then he returned to Bristol, implemented the changes and a few weeks later sent me the final draft.

The crucial meeting with the Board's Play Selection Committee was itself dramatic enough to go straight on stage. It was convened hastily one afternoon in the office of the Chairman, George Middleton, at the request of the Vice-Chairman, Lord Taylor. It was he who had written to me after *Little Malcolm*. He had been made a peer by the Labour Government for his services to the Co-operative Movement, and he was a decent enough man but with a stubborn belief in the correctness of his own artistic judgements. In his view inviting controversy or challenging public taste was not what a theatre was for. We knew he disliked the play, but not yet how much. Others present were Colin Chandler, who ran the drama school and who was passionately pro, and Michael Goldberg, over whose view there hung a question mark. The floating voter was the Chairman, who, inclining to a lack of confidence in his own judgement, usually took his cue either from the Vice-Chairman or Michael. I went into the meeting with our young front-of-house manager, Andrew Leigh, coldly resolved that this time I would use the threat of resignation as a weapon. It soon transpired that I was not alone in this tactic. Tom Taylor was the first to speak. He described the play as a disgrace, a travesty in appalling taste that made cruel fun of the disabled, and one which if performed on the stage of the Citizens' would force him to consider his position as Vice-Chairman.

Next to speak was Colin Chandler, but he was so angry with what he saw as a gross misunderstanding of the play that it undermined his effectiveness as an advocate. Besides, from the others' point of view Colin, with his drama school connection, was a little too close to the artistic side of the business to be entirely sound. His defence of the play became a kind of furious splutter which trailed away into silence. Our eyes turned to the Chairman for his view, and he shifted uncomfortably in his seat before his own eyes turned in appeal to Michael Goldberg. Perhaps Michael would give us his opinion first. In his usual good-natured, commonsensical tones, Michael began to address the meeting, and he seemed mainly concerned with shifting the debate to a less rancorous level. He expressed sympathy for the distress the play had caused the Vice-Chairman and commended him and Colin for the sincerity with which they had presented their views. The tension in the room began to abate, and almost in spite of myself I settled back in my chair to observe the skill of a brilliant and humane conciliator. Very gently he turned the argument towards the play itself. Certainly it was shocking, and certainly it had the power to give offence, but was this because it was a bad play? Might it not be true that it was a very good play attempting to say something that had not been said before, and daring to say it in a way which was itself unprecedented?

Slowly it was becoming clear that Michael not only understood the material but wanted to see it staged at the Citizens' as much as anyone in the room. 'When something like this comes our way,' he concluded, 'we have a duty to do our best by it.' No one spoke. The Chairman started nodding slowly. 'I think Michael may have a point,' he said, and that was it: three in favour, one against. Four very busy men rose to get on with the rest of their lives. Michael dawdled behind as the others left the room. Alone with me and Andrew, his expression changed. Like a schoolboy's smirk, Michael's smile consisted of trying not to smile and failing hopelessly at it. His eyes had become slits of amusement and satisfaction. 'When you first came into this room, Michael,' he said to me, 'I wouldn't have given tuppence for your chances!' And later, as we were leaving, 'And believe you me *A Day in the Death of Joe Egg* is a much better play than *Sweet Bird of Youth*!'

We could now set about casting. For Bri, Peter suggested Joe Melia, whom he had seen on television and whom he thought had the right zest and comic intelligence. I proposed Zena Walker for Sheila; we'd been at drama school together and I knew her to be an actress of skill and feeling. The company manager, Tony Jones, insisted there was only one actress who could play the part of Bri's mother, the incomparable Joan Hickson. We started enquiries. I went to London to cast the visiting couple and found Michael Murray and Carole Boyer. Not one of these five actors turned us down. Believing in the play, they packed their bags and came to Glasgow for what little we could pay them, and I remain in their debt.

There was now the set to think about, but I already knew what it should look like: the sitting room of a Victorian terrace house, but painted all white and furnished colourfully for a few pounds from auctions and junk shops. I started discussions with our resident designer, Robin Pidcock. In my own rented flat, where I lived with Shirley and Conrad, there was a Victorian chaise longue which I thought, its back to the audience, would be perfect to lie the child on, partially concealed when she was on stage for long periods of time but not the focus of the action. Our landlady agreed to let us borrow it for the three-week run. That chaise longue would travel with us to London and eventually to New York, and in rental recover its value a hundred times over. When you're thinking about something all day long, ideas are waiting wherever you look. One Sunday a gifted local musician, Andy Park, who had a jazz group, was giving a concert of his own work at our studio theatre. He had barely started to play when it became obvious to me that music had to be an integral part of the production. Peter loved jazz; his brother played in a jazz band in Bristol, and for their generation of Englishmen nothing summed up provincial yearnings for a wider world more than some basement where jazz was played. With music we could get the show off to an unexpected start, challenging at once the received ideas surrounding its subject, and it would dramatise and heighten the play's mercurial changes of direction. Andy Park's score would also travel with us to New York, and I've had few surprises as pleasant as hearing it brought to incandescent life by the kind of virtuoso musicians available in that city.

By the time we started rehearsing, the whisper was around town that something controversial, and maybe extraordinary, was about to be unveiled at the Citizens'. In the theatre we seemed to be on a tiptoe of anticipatory excitement, and when I ran into someone along a corridor we would start grinning complicitly at each other as if we were both sitting on top of a whopping surprise. Peter was unable to get away from Bristol until the last few days of rehearsal, but I reported to him each night by telephone. He arrived at the theatre just as we were about to run the first half of the play. Only two people watched the rehearsal that afternoon, the author and the director, sitting a few feet away from each other in a sea of empty seats, both as focused on the stage as if we were looking at our futures. When I turned to Peter at the end of the act he had tears streaming down his face, and was reaching for a handkerchief to wipe them away. 'Don't!' I said. 'Come into the green room and let Joe and Zena see you just as you are.' So a sniffing, swallowing Peter, who had never once been able to shed a tear over the real-life Joe Egg, but whose feelings this performance of his own story had unlocked, presented himself to the cast and said a few eloquent words. But for all of us those tears were praise enough.

Peter was again staying with us, and when we joined Shirley at the flat afterwards she complimented him on his final draft. 'All your old man,' he replied, which was nice of him but not remotely the case. *A Day in the Death of Joe Egg* is truly Peter's play. He had laboured on it for over a year, transmuting private distress into a liberating public event, in which people all over the world have been able to share. I, on the other hand, had had some sharp insights over a couple of hours one afternoon and passed them on. What I can perhaps claim for my interventions is that without them the play might have had more difficulty finding its way to the stage, nor would it have been able to reach out to the wider audience. And for me there was something almost poetically apt about this point we had both reached in our lives – two friends who had shared an idea of theatre over many years. Now one of them had written a play and the other had been able to give it a production in which we could celebrate those ideas beyond our best hopes. We had, as it were, given each other the present of success. Not that Peter's luck wouldn't have changed. He already had a reputation as a television dramatist, and he was too hard-working and gifted to remain overlooked by the theatre. Nor do I think that one way or another I would have been denied advancement. But at Glasgow this congruence of our fortunes had the perfect shape of a happy ending.

The first night was quite extraordinary and quite strange. We began by playing to two distinct audiences. Downstairs sat the members of the Board in their customary seats, surrounded by other regular supporters of a similar age and background. Those of us who actually worked in the building had chosen, along with our friends, to watch the play from the circle. Above us the gallery was packed with students, many of them from the drama school, and they were there to offer support. Having some idea of what lay ahead, they responded with almost hysterical force to the comedy in the early part of the play. Then Joe Melia left the stage and reappeared a moment later pushing on his rag-doll of a child in her wheelchair. The theatre was now so absolutely silent it was as if the air had been sucked out of the building and we were all sitting there in a vacuum. I was rigid in my seat wondering if the audience would ever make a sound again, or whether the rest of the evening would be received in this thunder of silence. On went the play and Joe and Zena Walker set about the business of ministering to their daughter, talking to her and caring for her just as if she was a child like any other.

The house began to comprehend that what was foreign and perhaps a little frightening for them was perfectly ordinary to these on-stage parents. This is what life had dealt them and they were getting on with it as best they could. Very cautiously the laughter started again, first in the gallery then little by little in the rest of the house, as the audience was forced to acknowledge the honesty of what they were watching and the skill with which it was being represented. In these parts Joe and Zena were to give the performances of their lives. My advice to both of them had been to avoid self-pity or any appeal for an audience's sympathy: let them come to you, which they will if we don't ask them to. Other actors in the role of Bri have made the decision to play the pain of the character's predicament. Joe, like Peter Nichols in life, didn't do this. He zigzagged through the play on a blast of nervous energy and never once dropped the mask of the obsessive joker; this told you everything you needed to know about what he was concealing, and underlined the play's paradoxical embrace of wild comedy and anguish. Both actors brought the love they felt for their own young children to bear on their parts, and Zena's performance, never remotely sentimental, had a transparency and a rawness of feeling that it sometimes seemed almost indelicate to watch. But it was impossible to turn your face away from a rendering of such talent.

Over the next few days our Scottish notices came in and they were uniform raves. Perhaps the best of all was in *The Guardian*, but this was in the paper's northern edition which no one in London would see. I sat at my desk in the office at the theatre with the arts page spread out in front of me. If the play was to have an extended life this had to be read down south. Long-distance dialling had only just come in, and I felt sick with apprehension as I picked my way carefully through the code which would connect me to the newspaper. For all I knew this could be make or break for all of us. Put through to the Arts Editor, my espousal of the play came out in a rush, but the voice at the other end sounded surprisingly amenable. Yes, he said, he'd certainly be prepared to reprint the notice in the London edition.

Within a week all the important calls were incoming. Kenneth Tynan rang me one morning to say he'd seen the review and could the National Theatre have a look at the script? He was back on the line within days to say he thought the play was wonderful, and so did Sir Laurence, who had read it in his dressing room as a matter of urgency between a matinee and an evening performance. The National wanted to do a production cast from their own company. By that time we'd already had two other offers, the one I favoured being from Albert Finney's Memorial Enterprises. It was ultimately the author's decision but Peter agreed with me, thus ensuring the continued involvement of our leading actors and, not least, the play's director. However, Peter was so encouraged by the National's interest that he told them he would write his next play with them in mind.

Getting the play to London was proving surprisingly easy, notwithstanding these telephone calls which would have me concentrating so hard that I could feel little springs of sweat prickling down my back. *The Observer* had now followed *The Guardian*'s lead, and dispatched its drama critic, Ronald Bryden, to Glasgow to review us. This was another rave and put the seal on our hopes, though I was a little miffed that all aspects of the production – the music, the staging and so on – were described as though they were attributes of the script. (This, I would soon learn, was one of the penalties of directing new work. There are many more compensations.) However, this was a time in my life when I had only to tap once on a door for it to open. The exceptional luck that eluded me as an actor was there in abundance the moment I began directing. After many collisions and ricochets, that miraculous billiard shot was coming to a conclusion, and all over the table balls were gliding towards the pockets for which they were intended. I was helping to run a theatre, *Joe Egg* was on its way first to London, then New York, and my novel was on the point of being accepted for publication. With each of these steps I would recover a little more of my health.

The staging of a play has often been represented as a process that involves rivalry and bitter intrigue. This has not been my experience, particularly when doing the work that has most engaged me. The sense of aspiration and the energy levels have been so high, the mutual dependence so readily acknowledged, that they have more often been periods of the greatest generosity. On an opening night the vision, thought and application of a variety of people with a variety of skills coalesce in an event which, amazingly, the outside world sometimes deems to have value. Acceptance of your best work can bring with it one of those rare but empowering moments of transition, from one state to a better one, which the American writer Emerson thought gave a life a shape and, for a little while at least, a point. These highs never last long, two or three days perhaps, but for a brief spell there is an apprehension of life's prodigality. Such feelings will soon mutate into something less pristine – self-satisfaction or complacency, even conceit – whereupon the experience has lost its value. But while it lasts it is a little like sprouting wings.

Trouble in the theatre, if it comes at all, is more likely to make an appearance when the rehearsal period has retreated into the past. That early fervour and goodwill have gone out with the tide, and the individual's memory of the event begins to be tailored around his own contribution to it. It is then that claims are made, and credit taken or blame apportioned. At this point the advantages of a sound contract become apparent. All of us in the theatre, to a lesser or greater degree, collude in this resentment but even to be victimised by it is rarely too high a price to pay for what went before. The trouble is, like life itself, the overall experience tends to conclude with the bad bit.

One morning, as *Joe Egg* was coming to the end of its Glasgow run, I had a telephone call from Peter down south. It took him a while to come to the point, and he sounded a little odd as if he was speaking at the behest of another person. But who? His agent? His wife? Eventually he began: there had originally been only five copies of the second draft on which we'd worked together. He'd managed to track down four of these copies and they had been returned to him. Mine was the only copy still unaccounted for and would I please put it in the post? (This, of course, was before the photocopying machine had become available.) I reminded him I no longer had it. We'd sent it to the Lord Chamberlain's office to anticipate any cuts the censor might insist on when we had a draft ready for performance. 'Oh yes,' he remembered. 'It's just that we don't want the old version floating around for anyone to see.' I didn't say anything. I had become alert in a way I would have preferred not to, because I could think of only one reason why he might want all copies of that second draft withdrawn from circulation.

Some weeks later I learnt that the play was to be published. I wondered if Peter would include me in any acknowledgements. Many years later when I made similar, though less crucial, contributions to the first draft of another play, the author did so as a matter of course. In the published *Joe Egg* there was nothing. Good fortune, as always double-edged, turned out to be the beginning of our long drift towards estrangement. Doubtless I played my part in this as well as Peter and, as mutual friends will testify, there is comedy mixed up in our escalating squabbles along with regret. We are now both in our mid-seventies, and it has been just recently that Peter has begun to speak generously about the work we did together in Glasgow so long ago.

*A Day in the Death of Joe Egg* opened in London, and the next morning Irving Wardle in *The Times* wrote, 'This is one of the rare occasions on which audiences can feel the earth moving under their feet,' and he concluded, 'This is not avant-garde writing. It is addressed to the general civic conscience, and it endows the random audience with a sense of a common human bond.' We had been understood. Laurence Olivier saw the performance and wrote me a letter in his customary florid manner, which touched and amused me. 'I do hope that next time fate steers our orbits in the same direction it will allow us to collide. Yours ever affectionately and with most heartfelt congratulations.

Larry O.' The collision to which he referred took place sooner than either of us were expecting. Peter Nichols gave his next play, *The National Health*, to the National Theatre, and I directed it for them. Like its predecessor it both won an *Evening Standard* Award for Best Play and was sold to the movies. A year or so later I was asked to join the National Theatre as an Associate Director; and a good point to conclude this book, because it brings the story full circle, might be the National Theatre production of *Long Day's Journey into Night*. It was to give me my sharpest perception of success, and allow me – because, like the play I was directing, I was not English – to make a particular contribution to the theatre of the country which had adopted me.

It is the opening night. On stage are a sublime quartet of actors – Ronald Pickup, Denis Quilley, Constance Cummings and, making a phenomenal and unexpected comeback from ill health, Laurence Olivier. Mary Tyrone has just spoken the last lines of that great play: 'Then in the spring something happened to me. Yes, I remember. I fell in love with James Tyrone and was so happy for a time.' I had asked for a quick curtain, severing the audience from the ongoing life of the stricken family with whom they have been so intimately involved for over four hours. Down it came, falling like a blade, and there was a breath of absolute quiet before the applause broke. In that suspended few seconds, that moment of transition, I felt as safe, as at liberty, as I ever would.

# Index